ACTION

PERSONAL TRAINER CERTIFICATION

www.ActionCertification.org

Table of Contents

Chapter 1: The Science of Exercise 1

The Importance of Understanding the Science of Exercise 2

Nervous System 3
Central Nervous System 5
Peripheral Nervous System 5
Skeletal System 6
Bones 6
Joints 7
Muscular System 8
Muscle Fibers 13
Cardiorespiratory System 14
Heart 15
Blood 16
Lungs 17
Energy Production 17
ATP 18
Glycolysis 19

Summary 20

Review Questions 20

References 22

Chapter 2: Biomechanics 23

What Is Biomechanics? 24

The Importance of Biomechanics 25

Biomechanics and Exercise 26
Warm-Up 27
Cool-Down 28
Motion and Kinematics 29
Forces 30
Internal Forces 31
External Forces 32
Inertia 32
Stability of Equilibrium 33

Anatomic Locations 34
Planes of Motion 35
Range of Motion 37

Muscle Actions...38

Modes of Muscle Strength 40

Motor Control 42
    Proprioception 43
    Motor Learning...45

Review Questions...48

References 49

Chapter 3: Client Assessment 51

The Importance of a Client Assessment 52

The General History Section of the Initial Client Assessment......................53
    Occupation 53
    Lifestyle 54

The Medical History Section of the Initial Client Assessment 55
    Injuries...55
    Surgeries 56
    Diseases and Medical Conditions...56
    Medications...57

Using a Questionnaire 58
    Example of Initial Client Assessment Form 58

The ACTION Personal Training System Health Screening 59
    PAR-Q..59
    PAR-Q, PARMED-X and PARMED-X for Pregnancy Printable Forms...........60
    Lifestyle Questionnaire...61
    Medical Screening 62

The Physical Assessment Section 63
    Pulse...63
    Blood Pressure 64
    Flexibility...65
    Posture...66
    Body Fat...67
    Body Mass Index (BMI)..68
    Step Test..69
    Walk Test...70
    Muscular Performance...71

How Thorough Should Each Initial Assessment Be? 73

Personalizing or Designing Custom Test 74

The ACTION Personal Training System Assessment Tools 77
Body Composition 77
Cardiovascular Assessment 80
Strength Assessment 83
Ease of Movement Assessment 85
Functional Assessment 87
Digital Posture Analysis 91

Tracking Client Progress Using the ACTION Personal Training System 93
Measurement Tracking 94
Fitness Assessment Tracking 95
Nutritional Tracking 96
Competition Tracking 97

Summary 98

Review Questions 99

References 100

Chapter 4: Introduction to Designing Programs 101

Introduction to Designing Programs 102

The ACTION Personal Training System Goals and Preferences 103
Experience and Goals 103
Weight Loss Goals 104
Resistance Training Preferences 106
Cardio Preferences 107
Schedule Preferences 108

Program Design 109
Health Precautions to Consider when Designing a Program 110
Avoiding Overexertion and Injury 111
Signs of Dangerous Dysfunctional Breathing 112
Avoiding Discouragement 113

Aerobic Programs for Beginners 113

Physiological Factors to Consider in Designing Programs 114
Types of Muscle Actions 114
Energy Usage 115
The Kinetic Chain 115
Proper Positioning 115

Types of Training Used in Exercise Program Design 116

Principles of Exercise Training..118
    Target Heart Rate 119
    Measuring Exercise Intensity..120
    Measuring Caloric Use...121
    Principles of Resistance Training (RT)..................................122
    Determining Resistance...123
    Determining Rest Periods..124
    Resistance Training Modalities 125
    Periodization..126
    Ways to Vary Volume and Intensity....................................127
    Overtraining..127

Resistance Program Design Using the ACTION Personal Training System...129
    Setting and Understanding Client Access Levels 129
    Prerequisites to Building a Program.....................................130
    Creating Your Own Custom Exercises..................................131
    Program Design..132
    Program Design Options 134
    Editing Programs..135
    Workout Tracking 137

Tracking Cardiovascular Activity Using the ACTION Personal Training System 138
    Cardio Program 138

Summary 139

Review Questions..139

References 140

Chapter 5: Flexibility..143

The Warm-Up...144
    What is a Warm-Up? 144
    Benefits of a Warm-Up..144
    Warm-Up Considerations 145

Types of Warm-Ups..145
    General Warm-Up...145
    Activity-Specific Warm-Up 146
    Passive Warm-Up 146

Warm-Ups and Stretching 146

Flexibility 147
    What is Flexibility? 147
    The Importance of Flexibility...147
    The Science of Flexibility 148

Types of Flexibility..149
Corrective Flexibility...149
Active Flexibility 150
Functional Flexibility 150

Stretching Techniques 151
Static Stretching...151
Passive Stretching 153
Active and Active Assistive Stretching.......................................153
Proprioceptive Neuromuscular Facilitation Stretching...............155
Dynamic and Ballistic Stretching..155

Precautions and Safety...157
Types of Stretches..157

Developing the Program...159
Measuring Flexibility 161

Summary 161

Review Questions..162

References 163

Chapter 6: Program Design Elements 165

Cardiorespiratory Conditioning..166
The Importance of Cardiorespiratory Fitness 166

Training Design...167

Postural Considerations...168

Smart Progression 168
Interval Training...169

Interval Training Model 170

Stage Training..171

Circuit Training 171
Fat Burning..172

Muscular Strength..173
Endurance Conditioning..175
The Adaptation of Strength Training 177

Flexibility Training 179
Types of Stretching 180

Things to Avoid 182
Postural Muscle Imbalance 182

Balance, Agility, Speed 183
    Balance.. 184
    Balance Training.. 184
    Coordination and Speed.. 186
    Sensory Function.. 188
    Speed 189

Summary 189

Review Questions... 190

References 191

Chapter 7: Warning Signs 193

The Warning Signs that Can Mean Trouble 194
    Muscle Cramps 195
    Dehydration 196
    Heat Exhaustion 199
    Heat Stroke.. 200

How to Respond to Various Events 202
    Dehydration that Leads to a Loss of Performance and Energy................ 202
    Dehydration and Muscle Cramps.. 202
    Heat Exhaustion that Causes Light-headedness, Dizziness and Cold, Clammy Skin...... 204
    Heat Exhaustion that Causes Nausea and Headaches 204
    Heat Stroke, High Body Temperature and Dry Skin 204
    Heat Stroke that Causes Confusion and Unconsciousness 205

Summary 208

Review Questions... 208

References 209

Chapter 8: Special Populations 211

Introduction to Special Populations... 212

Pregnant Women 212
    Designing a Safe Exercise Plan During Pregnancy................................... 213
    Exercises to Perform and Avoid 214
    Safety Precautions 216

Seniors.. 217
    Exercises to Perform and Avoid 217
    Safety Precautions 220

Youths **221**
Training Programs and Supervision 222
Preventing and Controlling Childhood Obesity... 222
Safety Precautions 223

Injured Persons **224**
Exercising with an Injury 224
Exercising after an Injury... 225
Exercises to Perform and Avoid 225
Safety Precautions 226

Persons with Specific Medical Conditions **226**
Arthritis.. 226
Asthma... 229
Preparing for Exercise... 229
Diabetes Mellitus 231

Hypertension **235**
Monitoring Blood Pressure.. 236
Types of Exercises for Persons with Hypertension 236

Summary **238**

Review Questions... **238**

References **239**

Chapter 9: Nutrition 243

Introduction to Nutrition... **244**
Recommended Caloric Intake.. 245
Nutrition for Working Out... 247

Carbohydrates.. **249**
Recommended Carbohydrate Intake 250
Types of Carbohydrates... 251
Carbohydrates for Working Out... 252
Alcohol as a Carbohydrate?.. 253

Fats **254**
The Role of Fats in the Body 254
Types of Fats.. 256
Triglycerides... *256*
Unsaturated Fats.. *256*
Trans Fats... *257*
Saturated Fats.. *257*
Cholesterol.. *257*

Problems with Fats..258
   Metabolic Syndrome 258
   Obesity..258
   Insulin Resistance...259
   Heart Disease 259
Fat Requirements...259

Protein 260
Protein Digestion...260
Factors that Affect Protein Requirements 262

Proper Hydration...263
Sports Drinks vs. Water 264
Signs of Dehydration..265
Hydration to Maximize Training...266

Supplements 267

Types of Supplements 268

Nutritional Programming with the ACTION Personal Training System ..273
Setting Client Nutritional Preferences 273
Prerequisites to Building a Nutritional Program..................................274
Adding Custom Foods and Recipes..274
Building a Nutrition Program..276
Using the Nutrition Program...278
Searching Recipes 280
Favorite Recipes...281
Cookbooks and Grocery Lists..282
Micronutrient Analysis 283
Nutritional Tracking...284

Summary 285

Review Questions..286

References 287

Chapter 10: Legal/Business...291

Legal Issues 292
Slip and Fall..293
Equipment Usage 294
Supplements..295
Sexual Harassment 296
Personal Trainer Qualifications 297
Emergency Response..298
Confidentiality 298

Risk Management 299
Proper Education 299
Appropriate Training for Each Client 300
Limiting Liability Through Avoidance, Retention, Reduction and Transfer ... 301
Proper Conduct 302
Proper Training Area 302
Documentation 302

Selling Your Services 303
Marketing Your Business 303
Determining the Cost of Your Service 305

Retaining Clients 306
READ—Rapport, Empathy, Assessment and Development 307
Customer Service 308
Key Points for Success 309
Referrals 310
Other Incentives 311
Non-Compete Clauses 311

Expanding Your Business 311
Organizing Your Business 312
The Business Plan 313
The Budget 314
Establishing Policies 314
Clients 315
Advertisement 316
Profits 317

Summary 318

Review Questions 319

References 321

Chapter 1: The Science of Exercise

Topics Covered

The Importance of Understanding the Science of Exercise

Nervous System

Central Nervous System
Peripheral Nervous System

Skeletal System

Bones

Joints

Muscular System

Muscle Fibers

Cardiorespiratory System

Heart

Blood

Lungs

Energy Production
ATP
Glycolysis

The Importance of Understanding the Science of Exercise

Training or exercise should be a positive and beneficial part of life. It is a proven fact that exercise improves a person's overall health when done on a regular basis. Besides its use in maintaining and losing weight, exercise is known to improve the heart and blood system and to enhance muscular athletic ability. It also prevents the onset of brain diseases and boosts the effectiveness of the immune system. These beneficial results are due to the many physical changes that occur within the body during exercise.

Over time with regular exercise, the blood supply to the active muscles improves, which causes the capillaries to respond more quickly to the requirements of the muscles. Physical activity also enhances the mechanical effectiveness of the heart by enhancing the volume of blood that can be pumped. Due to this, training and exercise helps the heart learn to more quickly adapt to exertion. It also increases the actual mechanical strength of the muscle fiber and its surrounding membrane, allowing the heart to withstand the stresses and strains of intense effort without injury.

Exercise has also been known to strengthen bones by causing an increase in the bone mineral density by increasing the rate at which minerals like calcium are deposited in the bones. Since bones naturally become weaker as people age, older adults are at a high risk for bone fractures. However, moderate to strenuous exercise has been known to reduce the risk of older adults getting a fracture in the heels, hips and other bones.

Additionally, exercise protects the brain and nervous system and helps to improve brain and nerve function. Research has shown that regular exercise can protect cells in the brain and nerves from the injury or erosion that normally occurs with neurodegenerative and neuromuscular disorders like Alzheimer's and MS (multiple sclerosis). This means that exercise can also minimize the risk of dementia. In addition, exercise and other physical activity can enhance nerve growth factors which are known to support the endurance and growth of several nerve cells. This stimulation of nerve cell growth ultimately leads to increased brain functioning through improvement of certain types of learning. This exercise-induced improvement in mental health also helps to prevent depression.

Exercising on a regular basis can also boost the immune system, a natural defense mechanism used to ward off foreign organisms, viruses and chemicals. Though exercise does not enhance the normal functioning of the immune system, exercise does strengthen it in times of illness or chronic disease such as obesity, cardiovascular disease, diabetes and heart disease. Exercise is believed to encourage strong immune responses by increasing antibody and immune cell responses. There has also been scientific data suggesting additional exercise-induced immune responses may be an indirect consequence of the brain and nervous system benefits of exercise.

> Exercising on a regular basis can also boost the immune system.

Because physical activity leads to physiological changes in the body, it is important for physical trainers to understand more about exercise physiology, the study of the body's responses and adaptation to the stress of exercise. The major systems of the body each have their individual roles during exercise performance and they work interactively to respond to exercise. All these factors should be taken into consideration when planning an exercise training program. This chapter will cover details on aspects of the nervous system, skeletal system, muscular system and cardio-respiratory system.

Nervous System

The nervous system serves as the control center of the body by integrating mass communication networks consisting of billions of nerve cells called neurons, which are designed to convey information. The three major functions of the nervous system are sensory, integrative and motor functioning. The ultimate purpose of this neural network is to gather information about our inner and external surroundings (sensory function), process and interpret the information (integrative function), and then respond to these stimuli (motor function). The messages are relayed back and forth between different parts of the body.

The neuron is the functional unit of the nervous system and the merging of these cells, called neurons, creates the nerves of the body. The structure of neurons allows for very quick communication to and from the cell as well as continuous conduction of signals across the neuron. A neuron's main component is a cell body, or soma, which contains the organelles important to the proper functioning of this cell. A long branch called the axon projects out of the soma and feeds information through nerve impulses to muscles, organs and other neurons. Shorter branches called dendrites project from the soma, bringing information from other neurons of the nervous system.

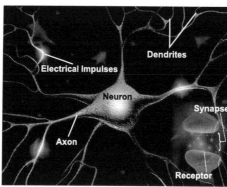

All the communication occurs across junctions referred to as synapses, which occur either between neurons or between a neuron and another cell type. A synapse is just a tiny empty space between two axons or dendrites from different cells. Within these synapses, neurotransmitters, the major chemical messengers of the nervous system, are released from the neurons before the synapse and bind to the receiving cells located after the synapse. This stimulates a signal that is called an action potential, which travels to the receiving cell, called a receptor, and then on to the cells that act on the signal in the desired location. This is how the continuation signal the neuron was transmitting makes it to the end location. For example, a signal to move your finger would travel from the brain, through many neurons and finally to the muscle in your finger.

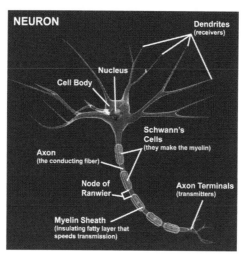

Neurons are usually covered in a layer of insulation called myelin and are therefore said to be myelinated or covered in a myelin sheath. This insulation helps signals to be transmitted faster from one nerve cell to another. In the brain, many nerve cells are not myelinated since they are located close together. But nerve cells that have long axons or dendrites need myelin to speed up the transmission time for their signals.

The different kinds of neurons are interneurons, motor neurons and sensory neurons. Interneurons transmit signals from one neuron to another neuron. Motor neurons send signals from the spinal cord or the brain to other areas of the body. Sensory neurons send signals from areas of the body to either the spinal cord or to the brain.

The nervous system is composed of two major compartments: the central nervous system (CNS) and the peripheral nervous system (PNS). The brain and the spinal cord, a long tubular continuation of the brain, are collectively known as the CNS. This is the source of conscious and unconscious thoughts, moods and emotions. The PNS is comprised of all the nerves in the body, including the cranial and spinal nerves.

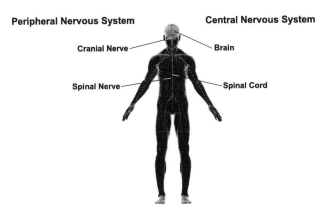

Peripheral Nervous System
Cranial Nerve
Spinal Nerve

Central Nervous System
Brain
Spinal Cord

Central Nervous System

The four major sections of the brain are the cerebrum, diencephalons, cerebellum and the brain stem. The cerebrum is the largest part of the brain, comprising 85% of the brain's total weight. The cerebrum is divided into left and right hemispheres that communicate with each other to control muscles and organs as

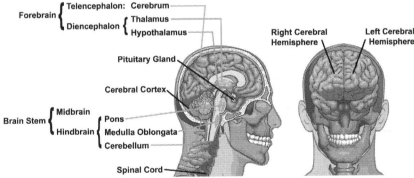

Forebrain { Telencephalon: Cerebrum
Diencephalon { Thalamus
Hypothalamus

Pituitary Gland
Cerebral Cortex

Brain Stem { Midbrain
Hindbrain { Pons
Medulla Oblongata
Cerebellum

Spinal Cord

Right Cerebral Hemisphere
Left Cerebral Hemisphere

well as thought, hearing and language. The outer portion of the cerebrum is called the cerebral cortex, which is primarily gray matter containing nerve cells.

The central part of the brain is the diencephalon, which includes glands important for the release or regulation of hormones. The cerebellum is located at the rear of the brain and is similar in function to the cerebrum but

controls balance, posture and coordination. The brain stem connects the cerebrum and cerebellum to the spinal cord and is the center for the control of visual and auditory reflexes, heart rate, blood pressure and breathing. The entire brain is protected by three layers of membranes called meninges, which are located just under the skull. The spinal cord branches out from the brain stem and its function is to send, receive and interpret nerve signals traveling between the brain and the rest of the body.

Peripheral Nervous System

The PNS is further divided into the voluntary nervous system (somatic) and the involuntary nervous system (autonomic). The somatic system signals skeletal muscles to control voluntary movement. The autonomic system, on the other hand, regulates the contraction of internal organs and therefore controls involuntary

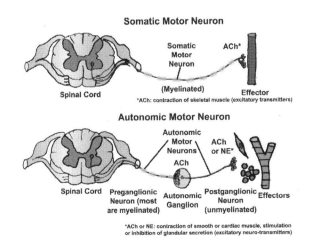

Somatic Motor Neuron
Somatic Motor Neuron
ACh*
(Myelinated)
Spinal Cord
Effector
*ACh: contraction of skeletal muscle (excitatory transmitters)

Autonomic Motor Neuron
Autonomic Motor Neurons
ACh or NE*
ACh
Spinal Cord
Preganglionic Neuron (most are myelinated)
Autonomic Ganglion
Postganglionic Neuron (unmyelinated)
Effectors
*ACh or NE: contraction of smooth or cardiac muscle, stimulation or inhibition of glandular secretion (excitatory neuro-transmitters)

physiological processes like heart rate, digestion and breathing. Since these processes could either be accelerated or decelerated, two distinct pathways of the autonomic nervous system (ANS) are present. The sympathetic ANS kicks in under stress conditions and responds accordingly, usually accelerating bodily functions like heart rate, while the parasympathetic pathways usually slow down bodily functions in rest conditions.

> When beginning an exercise program, it is important that the nervous system be properly trained.

When beginning an exercise program, it is important that the nervous system be properly trained to ensure that the right movement patterns are being developed. All movement within in the body is directly associated with the nervous system. This process will help improve performance and decrease the risk of injuries. For example, mechanoreceptors, the primary neurons important to fitness and physical movement, respond to mechanical forces. These receptors, found in muscles, tendons and ligaments, are responsible for sensing distortion in tissues, such as tension induced by exercise.

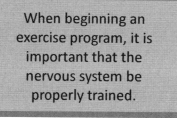

Skeletal System

The major function of the skeletal system is to provide form and shape to the body, thereby giving protection and support, plus allowing bodily movement. The skeletal system also helps in producing blood and storing minerals for the homeostasis of the body. The skeletal system determines our stature and the positioning of our bones determines our shape and size.

Our skeletal system is separated into two parts, the appendicular and the axial skeletal systems. The axial skeleton consists of the skull, rib cage and our vertebral column; the appendicular skeleton includes our upper and lower extremities.

Bones

Bones also provide protection for internal organs. For example, the ribcage protects the heart and lungs in the chest cavity. Nutrients and blood constituents are provided to the body from bone. Our bones form junctions, referred to as joints, which are linked by our connective tissue and muscles, and they are the sites where movement due to muscle contraction takes place.

In the skeletal system there are approximately 206 bones, 177 of which are used in voluntary movement. Our bones provide us with two primary functions during movement: support and leverage. Bones are the support system for soft tissues. Posture is an essential component of the support system provided by our bones and is essential for the allocation of resources within the body. With regard to leverage, our bones act like rigid levers, altering the direction and force exerted by our muscles.

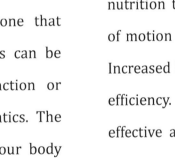

Pivot Joint

Ball and Socket Joint

Hinge Joint

Ellipsoid Joint

Saddle Joint

Gliding Joint

Joints

Our joints are formed by one bone that articulates with another bone. Joints can be categorized by their structure, function or movement, known as arthrokinemeatics. The joints that are most affiliated with our body movement are known as the synovial joints. These joints are held by a joint capsule and ligaments. They consist of roughly 80% of the joints within the body and have a large capacity for motion.

During a roll movement—especially during exercise—a bone in the joint rolls across the surface of another, similar to the tire of a motor bike that rolls down a road. A good example of this movement in our body is during a knee extension when the tibial condyles joint slides across to what is known as the femoral condyles joint. The next common movement is called the spin movement. This is when one joint surface rotates on another, similar to twisting a lid off a jar of spaghetti sauce. An example of this movement is when the forearm is rotated from the hand facing down to the hand facing up.

Stretching is the best exercise for increasing nutrition to the joints. Flexibility is the range of motion (ROM) available to a joint or joints. Increased ROM can provide greater mechanical efficiency. This efficiency results in more effective and safer movement. A mobile joint moves more easily through a range of motion and it requires less energy. Healthy flexibility means the capacity to move freely in all desired directions. The movement should be restricted to the intended movement capabilities or to the joint's functional range of motion (FROM).

> Stretching is the best exercise for increasing nutrition to the joints.

Muscular System

The forces that help the body perform physical activity are supplied by the muscular system. Muscle cells, also known as fibers, are multinucleated and connected in cylindrical bundles or individual cells. A single muscle is built from many bundles of muscle fibers called fascicule. Connective tissues run from one end of the muscle to the other, binding cells together and giving rise to muscle fiber bundles.

Muscle tissue is categorized into three types according to function and structure: cardiac, smooth and skeletal. As the names suggest, cardiac muscle is exclusively found in the walls of the heart and smooth muscle composes the epithelial of other hollow organs. Both of these muscle groups are under involuntary control. Skeletal muscle, however, is attached to the skeleton and is under voluntary control. Due to the important role of skeletal muscle in exercise and fitness, the following section reports more on the structure and function of skeletal muscle.

Skeletal muscle is composed of many thread-like striations and is attached to the skeleton. The sarcomere is the basic contractile unit of the myofibril, expanding from a Z line to the next closest Z line. Sarcomeres are composed of alternating large myosin and thin actin strands made of protein.

Myosin develops in the middle of every M line, a line that runs the length of myofibrils. The actin strands develop a Z shaped pattern down the points that are anchored, commonly called a Z line, which is characterized by having a darker color than other areas. When stimulation occurs and an action potential is received, the skeletal muscles carry out a contraction by decreasing every sarcomere. The easiest way to understand contraction is probably through the sliding filament model of

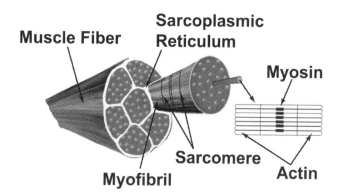

contraction in a muscle. Actin and myosin fibers overlap in a contractile motion toward each other.

Myosin filaments have club-shaped heads that project toward the actin filaments. Larger structures, known as myosin heads, are found along the myosin filament and give attachment points on binding sites for the actin filaments.

Myosin heads move in a synchronized manner toward the center of the sarcomere. They then detach and reattach to the closest active site of the actin filament. This is known as a "ratchet type drive system." As a result, this process uses up large quantities of adenosine triphosphate (ATP).

Where does the energy for contraction come from? It comes directly from ATP, which is the energy source of the cell. The job of ATP is to link the cross bridges among myosin heads and actin filaments. Energy powers the twisting of the myosin head. When used up, ATP converts to adenosine diphosphate (ADP). A person's muscles accumulate a small amount of ATP by constantly reusing the ADP and converting it back into ATP quickly. Inside muscle tissues there is a storage supply of a high-speed recharge chemical called creatine phosphate. This assists in producing the fast renewal of ADP into ATP.

What happens when a muscle needs to contract? A muscle is stimulated to contract when calcium is released from the sarcoplasmic reticulum into the sarcomere. Calcium ions are needed for every cycle of the sarcomere. It is calcium that reveals the actin binding sites. When a muscle does not need to contract, calcium ions are drawn out from the sarcomere and are stored back in the sarcoplasmic reticulum.

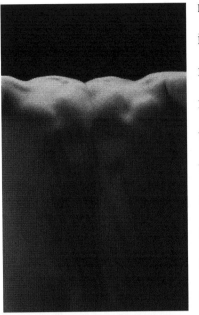

A muscle is stimulated to contract when calcium is released.

As a whole unit, skeletal muscles produce movement by pulling on the skeleton in a nervous system-controlled manner. When a muscle shortens, it moves a bone by pulling on the tendons which attach the muscle to the bone. The integration of bones, skeletal muscles and joints create apparent movements like running and walking. Skeletal muscles can even generate movements that are more subtle, which result in respiration, eye movements and facial expressions. The number of skeletal muscles used during a workout depends entirely on which exercises are chosen and the methods used during their implementation. This determines which muscles and how many are involved in the particular physical activity.

The skeletal muscles are grouped together, though this does not mean that they function together. They can either function separately or in groups along with other muscles. Power and muscle force are formed by the action of skeletal muscles. Moreover, muscle contraction movement can fulfill several other vital functions in the human body, like heat production, posture and joint stability. Sitting and standing with posture can be accomplished by contraction of muscles.

As soon as the nervous system triggers movement in the body, the entire muscle does not respond because a muscle has several motor units (a motor neuron and the muscle fibers it innervates) and the movement may require just a small part of the muscle. All of the fibers contract when a motor unit is stimulated. Clusters of motor units work in unison to manage the contractions of a muscle. Each fiber within the motor unit moves simultaneously. One individual muscle might have several motor units and the nervous system may contact many or a small percentage of them. The frequency at which the motor units fire is variable; it can be increased or decreased to help control force production. Force regulation is often referred to as force gradation—this is what allows people to control their body movements. By combining recruitment of motor units and the speed of their firing, patterns of neural discharge allow a vast selection of weak to strong contractions.

There are three muscle actions: concentric muscle actions, eccentric muscle actions and isometric (static) muscle actions. The concentric muscle actions, referred to as muscle contractions, happen when the muscle fibers are shortened. Eccentric muscle actions generate force continuously during regular body movements and this tension causes the muscles to lengthen. An example of this would be the movement of the quadriceps when a person walks down a steep hill. Other examples would be when a person sits down on a bench or the action of the forearm flexor muscles when throwing a ball. Day-to-day tasks such as walking or jogging cause spur-of-the-moment actions that are both eccentric and concentric. Isometric (static) muscle actions are a form of muscular activity that causes tension in the muscle; however, this action does not shorten or lengthen the muscle.

When a person begins body training, the blood supply to active muscles improves and the capillaries begin to respond at a fast pace. Experts have determined that an increased amount of alkali is placed in the fibers to defuse the acid that develops by physical force. An increased amount of glycogen is apparently placed in muscles to store energy, thereby allowing the nervous system which controls the muscles to work more efficiently. This is why the recovery process seems to accelerate during training. Also, during training, the mechanical strength of both the muscle fiber and the membrane (sarcolemma) is enlarged so that they have the ability to stand the aggressive action of exercise without damage.

Muscle damage is often the result of aggressive training, which can cause a breakdown of muscle fibers. In fact, aggressive training does not cause a muscle to grow or the nervous system to adapt. A good example of this would be when a person overstretches a muscle. If the muscle becomes damaged it will cause soreness and pain. Damaging a muscle during exercise doesn't lead to nervous system adaptations. The damage lessens the blood supply to the scarred area because of buildup of trauma; therefore, the fibers become more prone to repeated injury.

There are three types of muscle pain that people encounter after a workout. Soreness, often accompanied by a burning sensation, can be experienced after high-impact resistance training, cardiorespiratory conditioning or even after cooling off following a high-impact exercise session. Soreness is due to an accumulation of lactic acid during anaerobic effort. It is important to note that lactic acid is

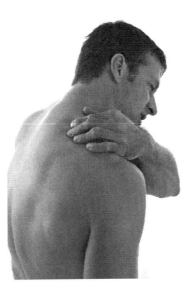

Skeletal muscles are consistently making extremely fine adjustments.

not considered a waste product; it is a by-product of anaerobic effort. The majority of lactic acid buildup normally dissolves within 30 to 60 minutes.

According to physiologists, lactate buildup is not associated with post-exercise soreness and pain that happens 24 to 48 hours after ending a normal training session. When enough oxygen is present, lactate is metabolized and can actually be used as energy. The remaining two types of soreness can happen for a prolonged amount of time right after finishing a workout. Muscle and joint soreness may develop a few hours after a workout, followed by a Delayed-Onset Muscle Soreness (DOMS) which can last for a few days. DOMS can happen when a person begins exercising after stopping for a while—the body is simply adjusting to the exercise.

Skeletal muscles are consistently making extremely fine adjustments which hold the human body in positions that are stationary. The muscle tendons extend over body joints, contributing to the stability of joints. This is particularly obvious in the shoulder and knee joints, where muscle tendons are a serious factor in the stabilization of the joints. To maintain the temperature of the body, heat production is a vital muscle by-product for metabolism. In fact, muscular contraction produces approximately 85% of the body's heat.

There are two different fiber types in the muscles of the body: "slow twitch," or Type I, and "fast twitch," or Type II. More power is generated as the fibers of muscles move more rapidly. In regards to fitness training that requires endurance and stamina, slow twitch muscle fibers are utilized. Fast twitch muscle fibers are used for strength and intensity involved in fitness training. In simpler terms, slow twitch fibers are considered low threshold because they are the first muscle fibers to be recruited for physical activity, while fast twitch fibers are considered high threshold because they are only recruited under intense conditions. Slow-twitch muscles are found more in muscles like postural muscles. These slow-twitch muscles must sustain contractions for long times without fatigue. They depend relatively more on fats for energy.

Comparison of Slow- and Fast-Twitch Muscles:

	Slow-Twitch	Fast-Twitch
Twitch Rate	Slow	Fast
Glycogen Content	Low	High
Glycolytic Capacity	Low	High
Fatigue Resistance	High	Low
Respiration Type	Aerobic	Anaerobic
Capillary Supply	High	Low

During a customized fitness training program that consists of aerobic and anaerobic exercises, various types of muscles are used. Weightlifters and bodybuilders use fast twitch muscle fibers, which provide brief bursts of strength, whereas marathon runners, hikers, bicyclists and walkers utilize slow twitch muscle fibers, which do not fatigue quickly.

Fast twitch fibers do not require oxygen; instead they utilize sugars to produce body fuel for optimal force and quick action involved in fitness training for strength. Slow fibers normally employ oxygen-utilizing (or aerobic

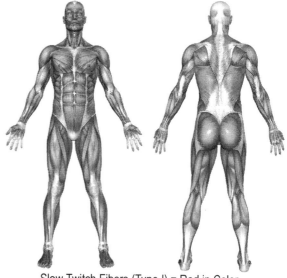

Slow Twitch Fibers (Type I) = Red in Color
Fast Twitch Fibers (Type II) = White in Color

pathways) to fuel activities that require lots of stamina and endurance. Research has shown that endurance athletes, like long-distance runners, produce less of a protein made mostly by fast twitch fibers due to a genetic mutation. Sprinters and other athletes that rely on quick bursts of energy, however, less frequently have this mutation.

Within the duration of eccentric (fast twitch) contraction, a muscle extends while under any tension because an opposite force is greater than force produced by muscle. Instead of working to pull any joint in a direction of muscle contraction, muscles decelerate the body joint at an end of any movement or else control repositioning of any load. This happens involuntarily, such as attempting to move much too heavy weight for muscles to lift, or voluntarily, such as smoothing out movement with muscles. During the short term, strength training involves contractions that are both concentric (slow twitch) and eccentric, which appears to enhance the strength of muscles more than fitness training with concentric contractions alone.

> Virtually any movement of routine action involves eccentric contractions.

To safeguard body joints from any damage, eccentric contractions generally occur as a brake-like force on the opposition to a contraction that's concentric. Virtually any movement of routine action involves eccentric contractions assisting in the maintenance of smooth body motions. Eccentric contractions can also slow down rapid muscle movements like a throw or a punch. An aspect of training for these rapid movements, like pitching a baseball or throwing a boxing jab, entails diminishing braking on an eccentric level. This allows a much greater power to develop during movement. Eccentric contractions are still being studied and researched for an ability to hasten rehabilitation of injured or weak tendons. For example, Achilles tendonitis has been proven to derive therapeutic benefits from high load eccentric contractions.

Muscle Fibers

Protein filaments make up the muscle fibers. Warm-up exercises increase muscle temperatures, which allow for greater mechanical efficiency. This efficiency is achieved by lowered viscous resistance within muscles, which helps to decrease the viscosity of the muscle. In turn, this helps protein filaments that make up muscle fibers to contract with less resistance, thus increasing the movement of the muscles.

Muscle fibers are specialized cells which are controlled by the nervous system. The chief function of these fibers is muscle contractibility. Where attached to internal organs, blood vessels or bones, muscles are liable for movement. Almost all bodily movements result from contractions of the muscles. Of course there are exceptions, such as cilia action, flagellum on cells of sperm, and movements of amoeboid of several white blood cells.

Cardiorespiratory System

The cardiorespiratory system is an umbrella term for the entire respiratory and cardiovascular systems. Acting together they offer oxygen, protective agents and nutrients to the tissues of the kinetic chain, a term referring to the muscular, articular and neural systems. The kinetic chain is also a mechanism for removing waste by-products. Basically the cardiorespiratory system is the support system for the kinetic chain to produce movement.

Lungs

Heart

Veins

Arteries

The cardiovascular system has three components: the heart, the blood vessels carrying blood between the heart and tissues, and the blood itself. The cardiovascular system plays an important role in maintaining homeostasis in the body. It also helps with continuation of normal function during exercise and rest. The cardiovascular system is accountable for the following seven functions in the body:

> The cardiovascular system helps with continuation of normal function during exercise and rest.

- Transportation of oxygenated blood from the lungs to different parts of the body and deoxygenated blood back to the lungs.

- Distribution of nutrients (e.g., free fatty acids, glucose and amino acids) to cells.

- Removal of end products and metabolic waste products (carbon dioxide, lactate and urea) from the periphery for reuse or elimination.

- Regulation of pH to control alkalosis and acidosis.

- Transportation of enzymes and hormones to control physiological function.

- Maintenance of fluid volume which helps in preventing dehydration.

- Maintenance of body temperature by absorbing and redistributing heat.

The respiratory system is often referred to as the pulmonary system and is made up of soft tissues and skeletal structures. The major role of the respiratory system is to make sure all cells function properly. This system works closely with the cardiovascular system to accomplish this task. It also provides a means of gathering oxygen from the environment and conveying it to the blood

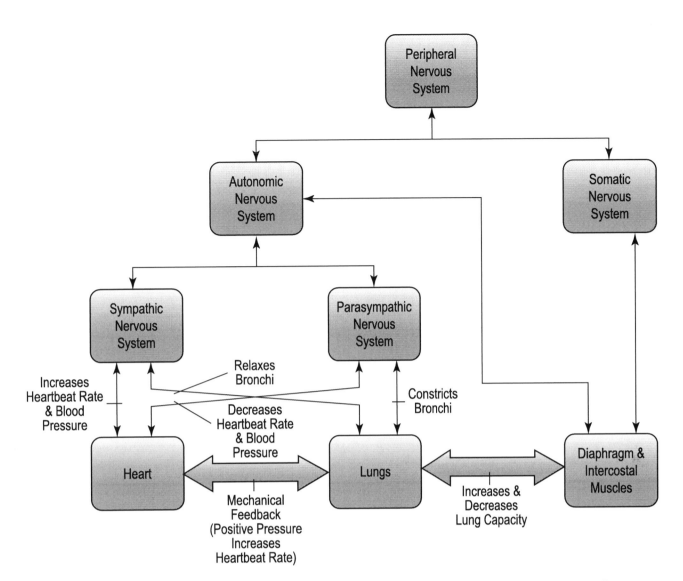

stream. In order to accomplish the movement of air in, out and through the body, the functionality of the respiratory and respiratory passageways must be integrated.

The primary respiratory muscles are the external intercostals and diaphragm, which help normal breathing, while the secondary respiratory muscles (pectorals minor and scalenes) aid in heavy, deep or forced breathing. All the structures that air travels through before entering the two respiratory passageways are called conduction passageways. The respiratory passageways collect the air coming from conduction passageways. Respiratory passageways allow oxygen and carbon dioxide to go in and out of the blood.

Heart

The heart is a muscular pump. It rhythmically contracts to push blood throughout the body. It is located in the center of the chest and is flanked by the lungs. The heart weighs about 300 grams, with an average size of an adult fist. Clients should be advised for medical checkup for diagnosing heart disease before selecting any kind of exercise or training program.

The heart is composed of four hollow chambers. Valves separate each chamber from one another and from the arteries and major veins, which prevents backflow or spillage of blood back into the chambers. These chambers are divided into two interdependent but separate pumps on both sides. The interatrial spectum separates these two pumps. Each side of the heart has two chambers: an atrium and a ventricle. The right ventricle receives deoxygenated blood coming from the right atrium then pumps the deoxygenated blood to the lungs. The reoxygenated blood coming from the lungs is received by the left atrium and then goes to the left ventricle. When the left ventricle contracts, it pushes the blood from the heart and distributes it to the body's tissues. The amount of blood pumped out with each contraction of the ventricle is known as the stroke volume. Additionally, an adequate oxygen supply is critical for myocardium because, compared to skeletal muscle, heart tissue has a very limited ability to generate energy anaerobically.

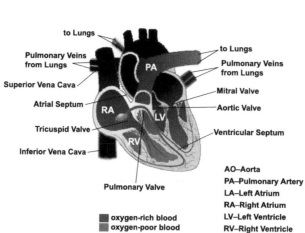

to Lungs
Pulmonary Veins from Lungs
Superior Vena Cava
Atrial Septum
Tricuspid Valve
Inferior Vena Cava
PA
RA
LV
RV
to Lungs
Pulmonary Veins from Lungs
Mitral Valve
Aortic Valve
Ventricular Septum
Pulmonary Valve

AO–Aorta
PA–Pulmonary Artery
LA–Left Atrium
RA–Right Atrium
LV–Left Ventricle
RV–Right Ventricle

oxygen-rich blood
oxygen-poor blood

Blood

Blood transports the necessary oxygen to tissues and gathers waste products from all tissues. It also transports hormones and delivers nutrients from the gastrointestinal tract to specific tissues. Blood provides a means to regulate the temperature of the body through its conduction of heat, primarily due to its water content and its flow path. Blood travels close to the skin which helps to give off heat or cool the skin, depending on the environment. The regulation of the body's water content and acid balance is based on pH values and is dependent on the blood. The clotting mechanism of blood provides protection from excessive blood loss by sealing off damaged tissue. Blood also generates specialized immune cells to fight against foreign toxins within the body, leading to a decrease in illnesses. Ironically, by the same mechanism, blood can promote the spread of foreign organisms that invade the body.

The ventricles of the heart pump and disperse the blood throughout

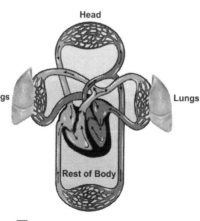

Head
Lungs
Lungs
Rest of Body

Blood carrying oxygen in arteries
Blood carrying carbon dioxide in veins

the body. Simultaneously the blood is also re-entering the heart. For proper circulation of blood throughout the body and back to the heart there must be a network through which blood can travel. This network is composed of blood vessels. Arteries are the vessels that carry blood from the heart to the entire body. Arteries are typically large and elastic and are further divided into medium-sized muscular arteries, which again branch into small arteries called arterioles. These arterioles are again divided into capillaries, which help the exchange of nutrients, oxygen, waste products and hormones. Veins are the blood vessels that carry blood back to the heart. The waste products collected in capillaries are transported for cleaning purposes by the veins.

Lungs

The two lungs, located in the chest cavity, are essential respiratory organs. Though humans have two lungs, they are non-identical and differ in size. The left lung is typically smaller than the right lung. Lungs bring oxygen into the body and remove carbon dioxide from the body. Deoxygenated blood coming from the right ventricle of the heart

is saturated by the lungs with incoming oxygen. Breathing, or ventilation, is the actual process of moving air in and out of the body.

Breathing is divided into two phases: inspiration and expiration. Inspiratory ventilation is active while expiratory ventilation can be both active and passive. When you inhale the diaphragm contracts and flattens out. Also the rib muscles lift the ribs up and outward. Thus the lungs get more space to grow larger and fill up with air. The process is reversed during expiration. The diaphragm relaxes, moves up and pushes the air out of the lungs. The rib muscles also relax and they move in. Now the lungs have smaller space, causing the air to push out.

Patients having problems with their lungs find difficulty with exercise. Training helps to strengthen the lungs and muscles, improve endurance and reduce breathlessness.

Energy Production

Energy is the capacity to do work. Chemical energy obtained from food is converted to mechanical energy that then fuels physical activity, often in the form of muscle contractions. When energy is used, it is referred to as AN energy utilizing reaction. In other words, energy is

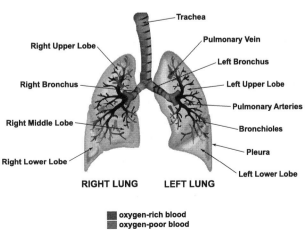

Trachea
Pulmonary Vein
Right Upper Lobe
Left Bronchus
Right Bronchus
Left Upper Lobe
Right Middle Lobe
Pulmonary Arteries
Bronchioles
Right Lower Lobe
Pleura
Left Lower Lobe

RIGHT LUNG   LEFT LUNG

■ oxygen-rich blood
■ oxygen-poor blood

collected from an energy utilizing source (the breakdown of food) by some storage unit and then transferred to a site that can use this energy.

Energy is generated from fat, carbohydrates and protein gathered from consumed food, and it can be produced aerobically (with oxygen) and anaerobically (without oxygen). The intensity of activity determines which energy system will predominate. The aerobic energy system contributes toward certain goals, while the anaerobic system can be trained for other goals. There are three energy systems for the body which are:

> **Energy is generated from fat, carbohydrates and protein.**

- Immediate Energy (ATP-CP system)
- Short term Energy (Lactic acid or Glycolytic system)
- Long term energy (Aerobic or Oxidative system)

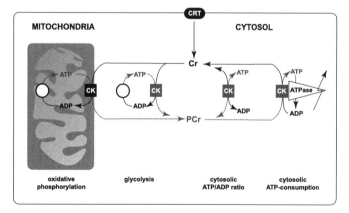

As each name suggests, each energy system relates to different activity times. The ATP-CP system is used for activity up to 10 seconds while glycolysis fuels activity up to about one minute.

Oxidative energy production is the major source of energy for greater than two minutes worth of activity.

The ATP-CP system is inefficient in producing large amounts of ATP so training these systems is neither easy nor enjoyable for most clients. The glycolytic system can generate a greater amount of energy than the ATP-CP system but it is very limited. Many training programs give more importance to this system compared to the ATP-CP system because a typical repetition range of 8 to 12 repetitions falls within this time frame. For long-term energy an oxidative system is needed. It depends mainly on fats and carbohydrates for generating ATP. Energy is produced more slowly in this system compared to other systems, because it requires a larger amount of oxygen to meet the muscular needs of exercise. Even though this is the slowest system, it produces the greatest amount of ATP. In this system, 1 glucose molecule generates 36 ATP molecules and in certain circumstances can possibly generate up to 38 ATP molecules.

ATP

Adenosine triphosphate (ATP) is the storage and transfer unit of energy within the cells of the body. Because of this, ATP is called "the energy currency" of the cell. At any one time the amount of ATP stored in the body is very small so the body needs to resynthesize ATP continuously.

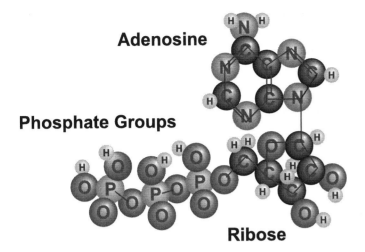

Adenosine

Phosphate Groups

Ribose

ATP is structurally composed of a nitrogen based compound, adenine, a five-carbon sugar called ribose and three phosphates. ATP has the ability to store great amounts of energy in the chemical bonds of the phosphates. Essentially this is the energy needed for the muscle contractions which create physical activity. The natural supply of ATP in each cell is inadequate; therefore, cells must have a means of generating more.

Glycolysis

Glycolysis typically takes place in the initial stage of respiration in the presence of oxygen but can also occur without oxygen present. The breakdown of carbohydrates (glucose) rapidly produces ATP. This metabolic pathway occurs in almost every cell. Through anaerobic glycolysis one glucose molecule will produce two ATP molecules while aerobic respiration

can produce many more high-energy ATP molecules. The anaerobic glycolytic system is called the short-term energy system and is used for high intensity efforts in a short period of time.

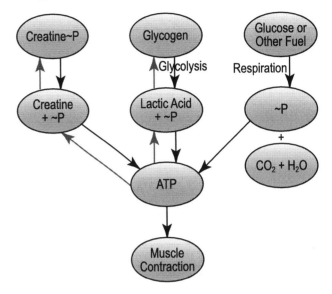

For example, anaerobic glycolysis is needed for passing a participant in a 5 kilometer race with a 60 second burst of speed.

Pyruvate is one of the by-products of this process. Two molecules of pyruvic acid are

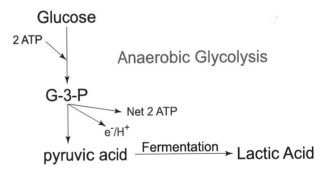

Fermentation permits more glycolysis by removing the product of glycolysis, pyruvic acid. Eventually lactic acid builds up and contributes to muscle fatigue.

usually oxidized from a single molecule of glucose. A build up of lactic acid will occur if pyruvate cannot be rapidly utilized by the muscle cell. A large accumulation of lactic acid triggers a drop in the pH of muscle cells, making them acidic and possibly interfering with muscle contractions. It may cause a burning sensation in the exercising muscles and should lead to stopping the activity or decreasing the intensity of the activity.

Summary

All systems in the human body are related. The harmonious functioning of all these systems is necessary for good health. The exercises or training programs selected must not destroy the original harmony present in the human body. For example, alterations in breathing patterns may have a direct impact on the  components of the kinetic chain and may lead to dysfunction. If the breathing patterns become shallower, the body uses secondary respiratory muscles more than the diaphragm. It may negatively impact posture. This may also cause excessive muscular tension which results in light-headedness, headaches and dizziness. Short shallow breaths can also lead to altered carbon dioxide and oxygen blood content. It may cause feelings of anxiety. Inadequate oxygen which causes retention of metabolic waste within muscles can create stiff joints and muscles.

When a client's goal is health and fitness, the personal trainer has to be aware of different kinds of exercise. A personal trainer should understand the roles of the cardiovascular and respiratory systems in exercise selection and programming. The cardiovascular system is very influential in the body's ability to consume oxygen. The personal trainer should also be aware of the science associated with energy production to effectively use it for the training of clients. To achieve specific results, the clients should have the ability to train and influence all three energy systems.

Review Questions

1. Which of the following is not a component of the cardiovascular system?

   a) The heart

   b) Blood

   c) Blood vessels

   d) Lungs

2. What are the three functions of the nervous system? _____

   _____

   _____

3. The sensory neurons transmit nerve impulses to which structures?

   a) Other neurons

   b) The brain

   c) The spinal cord

   d) The brain and the spinal cord

4. One of the main purposes of exercise is to exert the cardiovascular and respiratory systems. True or False? _____

5. What are the three systems that are collectively referred to as the kinetic chain? _____

   _____

   _____

6. Is the oxidative system for producing aerobic energy or anaerobic energy? _____

   _____

   _____

7. Which energy system is needed for running up a 100-yard hill as fast as possible?

   a) Oxidative system

   b) ATP-CP system

   c) Anaerobic Glycolysis/lactic acid system

8. What is the function of the ATP-CP system?

   a) To provide energy all the time

   b) To provide energy for low intensity long workouts

   c) To provide energy for high intensity short workouts

   d) All of the above

9. Which of the following is NOT an organ or tissue required to work intensely during a workout?

   a) Heart

   b) Lungs

   c) Muscle

   d) None of the above

10. A personal trainer can cause a client injury with an inappropriate workout if the trainer is not aware of how the body works. True or False? _____

Answers:

1. d) Lungs.

2. 1) To gather information about our inner and external surroundings (sensory function), 2) to process and interpret the information (integrative function) and 3) to respond to these stimuli (motor function).

3. d) The brain and the spinal cord.

4. True.

5. The muscular, articular and neural systems.

6. Aerobic energy.

7. b) The ATP-CP system.

8. c) To provide energy for high intensity short workouts.

9. d) None of the above.

10. True.

References

Blumenthal JA, Babyak MA, Carney RM, Huber M, Saab PG, Burg MM, Sheps D, Powell L, Taylor CB, Kaufmann PG. Exercise, depression and mortality after myocardial infarction in the ENRICHED trial. *Medicine and Science in Sports and Exercise.* 2004;36(5):746-55.

Kai MC, Anderson M, Lau EM. Exercise interventions: defusing the world's osteoporosis time bomb. *Bulletin of the World Health Organization.* 2003;81(11):827-30.

Lange-Asschenfeldt C, Kojda G. Alzheimer's disease, cerebrovascular dysfunction and the benefits of exercise: from vessels to neurons. *Experimental Gerontology.* 2008;43(6):499-504.

Rogers CJ, Zaharoff DA, Hance KW, Perkins SN, Hursting SD, Schlom J, Greiner JW. Exercise enhances vaccine-induced antigen-specific T cell responses. *Vaccine.* 2008;26(42):5407-15.

Santana-Sosa E, Barriopedro MI, López-Mojares LM, Pérez M, Lucia A. Exercise Training is Beneficial for Alzheimer's Patients. *International Journal of Sports Medicine.* 2008; 29(10):845-50.

Takahashi T, Arai Y, Hara M, Ohshima K, Koya S, Yamanishi T. Effects of resistance training on physical fitness, muscle strength and natural killer cell activity in female university students. *Japanese Journal of Hygiene.* 2008;63(3):642-50.

Yang N, MacArthur DG, Gulbin JP, Hahn AG, Beggs AH, Easteal S, North K. ACTN3 Genotype is Associated with Human Elite Athletic Performance. *Am J Hum Genet.* 2003;73(3):627-31.

Chapter 2: Biomechanics

Topics Covered

What Is Biomechanics?

The Importance of Biomechanics

Biomechanics and Exercise

Warm-Up

Cool-Down

Motion and Kinematics

Forces
Internal Forces
External Forces
Inertia

Stability of Equilibrium

Anatomic Locations

Planes of Motion

Range of Motion

Muscle Actions

Modes of Muscle Strength

Motor Control

Proprioception

Motor Learning

What Is Biomechanics?

Mechanics is the science studying the motion of objects and the forces that cause the motion. Mechanics is often divided into three main areas including rigid body mechanics, deformable-body mechanics and fluid mechanics. In rigid-body mechanics, the object in question is treated as rigid and the forces that act on the object are studied. In other words, the object does not deform by bending, stretching or condensing. Rigid-body mechanics is often subdivided into the study of statics and dynamics. Statics is the mechanics of objects at rest or moving at an unchanging velocity. On the contrary, the mechanics of dynamics looks at objects that are in accelerated motion.

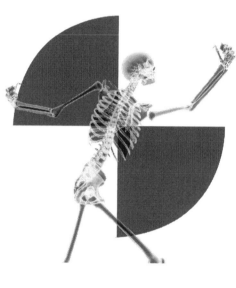

Segments of the body are often considered rigid elements, linked by bendable joints but this is not truly the case. Deformable-body mechanics and fluid mechanics are more applicable to dynamic biological systems. How forces are distributed within an object at the lowest levels encompasses deformable-body mechanics. So if the object is the body, the science of deformable-body mechanics would look at the effect of external forces on tissues and organ systems. As the name suggests, fluid mechanics deals with the forces of fluids on and within the body such as blood flowing past heart valves and the effects of swimming on the body.

The study of biomechanics is relatively new to the field of science and medicine. Biomechanics is the use of engineering principles, such as fluid mechanics and thermodynamics, and applying them to biological organisms. Biomechanics also incorporates mathematics and therefore mathematical concepts like calculus and vector algebra. These physical and mathematical principles are applied to the conception, design, development and analysis of equipment and systems in biology. Therefore, biomechanics is simply the mechanics of tissues, joints and human movement. As a study on how the body moves much like a machine, with principles of physics intertwined, biomechanics includes how "living forces interact within a living body." Research in sports biomechanics may take the form of describing movement for the enhancement of performance. Biomechanics is also often applied to sports medicine in the prevention of sports-related injuries. To accomplish this, computer modeling simulation of the body is used to aid in the study of biomechanics.

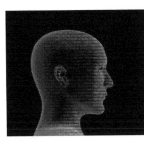

The Importance of Biomechanics

Virtually all modern advancements of medical science and technology have involved biomechanics. Because of this, biomechanics is thought to have made significant contributions to the health sciences. Developments in the field of biomechanics have improved our understanding of normal and malignant tissue abnormalities, the mechanics of neuromuscular control, and the mechanics of lung and cardiovascular function.

Biomechanics plays an important role in growth, development, tissue remodeling and physiological homeostasis. Molecular biology deals heavily with the formation, design, function and production of molecules, which are all biomechanical characteristics. For example, mechanical forces stimulate bone growth and determine how big and strong bones need to be to carry weight. Biomechanics also plays a role in some disease states by either being involved in the onset of disease or being used to treat the diseases or other illnesses. For example, biomechanical principles are involved in the ocular disease glaucoma. The eye is internally pressurized and that pressure can become elevated. This can then lead to damage of the optic nerve and eventual blindness if left untreated. On the other hand, the study of biomechanics can help in the design of implants and prosthetic devices that have mechanical function like artificial hips and hearts used in transplantation to correct biological dysfunctions.

One of the ultimate goals of biomechanics as it relates to exercise and sports is the improvement of performance. The most common way to improve performance is to develop training techniques. Biomechanics is most useful when the dominant factor has to do with the action of movements and not physical structure or physiological capacity. Using biomechanics to improve performance may be accomplished in several ways. A trainer or coach may use biomechanics to correct skeletal or joint action to improve skill. In addition, a biomechanical researcher may discover new techniques that can be used to perform skills.

Biomechanics may also prove to be useful in improving the design of sports equipment. An example of this is the production of lighter and more aerodynamic javelins or tennis racquets. Additionally, biomechanics has the potential to lead to improvements in athletic performance through advanced strength training. Biomechanical analysis can uncover technique deficiencies and identify the type of training that a person requires in order to correct such problems. For example, a person may lack strength and endurance in certain muscle groups or in their speed of movement. Knowledge of the biomechanical properties of muscle groups and movement can allow trainers and

Warm-up exercises for 5 to 10 minutes gently get the blood circulating.

coaches to easily detect setbacks and adjust training regimens accordingly.

Other goals of exercise and sport biomechanics include injury prevention and rehabilitation. Biomechanics can be useful in determining what forces caused

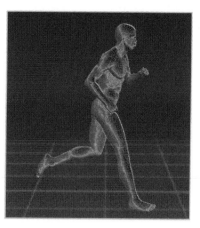

an injury and thus how to prevent this injury from reoccurring. Furthermore, figuring out what exercises aid the rehabilitation process after an injury may also be possible through biomechanics. This is directly related to improving athletic performance since the development of new techniques and equipment that prevent and treat injuries are essential. Determining how to decrease the impact of forces for a gymnast's landing or creating shoes that are not stiff for runners are also examples of how biomechanics can reduce injuries.

Biomechanics and Exercise

Understanding how the body works when it moves in a certain way or with certain intensity is possible by studying a never-ending circle called the "human movement efficiency" circle. Regardless of "how" energy is used, biomechanics also involves the "where" of energy usage and how that energy intermingles with the realm of physics, such as motion through skeletal muscles.

In general, muscles are composed of millions of fibers, which need to be warmed up and cooled down

Cool-down exercises slow the heart rate and stretch warm muscles.

to prevent muscle damage. These fibers are wrapped by fascia, or connective tissue, called endomysium. Endomysium forms bundles that are surrounded by another layer of tissue called the perimysium. The perimysium is covered by a fibrous facial layer, named the epimysium. This layer of tissue extends from the tendons that connect bones to muscles. Moreover, the area where the muscle attaches to a moveable skeletal structure (e.g., elbow) is called the insertion. An origin is defined as the area of the body where tendons attach to immobile skeletal structures.

It is well known that muscles need oxygen, but it must be noted that special mechanics are involved in the process that enables muscles to attain oxygen. More detailed components of muscle structure, its relation to the nervous system, and how muscle structure stimulates motion are also factors for both anatomy and biomechanics.

Blood cells release oxygen more rapidly at higher temperatures.

Warm-Up

Like many machines, the human body must also warm up before sharply accelerating. There are typically five biomechanical benefits of warming up. Cardiorespiratory enhancements are the first benefit of a good warm-up because it leads to less stress on a client's lungs and heart.

A proper warm-up raises the body temperature, which is beneficial because blood cells release oxygen more rapidly at higher temperatures. This leads to increased utilization of oxygen for the muscles.

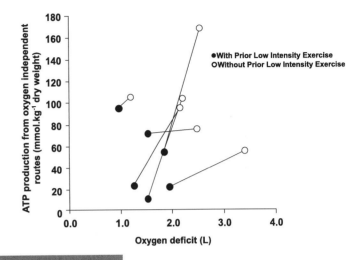

Low Intensity Exercise Chart— Effects of warm-up exercise on oxygen-independent ATP re-synthesis and the oxygen deficit. Shown is ATP re-synthesis from oxygen-independent routes following 1 minute of moderate-intensity exercise (75% of VO$_2$max) and the calculated oxygen deficit over the same period in individuals (n=6) who had performed 10 minutes of low-intensity exercise (55% of VO$_2$max) and 3 minutes of passive recovery before the moderate-intensity exercise (●), compared with values obtained in the absence of prior low-intensity exercise (O)

Secondly, blood flow to active muscles increases during a warm-up and prevents premature fatigue during the workout, not

27

to mention lactic acid buildup. Lactic acid is produced in muscle tissue during exercise, but causes muscle fatigue and cramps when large amounts accumulate. The steady flow of blood to active muscles is due to vasodilatation, which is an increase in the diameter of blood vessels in order to accelerate the passage of blood. Exercising and warming up leads to an increase in the body's core temperature. This increase in temperature causes large amounts of blood to circulate within the body quickly. Increased blood flow means more oxygen is available to tissues. In addition, proper blood circulation hinders the accumulation of lactic acid, promotes the removal of metabolic by-products, and stimulates the release of nutrient-filled fuel for active muscles.

Thirdly, as mentioned before, a heightened body temperature can be biologically beneficial. For instance, less muscle injuries occur when the body temperature rises in response to warming up or exercising. With an increased temperature, muscles become "stretchy" or more flexible, which makes it more difficult to tear muscle fibers and decreases the occurrence of injuries. Additionally, the fluidity of muscle fluids increases as body temperature elevates. This allows proteins such as actin and myosin, which make up muscle fibers, to move more freely and allow muscles to contract with less resistance. Besides the muscular benefits, joints are lubricated during warm-ups and allow movements to be carried out easily.

> With an increased temperature, muscles become "stretchy" or more flexible, which makes it more difficult to tear muscle fibers and decreases the occurrence of injuries.

Fourthly, warming up enhances motor skills and brain transmissions for continuous activity. With nervous impulses moving faster, muscle movements are made with more ease. Lastly, symptoms of stress, pain or any discomfort felt by the client from the skeletal muscles or cardiovascular systems are increased. Ironically, this can be beneficial to physical training. If these symptoms occur during or toward the end of a workout, they can be taken as normal signs of fatigue. In such cases, the trainer can assume that the current routine will not irritate any current bodily ailments and should be continued.

However, if bodily ailments present themselves after a workout as a result of excessive movement and weight training, then the client will not benefit from the regimen and a different workout routine should be designed.

Cool-Down

Just as a warm-up is crucial to any physical activity, a "cool-down" is just as important. There are explicitly four reasons why this is the case. The first reason is that cooling down delays the onset of muscle soreness after activity by reducing lactic acid buildup. Although the majority of muscle soreness is caused by irritated muscle tissue fibers from the activity itself, it has been proven that lactic acid can induce further irritation.

Secondly, if an exercise is stopped abruptly without a proper cool-down period, blood pools in the lower extremities or limbs, a phenomenon known as venous pool. When this happens, blood supply to the heart is compromised. Moreover, the heart is still pumping hard from the activity that was being performed. When both situations occur simultaneously, the heart is in dire need of oxygen, but is not be able to attain adequate quantities of oxygenated blood because blood has begun to accumulate in the lower limbs. This leads to dizziness and possibly fainting.

Thirdly, consistent with minimizing muscle soreness, cooling down can keep muscle fibers warm for a lengthened amount of time because muscle fibers are gently stretched after the workout. The warmer the tissue fibers are, the less likely

> Cooling down can keep muscle fibers warm for a lengthened amount of time because muscle fibers are gently stretched after the workout.

they will tear. A sudden increase or decrease in temperature will also cause similar tearing, so the cool-down period allows the temperature to decrease slowly.

Fourthly, excess adrenaline released during exercise can be used up during the cool-down period. When blood carries unused adrenaline, the heart becomes stressed. By cooling down, a client's body will not be as physically stressed after a workout. Until now, through understanding biomechanics, many physical trainers understood how to turn a client's engine "on" and "off". However, now biomechanics can also help trainers understand how to keep the engine in good condition when it is on and off.

Motion and Kinematics

Completely understanding the human body and the energy used in movement is the key to proper physical training and the improvement of fitness. In the field of mechanics, the analysis of motion has physical as well as geometric (mathematic) properties. The physical aspects primarily deal with the forces involved in movement and activity. These forces, both internal and external, act on different points on the body and influence specific motion. Geometrical (mathematical) descriptions of motion involve location and orientation.

The study of human motion itself is often referred to as kinematics. Kinematics also describes and analyzes motion without reference to mass, force or other circumstances leading to motion. Kinematics involves five primary variables including the timing of movement, positioning, rearrangement, speed and acceleration.

Timing provides a measurement of how long a movement lasts. This variable becomes important when determining the mechanical response to internal and external forces on the body. The position of the body during the movement determines the likelihood of an injury occurring. For instance, forces acting on a hyper-extended (straight) arm will be different from the forces acting on a flexed (bent) arm. In terms of rearrangement, linear rearrangement measures the movement from one location to another, typically in a straight line, while angular rearrangement involves the rotation of the body. Related to this variable is speed (velocity) or the measure of how fast a part of the body

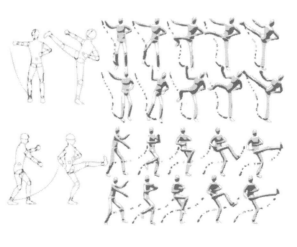

is moved. Similar to rearrangement, speed can be averaged as linear speed or angular speed. Lastly, acceleration measures how quickly speed has changed. Linear acceleration measures the change in linear speed (in a straight line) and angular acceleration notes the change in angular speed (e.g., a circular movement). Virtually all body movements involve acceleration. During running and jumping, the arms and legs are constantly accelerating rather than maintaining a constant rate of motion.

Judgments regarding normal and abnormal motion also use kinematics. Geometrical (mathematical) parameters like length, rearrangement and angle can be used to evaluate, for instance, a person's walking patterns. In this case, kinematics can be used on each body segment or on the body as a whole. The use of kinematics can then be helpful in diagnosing locomotor problems and deciding which treatment regimens and movement therapy would be most beneficial.

Forces

Mechanics deals a lot with energy, such as where it goes and how it is used. Most of the dynamic forces involved in biomechanics and around any living system are kinetic energy. Kinetic energy is the energy of motion. This area of kinetics studies the relationship between an object's movement and what caused it. For example, when there is extra energy associated with an object like a ball that is tossed, the ball will move in a certain direction. The energy used to move the ball is a form of kinetic energy. In terms of biological systems, kinetics examines the energy that causes the body to move. The size of the force is directly related to the weight of the object and how its motion will change. Additionally, just as force is required to start motion, it is also needed to stop motion.

In simple terms, a force is a push or pull on an object. Force can cause an object to start, stop, move faster or slower or change directions in movement. A force always exists between two objects whenever an interaction is initiated. Forces can be classified as internal and external, depending on the source of the force.

Internal Forces

Internal forces act within the object (e.g., the body)

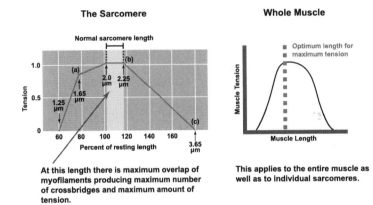

Relationship of Tension to Muscle Length

being studied. The force acts on different parts of the body but does not necessarily affect the motion of the whole body. For example, muscles pull on tendons which conversely pull on bones. The pulling force that acts on an internal structure is called a tensile force. The structure being acted on is said to be under tension. The pushing forces are referred to as compressive forces, which are forces that press objects together. In this case, the structure being acted upon is under compression. In situations where the tensile or compressive force is greater than what the object can withstand, the structure fails and can break. When this occurs in the body, muscles, joints, ligaments and bones can be damaged. Knowledge of internal forces that can affect the body when it is in motion is important for the prevention of injury.

Muscles are often thought of as the structures that produce the force in the body that leads to motion. This is mainly because muscles produce motion in the limbs of the body. However, muscles only produce internal movements (forces) and are incapable of producing changes in motion without external forces that act on the body. In other words, the body can only cause changes in motion if it pushes or pulls against an external force.

External Forces

External forces on an object are due to the influence of the surrounding environment. External forces can either be contact forces, which occur when objects physically touch each other, or non-contact forces, forces between objects that are not touching. The most common forces are contact forces. Pushing on a weight machine is an example of an external force. Magnetic, electrical and gravitational forces are all non-contact forces. Friction, another non-contact external force, is an important force in every movement. Basic activities like walking or jogging require frictional forces. For instance, shoes provide the proper frictional force between the surface of the feet and the ground or floor.

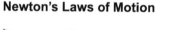

Pushing on a weight machine is an example of an external force. Magnetic, electrical and gravitational forces are all non-contact forces.

Inertia

Inertia is the property of an object to resist changes in its motion. This outlines an important relationship between force and motion. A more detailed explanation of inertia is given in Newton's first law of motion. This law states that "a body which is at rest will remain at rest unless some external force is applied to it, and a body which is moving at a constant speed in a straight line will continue to do so unless some external force is applied to it." In other words, static objects have to be pushed or pulled to be moved. However, it

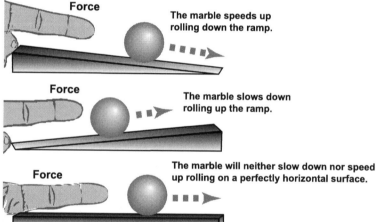

Newton's Laws of Motion

Force — The marble speeds up rolling down the ramp.

Force — The marble slows down rolling up the ramp.

Force — The marble will neither slow down nor speed up rolling on a perfectly horizontal surface.

is thought that when an object is pushed across a floor it would eventually come to a stop. The object stops when the force is removed because there is also an opposite force on the object (e.g., gravity or friction). The opposite force is primarily due to friction between the two surfaces.

Friction is defined as the resistance between two surfaces that are in contact with one another. When friction is reduced, possibly through the polishing of the surface, the pushed object has the potential to travel farther along the surface. The second part of the theory of inertia demonstrates a situation where there is no resistance due to friction or air resistance. In this case, the object will continue to move if it does not come in contact with another object or if the surface is never-ending.

Intuitively, heavier objects have more inertia (resistance) than lighter objects. However, the measure of inertia is not weight but rather mass. Weight is the measure of the force of gravity acting on an object. Mass is defined as the amount of matter in an object (an object's composition) and corresponds more closely to inertia. In situations where gravity is negligible, the weight of someone or something would change but not the mass. For example, in space, gravity does not pull objects down so objects float and appear to be weightless. However, in reality the object's composition has not changed. This becomes important in sports and exercise when a person has to change the motion of a piece of exercise equipment or parts of the body. The mass and inertia (resistance) of the equipment and the body will determine the effort that is required to get the object moving or stop the object from moving.

Stability of Equilibrium

When the body is at rest or moving at a constant speed, the body is said to be in equilibrium. The major characteristic of equilibrium is that the overall force on the body in all directions is zero. This means that the rightward forces on the object are balanced by the leftward forces and the upward forces are balanced by the downward forces.

Equilibrium Types

Stable

Unstable

Neutral

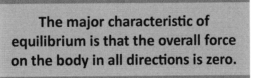

There are three types of equilibrium for an object depending on the stability of the body. These classes are stable equilibrium, unstable equilibrium and neutral equilibrium. For stable equilibrium to occur, a slight disturbance must generate a force that restores the object to its equilibrium position. When a force causes an object to move away from its equilibrium, it is known as unstable equilibrium. Neutral equilibrium occurs when there are no forces acting on an object.

Many everyday objects are constantly in a state of equilibrium because of friction. An object may rely on the friction of a surface to prevent it from

> The major characteristic of equilibrium is that the overall force on the body in all directions is zero.

moving. If the surface that the object was on was frictionless, even the smallest force would cause a large object to slide in a particular direction.

The two important aspects of equilibrium in the human body are intrinsic (inward) and extrinsic (outward) stability. For intrinsic stability to occur, the segments of the body need to be balanced. The body has intrinsic muscular actions that control and stabilize an erect human body around the joints of the spine and the limbs. This stability requires a constant, conscious state that is controlled by the brain and spinal cord (central nervous system). The stability of the whole body, with respect to objects that are supporting it, is extrinsic stability. For example, a person standing on the ground uses the ground to support the body, similar to a chair that a person may be occupying.

Anatomic Locations

Biomechanics involves another field called kinesiology. Kinesiology emphasizes biomechanics when it comes to the muscular and skeletal system, not to mention the joints. Physical trainers commonly use kinesiology to

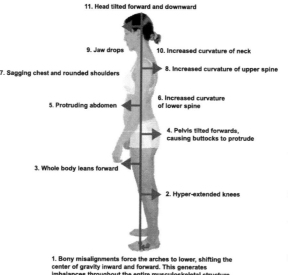

11. Head tilted forward and downward
9. Jaw drops
10. Increased curvature of neck
8. Increased curvature of upper spine
7. Sagging chest and rounded shoulders
6. Increased curvature of lower spine
5. Protruding abdomen
4. Pelvis tilted forwards, causing buttocks to protrude
3. Whole body leans forward
2. Hyper-extended knees
1. Bony misalignments force the arches to lower, shifting the center of gravity inward and forward. This generates imbalances throughout the entire musculoskeletal structure.

deal with body posture and alignment. When it comes to body posture, anatomical (bodily) positions refer to reference points. Often times it is important to be able to identify relative locations on the body and be able to access these points on other people.

Anatomical (bodily) locations relate the regions and specific arrangement of different body parts to the actual position of the body. Such reference points are meant to expose special relationships between how bones, muscles and joints are configured. Universally, the most common position of reference is known as the basic anatomic position. This is when one is standing facing forward with feet together and hands at the side. The feet and palms of the hands are also faced forward.

Anatomical locations include the superior (upper), inferior (lower), proximal (toward center), distal (away from center), anterior (front), posterior (back), medial (middle), lateral (side), contralateral (opposite side) and ipsilateral (same side) positions. Superior refers to the upper parts of the body and inferior the lower parts. For example, the knee is said to be superior to the ankle and the hand is inferior to the shoulder. The area close to the center of the body or midline is known as proximal. Distal is the position farthest from the center. The front of the body is the anterior side and the back of the body is the posterior side. Medial refers to the middle of the body or the point where the body can be divided into two halves. Lateral refers to one side of the body. The right foot is said to be contralateral to the left foot; however, the right foot is ipsilateral to the right hand.

Some people have common natural body positions that cannot conform to the basic anatomic position. One of these conditions is known as valgus or the outward curve of a limb. Conversely, there is varus or the inward curving of a body part. Simply stated, these anatomical conditions are referred to as being "bowlegged" and "knock-kneed," respectively.

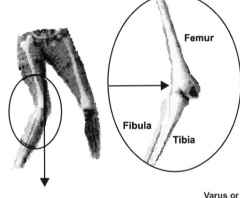

Varus or bowlegged deformity

(body positions) applies the knowledge of axes rotation and muscle position to determine which muscles may contribute to motion in a particular direction. Knowledge of how the body moves in relation to its spine, muscles and joints can help a trainer design routines that will be beneficial for the client. Motion at the joints in a particular direction often occurs by rotating the joint approximately 90° or in other words, up and down. This action is called joint motion, another understanding of how a client's body moves and works.

Both kinesiology and biomechanics lead to the understanding of planes of motion. In this case plane means direction. The planes of motion refer to the three basic imaginary planes that meet at one point in the body. Though motion is said to occur in a specific plane, motion does not strictly occur in one plane of motion, but rather in multiple planes. These planes include the sagittal plane, frontal plane and the traverse plane. The sagittal plane divides the body into the right and left sides. The frontal plane, also known as the

Planes of Motion

Human movement in the three dimensions is based on a system of planes (flat surfaces) and axes (e.g., the spine). Functional anatomy

Frontal

Sagittal

Transverse

coronal plane, separates the body into front and back sections. Lastly, the upper and lower areas of the body are designated by the traverse plane.

The sagittal plane separates a client's body into a right side and a left side. This plane is used to perform most activities because it permits the flexing and extending of muscles. Flexing basically means "the bending of" and extensions are the "straightening of." Flexing

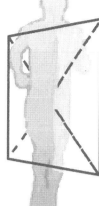

is movement toward the middle of the body that decreases the angle between the two moving segments of the body. This movement is typically directed toward the upper parts of the body such as the head, neck, trunk, upper extremities and hips. Movements of the lower extremities such as the knees, ankles and toes also move along the sagittal plane. Injuries often occur when joints and muscles are improperly flexed or overextended. Hyperflexion refers to flexing a part of the body too hard or beyond its normal limits. Extending a body part beyond its normal range is known as hyperextension.

The frontal plane involves movements from the front and back of the body. Movements include those that are related

to the trunk, the flexing of the spine, and ankle and foot flexing, as well as abduction and adduction. Abduction simply refers to a sideways movement of a limb away from the body, whereas adduction is the movement that returns the limb to its original position. Hyperabduction and hyperadduction are movements that push limbs beyond their limits. This is usually when injuries occur. Side lunges and side lateral raises are examples of frontal plane movements.

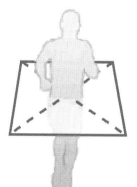

Lastly, the transverse plane separates the body into an "upper" and "lower" half. This plane is considered rotational motion. Because this plane stresses movement along a vertical axis (the spine), internal and external rotations occur. Movements of the leg or arm in a horizontal direction are most common for this plane of motion. Examples of this motion include throwing a ball, swinging a bat and golfing. The foot is unique in that it has transverse plane abduction and adduction. When the toes are pointed outward and the foot is rotated outward, this motion is termed abduction. Pointing the toes inward and rotating the foot inward is termed adduction.

Range of Motion

Range of Motion (ROM) is a measure of the body's flexibility by observing the number of degrees the body can move through a set of neutral positions and exercises. The anatomical reference position aids in accurate measurements of the range of motion. The ROM at the joints is

often considered since the majority of movement in the body occurs at the joints. The body as a whole or specific motion at the joints can occur through rearrangement, rotation or by some combination of the two movements.

A motion of the body that moves all points on straight lines over an identical distance is called linear movement or rearrangement. Simply stated, rearrangement is a movement of the body that changes the final position of the body. For example, when a person throws a baseball, the body's position completely changes after the ball is thrown.

Rotation is different from rearrangement. It is the movement of an object in circles. This movement

occurs with a constant angle of rotation around the center of the body. The rotation has a specific direction and may be positive or negative, depending on the reference point. A positive rotation is in a counterclockwise direction while a negative rotation is in a clockwise direction.

For example, spinning a basketball on a finger is a rotating motion.

In terms of joint movement, the pivot point is the point around which the joints rotate. The fundamental movements at the pivot point are the roll, slide and spin. The majority of the body's movements are due to motions at the pivot points, or junctions, of the joints. A limited ROM in this area can be caused by muscle weakness, nerve and spinal damage or even arthritis. Rotation of the trunk, or axial rotation, is another common activity of

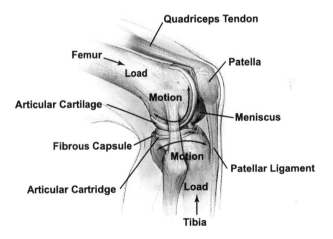

daily life. Many activities require the rotation of the trunk through various degrees.

The difference between rotation and rearrangement is easy to differentiate. When rearrangement occurs, the whole object moves to an entirely new position. When rotation occurs, the object remains in the same place and just moves around a fixed axis. However, as the body moves, rearrangement and rotation are often combined. A body can begin an action by rotating and then start to move along a straight line during the second part of the action. The movement that needs to be carried out determines whether or not the body will rotate or be rearranged.

Two major terms that define motion and describe rotation include pronation (downward motion) and supination (upward motion). These movements occur in the forearm and the foot. In the hand and forearm, pronation occurs when the palms are rotated in a downward position. The rotation of the foot in a direction that causes more weight to be supported on the inside of the foot is also pronation. Supination is a rotation that causes the palms to face upward or when the foot is rotated to cause weight to be on the outside of the foot.

Muscle Actions

Overall, biomechanics research can improve exercise performance and conditioning of muscles. Muscle action is the activation of

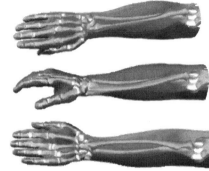

Pronation

Supination

Isometric Contraction
Muscle contracts but does not shorten

No Movement
(a)

Concentric Contraction

Movement

(b)

Eccentric Contraction

Movement

(c)

muscles by the nervous system. This contributes to overall movement and stabilization. Bodily movements are due to the contraction of skeletal muscle, force and work generated by the body.

During typical strength training, various muscle groups contract hundreds of times to move the body. Muscles produce a variety of actions to manipulate the external forces that act on them, such as gravity and external resistance. There are three muscle actions: concentric muscle actions, eccentric muscle actions and isometric (static) muscle actions. Often, day-to-day tasks such as walking or jogging cause spur of the moment actions that are a combination of all three of the muscle actions.

Isometric literally means "same length" and an isometric muscle action occurs if the measurement of the force acting on the muscle is exactly equal to the force of the muscle's resistance. In other words, the muscle is exerting a force equal to what is placed on it. In this case, the muscle generates force and attempts to shorten but cannot overcome the external resistance.

An isometric muscle action does not cause a change in the length of the muscle fiber. However, there will be some shortening of elastic structures such as tendons and connective tissue. Because there is no overall shortening of the muscle, this action is considered to be a stabilizing contraction. This type of muscle action allows a person to hold a position for a relatively long period of time. 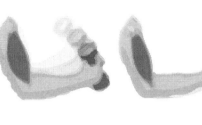 A bodybuilder's pose is a great example of an isometric contraction.

Clinically, isometrics are used during the early phases of rehabilitation when movement has to be limited to prevent further injury. Isometric training is also important for people participating in activities that need the static (fixed) muscle contraction. Activities like surfing, rock climbing and skiing often require the ability to maintain prolonged static positions. Practice in maintaining an isometric hold on a climber's wall or doing a pull-up can maximize isometric strength  training. Relatively very few athletic activities involve isometric muscle actions so isometric strength does not completely predict success in all sporting activities.

Concentric muscle action occurs when the force generated by the muscle is sufficient to overcome any resistance. The force that develops depends on the muscle tension needed to move the load and varies with joint position. This ultimately causes the muscle-tendon unit to shorten. Concentric actions are often referred to as the positive phases of repetition or most simply, muscle contractions. An arm curl with a dumbbell is an example of a concentric muscle action. Most people focus heavily on this muscle action and neglect the others. However, it is the combined action of all three contractions that are necessary and important.

After an arm curl, the lowering of the dumbbell causes the muscle to lengthen. This lengthening of an activated muscle is known as an eccentric muscle action. In this case, the force generated by the muscle is not enough to overcome the resistance being placed on it. Eccentric muscle 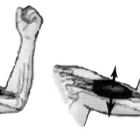 actions are considered to be muscle actions that generate force continuously during regular body movements. An example of this would be the movement of the quadriceps when a person walks down a steep hill. Other examples include when a person sits down on a bench or the action of the forearm muscles when a ball is thrown.

Within the duration of an eccentric (fast twitch) contraction, a muscle extends when it is under tension because the opposite force is greater than the force produced by the muscle. Instead of working to pull the joint in the direction of the muscle contraction, muscles relax the joint at the end of the movement. This allows the joint to be ready to repeat the movement and prevents injury. Injuries can happen involuntarily, when a person attempts to move objects that are too heavy, or voluntarily, when the body can accommodate the weight that is being lifted.

Eccentric contractions generally happen with any abrupt force in opposition to a concentric contraction in order to secure the body's joints from any damage. Virtually any routine movement involves eccentric contractions, which assist in the maintenance of smooth body motions. Eccentric contractions can also slow down rapid muscle movements like a throw or a punch. An aspect of training for these rapid movements, like pitching a baseball or throwing a boxing jab, is being able to increase the body's ability to carry out a movement with much greater power while being able to stop the movement on a moment's notice. Eccentric contractions are still being studied and researched for the

Constant Load

Eccentric Action

ability to hasten rehabilitation of injured or weak tendons. For example, Achilles tendonitis has been proven to derive therapeutic benefits from high load eccentric contractions.

There has been much debate over the importance of all three of these muscle contractions in strength training. Research attempts to determine which muscle contraction leads to significant increases in strength and muscle mass. Eccentric and concentric muscle contractions have been found to produce greater force than isometric muscle contractions and thus it has been hypothesized that these actions are more important. While researchers have found that training with a focus on isometric muscle contractions increases muscle strength and size, this impact has only been proven with respect to specific joint angles. Isometric training can therefore be beneficial, but it is important that all three muscle actions be included in a workout routine for better muscle training.

> Eccentric and concentric muscle contractions have been found to produce greater force than isometric muscle contractions.

Modes of Muscle Strength

Muscle strength is one of the major components of physical fitness. It refers to the maximum amount of force that a muscle can exert or the capacity of a muscle to develop voluntary tension. This tension is often used to further increase the strength of muscles. Strength training is often used for conditioning, reducing fatigue and preventing muscle soreness as well as in instances of rehabilitation of injured athletes. Increasing aspects of muscle strength training have been attributed to high levels of athletic performance.

A common clinical method to determine muscle strength is the manual muscle test

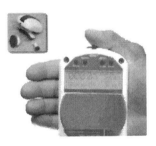

(MMT), which is used to determine the capability of muscles or groups of muscles to provide support and movement. A MMT is also a non-invasive way to assess physical weakness, faulty posture, muscle imbalance and sensitivities in the neuromuscular (nerve and muscle) system.

Almost all modes of muscular strength are related to each other and are related to various forms of muscle actions. All these modes can be conducted through weight training and exercises which use the body weight as resistance. Muscular strengthening is usually measured in linear or rotational force and includes isometric, isokinetic and isotonic modes.

Contraction against a fixed, immovable object is involved in the isometric mode of muscle strength testing. As with isometric muscle action, this is a static (fixed) exercise that occurs when a muscle contracts without an observable change in length. Although no physical work is being performed, this strength training mode generates a great deal of tension and force. Ideally, muscles that are contracting isometrically can be held against an object that produces resistance for at least six seconds to allow peak tension in the muscle to develop. These exercises are especially

Isometric Test Positions

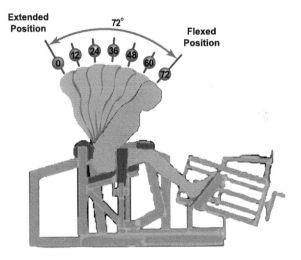

beneficial in the early rehabilitation process for clients after injury when other modes of strength training maybe too painful.

Isotonics are carried out against a constant or even variable force to lengthen or shorten muscles through a specific range of motion. Due to this, concentric and eccentric muscle actions are a major part of isotonic strength training. Isotonic muscle strengthening occurs by lifting free weights and through many other basic movements. Other examples of isotonic exercises include hip extensions, hip abductions and knee extensions.

Isokinetics is exercising with a constant resistance and a fixed speed. It can also be simply defined as "constant speed". Isokinetic techniques test joint movement rather than a specific muscle group. Isokinetic actions are performed on a dynamometer, a device that accommodates the resistance based on the amount of force produced. This ultimately allows the movement to occur at a constant speed regardless of force. The major advantage of isokinetics over isometric strength training is that maximum force, called peak force, is produced throughout

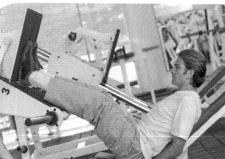

the entire range of motion. Many machines used for isokinetic strength training are capable of concentric and eccentric training and achieve isokinetic exercise by changing the resistance as the muscle contracts or expands. Due the limited motility and the narrow bench of these machines, this mode of exercise may be difficult initially.

Motor Control

The body must be able to exhibit precise control over its segments. This segmental control incorporates processes involving all components of the nerve, skeletal and muscular systems to produce deliberate and effective motor responses. Motor control is simply the ability to regulate and direct movement. The concept of motor control addresses how the central nervous system (CNS) organizes and controls the series of individual muscles and joints. It also explains how sensory information from the environment influences movement. Motor control is usually studied in relation to specific activities and how control processes work.

Muscle synergy, sequential activation of muscle groups, is one of the most important concepts in motor control. Muscles do not act alone but are recruited by the CNS in groups. In other words, these muscle groups operate as a functional unit to become automatic and effortless. The term used to define the functional grouping of muscles is synergy.

These recruited muscle groups transmit force onto their respective bone based on the particular muscle-bone attachment sites and the angle of attachment. This ultimately creates movement in the joints. Known as a force-couple, the sequential action of the muscle is responsible for this movement. The resultant motion depends on the structure of the joint and the distinct pull of each muscle involved.

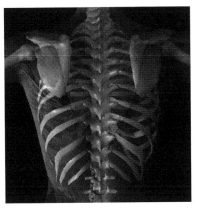

Proprioception

Motor control often involves cognition (learning and reasoning) and areas of perception known as proprioception. Proprioception is being able to sense the location and position of parts of the body in relation to each other and the body as a whole. It is the ability to know if the body is in motion and, when it is, where each part is located during the movements. In order to accomplish this, sensory cues are obtained from muscular, skin, joint, tendon and ligament tissues. These inputs are then processed as sensory information (e.g., touch and sight) in the brain and spinal cord to regulate reflexes and motor control. Though the initial sensing of the position of limbs in space was referred to as proprioception, the definition of this system has been expanded to the interaction between the sensory pathways and the motor system. The combination of the sensory and motor system is also known as the sensorimotor system.

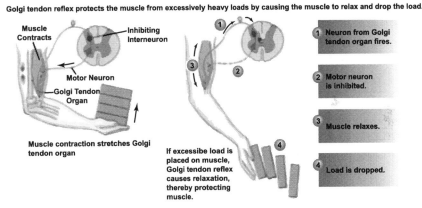

Golgi tendon reflex protects the muscle from excessively heavy loads by causing the muscle to relax and drop the load.

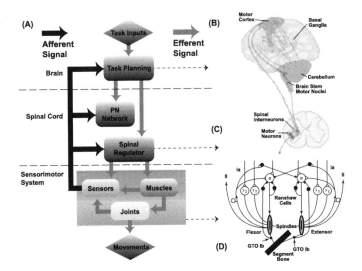

Proprioceptors, specialized nerve endings, are located deep within the tissues of muscles, tendons and joints. These are the nerves that respond to the subconscious sense of position and movement, and they also sense tissue deformations. With any change in tissue pressure or if deformities develop, these nerves send a signal to the brain and spinal cord (central nervous system).

The two major categories of proprioceptors are muscle cells, which are located in the belly of the muscle, and the tendon cells, which are located in the area where muscle fibers attach to tendon tissue. Muscle cells relay information directly to the spinal cord from muscle fibers. Tendon cells monitor the amount of tension in muscle cells that builds during stretching and contracting.

There are three main groups of proprioceptors -ligament, joint and skin proprioceptors; neck and inner ear proprioceptors; and muscle proprioceptors. Proprioceptors in the skin, joints and ligaments send signals to the brain when pressure changes or an injury occurs. The neck contains an extremely large number of proprioceptors that are responsible for stabilizing the head upon the neck and the neck upon the body. The proprioceptors in the inner ear give the body a sense of equilibrium or balance. This is accomplished by nerves that measure the movement of fluid in the ear and send a signal to the nervous system that controls the head's position and its ability to move properly. Through muscle contractions, the muscle proprioceptors are directly involved in human posture and movement.

When a part of the body is stimulated, the signal is received at three separate places—the visual system, the inner ear system and the sensory cell system. Importantly, the sensory cells act as the transporters of mechanical energy and provide a sense of position and conscious awareness by initiating reflexes that stabilize joints during a movement. Next, the message is transferred to the brain and spinal cord where it is processed at one of three levels of motor control. The first

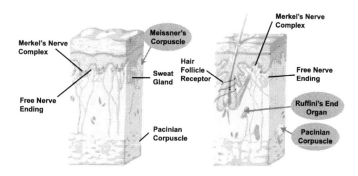

level of motor control is a fast, reflex response at the spinal cord level, necessary for protective reflexive joint stabilization and the prevention of injuries in the skeletal system. The second level of motor control involves the lower parts of the brain (e.g., brain stem). This part of the brain processes higher commands and is involved in the timing of motor activities, learning of planned movement and control of prolonged and repetitive movements. Thirdly, processing at the cerebral level controls voluntary motion. Cerebral refers to the two halves of the brain, which are the dominant parts of the central nervous system.

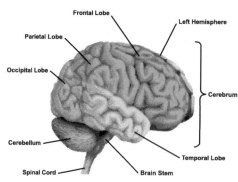

The task of defining proprioception has always been controversial; however, there are various accepted methods used to assess the proprioceptive control of the joints. This includes assessing joint position. In this assessment, the limb is set at a certain angle. The subject is then asked to recreate this angle. The deviation from the actual angle determines the brain" ability to sense the joint position.

Another method to access proprioception is the perception of passive movement. In this method, the ability to detect movement of the limbs is tested. The subject's eyes are covered and a limb is placed at a certain angle. The limb is then slowly moved and the subject is asked to indicate when motion is first detected. The measurement of the distance traveled between the time motion started and when it was first detected is recorded and assessed. Additional tests include reaction time of reflexes and balance assessment for postural control.

Gender differences in proprioception have also been examined. Female athletes are thought to have deficits in proprioception, evidenced by a four- to sixfold higher incidence of knee injuries compared to their male counterparts. Other studies, however, have shown no differences in aspects of proprioception between genders.

Overall, differences in other aspects of motor control between men and women are controversial.

Motor Learning

Motor learning is incorporating motor control processes with experiences. The combination of these processes leads to an increase in the ability to develop skilled movements. After repeated experience with a particular motion, one learns to perform the movement more efficiently. Motor learning teaches the body and body parts to work correctly and sequentially. Examples of this include throwing a ball or climbing trees. Motor learning is also critical for the reflex response.

Storing exercise routines in one's memory is necessary to develop motor learning skills. Feedback (memory) is a circular process in which the movement of the body is returned to the brain for processing. Feedback also uses the senses (e.g., sight and sound) to aid in motor patterns and allows efficient movements to be carried out. There are two major forms of feedback – internal feedback and external feedback.

Internal feedback is also referred to as sensory (senses) feedback. This is a process in which sensory information such as sound is used by the body to monitor movement as well as the external environment. Information from

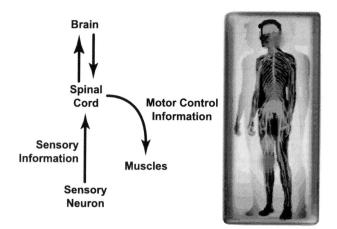

posture, external forces and kinematics is used to guide movement patterns. This is one of the reasons why it is important to have proper form when exercising: it ensures that the sensory feedback is transmitting correct information to the brain.

External feedback is provided by external sources such as monitoring equipment, audio/visual devices, a health care professional or a personal trainer. External feedback provides information on whether movement patterns are correct or incorrect and associates such movements with internal feelings. External feedback can be in the form of processing physical performance or processing the results of an exercise routine. Analyzing physical performance provides information about the quality of the movement. For instance, whether or not the body is in the correct position during

an exercise routine. Analyzing the results of an exercise routine allows the client and trainer to determine if the regimen is producing the desired results. All forms of external feedback, however, allow for the correction of performance errors and improve efficiency.

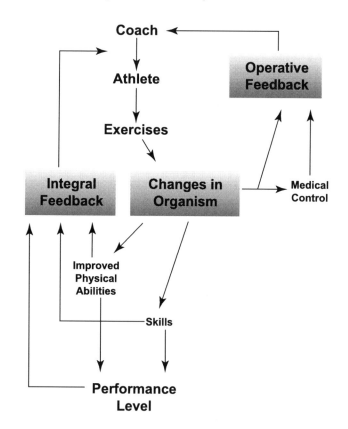

Biomechanics is a relatively new field that includes applying principles of physics to the human body and biological systems. Biomechanics is often used to develop a better understanding of biological processes and exercise science through the study of motion, forces and the structure of the body. Biomechanics is often a useful tool for physical educators and athletic trainers. Applications of biomechanics include performance improvement or the reduction of injuries. Many aspects of rehabilitation after injury involve knowledge of biomechanical principles.

Exercise and sports biomechanics primarily contain aspects from the branch of mechanics known as rigid-body mechanics. The subdivisions of rigid-body mechanics include analyzing the body's movements mathematically (statistics) and forces that cause movement (dynamics). Kinematics, the study of the motion in the body, is a major component of dynamics. Major mechanical concepts used in biomechanics include force, mass and inertia (the body's resistance a change in force). There are both external and internal forces that influence motion in general. These forces can be caused by direct contact of another object with the body or by forces found in daily life, like gravity and friction.

The body is in a constant state of motion that is controlled subconsciously when the body is at rest. The body is complex and moves in three dimensions through a system of planes and axes. This allows the body to create various movements and attain a wide range of motion. Joints, in particular, enhance the body's ability to carry out specific movements.

> **The body is in a constant state of motion that is controlled subconsciously when the body is at rest.**

Muscles may contract concentrically, eccentrically or isometrically, depending on the relationship between forces like tension and resistance. Muscle actions also differ depending on whether they are dynamic (moving) or static (still). Muscles move in functional groups known as synergies, the sequential order of muscle movements, to produce these distinct contractions. Motor control, involving the neuromuscular system, is important in regulating and directing deliberate movement. The neuromuscular system involves the relationship between muscles and nerves. Proprioception is also essential for sensing the location, orientation and movement of the body using internal stimuli. Motor learning allows muscles to properly conduct repetitive movements.

Review Questions

1. Which of the following is a not part of the study of biomechanics?

   a) Physics; fluid mechanics and thermodynamics (the study of energy)

   b) Biology; understanding tendons and muscles

   c) Mathematics; calculus and algebra

   d) Chemistry; the production of hormones during exercise

2. Kinematics is the study of human motion. True or False? _____

3. What are three of the biomechanical processes that occur during a warm-up exercise? ___

   _____

   _____

4. What are the three groups of proprioceptors?_____

   _____

   _____

5. As you walk from one end of the room to another, what forces are influencing your movement?

   a) Gravity

   b) Friction

   c) Tension

   d) All of the above

6. What is the opposite of the motion pronation (to turn the palms face down)?

   _____

   _____

7. What are the three planes of motion that intersect (meet at one point) in the body?

   _____

   _____

8. Concentric, eccentric and isometric/static are the names of three major types of what? _

   _____

   _____

9. How is muscle strength typically measured?_____

   _____

   _____

10. What system of the body plays a role in proprioception (perception of an object's position)?

    a) Nervous system

    b) Cardiorespiratory system

    c) Immune system

    d) Digestive system

Answers

1. d) Chemistry; the production of hormones during exercise.
2. True.
3. Any three of these -1) Cardiorespiratory changes (increased utilization of oxygen by muscles); 2) increased blood flow to active muscles; 3) increased body temperature; 4) enhanced motor skills and brain transmissions with nervous impulses moving faster; and 5) increased discomfort from muscles and cardiorespiratory system.
4. 1) Ligament, joint and skin proprioceptors; 2) neck and inner ear proprioceptors; and 3) muscle proprioceptors.
5. d) All of the above.
6. Supination.
7. 1) The sagittal plane; 2) the frontal plane; and 3) the traverse plane.
8. Muscle action.
9. The manual muscle test (MMT).
10. a) Nervous system.

References

Bensoussan L, Viton JM, Barotsis N, Delarque A. Evaluation of patients with gait abnormalities in physical and rehabilitation medicine settings. *Journal of Rehabilitation Medicine.* 2008;40(7):497-507.

Blumenthal JA, Babyak MA, Carney RM, Huber M, Saab PG, Burg MM, Sheps D, Powell L, Taylor CB, Kaufmann PG. Exercise, depression and mortality after myocardial infarction in the ENRICHED trial. *Medicine and Science in Sports and Exercise.* 2004;36(5):746-55.

Clark FJ, Grigg P, Chapin JW. The contribution of articular receptors to proprioception with the fingers in humans. *Journal of Neurophysiology.* 1989;61(1):186-93.

Drury DG. Strength and proprioception. *Orthopedic Physical Therapy Clinic.* 2000;9(4):549-61.

Famuła A, Nowotny-Czupryna O, Brzek A, Nowotny J, Kita B. Telereceptive and proprioceptive control of balance vs. Body stability in elderly people. *Orthopedic Traumatology Rehabilitation.* 2008;10(4):379-90.

Hewet TE, Paterno MV, Myer GD. Strategies for enhancing proprioception and neuromuscular control of the knee. *Clinical Orthopedic Related Research*. 2002;(402):76-94.

Kai MC, Anderson M, Lau EM. Exercise interventions: defusing the world's osteoporosis time bomb. *Bulletin of the World Health Organization*. 2003;81(11):827-30.

Lange-Asschenfeldt C, Kojda G. Alzheimer's disease, cerebrovascular dysfunction and the benefits of exercise: from vessels to neurons. *Experimental Gerontology*. 2008;43(6):499-504.

Rogers CJ, Zaharoff DA, Hance KW, Perkins SN, Hursting SD, Schlom J, Greiner JW. Exercise enhances vaccine-induced antigen-specific T cell responses. *Vaccine*. 2008;26(42):5407-15.

Rossi-Durand C. Proprioception and myoclonus. *Neurophysiology Clinic*. 2006;36(5-6):299-308.

Santana-Sosa E, Barriopedro MI, López-Mojares LM, Pérez M, Lucia A. Exercise Training is Beneficial for Alzheimer's Patients. *International Journal of Sports Medicine*. 2008;29(10):845-50.

Stuempfle KJ, Drury DG, Wilson AL. Effect of load position on physiological and perceptual responses during load carriage with an internal frame backpack. *Ergonomics*. 2004;47(7):784-89.

Takahashi T, Arai Y, Hara M, Ohshima K, Koya S, Yamanishi T. Effects of resistance training on physical fitness, muscle strength and natural killer cell activity in female university students. *Japanese Journal of Hygiene*. 2008;63(3):642-50.

Chapter 3: Client Assessment

Topics Covered

The Importance of a Client Assessment

The General History Section of the Initial Client Assessment
Occupation
Lifestyle

The Medical History Section of the Initial Client Assessment
Injuries
Surgeries
Diseases and Medical Conditions
Medications

Using a Questionnaire
Example of Initial Client Assessment Form

The Physical Assessment Section
Pulse
Blood Pressure
Flexibility
Posture
Body Fat
Body Mass Index (BMI)
Step Test
Walk Test
Muscular Performance

How Thorough Should Each Initial Assessment Be?

Personalizing or Designing Custom Test

The Importance of a Client Assessment

A fitness assessment is an essential part of the design of a healthy and effective fitness and/or weight loss program for individuals. Fitness assessments can provide an estimated measure of a client's fitness level by measuring cardiorespiratory endurance, muscular endurance, strength, flexibility and body composition. The results of an assessment reveal a client's current level of fitness and can be used to tailor an exercise program that fits the client's specific needs.

Trainers should give pre-testing questionnaires that include surveys of medical history as well as current lifestyle and fitness activities to client's before assessments.

These questionnaires help a trainer understand a client's lifestyle and medical history, since these may significantly affect a client's exercise program. Once the initial assessment has been performed, consistently monitoring and recording new results can also reveal areas of weakness that need improvement. Positive results on follow-up tests can also be used as a motivational tool.

One of the most important aspects of a fitness assessment is determining whether the use of a personal trainer is necessary. A personal trainer guides and molds the exercise regimen that is best for a client. However, in order for a trainer to successfully design an individualized regimen, it is imperative to have accurate and up-to-date information from an initial fitness assessment. This initial assessment should be performed prior to the personal trainer's recommendation of an exercise routine.. Personal trainers should also always advise clients to get approval or a clean bill of health from their primary care physician before starting any exercise program.

This chapter will discuss areas covered during the overall assessment. The first part of the assessment usually involves acquiring information about the client's general history, such as occupation and habits. A personal trainer needs to know if a client sits in front of a computer all day or is constantly on the move. Information like hobbies, regular activities and nutrition are also evaluated to assess the client's lifestyle. Next, the client's medical history is recorded, which includes injuries, surgeries, diseases/conditions and medications.

In some cases, issues of concern are revealed during the fitness assessment and the personal trainer may need to ask the client to get medical clearance prior to making any exercise recommendations. Once the assessment is complete, the personal trainer reviews each part of the evaluation in order to design an exercise regimen for the client that is as compatible with his lifestyle as possible. The personal trainer must discuss the assessment with his client and not simply read the responses on the questionnaire.

This chapter will point out crucial issues that a personal trainer should recognize during the initial assessment. Asking additional questions can reveal details that will ensure the optimum program design for the client. While it is well known that diet and exercise are foundations of healthier lifestyles,, the role of a personal

trainer is to add that special benefit that a client has been missing in order to reach weight-loss and/or fitness goals.

The General History Section of the Initial Client Assessment

Occupation

The first area covered during the initial client assessment is the client's occupation.

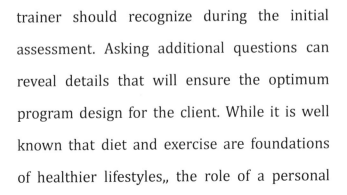

It is important to have an idea of the client's daily work routine so that the regimen can be scheduled around the client's current activities. If the client works 12 hours a day, a personal trainer can assume that this person hardly has time to eat, let alone work out. In these cases, the personal trainers must be creative and help clients manage exercise time efficiently. On the other hand, if the client is a stay-at-home parent, the personal trainer knows this schedule is just as challenging as that of a 12 hour worker's but possibly more flexible. Keep in mind that one of a personal trainer's tasks is to tailor-make an exercise routine that fits a client's lifestyle.

Working and daily lifestyle considerations are also important and should be included in the assessment. For example, the client should

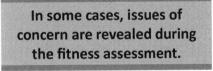
In some cases, issues of concern are revealed during the fitness assessment.

discuss whether or not there is time to take a brisk 20 minute walk during lunchtime. A stay-at-home parent may have an elliptical or treadmill in the home or be willing to invest in one. Some workplaces are equipped with fitness centers and this option could be considered in developing those clients' exercise routines. In recent years the rising cost of health insurance has prompted many employers to allow workout time or to even pay for memberships at fitness centers. Many people are not aware of all of the perks offered by their employer-generating this awareness can make a personal trainer's role more impactful and the task of developing the client's exercise routine much easier.

Another important detail to be discussed is the nature of the client's work or lifestyle. Factors to be noted when tailoring the client's workout include: repetitive movements throughout the day, the length of time spent standing during the day and the amount of time spent sitting each day. Recommending exercises that cause the client's to feel sore and unable to perform work duties should be avoided. Knowing how stressful the client's job is can also help the personal trainer determine which exercises can

The rising cost of health insurance has prompted many employers to allow workout time or to even pay for memberships at fitness centers.

increase mental endurance as well as physical endurance. The personal trainer should be as thorough as possible when collecting the client's information during the initial assessment.

Lifestyle

The lifestyle section of the initial client assessment is where the trainer gains the most personal information about their client. This section of the assessment reveals what the client does during free time as well as likes and dislikes. During this part of the evaluation, a personal trainer may discover that a client plays a certain sport occasionally. Sometimes people do not consider an occasional sporting activity (e.g., tennis or golf) as physical exercise because they do not do it regularly; however, a personal trainer may be able to assist a client in easily incorporating an occasional sporting activity into an exercise regimen. A study published in 2007 focused on the health benefits of tennis and showed that as little as 30 minutes of moderate tennis playing three times per week led to dramatic overall health benefits. If the personal trainer discovers the client does not have a hobby or activity that requires physical exertion, the personal trainer should recommend one for them.

Sessions with a personal trainer also provide a positive atmosphere for the client to ease into an exercise routine. Small changes to a client's routine lifestyle can produce great benefits over time. One small change easily incorporated into most lifestyles on a daily basis is taking the stairs. Taking the stairs at work or using the stairs when possible (e.g., in a shopping center) is a great way to enhance individual effort and increase one's fitness level. A study published in 2005 analyzed the effects of stair climbing in a group of non-active women. The women were told to start by taking one flight of stairs per day for week one and increasing this number to five flights a day by week seven. At the end of seven weeks, several of the women increased their ability to utilize oxygen, which is a direct measure of a person's physical fitness.

Another aspect of the lifestyle assessment is nutrition. This involves analyzing a client's eating habits. The trainer needs to know if the client typically eats on the run or prepares

homemade meals and takes time to sit and eat. Many working Americans eat on the run. With that in mind, the personal trainer needs to be familiar with types of foods that are healthy for people on the go. Most fast food restaurants' nutritional guides are on the Internet for downloading. The trainer should keep up-to-date with healthy eating guidelines in order to review them with clients. The trainer can also suggest that clients take healthy snacks to work or on outings instead of being tempted by unhealthy snacks in vending machines and convenience stores.

Sub-sections in the initial assessment for physical activities, hobbies and nutrition let the client know the type of information the trainer is seeking. This also helps the trainer remain organized. Properly evaluating client lifestyles enables trainers to design ways in which clients can make small adjustments to daily routines as well as adapt to exercise programs that will help them fulfill their fitness goals.

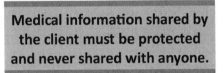

Medical information shared by the client must be protected and never shared with anyone.

The Medical History Section of the Initial Client Assessment

For the medical history portion of the assessment, the addition of a confidentiality clause should help put the client's mind at ease when revealing personal information. Medical information shared by the client must be protected and never shared with anyone.

Injuries

The client needs to disclose detailed information. Surprisingly, people tend to forget

55

old injuries that the personal trainer must take into account during the assessment. This is why a one-on-one session is better than just reading what your client filled out in the questionnaire.

If there are any new injuries (within the last year) the personal trainer may want the client to get a medical release form before beginning an exercise routine. The trainer also needs to make sure that on-going ailments are considered when designing or changing the client's workout. The proper regimen can speed up the recovery process. The personal trainer must get as much pertinent information from the client as possible. The initial client assessment is more than just a formality—it is a guide to the trainer's and client's success.

Surgeries

This section of the initial client assessment is fairly straightforward. In this day and age, many people have had surgical procedures and a personal trainer needs to know about them before recommending an exercise program. If a person had surgery that

left them unable to perform certain exercises, this is a significant fact for the trainer to record. Sometimes surgery can be performed without causing physical limitations, but the individual may have been left with more of a physiological problem such as becoming short of breath easily. No amount of information is too small to note and numerous questions regarding previous surgeries should be asked. If there is a surgical procedure the personal trainer is not familiar with, it is the personal trainer's responsibility to obtain more information about the procedure before recommending an exercise regimen.

Diseases and Medical Conditions

This area of the assessment covers chronic problems the client may have. Conditions such as shin splints, sciatica (lower back pain), arthritis (inflammation of the joints) and hypertension (high blood pressure) are common ailments. If the client has a disease or condition that the personal trainer is not familiar with, the trainer must obtain more information about it. Frequently, clients suffer from similar ailments and, if a trainer has already done research on a particular condition, this information can be used to help the trainer work quickly and efficiently with new clients.

When clients inform personal trainers that they are suffering from one or more ailments, trainers can respond accordingly by adding specific stretches that focus on problematic areas before and after workouts. Additional exercises, however, should not cause excess discomfort. If clients feel that the pain level experienced after workouts is too severe, they are less likely to continue.

A diagram of the body can also be included with the assessment so that the client can clearly identify the source of chronic pain or discomfort. Some people may not be familiar with anatomical terms and diagrams can aid them in showing trainers exactly where the pain is. However, personal trainers must not diagnose client ailments. If a client has unresolved issues, the trainer should recommend that the client see a doctor prior to beginning any fitness routine.

Medications

This section of the assessment informs the trainer about the medications a client is currently taking or has taken in the past, as well as those that cause the client allergic reactions.

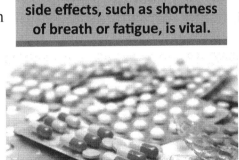

Knowing which drugs cause side effects, such as shortness of breath or fatigue, is vital.

As in the other sections, if the function of a certain drug is unknown the trainer must look into it. Knowing which drugs cause side effects, such as shortness of breath or fatigue, is vital.

One method of treatment for high-blood pressure, a common and often chronic problem among Americans, is the use of diuretics. Diuretics increase urine production and, by doing so, they remove excess water from the body. This is important for a personal trainer to know because a client taking this medication will probably sweat and urinate more frequently than normal. Increased sweating and urinating also increase the loss of electrolytes, so the trainer should recommend that the client bring not only water to workout sessions but also fluids for replenishing electrolytes, such as Gatorade.

Knowing the type of medications a client is allergic to is also important, so a section for allergies should be included in the medical section of the questionnaire. In addition to allergies cause by medications, environmental allergens need to be discussed. Whether or not a person is allergic to bee or wasp stings is a serious issue and, if so, not only should be written in the client's assessment, the trainer should also know if the client generally carries an Epipen. An Epipen is a self-administered shot of a hormone called epinephrine, a neurotransmitter that increases heart-rate and helps open airways. In an emergency, having this knowledge could save a client's life. This type of information can also help a personal trainer decide on a suitable location for a client's workout. Once again, obtaining as many details as possible is of the utmost importance for this section of the assessment.

Using a Questionnaire

In order to obtain as much information as possible, the personal trainer must be well prepared, organized and extremely detailed when performing the initial assessment. Most people already know that having a proper diet and exercising regularly are among the best ways to stay fit, but if they have decided to seek the advice of a personal trainer it is more than likely because they feel like they are not reaching their physical fitness goals. It is the duty of a personal trainer to create a specific exercise regimen that produces the positive results the client is seeking. Below is a guideline that can be used to design a questionnaire for the initial client assessment.

Example of Initial Client Assessment Form

Name_____

DOB _____

Address _____

_____

Home Phone_____

Cell _____

Emergency Contact _____

Phone _____

General History:

Occupation _____

_____

Work Conditions (standing, sitting, etc,) ____

_____

How many hours per week do you typically work? _____

What time do you normally have lunch?

_____

How long is your lunch break?_____

Are you opposed to working out at lunch?__

Is there a fitness center in your workplace?

_____

How stressful is your job?_____

Lifestyle

Hobbies _____

_____

Physical Activities (softball, tennis, etc.) ____

_____

_____

Nutrition (eat on the go or prepare meals) __

_____

Medical History:

Injuries and Dates_____

_____

Surgeries and Dates_____

_____

Conditions or Diseases (arthritis, hypertension,

etc.)_____

_____

Allergies _____

_____

Medications _____

_____

Exercise 1: Go through a client assessment with a classmate.

The ACTION Personal Training System Health Screening

The ACTION PTS Health Screening section is comprised of a series of questionnaires and screenings that you may use to evaluate your client's overall health and readiness for exercise.

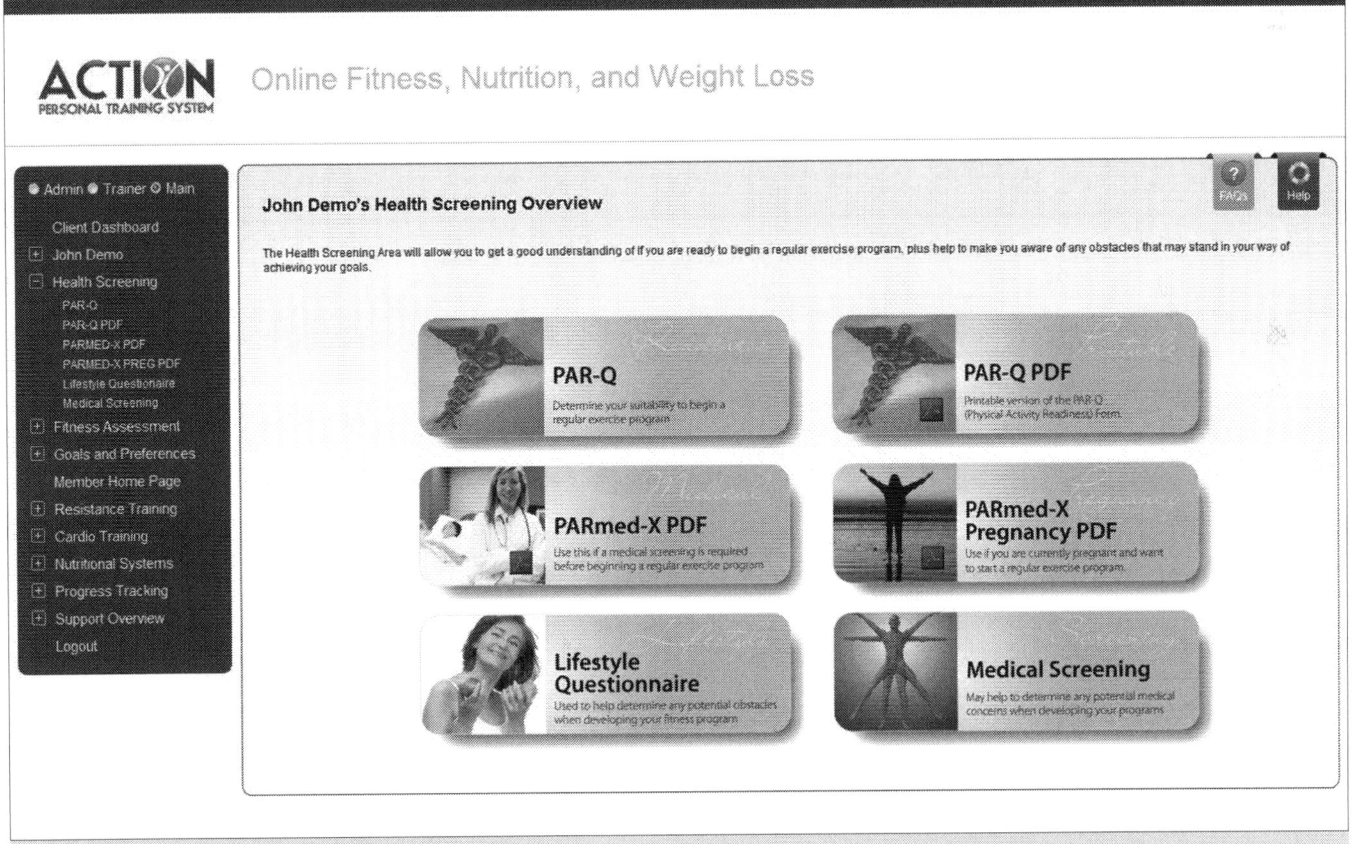

PAR-Q

The ACTION PTS Online Par-Q will allow you to perform a basic health screening on your client prior to beginning a physical fitness regimen. The Par-Q is a series of 7 basic health screening questions that will allow you to assess whether your client needs a medical clearance prior to starting their exercise routine. An answer of 'yes' to any of the 7 questions, will halt a client's progress through the initial setup and will require the completion of an extra waiver stating that they have received a physician's clearance. This should prompt you to send the client to their physician for a medical clearance.

ACTION PERSONAL TRAINING SYSTEM Online Fitness, Nutrition, and Weight Loss

● Admin ● Trainer ● Main

Client Dashboard
⊞ John Demo
⊟ Health Screening
   PAR-Q
   PAR-Q PDF
   PARMED-X PDF
   PARMED-X PREG PDF
   Lifestyle Questionaire
   Medical Screening
⊞ Fitness Assessment
⊞ Goals and Preferences
   Member Home Page
⊞ Resistance Training
⊞ Cardio Training
⊞ Nutritional Systems
⊞ Progress Tracking
⊞ Support Overview
   Logout

FAQs   Help

John Demo's Basic Physical Activity Readiness Form - PAR-Q

While this form will help screen for potential health issues, we always recommend consulting your doctor before starting a new physical activity regime.

Regular physical activity is fun and healthy, and increasingly more people are starting to become more active every day. Being more active is very safe for most people. However, some people should check with their doctor before they start becoming more physically active. If you are planning to become much more physically active than you are now, start by answering the seven questions in the box below. If you are between the ages of 15 and 69, the PAR-Q will tell you if you should check with your doctor before you start. If you are over 69 years of age, and you are not used to being very active, check with your doctor.

Common sense is your best guide when you answer these questions. Please read the questions carefully and answer each one honestly:

○ Yes ◉ No 1. Has your doctor ever told you that you have a heart condition and that you should only do physical activity recommended by a doctor?

○ Yes ◉ No 2. Do you feel pain in your chest when you do physical activity?

○ Yes ◉ No 3. In the past month, have you had chest pain when you were <u>not</u> doing physical activity?

○ Yes ◉ No 4. Do you lose your balance because of dizziness or do you ever lose consciousness?

○ Yes ◉ No 5. Do you have a bone or joint problem (for example, back, knee or hip) that could be made worse by a change in your physical activity?

○ Yes ◉ No 6. Is your doctor currently prescribing drugs (for example, water pills) for your blood pressure or heart condition?

○ Yes ◉ No 7. Do you know of any other reason why you should not do physical activity?

If you answered YES to one or more questions, talk with your doctor by phone or in person BEFORE you start becoming much more physically active or BEFORE you have a fitness appraisal. Tell you doctor about the PAR-Q and which questions you answered YES.

- You may be able to do any activity you want - as long as you start slowly and build up gradually. Or, you may need to restrict your activities to those which are safe for you. Talk with your doctor about the kinds of activities you wish to participate in and follow his/her advice.
- Find out which community programs are safe and helpful for you.

If you answered NO honestly to all PAR-Q questions, you can be reasonably sure that you can:

- start becoming much more physically active - begin slowly and build up gradually. This is the safest and easiest way to go.
- take part in a fitness appraisal - this is an excellent way to determine your basic fitness so that you can plan the best way for you to live actively. It is also highly recommended that you have your blood pressure evaluated. If your reading is over 144 / 94, talk with your doctor before you start becoming much more physically active.

Save

PAR-Q, PARMED-X and PARMED-X for Pregnancy Printable Forms

There are also several printable versions of the Health Screening forms including:

PAR-Q — to give you the option of printing the PAR-Q form to have the client complete and sign it.

PARMED-X — Clients in need of a medical clearance can be printed a PARMED-X to be taken to their physician for approval.

PARMED-X for Pregnancy — A client who is pregnant and who did NOT exercise regularly prior to becoming pregnant should be sent to their physician with a printed PARMED-X for Pregnancy.

Lifestyle Questionnaire

The Lifestyle Questionnaire is designed to give you background information about your client's health, fitness, and nutritional habits. The form has a series of basic questions that you can use to develop an overall picture of your client's current health and wellness.

ACTION PERSONAL TRAINING SYSTEM

Online Fitness, Nutrition, and Weight Loss

● Admin ● Trainer ◉ Main

- Client Dashboard
- ⊞ John Demo
- ⊟ Health Screening
  - PAR-Q
  - PAR-Q PDF
  - PARMED-X PDF
  - PARMED-X PREG PDF
  - **Lifestyle Questionnaire**
  - Medical Screening
- ⊞ Fitness Assessment
- ⊞ Goals and Preferences
- Member Home Page
- ⊞ Resistance Training
- ⊞ Cardio Training
- ⊞ Nutritional Systems
- ⊞ Progress Tracking
- ⊞ Support Overview
- Logout

? FAQs   ○ Help

John Demo's Lifestyle Questionaire

One a scale of 1 (worst ever) to 10 (best ever), how would you rate your current level of fitness? `7 ▼`

How many times per week do you typically take part in physical activities? `6-7 ▼`

If you are presently inactive, when was the last time you exercised regularly? `▼`

If you are presently active, what sorts of activities are you involved in?

Strength Training	`4 ▼` x / week	`0.50 ▼` hr(s)	`High ▼` intensity
Cardio Training	`6 ▼` x / week	`0.50 ▼` hr(s)	`High ▼` intensity
Flexibility Training	`2 ▼` x / week	`0.25 ▼` hr(s)	`Low ▼` intensity

On a scale of 1 (poor) to 10 (excellent) how would you rate your current eating habits? `7 ▼`

On average how many cigarettes do you smoke a day? `0 ▼`

On average how many hours do you sleep per night? `7.0 ▼`

Do you currently work at a job that requires you to perform constant repetitive motions (e.g. construction, cashier)? ☐

If Yes, please explain job:

On a scale of 1 (low) to 10 (high) how would you rate your stress level? `5 ▼`

List your 3 biggest sources of stress:

Bills

Job

Weight

Please describe any medications or prescriptions you take on a regular basis, what it is for, and how it effects your ability to exercise.

Do you feel you have any obstacles (actions, behaviors, or activities) that may impede your progress towards accomplishing your goals? For example: inconsistency, not prioritizing your health, not changing your workout program.

Save

61

Medical Screening

The Medical Screening form provides emergency contact and physician's information as well as a more detailed idea of the client's medical history. The form is broken into sections covering the client's General Medical Background, Lifestyle and Dietary Factors, Cardiovascular Screening, Musculoskeletal Conditions, and Nutritional Information, as well as an area for them to provide any additional information they see necessary.

ACTION PERSONAL TRAINING SYSTEM
Online Fitness, Nutrition, and Weight Loss

● Admin ● Trainer ◉ Main

Client Dashboard
⊞ John Demo
⊟ Health Screening
 PAR-Q
 PAR-Q PDF
 PARMED-X PDF
 PARMED-X PREG PDF
 Lifestyle Questionaire
 Medical Screening
⊞ Fitness Assessment
⊞ Goals and Preferences
 Member Home Page
⊞ Resistance Training
⊞ Cardio Training
⊞ Nutritional Systems
⊞ Progress Tracking
⊞ Support Overview
 Logout

John Demo's Medical Screening

In case of emergency, please notify:

Name	Janet Demo
Relationship	Wife
Address	
Phone 1	123-456-7890
Phone 2	
Physician Name	Dr. Demo
Physician Phone	987-654-3210

Save

You are 39 years old

Do you experience any sharp pain or extreme tightness in your chest when you are hit with a cold blast of air?	◯ Yes ◉ No
Have you ever experienced a rapid heartbeat or palpitations?	◯ Yes ◉ No
Have you ever had a real or suspected heart attack, coronary occlusion, myocardial infarction, coronary insufficiency, or thrombosis?	◯ Yes ◉ No
Have you ever had rheumatic fever?	◯ Yes ◉ No
Do you have diabetes, hypertension, or high blood pressure?	◯ Yes ◉ No
Does anyone in your family have diabetes, hypertension, or high blood pressure?	◯ Yes ◉ No
Has more than one blood relative (parent, sibling, first cousin) had a heart attack or coronary artery disease before the age of 60?	◯ Yes ◉ No
Have you ever taken medications for or been on a special diet to lower your cholesterol?	◯ Yes ◉ No
Have you ever taken any drugs for your heart?	◯ Yes ◉ No
Have you ever taken nitroglycerine of any other tablets for chest pain—tablets you take by placing under the tongue?	◯ Yes ◉ No
Are you overweight?	◯ Yes ◉ No
Are you under a lot of stress?	◯ Yes ◉ No
Do you drink excessively?	◯ Yes ◉ No
Are you unaccustomed to vigorous exercise?	◯ Yes ◉ No

Are you under the care of a physician, chiropractor, or other health care professional for any reason? If Yes, list reason below:

◯ Yes ◉ No

Are you currently taking any medications? If Yes, list Type, Dosage/Frequency, and Reason for Taking below:

◯ Yes ◉ No

Please list any allergies below:

Save

If there is family history for any condition, please check the box to the left. If you are personally experiencing any of these conditions, fill the information in on the line to the right.

☑ Asthma:

☑ Respiratory/Pulmonary Conditions:

☑ Diabetes:

 Type I:

 Type II:

 Other:

The Physical Assessment Section

Once the initial questionnaire is complete, a thorough assessment of the client's physical status needs to be performed. This part of the assessment includes several areas such as checking the client's pulse and blood pressure. These vital signs, in addition to other areas of physical fitness, will be discussed in detail in the following sections.

Before an assessment is performed, the client should be told to avoid eating or smoking for at least four hours prior to the assessment. This is recommended but certainly not required. The client should also avoid performing both cardiovascular and weight training exercises at least 12 hours prior in order for the trainer to get an accurate perspective of the client's physical capabilities.

Pulse

Pulse is the frequency of the heart beat. Arteries, which are blood vessels that carry oxygenated blood away from the heart to the rest of the body, produce a continuous pulse. Checking the pulse is an easy way to determine one's current heart rate, or the number of heartbeats per minute (BPM), and it is easy to

calculate: count the number of heart beats for 10 seconds then multiply by 6. The final number represents the current heart rate. To determine

Pulse taken at the neck (above).

Pulse taken at the wrist.

the heart rate during exercise, the activity should be interrupted and the pulse taken quickly to acquire the number of heart beats per minute (BPM) accurately. The pulse is normally lower when an individual is resting, but it increases during activity. This is primarily because more oxygen-rich blood is needed during exercise or other activity.

A pulse can usually be felt in any place on the body where an artery can be compressed against a bone, but it is most often located in two areas. The first site is at the thumb side of the wrist

> **Why do we care?**
> Because the pulse can be used as an advanced warning of impending illness. An increase of 10 BPM or more from normal rate can indicate health problems. Medications can also affect one's heart rate.

right below the base of the thumb (radial pulse). The second is on the neck just below the jaw along the windpipe and throat (carotid pulse).

The tips of both the index and third finger are used to find the artery and a watch is generally used to track the time.

Heart rates generally vary from person to person and also depend on a person's age. The heart rates of infants and children are higher than that of adults age 18 and over. The resting heart rate for an adult is between 60-100 BPM, with the average heart rate being approximately 70 BPM. The heart rate of a child is normally 70-120 BPM, while an infant's heart rate can be typically between 100-160 BPM. Performing exercises that causes the pulse to exceed 85% of maximum heart rate is not recommended. The maximum heart rate and the optimal exercise heart rate can be predicted using the following equation:

Maximum heart rate = 220 – your age

Exercise heart rate = Resting heart rate + [0.6 x (maximum heart rate-resting heart rate)]

> **Exam Alert:**
> **What are two ways your pulse can be taken?**

Blood Pressure

Blood pressure is the pressure of the blood against the walls of the arteries. This is created by two forces: the force of the heart pumping blood into the arteries throughout the body and the resistance from these arteries. Blood pressure is highest during activity and falls when resting or sleeping. Not only does blood pressure change throughout the day, it also responds to changes in emotion, such as feeling nervous or fearful.

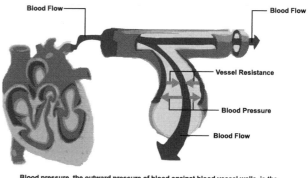

Blood pressure, the outward pressure of blood against blood vessel walls, is the product of blood flow from the heart and inward resistance of blood vessel walls.

Blood pressure is denoted as a reading of two numbers and measured in millimeter mercury (mmHg). The first number is the systolic pressure which indicates the pressure of the contracting heart. The second number is the diastolic pressure which indicates the pressure of the heart when it is relaxing between beats. Your systolic pressure is said to be "over" your diastolic pressure (i.e., 145/75 or 145 over 75 mmHg). Normal blood pressure for adults is considered to be 120 over 80 mmHg, though there are some considerations to this rule. Medication for high blood pressure, a short-term illness or medical conditions such as diabetes and kidney disease can affect blood pressure. In addition, athletes tend to have lower blood pressures. The chart gives an indication of blood pressure ranges and the risk of high blood pressure:

Blood Pressure Category	Systolic (First Number)	Diastolic (Second Number)
Average	<120	<80
Elevated	120-139	80-89

Hypertensive	Systolic	Diastolic
Phase I	140-159	90-99
Phase II	≥160	≥100

The regulation of blood pressure is dependent on two factors. One factor is the amount of blood being pumped by the heart (cardiac output).

Why do we care?
High blood pressure carries
with it a risk of heart disease.

The other is resistance to blood flow from the arterial wall (peripheral resistance). The reason for high blood pressure is an increase in one of these factors or a combination of the two. The brain also regulates blood pressure through the nervous system. The tone of the blood vessels is regulated by the sympathetic nervous system which increases blood pressure. Conversely, the parasympathetic nervous system lowers blood pressure. Both systems are perpetually active and they modulate constantly to regulate blood pressure.

Exam Alert:
How does the body
regulate blood pressure?

Flexibility

Flexibility is the ability of the body to adjust to various positions and is the key element to overall physical fitness. It is usually defined as the range of motion for a given joint and the ability of the joint to adapt to changing requirements from the body. Usually, the best way to increase flexibility is through consistent training. Flexibility training typically focuses on breathing to bring about greater muscle relaxation and correct body positioning.

Warmed-up muscles are easier to stretch. Stretches should be held for 10–60 seconds to guarantee an increase in flexibility. Increased flexibility has benefits that include improved circulation, breathing and coordination, as well as preventing injuries that may occur during day-to-day activities. Lower back and hamstring flexibility are especially crucial in preventing back pain and lower back injuries.

The most common way to test flexibility is by performing a flexibility stretch test or the sit-and-reach test. To perform the stretch test, the individual sits on the floor with a measuring stick or tape between the legs and then reaches forward as far as possible. The distance of the stretch is measured in inches and evaluated based on a comparison to average flexibility ratings. The chart on this page shows how different levels of flexibility are rated.

The sit-and-reach test utilizes a sit-and-reach box or alternatively, a ruler placed and held between the feet. The subject sits on the floor, removes shoes and places the sole of each foot against the box approximately shoulder width apart. The tester presses both knees against the floor and instructs the subject to reach forward as far as possible along the measuring line. Both palms should be face down, with one hand placed on top of the other. The subject is allowed three

> **Why do we care?**
> Inflexibility increases the risk of joint and muscle injury. Flexible muscles can improve athletic performance because activities become easier and less exhausting.

practice reaches and on the fourth reach, the position is held for a minimum of two seconds and recorded. There should be no jerky movements and the legs should remain flat. In order to rate the level of flexibility form the sit-and-reach test, the distance reached is recorded

to the nearest half-inch or centimeter and compared to a scale.

The sit-and-reach test is a reliable measure of hamstring and lower-back flexibility, which can be used to estimate an individual's overall level of flexibility. Results may differ depending on the amount of time the individual spent warming up before the test was performed. In order to keep data consistent, testers should ensure that the same protocol is used for each test. One advantage to the sit-and-reach test is the ease with which it can be used. However, a proper sit-and-reach box may be difficult to obtain and tests measured with a ruler would more than likely be less accurate.

Flexibility Rating Chart

Performance	Males	Females
Exceptional	20.5-23 in.	23-24.5 in.
Excellent	17.5-20 in.	20-22.5 in.
Good	15.5-17 in.	18.5-19.5 in.
Fair	13.5-15 in.	16.5-18 in.
Poor	10.5-13 in.	14.5-16 in.
Below Poor	7-10 in.	12.5-14 in.

Posture

Posture involves keeping the body straight and upright while performing daily activities such as sitting, walking and sleeping. Bad posture can be developed by sitting for long periods of time, working at the computer for more than eight hours a day, and standing or driving for a long time. Achieving good posture involves training the body to conform to a position that causes the least amount of strain on the body. Proper

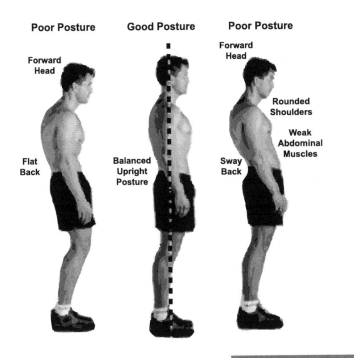

Poor Posture — Forward Head — Flat Back

Good Posture — Balanced Upright Posture

Poor Posture — Forward Head — Rounded Shoulders — Weak Abdominal Muscles — Sway Back

posture also involves keeping bones and joints aligned and decreasing unnecessary wear

> **Maintaining good posture prevents the spine from becoming fixed in an abnormal position.**

and tear on the joints. In addition, maintaining good posture prevents the spine from becoming fixed in an abnormal position. After an individual learns how to correct bad posture, maintaining good posture becomes automatic and requires little to no effort.

Requirements for good posture include sitting and standing properly with the back straight and the shoulders upright. The body weight should be evenly distributed on both hips. Lifting objects correctly is also good for maintaining correct posture. Having firm footing with a wide stance

and keeping the back straight are both important elements of proper lifting. While standing close to the object, the individual should bend at the knees and hips and then lift upward without jerking. In addition, supportive footwear can be worn when standing for prolonged periods of time or lifting heavy objects. However, shoes that can affect the body's center of gravity and change the alignment of the body should be avoided.

Body Fat

Body fat is the percentage of fat the body contains. For example, a 150 pound person with 10% body fat has 15 pounds of body fat. The other 135 pounds is lean body mass and a combination of bone, muscle, organ tissue, blood, etc. When a person expresses a desire to lose weight, this usually means a desire to lose body fat. However, a small amount of body fat is necessary. This small amount of essential fat is needed to help regulate body temperature, protect and insulate organs and serve as an energy source.

% of Body Fat		
Classification	Males	Females
Slim	2-4	10-12
Athletic	6-13	14-20
Fit	14-17	21-24
Average	18-25	25-31
Overweight	25+	32+

A number of tests are used to measure body fat. One common method is the pinch test, which estimates body fat by skinfold thickness. The skin is pinched at three to nine different anatomical sites on the body such as the tricep, bicep, abdominal and thigh. The pinch raises a double layer of skin and the underlying adipose (fat) tissue but not the muscle. Skinfold calipers are used to take a reading in millimeters. Usually the sum of seven skinfold readings is calculated. Following is a table that rates the sums of several pinch tests.

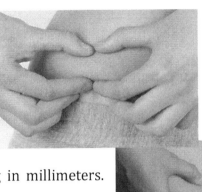

Fitness		Very Good	Good	Normal	Below Normal	Poor
Average	Males	60-80	81-90	91-110	111-150	>150
	Females	70-90	91-100	101-120	121-150	>150
Athlete	Males	40-60	61-80	81-100	101-130	>130
	Females	50-70	71-85	86-110	111-130	>130

Body Mass Index (BMI)

Units	How to Calculate
Using kilograms (kg) and meters (m)	BMI = weight (kg) / [height (m)]² *For height taken in centimeters (cm), dividing height in cm by 100 gives height in meters.
Using pounds (lb) and inches (in)	BMI = weight (lb) / [height (in)]² x 703

Body Mass Index (BMI) provides an indication of what body weight should be according to height. BMI is considered as an alternative to measuring body fat and is used quite often to determine which people belong to certain weight categories (e.g., underweight, average, overweight, obese). It is also used to indicate whether or not a person has weight-related health problems such as heart disease or diabetes. However, additional assessments such as measuring skinfold thickness, evaluating diet and exercise regimen, measuring blood pressure and getting family history are needed to determine if a person is at potential risk for developing weight-related health problems.

BMI is calculated in a similar way for adults and children; however, the interpretations of the BMI often differ. BMI is also dependent on age, race and gender. For instance, it is typical for women to have more body fat than men. Also, as the body ages, the amount of body fat tends to increase. The first test usually conducted after a BMI evaluation is the measurement of an individual's waist circumference to determine the amount of abdominal fat. If a person has a relatively high BMI but a small degree of abdominal fat, the person is not considered at risk of developing health problems. If the BMI calculated for an individual falls into the danger zone (e.g., overweight or obese) and the person has two or more risks factors such as high cholesterol or hypertension, then weight loss is recommended to reduce health problems.

Weight in Pounds

Height in Feet and Inches	120	130	140	150	160	170	180	190	200	210	220	230	240	250
4'6"	29	31	34	36	39	41	43	46	48	51	53	56	58	60
4'8"	27	29	31	34	36	38	40	43	45	47	49	52	54	56
4'10"	25	27	29	31	34	36	38	40	42	44	46	48	50	52
5'0"	23	25	27	29	31	33	35	37	39	41	43	45	47	49
5'2"	22	24	26	27	29	31	33	35	37	38	40	42	44	46
5'4"	21	22	24	26	28	29	31	33	34	36	38	40	41	43
5'6"	19	21	23	24	26	27	29	31	32	34	36	37	39	40
5'8"	18	20	21	23	24	26	27	29	30	32	34	35	37	38
5'10"	17	19	20	22	23	24	26	27	29	30	32	33	35	36
6'0"	16	18	19	20	22	23	24	26	27	28	30	31	33	34
6'2"	15	17	18	19	21	22	23	24	26	27	28	30	31	32
6'4"	15	16	17	18	20	21	22	23	24	26	27	28	29	30
6'6"	14	15	16	17	19	20	21	22	23	24	25	27	28	29
6'8"	13	14	15	17	18	19	20	21	22	23	24	25	26	28

■ Underweight ■ Healthy Weight ■ Overweight □ Obese

There are limitations associated with using BMI to determine ideal body weight and composition. From a BMI calculation it is not clear if an individual's actual weight has to do with the amount of fatty tissue or lean muscle content. It is also hard to determine whether changes in BMI over time are due to a change in fat or muscle content. Athletes typically have high BMIs because of their increased muscle mass and not because of body fat.

Step Test

The step test is designed to measure cardiovascular endurance and assess overall aerobic capacity. Cardiorespiratory and endurance tests measure the ability of the lungs and heart to absorb, transport and utilize oxygen. Fit individuals are able to use larger muscle groups for prolonged periods of time at a moderate to high intensity. Lower levels of

cardiorespiratory fitness are associated with an increased risk of developing cardiovascular and respiratory diseases that may lead to premature death. Conversely, higher levels of cardiorespiratory fitness are associated with a decreased risk of death due to cardiovascular disease, as well as improved quality of sleep and immunity.

The Harvard step test, also known simply as the step test, and the bike test are the two most commonly used cardiorespiratory and endurance tests. The test used in a certain facility is based on the equipment available and number of people being tested. This step test is efficient even when there is minimal equipment present and can be done in almost any location. This test measures a person's ability to exercise continuously for extended periods of time without becoming extremely tired.

The test uses a 12-inch high bench or step as the primary tool. The individual steps on and off the bench or step for 3 minutes. More specifically, the individual should step one foot up and bring the other up, then step down in the same manner, maintaining a steady pace. After 3 minutes of stepping, the client's heart rate is checked during what is called the recovery period. This just means that the heart rate is checked about 1 minute after finishing the exercise and the number is compared to normal values that have been previously established. The closer the active heart rate is to the normal resting heart rate, the more fit the individual is.

> It is important that any participant in this test warms up and stretches for at least 4-5 minutes.

Heart Rates after 3 Minute Step Test (Males)*

Age	18-25	26-35	36-45	46-55	56-65	>65
Good to Excellent	<84	<86	<90	<93	<96	<102
Average to Above Average	85-100	87-103	91-106	94-112	97-115	103-118
Poor to Fair	>101	>104	>107	>113	>116	>119

Heart Rates after 3 Minute Step Test (Females)*

Age	18-25	26-35	36-45	46-55	56-65	>65
Good to Excellent	<93	<94	<96	<101	<103	<105
Average to Above Average	94-110	95-111	97-119	102-124	104-126	106-130
Poor to Fair	>111	>112	>120	>125	>127	>131

*Using a 60 second pulse count

Walk Test

Aerobic fitness is a good indicator of overall fitness. For the 1 mile walk test, the course needs to be smooth and flat—ideally a ¼ mile track. It is important that any participant in this test warms up and stretches for at least 4-5 minutes, paying special attention to stretching the leg muscles. An individual walks 1 mile as quickly as possible while maintaining a steady walking pace. The test is scored in minutes and seconds and the heart rate is recorded after completion of the walk test. Similar to the step test, an active heart rate that is close to the normal resting heart rate means the individual is in good shape.

This test also provides an estimation of an individual's VO_2 max, or the maximum oxygen consumption. In more specific terms, VO_2 max is an indicator of the maximum amount of oxygen that an individual can take in and utilize during exercise. This value can be calculated using the Rockport Fitness Walking Test equation. VO_2 max is measured in milliliters of oxygen consumed per kilogram of body weight per minute. This value also reflects the physical and cardiorespiratory endurance of an individual.

Personal trainers often measure the VO_2 max of athletes to determine how much oxygen they utilize during their workouts. This is normally done by using the "beep test," also known as the multi-stage fitness test. This test is commonly used for sports like hockey, soccer, rugby, football, cross-country and cricket to measure the cardiorespiratory fitness of athletes. The test consists of an athlete running between two points that are 20 meters apart. The running activity is synchronized to pre-recorded "beeps" that are played at set intervals. The intervals become increasingly shorter and the beeps are played faster until the athlete can no longer keep up the pace.

There are currently 23 levels in the beep test, although some tests may only go up to level 17. The beep test is easy to perform as the audio track can be played in mp3 format, which also decreases the risk of malfunctions from cassette tapes or compact disks. The beep test is not recommended for a person just starting a fitness program, but would be a good tool for active individuals interested in developing higher levels of cardiorespiratory fitness.

Exam Alert:
In terms of fitness, what is VO$_2$
and what does it measure?

Time (minutes and seconds) for Walk Test (Males)						
Age	20-29	30-39	40-49	50-59	60-69	>70
Excellent	<11:54	<12:24	<12:54	<13:24	<14:06	<15:06
Good	11:54-13:00	12:24-13:30	12:54-14:00	13:24-14:24	14:06-15:12	15:06-15:48
Average	13:01-13:42	13:31-14:12	14:01-14:42	14:25-15:12	15:13-16:18	15:49-18:48
Fair	13:43-14:30	14:13-15:00	14:43-15:30	15:13-16:30	16:19-17:18	18:49-20:18
Poor	>14:30	>15:00	>15:30	>16:30	>17:18	>20:18

Time (minutes and seconds) for Walk Test (Females)						
Age	20-29	30-39	40-49	50-59	60-69	>70
Excellent	<13:12	<13:42	<14:12	<14:42	<15:06	<18:18
Good	13:12-14:06	13:42-14:36	14:12-15:06	14:42-15:36	15:06-16:18	18:18-20:00
Average	14:07-15:06	14:37-15:36	15:07-16:06	15:37-17:00	16:19-17:30	20:01-21:48
Fair	15:07-16:30	15:37-17:00	16:07-17:30	17:01-18:06	17:31-19:12	21:49-24:06
Poor	>16:30	>17:00	>17:30	>18:06	>19:12	>24:06

Muscular Performance

Muscular performance is tested by using various forms of fitness and strength training exercises. These exercises include the bench press, squats, ab crunches, push-ups and sit-ups. The bench press evaluates upper body strength and entails an individual lying on the back, lowering a weight to the chest level, and then pushing it back up with arms straight and elbows

locked. The push-up test also evaluates muscular strength and endurance in the upper body. Men and women usually adapt to different floor positions while doing push-ups. Men are typically fully extended with only the hands and toes in contact with the floor while women often use a modified version of the push-up position in which the knees are bent and touch the floor. Push-ups are counted until muscle fatigue and exhaustion sets in and then evaluated based on number accomplished.

Push-up Test (Averaged for Males and Females)

Age	17-19	20-29	30-39	40-49	50-59	60-65
Excellent	>35	>36	>37	>31	>25	>23
Good	21-35	23-36	22-37	18-31	15-25	13-23
Average	6-20	7-22	5-21	4-17	3-14	2-12
Poor	2-5	2-6	1-4	1-3	1-2	1
Very Poor	0-1	0-1	0	0	0	0

The sit-up test, or curl-up test, also evaluates muscular endurance by testing the strength of an individual's abdominal muscles. Abdominal strength is important for stabilizing the body and maintaining good posture during exercise. To perform the sit-up test an individual lies on the back with the knees bent. The feet are pressed to the ground and the hands are resting on the thighs. Next, the individual slightly raises the upper body toward the ceiling while keeping the lower back pressed against the floor and then slowly lies back down. It is important not to lift the torso by pulling the neck and to keep the lower back on the floor to avoid injuries. The number of sit-ups an individual can do in one minute is counted and compared to average values.

1 Minute Sit-up Test (Males)

Age	18-25	26-35	36-45	46-55	56-65	>65
Excellent	>49	>45	>41	>35	>31	>28
Good	39-49	35-45	30-41	25-35	21-31	19-28
Average	31-38	29-34	23-29	18-24	13-20	11-18
Poor	25-30	22-28	17-22	13-17	9-12	7-10
Very Poor	<25	<22	<17	<13	<9	<7

1 Minute Sit-up Test (Females)

Age	18-25	26-35	36-45	46-55	56-65	>65
Excellent	>43	>39	>33	>27	>24	>23
Good	33-43	29-39	23-33	18-27	13-24	14-23
Average	25-32	21-28	15-22	10-17	7-12	5-13
Poor	18-24	13-20	7-14	5-9	3-6	2-4
Very Poor	<18	<13	<7	<5	<3	<2

Squats focus more on strength training of the lower body. The squat test is performed by bending the knees and hips, lowering the torso between the legs with the glutes near the heels, and standing again to straighten up the body. This exercise can be done with weights to enhance muscle strength and development or without weights.

Squat Test (Males)

Age	18-25	26-35	36-45	46-55	56-65	>65
Excellent	>49	>45	>41	>35	>31	>28
Good	39-49	35-45	30-41	25-35	21-31	19-28
Average	31-38	29-34	23-29	18-24	13-20	11-18
Poor	25-30	22-28	17-22	13-17	9-12	7-10
Very Poor	<25	<22	<17	<13	<9	<7

Squat Test (Females)						
Age	18-25	26-35	36-45	46-55	56-65	>65
Excellent	>43	>39	>33	>27	>24	>23
Good	33-43	29-39	23-33	18-27	13-24	14-23
Average	25-32	21-28	15-22	10-17	7-12	5-13
Poor	18-24	13-20	7-14	5-9	3-6	2-4
Very Poor	<18	<13	<7	<5	<3	<2

Muscular performance tests measure both muscle endurance and muscle strength. Muscle

endurance is the ability for a muscle or muscle group to exert force repeatedly. Muscle strength is the ability for a muscle or muscle group to exert maximal force in a single repetition. Health related benefits of proper muscle fitness include a better resting metabolic rate, which means muscles burn more fat calories even when an individual is at rest. Healthy muscles also improve bone mass and glucose (sugar) tolerance. Improving bone mass and tolerance to glucose can decrease the risk of developing diseases such as osteoporosis and Type II Diabetes.

How Thorough Should Each Initial Assessment Be?

After learning the many benefits of conducting detailed personal and physical assessments, personal trainers may decide that detailed assessments are required for every new client. However, a trainer can decide whether a thorough personal and physical assessment is necessary and right for every client on an individual basis. The first step is for the trainer to gather necessary information about the client through the initial interview and conversation, in addition to any questionnaires that need to be filled out. The evaluation and interview, coupled with a visual assessment of the client. should in most cases provide the information needed to determine what type of exercise routine is right for that person without having to complete the full physical assessment. In cases like these, the trainer can also decide whether or not to omit certain parts of the physical assessment.

> A trainer can decide whether a thorough personal and physical assessment is necessary and right for every client on an individual basis.

Here is an example: John is a new client in his early 40s who describes himself on his self-evaluations as a "couch potato" and admits he performs minimal to no cardiorespiratory exercises. Visually, he is slightly overweight and he discussed his poor eating habits during the interview. He decided to start a personal training regimen in order to lose weight and increase his cardiorespiratory health. In John's case, a full physical assessment would probably not be a good idea because it may put John under unnecessary stress and pressure that could discourage him from starting a fitness program. The trainer would not necessarily need the physical assessment to determine John's current fitness level and could deduce that John will need to start at a low intensity because he is not currently exercising. In this case, knowing John's medical history, family history, height, weight and BMI may be enough to design an exercise regimen for him.

In another case, the trainer may have a female client who has an average weight and exercises at a moderate level three times a week. She is interested in beginning a fitness program that will encourage her to exercise more frequently and produce visible results since she says she has not seen any improvement in the last few months. This client is a good candidate for a full physical assessment to determine a starting point for her fitness program. Calculating her BMI, muscle strength and endurance, and performing at least one cardiorespiratory exam is a good idea as it allows both the trainer and client to discover her strengths and weaknesses. In this case, the trainer may also want to see her current exercise routine as she may be exercising at an intensity that is too low to achieve results or performing the exercises incorrectly and putting herself at a risk for injury.

Most importantly, the trainer should be sure not to do any tests that may injure or embarrass the client. For example, an overweight client may feel extremely embarrassed if asked to perform a sit-up test during the initial assessment. A client who admits to having a poor fitness level may become discouraged with poor performance during physical tests. In some cases, the trainer may even have a client with pre-existing conditions that may affect their physical abilities and certain parts of the physical assessment may cause them further injury. It is best for the trainer to always use his judgment and avoid injury and embarrassment to the client.

Personalizing or Designing Custom Tests

Once the trainer has decided that a fitness assessment is right for a client, the trainer then needs to ascertain which specific tests are going to be the most helpful in determining a good fitness plan. The trainer also needs to decide when to perform both the initial assessment and follow-up physical assessment. Some clients, mainly those with poor fitness levels, may benefit from a few conditioning sessions before their physical assessment. This may even help reduce the risk of injury and embarrassment, especially in individuals who already exhibit low levels of self-esteem. In addition, the client's current physiological and emotional state should be considered when a physical assessment is scheduled.

Let us say the first session with John (40-year-old male client) consists of a short warm-up, stretching and a discussion of his expectations for the program. He mentions that he has slept poorly the night before and has not eaten for the day. These factors will more than likely influence his fitness assessment results. If he feels like he did poorly during the warm-up and stretching exercise, he may feel less motivated and display less effort during the physical assessment, which will result in lower scores. In John's case, a fitness assessment one or two weeks into his training program may be a better plan. After his initial assessment, a follow-up assessment six to eight weeks later will be sufficient because clients usually show the most significant changes and improvements during that time frame.

The personal trainer should also tailor the type of tests used according to the client's needs and

The client's current physiological and emotional state should be considered when a physical assessment is scheduled.

current conditions. There may be cases where certain tests need to be omitted or modified. For example, a trainer may have a female client in her 30s who would like to lose her pregnancy weight. She had a C-section during delivery and although she has received medical clearance from her doctor to start an exercise regimen, she has limited flexibility due to her procedure. In this case, a flexibility test such as the sit-and-reach test may injure the client if she is forced to stretch beyond her capabilities. Omitting that test until she begins her exercise routines and performing different assessment tests are going to be more beneficial for this client.

A personal trainer should also listen to his client's long-term goals and expectations. A client who wishes to build muscle mass and improve overall muscle tone is probably going to want muscle strength and endurance to be assessed immediately. Although the trainer may feel this is initially unnecessary, it may be important to the client especially if the client wants to set personal goals or know current fitness levels. A client may also want to avoid cardiorespiratory testing because it is seemingly irrelevant to the client's goals; however, in cases like these, it is important for the trainer to explain that cardiorespiratory assessments are necessary. On the other hand, some clients may not even want to know their initial weight or BMI because they may find it too discouraging. As their trainer, keeping the client's best interests in mind is a must and in this situation, the trainer can record the information without revealing it to the client. In addition, sometimes omitting a potentially embarrassing test is a better long-term choice than performing the test right away and deterring the client from returning.

Follow-up fitness tests can be performed at regular intervals or as little as once every six months. Some clients will prefer a more consistent routine so that they can quantitatively track their progress whereas others would prefer to get assessed as infrequently as possible. The six to eight week follow-up assessment is especially useful to show results to the client. However, if the assessments are too frequent and show little change, the client may get discouraged because results are not seen each time. A trainer can avoid these issues by performing different tests at different intervals. Tests like blood pressure or BMI are easy to measure. For comparing results, though, it is best to use the same tests in the same order as during previous assessments.

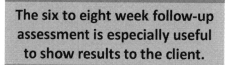

The six to eight week follow-up assessment is especially useful to show results to the client.

The order of the fitness assessment tests is also important. Here is the recommended order:

1. Non-fatiguing tests (height/weight measurements, skinfolds, vertical and broad jumps)
2. Agility tests
3. Maximal strength and power tests
4. Sprint tests
5. Muscular endurance tests
6. Flexibility tests

Warm-up and cool-down stretching exercises are recommended before and after the assessment in order to prevent muscle tearing and injury.

The different tests used to measure similar aspects are important as well. Beginning clients with lower levels of fitness do not need to perform a beep test to measure cardiorespiratory health. Instead they would benefit more from the walking test. This is a test for less active individuals and basically consists of walking a mile at the fastest comfortable pace and recording their heart rate after the walk. The trainer could then calculate the VO_2 max with a simple formula. There are also different kinds of flexibility tests besides the sit-and-reach test. For example, the trunk rotation test or groin flexibility test can be used to measure flexibility in patients who have a limited range of motion. The most important points to remember are considering the client's strengths, weaknesses and pre-existing conditions when choosing the assessment tests.

The ACTION Personal Training System Assessment Tools

The ACTION PTS assessment tools are designed to allow you to establish a baseline starting point for your clients as well as track their progress over time. The assessment tools can also be used to effectively help you to build your personal training revenues by showing clients areas that they may need improvement in and therefore may require your services.

There are 7 different assessment tools available for you to use:

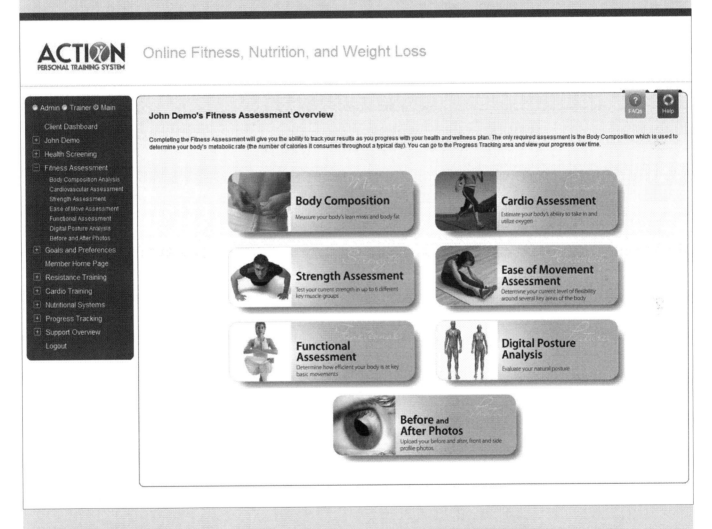

Body Composition

The ACTION PTS Body Composition will allow you to estimate the body fat and lean mass levels of your clients using a simple method of taking girth measurements. The Body Composition results are then used to determine caloric consumption values for your clients and may also be re-assessed over time and the progress recorded and tracked. There are several advantages of using this method of body composition estimate:

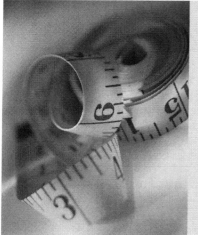

- Measurements are simple to take and may be done over clothing

- Simple measurements allow for greater consistency even with different trainers taking measurement samples

- Very unobtrusive and comfortable for the client

- Girth measurement method is extremely reflective of actual results achieved due to the direct correlation between weight and girth losses or gains, and body fat changes

- Only equipment required is a tape measure

There are 2 different methods for achieving this estimate:

Method 1: Girth Measurements

By imputing your client's height and weight, and the girth measurements of their shoulders, navel (umbilicus), waist, and hips, the software will determine an estimate of their overall lean mass and body fat values.

The following information will assist you in obtaining accurate measurements and therefore an accurate body composition. Girth measurements may be taken in inches (in) or centimetres (cm). Measurements may be done over or under clothing, but will typically be more accurate when done directly on the skin. If you need to take them over clothing please ensure it is as lightweight as possible and make sure similar clothing is worn each time measurements are taken.

Site 1 — Shoulders

This measurement is taken 1½" (4 cm) below the top of the shoulder. Ensure that the client is standing as upright as possible with the head up and the shoulders drawn back slightly. Where possible, use a mirror to assist you. Do not pull the measuring tape too tight.

Site 2 — Navel

This site is measured at the exact height of the navel (umbilicus). Ensure that the measuring tape remains level around the body. Do not pull the measuring tape too tight.

Site 3 — Waist

IMPORTANT — This site is measured at the **narrowest** point of the torso. For men this will often be just below the navel (1-2" or 2-5 cm) and for women just above the navel (1-2" or 2-5 cm), but this is not always the case. Do not pull the measuring tape too tight.

Site 4 — Hips

IMPORTANT — This site is measured at the **widest** point of the torso. Please ensure that the client's feet are together. The widest point of the torso will usually be across the gluteals but may also be slightly higher or lower. This measurement may or may not be where the actual hip joint is. Remember you are looking for the widest point. Do not pull the measuring tape too tight.

Method 2: Estimated Girth Measurements Using Clothing Size

You can use a dress size in the case of a female client, or pant and shirt size in the case if a male client, to estimate their girth measurements, and therefore their body composition. While this method may not be as accurate as the Girth Measurement method, it may prove to be more practical and possibly more comfortable for clients that are quite overweight, or are uncomfortable with having girth measurements done.

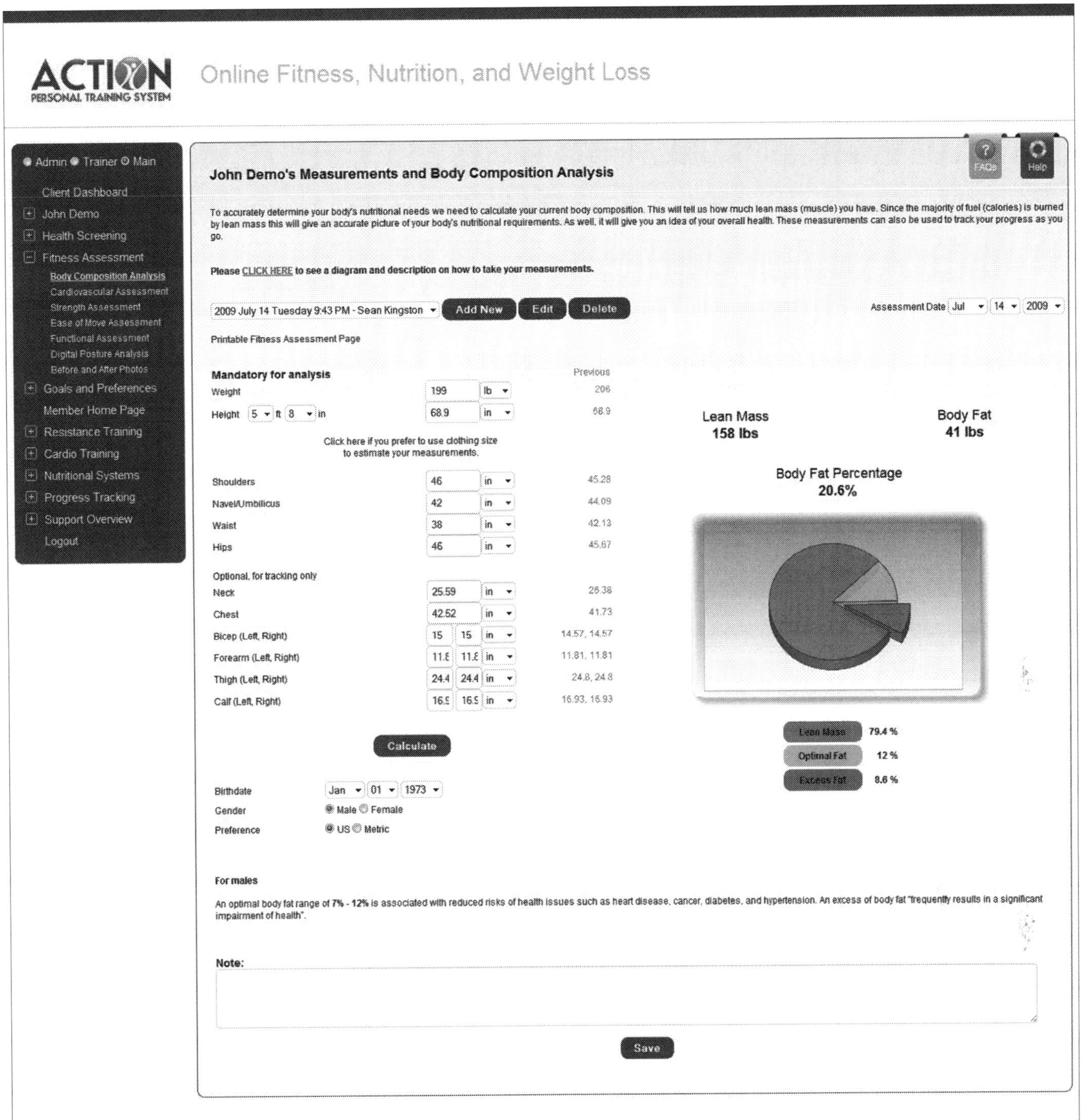

Online Fitness, Nutrition, and Weight Loss

John Demo's Measurements and Body Composition Analysis

To accurately determine your body's nutritional needs we need to calculate your current body composition. This will tell us how much lean mass (muscle) you have. Since the majority of fuel (calories) is burned by lean mass this will give an accurate picture of your body's nutritional requirements. As well, it will give you an idea of your overall health. These measurements can also be used to track your progress as you go.

Please CLICK HERE to see a diagram and description on how to take your measurements.

2009 July 14 Tuesday 9:43 PM - Sean Kingston ▾   **Add New**   **Edit**   **Delete**

Assessment Date   Jul ▾ 14 ▾ 2009 ▾

Printable Fitness Assessment Page

Mandatory for analysis			Previous
Weight	199	lb ▾	206
Height	5 ▾ ft 8 ▾ in	68.9	in ▾	68.9

Click here if you prefer to use clothing size to estimate your measurements.

Shoulders	46	in ▾	45.28
Navel/Umbilicus	42	in ▾	44.09
Waist	38	in ▾	42.13
Hips	46	in ▾	45.67

Optional, for tracking only

Neck	25.59	in ▾	26.38
Chest	42.52	in ▾	41.73
Bicep (Left, Right)	15	15	in ▾	14.57, 14.57
Forearm (Left, Right)	11.8	11.8	in ▾	11.81, 11.81
Thigh (Left, Right)	24.4	24.4	in ▾	24.8, 24.8
Calf (Left, Right)	16.9	16.9	in ▾	16.93, 16.93

Calculate

Birthdate	Jan ▾ 01 ▾ 1973 ▾
Gender	● Male ○ Female
Preference	● US ○ Metric

Lean Mass
158 lbs

Body Fat
41 lbs

Body Fat Percentage
20.6%

Lean Mass	79.4 %
Optimal Fat	12 %
Excess Fat	8.6 %

For males

An optimal body fat range of **7% - 12%** is associated with reduced risks of health issues such as heart disease, cancer, diabetes, and hypertension. An excess of body fat "frequently results in a significant impairment of health".

Note:

Save

Navigation sidebar:
- Admin ● Trainer ● Main
- Client Dashboard
- John Demo
- Health Screening
- Fitness Assessment
  - Body Composition Analysis
  - Cardiovascular Assessment
  - Strength Assessment
  - Ease of Move Assessment
  - Functional Assessment
  - Digital Posture Analysis
  - Before and After Photos
- Goals and Preferences
- Member Home Page
- Resistance Training
- Cardio Training
- Nutritional Systems
- Progress Tracking
- Support Overview
- Logout

Key Features of the ACTION Body Composition Page

A. Use the drop down to select, view, or edit any previous body composition completed with this client

Select 'Add New' if you want to begin a new body composition – you can change the Assessment Date using the field to the right if you have taken their measurements and are inputting them on a different date

Select 'Edit' to make changes to any previous body composition

Use the 'Delete' button to remove any previous body composition from the client's records

Use the 'Printable Fitness Assessment Page' link to open a separate window that you may print with all of the fitness assessment fields to record the data for input later

B. Use the drop downs to select either pounds (lb)or kilograms (kg) for the weight measurement and inches (in) or centimetres (cm) for the girth measurements.

If you have completed a previous Body Composition with this client, their previous measurements will be displayed

You can either input the height in feet (ft) and inches (in) on the left, or in total inches on the right

If you prefer to use clothing size to estimate the girth measurements click the link immediately below the height measurements to open a new window where you can input clothing size. The girth measurements will now be estimated by the system

Using the directions outlined above, input the girth measurements for the mandatory fields plus any optional measurements you would like to track

Once you have completed these steps, press the 'Calculate' button and the system will show the body composition results on the right

You may also view their progress over time in the 'Progress Tracking' section of the system

C. You can confirm or make changes to Birthdate, Gender, and Preference information here

D. If you would like to add any notes to be saved with this Body Composition you may do so in the 'Notes' field

Once you have completed the Body Composition click 'Save' to save the results to the client's profile

Cardiovascular Assessment

The ACTION PTS Cardiovascular Assessment will allow you to determine and record a resting heart rate and an estimate V02 Maximum value for your clients. These values can then be re-assessed over time and the progress recorded and tracked.

You can use the Master Preferences (see Appendix: Admin Menu: Settings and Tools) to select which cardiovascular test you would like set as the default, or if there are any tests you want removed as options to select.

Resting Heart Rate

The Resting heart Rate calculation may be determined in one of two ways:

1. Using the 15 second timer built into the software, simply enter the number of heartbeats that occur and use the system to calculate the client's resting heart rate

2. Use any other method you would prefer and enter the actual resting heart rate count

There are several methods you can use to determine an Estimated VO2 Maximum value:

Cooper 12 Minute Distance Test
For this test the object is to walk or run as far as you can in 12 minutes. It is best to use either an outdoor track of 440 yard (400 meters) length or a treadmill set to a 2% incline. Record the total distance covered in the 12 minutes. The system will calculate your estimated VO2 Max score

Rockport 1 Mile (1.6 km) Test
The object of this test is to walk or run for 1 mile (1.6 kilometres) and record your time in minutes and seconds and heart rate at the end. It is best to use either an outdoor track of 440 yard (400 meters) length or a treadmill set to a 2% incline. Record the total time and heart rate at the end of the test. The system will calculate your estimated VO2 Max score

Bruce Treadmill Test
For this test you must use a treadmill and adjust the speed and incline according to the chart below. The object is to keep going for as long as possible. This is an advanced test and should only be completed by persons with a high fitness level. Record the total time in minutes and seconds at the end of the test. The system will calculate your estimated VO2 Max score

Minute 00 — 1.7mph — @ 10% Incline
Minute 03 — 2.5mph — @ 12% Incline
Minute 06 — 3.4mph — @ 14% Incline
Minute 09 — 4.2mph — @ 16% Incline
Minute 12 — 5.0mph — @ 18% Incline
Minute 15 — 5.5mph — @ 20% Incline
Minute 18 — 6.0mph — @ 22% Incline
Minute 21 — 6.5mph — @ 24% Incline
Minute 24 — 7.0mph — @ 26% Incline

Direct Input Method (Other)
You can use any other method of preferences for determining estimated VO2 Maximum and simply enter the value into the system

Key Features of the ACTION Cardiovascular Assessment Page

A. Use the drop down to select, view, or edit any previous assessment completed with this client.

Select 'Add New' if you want to begin a new assessment – you can change the Assessment Date using the field to the right if you have completed the assessment previously and are inputting results on a different date.

Select 'Edit' to make changes to any previous assessment.

Use the 'Delete' button to remove any previous assessment from the client's records.

Use the 'Printable Fitness Assessment Page' link to open a separate window that you may print with all of the fitness assessment fields to record the data for input later

B. The diagrams will assist you in finding either the Carotid or Radial pulse.

Use the 15 second timer and enter the number of heartbeats recoded, then click the 'Calculate (bpm) from 15 Second Beat Count' button to have the software calculate the Resting Heart Rate.

Alternatively, you can enter the Resting Heart Rate directly

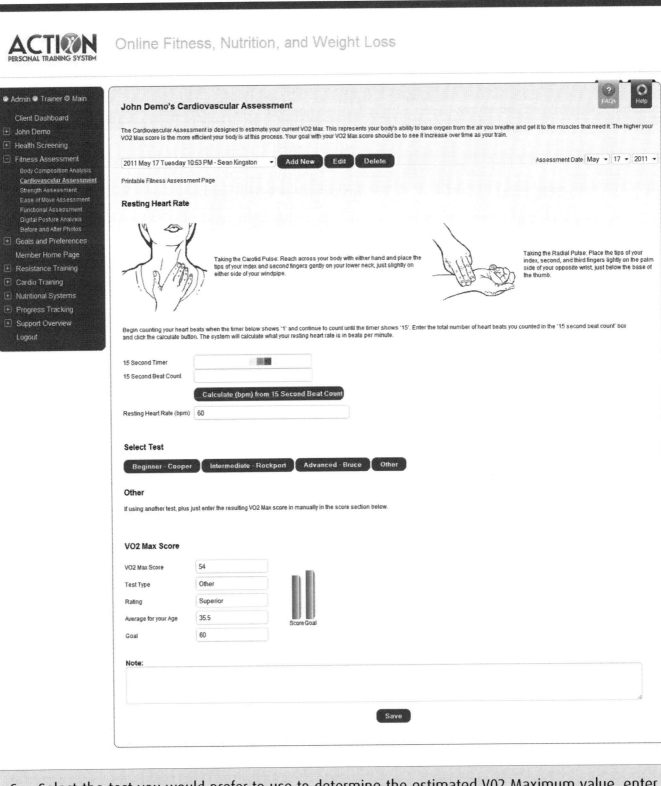

● Admin ● Trainer ⊙ Main

Client Dashboard
⊞ John Demo
⊞ Health Screening
⊟ Fitness Assessment
    Body Composition Analysis
    Cardiovascular Assessment
    Strength Assessment
    Ease of Move Assessment
    Functional Assessment
    Digital Posture Analysis
    Before and After Photos
⊞ Goals and Preferences
    Member Home Page
⊞ Resistance Training
⊞ Cardio Training
⊞ Nutritional Systems
⊞ Progress Tracking
⊞ Support Overview
    Logout

John Demo's Cardiovascular Assessment

The Cardiovascular Assessment is designed to estimate your current VO2 Max. This represents your body's ability to take oxygen from the air you breathe and get it to the muscles that need it. The higher your VO2 Max score is the more efficient your body is at this process. Your goal with your VO2 Max score should be to see it increase over time as your train.

2011 May 17 Tuesday 10:53 PM - Sean Kingston ▾   **Add New**   **Edit**   **Delete**   Assessment Date May ▾ 17 ▾ 2011 ▾

Printable Fitness Assessment Page

Resting Heart Rate

Taking the Carotid Pulse: Reach across your body with either hand and place the tips of your index and second fingers gently on your lower neck, just slightly on either side of your windpipe.

Taking the Radial Pulse: Place the tips of your index, second, and third fingers lightly on the palm side of your opposite wrist, just below the base of the thumb.

Begin counting your heart beats when the timer below shows '1' and continue to count until the timer shows '15'. Enter the total number of heart beats you counted in the '15 second beat count' box and click the calculate button. The system will calculate what your resting heart rate is in beats per minute.

15 Second Timer

15 Second Beat Count

        Calculate (bpm) from 15 Second Beat Count

Resting Heart Rate (bpm)   60

Select Test

Beginner - Cooper   Intermediate - Rockport   Advanced - Bruce   Other

Other

If using another test, plus just enter the resulting VO2 Max score in manually in the score section below.

VO2 Max Score

VO2 Max Score   54

Test Type   Other

Rating   Superior

Average for your Age   35.5

Goal   60

Score   Goal

Note:

        Save

C.   Select the test you would prefer to use to determine the estimated VO2 Maximum value, enter the appropriate data as outlined in the test description and click 'Calculate Score'.

The system will calculate the estimated VO2 Maximum as well as displaying the Test Type, Rating, and Average for your Age.

You can then input a goal for your client and the chart on the right will show a visual representation of where they are currently relative to their goal.

You may also view their progress over time in the 'Progress Tracking' section of the system

D. If you would like to add any notes to be saved with this assessment you may do so in the 'Notes' field.

Once you have completed the assessment click 'Save' to save the results to the client's profile

Strength Assessment

The ACTION PTS Strength Assessment will allow you to estimate a 1 Repetition Maximum value for each of the major muscle groups by using a test to exhaustion in a safe range of between 8 and 15 repetitions. These values can then be re-assessed over time and the progress recorded and tracked.

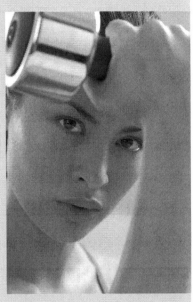

For each muscle group that you want to test you will be able to select from up to 3 different exercises (see Appendix: Admin Menu: Settings and Tools: Master Preferences for how to select the exercise choices). Once an exercise is selected, have the client perform a warm up set at light weight, then after a short rest have them perform 1 set using a weight that exhausts them between 8 and 15 repetitions. If they are unable to complete 8 repetitions you will need to reduce the weight, and if they are able to complete more than 15 repetitions before exhaustion then you will need to increase the weight.

Core exercises should be done using an isometric exercise and therefore you will record the time they are able to hold the isometric position. The system will not estimate a 1 Repetition Maximum for core exercises.

Key Features of the ACTION Strength Assessment Page

A. Use the drop down to select, view, or edit any previous assessment completed with this client.

Select 'Add New' if you want to begin a new assessment – you can change the Assessment Date using the field to the right if you have completed the assessment previously and are inputting results on a different date.

Select 'Edit' to make changes to any previous assessment.

Use the 'Delete' button to remove any previous assessment from the client's records.

Use the 'Printable Fitness Assessment Page' link to open a separate window that you may print with all of the fitness assessment fields to record the data for input later

B. Using the drop downs, select the exercise you would like to use for each muscle group that you will test. Record the amount of weight used for the test, using the drop down to select between lbs or kg.

Use the drop down to select the number of repetitions completed to exhaustion. The number of repetitions must be between 8 and 15.

Click the 'Calculate' button and the system will determine the 'Calculated Maximum' and a 'Goal Maximum' for each muscle group tested. The 'Goal Maximum' is simply an estimate and you may over-write this value with one of your choosing

C. The system will display a series of bar graphs displaying a visual representation of the client's current 1 repetition maximum score relative to their goal.

You may also view their progress over time in the 'Progress Tracking' section of the system

D. If you would like to add any notes to be saved with this assessment you may do so in the 'Notes' field.

Once you have completed the assessment click 'Save' to save the results to the client's profile

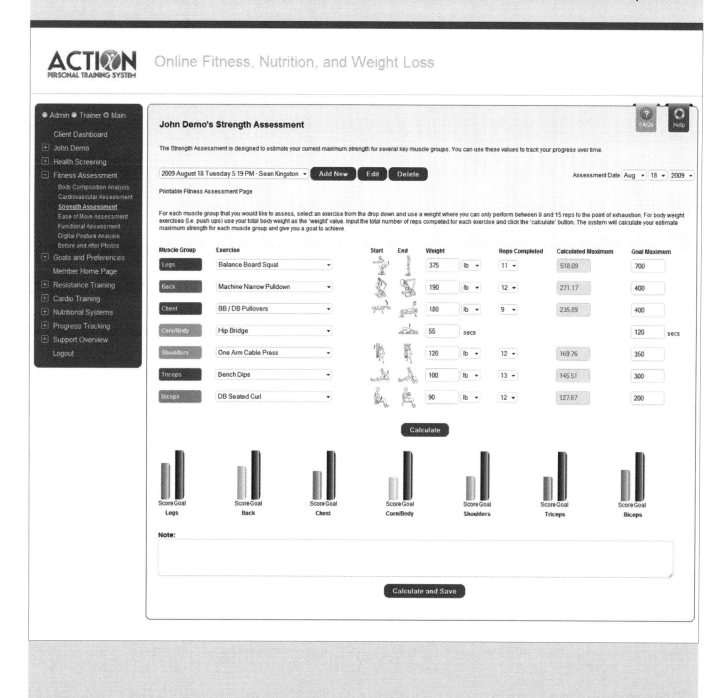

Ease of Movement Assessment

The ACTION PTS Ease of Movement Assessment is designed to test for functional range of motion across key joints and to check for even flexibility on both sides of the body. The goal should be to have ratings of 'Good' for all of the key joints in the body and to have even range of motion from side to side. Unbalanced range of motion from side to side can potentially lead to injuries. To perform the tests as accurately as possible it is suggested that a Goniometer is used to measure the joint angles for Straight Leg Raise, and Internal and External Hip Rotations.

Straight Leg Raise

The Straight Leg Raise should be performed with the client lying in a supine position with their arms to their sides. Starting with the right leg, slowly raise the leg, keeping the knee fully extended, as far as the client can comfortably go. Slowly lower and then repeat with the same leg. Using a Goniometer, measure the joint angle at the hip (from the floor where the ankle was when lying supping to the position the ankle is at the end) and record this value. Repeat with the left leg

Internal Hip Rotation

Begin with the client lying in a supine position with their arms to the sides. Slowly raise the right leg until it is perpendicular to the floor, bending the knee to a 90 degree angle. Slowly rotate the ankle away from the midline of the body, which will internally rotate the hip. Go as far as the client can comfortably move, then return to the start position and repeat with the same leg. Using a Goniometer, measure the joint angle by placing the Goniometer on the kneecap and measuring the angle from the midline of the body (original position of the ankle) to the ankle with the hip internally rotated. Repeat the procedure with the left leg

External Hip Rotation

Begin with the client lying in a supine position with their arms to the sides. Slowly raise the right leg until it is perpendicular to the floor, bending the knee to a 90 degree angle. Slowly rotate the ankle across the midline of the body, which will externally rotate the hip. Go as far as the client can comfortably move, then return to the start position and repeat with the same leg. Using a Goniometer, measure the joint angle by placing the Goniometer on the kneecap and measuring the angle from the midline of the body (original position of the ankle) to the ankle with the hip externally rotated. Repeat the procedure with the left leg

Quadriceps

With the client lying in a prone position, slowly draw the heel of the right leg towards the buttocks, bending at the knee, as far as the client can comfortably go. Return to the starting position and repeat with the same leg. Using a measuring tape or ruler, measure the distance between the heel and the buttock and record this measurement. Use a measurement of '0' if the heel touches the buttock. Repeat with the left leg

Shoulders

With the client standing, have them extend the right arm above the head and left arm towards the floor. Simultaneously have them drop their right hand behind their back while reaching up behind the body with the left hand with the goal being to touch the hands together. Using a measuring tape or ruler, measure the distance between the tips of the fingers of the right and left hand, and record this measurement. Use a measurement of '0' if the fingers are able to touch. Repeat with the arms in opposite positions for the left side

Key Features of the ACTION Ease of Movement Page

A. Use the drop down to select, view, or edit any previous assessment completed with this client.

Select 'Add New' if you want to begin a new assessment – you can change the Assessment Date using the field to the right if you have completed the assessment previously and are inputting results on a different date.

ACTION — Online Fitness, Nutrition, and Weight Loss
PERSONAL TRAINING SYSTEM

● Admin ● Trainer ○ Main

Client Dashboard
+ John Demo
+ Health Screening
− Fitness Assessment
   Body Composition Analysis
   Cardiovascular Assessment
   Strength Assessment
   Ease of Move Assessment
   Functional Assessment
   Digital Posture Analysis
   Before and After Photos
+ Goals and Preferences
   Member Home Page
+ Resistance Training
+ Cardio Training
+ Nutritional Systems
+ Progress Tracking
+ Support Overview
   Logout

John Demo's Ease of Movement Assessment

The Ease of Movement Assessment is designed to test for functional range of motion across key joints and to check for even flexibility on both sides of the body. Your goal should be to have ratings of 'Good' for all of the key joints in the body and to have even range of motion from side to side. Unbalanced range of motion from side to side can potentially lead to injuries.

2009 April 15 Wednesday 2:50 PM ▾ | Add New | Edit | Delete   Assessment Date Apr ▾ 15 ▾ 2009 ▾

Printable Fitness Assessment Page

Picture					Even from Side to Side
	Straight Leg Raise Right	77	degrees ▾	Good	
	Straight Leg Raise Left	62	degrees ▾	Satisfactory	No
	Internal Hip Rotation Right	45	degrees ▾	Good	
	Internal Hip Rotation Left	45	degrees ▾	Good	Yes
	External Hip Rotation Right	90	degrees ▾	Good	
	External Hip Rotation Left	45	degrees ▾	Good	No
	Quadriceps Right	1.18	in ▾	Good	
	Quadriceps Left	1.18	in ▾	Good	Yes
	Shoulders Right	2	in ▾	Needs Improvement	
	Shoulders Left	2.76	in ▾	Needs Improvement	Yes

Note:

| Calculate and Save |

Select 'Edit' to make changes to any previous assessment.

Use the 'Delete' button to remove any previous assessment from the client's records.

Use the 'Printable Fitness Assessment Page' link to open a separate window that you may print with all of the fitness assessment fields to record the data for input later

B. Record the joint angles and measurements for each of the various tests, using the drop down to select between inches and cm for the Quadriceps and Shoulder tests.

Click the 'Calculate and Save' button and the system will now display the results of the Ease of Movement test with a rating of 'Good', 'Satisfactory', or 'Needs Improvement', and a simple 'Yes' or 'No' rating for whether the joints are even from the right to left side.

You may view their progress over time in the 'Progress Tracking' section of the system

C. If you would like to add any notes to be saved with this assessment you may do so in the 'Notes' field.

Once you have completed the assessment click 'Save' to save the results to the client's profile

Functional Assessment

The ACTION PTS Functional Assessment is designed to test the body's overall core stability and endurance and the ability to perform basic tasks. It is comprised of two separate tests, the Squat test and the Marching test.

Squat Test

The squat test is performed starting with the client in a normal standing position and then performing 10 -12 basic body weight squats. The following criteria should be monitored and recorded:

Is full range of motion achieved (thighs parallel to floor)?

Full range of motion not achieved indicates possible:

- Tightness in lumbar-pelvic-hip complex
- Tightness in hamstrings
- Core weakness
- Poor balance and/or proprioception
- Lumber disk degeneration

Does the knee width remain constant?

Knee width changes indicate possible:

- Width decreases indicates possible:
  - Tightness in adductor muscles
  - Tightness in hip flexors
  - Prior hip / knee injury
- Width increases indicates possible:
  - Tightness in abductor muscles
  - Prior hip / knee injury

Does their weight shift from their heels to toes?

Weight shifts from heels indicates possible:

- Core weakness
- Tightness in hamstrings
- Postural issues
- Tightness in lumbar-pelvic-hip complex
- Poor balance and/or proprioception
- Inexperience with movement

Is there overall stability good?

Poor overall stability - indicates possible:

- Core weakness
- Poor balance and/or proprioception
- Inexperience with movement

Are they able to maintain a neutral spine position?

Unable to maintain neutral position (pelvic tilt) - indicates possible:

- Tightness in lumbar-pelvic-hip complex
- Tightness in hamstrings
- Core weakness
- Poor balance and/or proprioception
- Tightness in hip flexors

Marching Test

The Marching test begins with the client standing in the center of an open space, preferably somewhere as quiet as possible, and should be performed by marching on the spot at a pace of 2 steps per second bringing the knees to hip height. This test should be done for 1 minute with the EYES CLOSED. The objective of this test is to determine overall stability and muscular balance. Record the client's starting and finishing positions, including the direction and approximate degrees of rotation.

Forward movement indicates possible:

- Core weakness
- Tightness in lumbar-pelvic-hip complex
- Tightness in hamstrings
- Poor balance and/or proprioception

Right or left curve indicates possible:

- Curve right, right shoulder sitting lower than left
- Curve left, left shoulder sitting lower than right

Slight curve (less than 45°)

- Previous hip, knee, or back injury
- Core weakness
- Slight lateral pelvic tilt

Large curve (more than 45°)

- Limb length difference one leg slightly shorter than other
- Lateral head tilt to one side
- Core weakness
- Possible disk degeneration
- Possible spinal scoliosis
- Lateral pelvic tilt

Key Features of the ACTION Functional Assessment Page

A. Use the drop down to select, view, or edit any previous assessment completed with this client.

Select 'Add New' if you want to begin a new assessment – you can change the Assessment Date using the field to the right if you have completed the assessment previously and are inputting results on a different date.

Select 'Edit' to make changes to any previous assessment.

Use the 'Delete' button to remove any previous assessment from the client's records.

Use the 'Printable Fitness Assessment Page' link to open a separate window that you may print with all of the fitness assessment fields to record the data for input later

B. Have the client perform the Squat test and check the appropriate boxes for the parts of the test they are capable of completing properly

The system will display a score and a bar graph displaying a visual representation of the client's score and their goal

C. Have the client perform the Marching test and input their score based on how far they move from their starting position

D. You may view their progress over time in the 'Progress Tracking' section of the system

E. If you would like to add any notes to be saved with this assessment you may do so in the 'Notes' field.

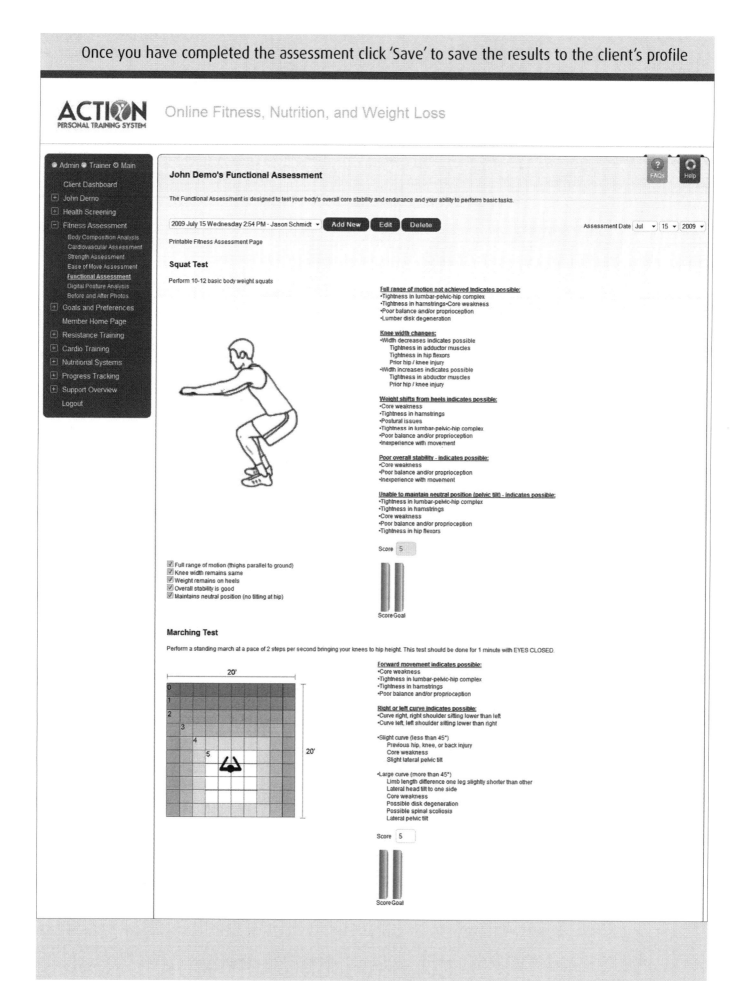

ACTION PERSONAL TRAINING SYSTEM

Online Fitness, Nutrition, and Weight Loss

● Admin ● Trainer ● Main

Client Dashboard
⊞ John Demo
⊞ Health Screening
⊟ Fitness Assessment
   Body Composition Analysis
   Cardiovascular Assessment
   Strength Assessment
   Ease of Move Assessment
   Functional Assessment
   Digital Posture Analysis
   Before and After Photos
⊞ Goals and Preferences
   Member Home Page
⊞ Resistance Training
⊞ Cardio Training
⊞ Nutritional Systems
⊞ Progress Tracking
⊞ Support Overview
   Logout

John Demo's Functional Assessment

The Functional Assessment is designed to test your body's overall core stability and endurance and your ability to perform basic tasks.

2009 July 15 Wednesday 2:54 PM - Jason Schmidt ▾ | Add New | Edit | Delete

Assessment Date Jul ▾ | 15 ▾ | 2009 ▾

Printable Fitness Assessment Page

Squat Test

Perform 10-12 basic body weight squats

Full range of motion not achieved indicates possible:
•Tightness in lumbar-pelvic-hip complex
•Tightness in hamstrings•Core weakness
•Poor balance and/or proprioception
•Lumber disk degeneration

Knee width changes:
•Width decreases indicates possible
   Tightness in adductor muscles
   Tightness in hip flexors
   Prior hip / knee injury
•Width increases indicates possible
   Tightness in abductor muscles
   Prior hip / knee injury

Weight shifts from heels indicates possible:
•Core weakness
•Tightness in hamstrings
•Postural issues
•Tightness in lumbar-pelvic-hip complex
•Poor balance and/or proprioception
•Inexperience with movement

Poor overall stability - indicates possible:
•Core weakness
•Poor balance and/or proprioception
•Inexperience with movement

Unable to maintain neutral position (pelvic tilt) - indicates possible:
•Tightness in lumbar-pelvic-hip complex
•Tightness in hamstrings
•Core weakness
•Poor balance and/or proprioception
•Tightness in hip flexors

Score 5

☑ Full range of motion (thighs parallel to ground)
☑ Knee width remains same
☑ Weight remains on heels
☑ Overall stability is good
☑ Maintains neutral position (no tilting at hip)

Score Goal

Marching Test

Perform a standing march at a pace of 2 steps per second bringing your knees to hip height. This test should be done for 1 minute with EYES CLOSED.

20'

20'

Forward movement indicates possible:
•Core weakness
•Tightness in lumbar-pelvic-hip complex
•Tightness in hamstrings
•Poor balance and/or proprioception

Right or left curve indicates possible:
•Curve right, right shoulder sitting lower than left
•Curve left, left shoulder sitting lower than right

•Slight curve (less than 45°)
   Previous hip, knee, or back injury
   Core weakness
   Slight lateral pelvic tilt

•Large curve (more than 45°)
   Limb length difference one leg slightly shorter than other
   Lateral head tilt to one side
   Core weakness
   Possible disk degeneration
   Possible spinal scoliosis
   Lateral pelvic tilt

Score 5

Score Goal

Digital Posture Analysis

The ACTION PTS Digital Posture Analysis is a basic postural assessment to help identify muscle imbalances, postural issues, core weaknesses, and other potential causes of long term problems. Please note that this is a very basic analysis and should not be relied upon to diagnose lordosis, scoliosis, or other potentially serious back conditions. To perform this test you must have a wall mounted or portable grid chart, a plumb line, and a digital camera. There are 2 components to this analysis, the Rear Profile and the Side Profile.

Rear Profile

Have the client stand facing the grid chart in a normal, relaxed stance, with the ankles evenly spaced on either side of the plumb line. Making sure you are centered on the chart, take a digital picture of the client, ensuring you are far enough away to get the client's entire body in the picture.

There are 5 criteria you are looking for on the rear profile:

1. Are the shoulders level and parallel to the ground?

2. Do the hands hang to the same height?

3. Are the hips level and parallel to the ground?

4. Are the knees at the same height?

5. Is the head upright with no tilt?

Each criterion that the client meets should be checked. The system keeps a running total of the score as boxes are checked.

Side Profile

Have the client stand centered on, but facing to the right of, the grid chart in a normal relaxed stance, with the ankles centered on the plumb line. Have the client close their eyes and relax forward, bending at the waist and extending their hands towards the floor and then return to an upright, relaxed position. Making sure you are centered on the chart, take a digital picture of the client, ensuring you are far enough away to get the client's entire body in the picture.

There are 5 criteria you are looking for on the side profile:

1. Are the ears, shoulders, hips, knees, and ankles aligned on the plumb line?

2. Do the hands hang in line with the front of the thighs?

3. Is the spine neutral with just a slight curvature?

4. Is the chin and jaw parallel to the ground?

5. Are the shoulders not rounded forward?

Each criterion that the client meets should be checked. The system keeps a running total of the score as boxes are checked.

Key Features of the ACTION Digital Posture Analysis Page

A.   Use the drop down to select, view, or edit any previous assessment completed with this client.

Select 'Add New' if you want to begin a new assessment – you can change the Assessment Date using the field to the right if you have completed the assessment previously and are inputting results on a different date.

Select 'Edit' to make changes to any previous assessment.

Use the 'Delete' button to remove any previous assessment from the client's records.

Use the 'Printable Fitness Assessment Page' link to open a separate window that you may print with all of the fitness assessment fields to record the data for input later

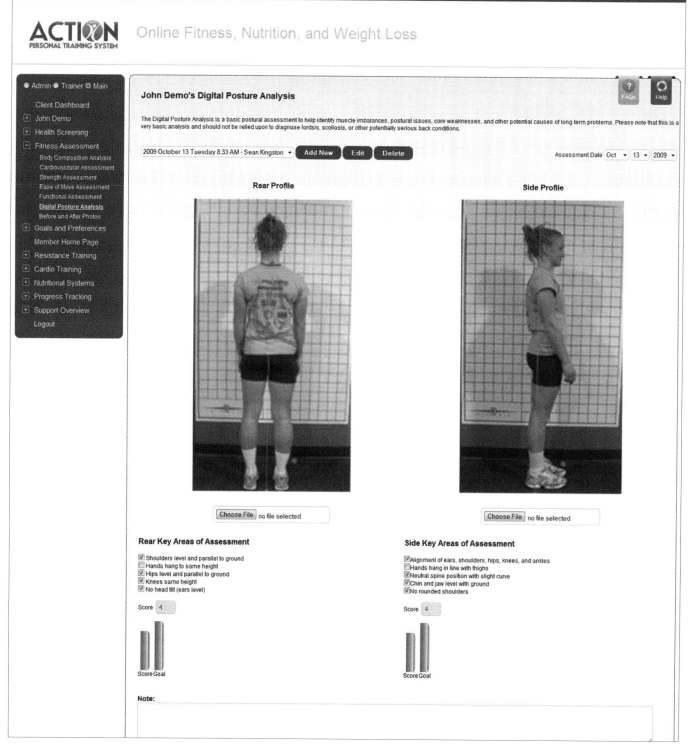

B. Using the 'Browse' or 'Choose File' button, upload the digital pictures of the client's rear and side profiles

C. Check each of the boxes that apply to the client's profile pictures. The system will keep a running total of their score from 0 to 5, with each checked box being worth a score of 1.

D. The system will display a series of bar graphs displaying a visual representation of the client's current score relative to their goal. You may view their progress over time in the 'Progress Tracking' section of the system

E. If you would like to add any notes to be saved with this assessment you may do so in the 'Notes' field.

Once you have completed the assessment click 'Save' to save the results to the client's profile

Tracking Client Progress Using the ACTION Personal Training System

The Progress Tracking Tools in the ACTION PTS are designed to allow you to visually track the progress of your clients. These tools are also accessible by your clients so they may view their progress as well. The Progress Tracking area is broken down into 4 key elements:

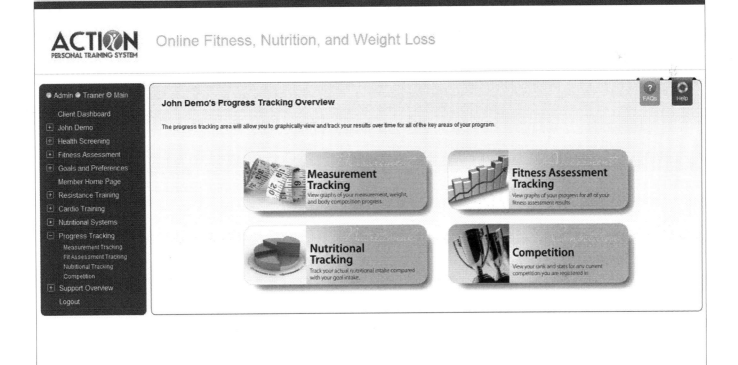

Measurement Tracking

Measurement Tracking is used to graph results of the Body Composition Fitness Assessment. There are trend charts for Body Fat Percentage, Weight, the 4 mandatory measurements used in the body composition (Shoulders, Navel, Waist and Hips), and the 4 option measurements (Biceps, Forearm, Thigh, Calf)

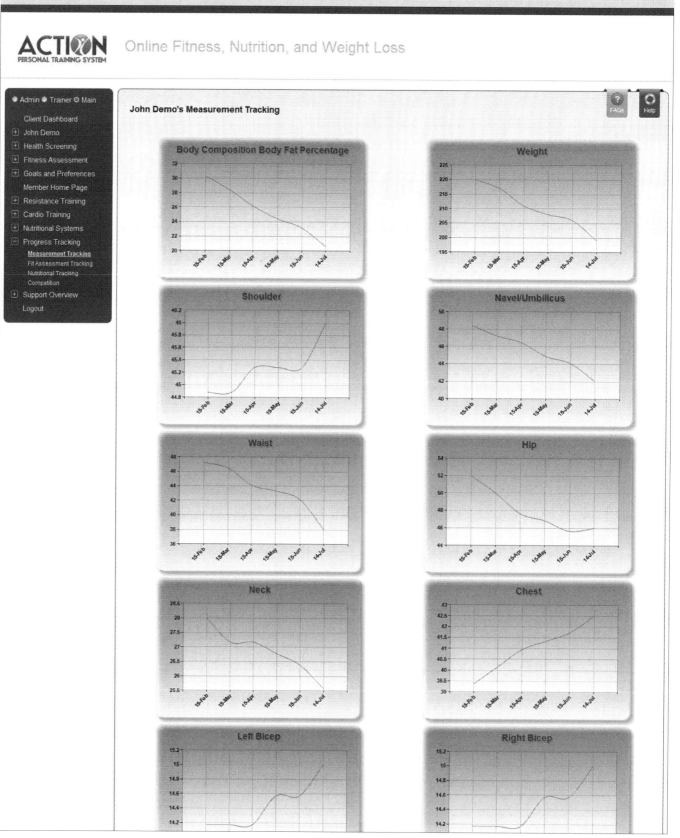

Fitness Assessment Tracking

Fitness Assessment Tracking will display trend graphs of the results of the Strength, Cardio, Postural, and Functional Assessments

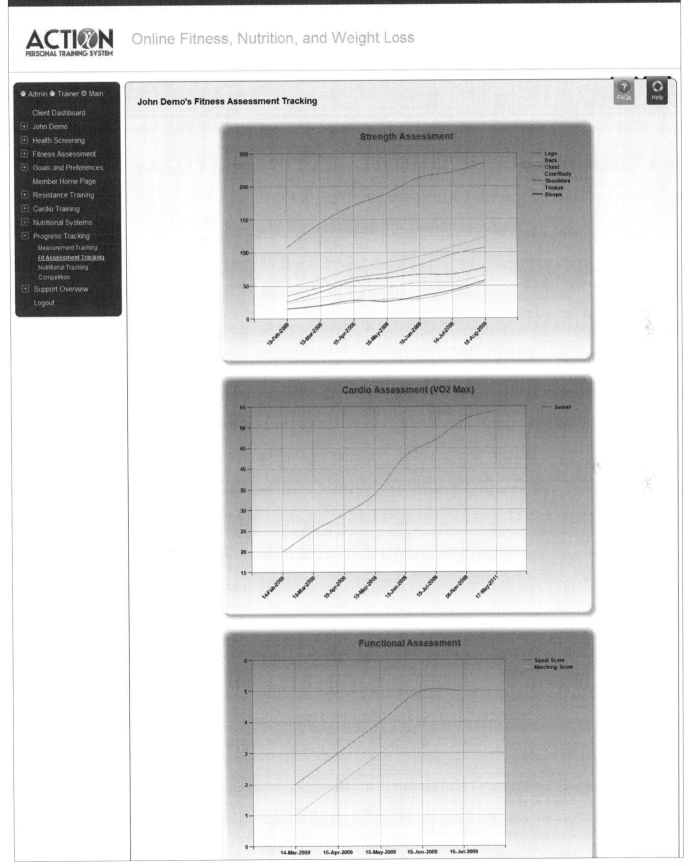

Nutritional Tracking

The Nutritional Tracking is separated into Calories, Fats, Carbs, and Protein and each of these has 'Daily' and 'Cumulative' graphs.
The Daily graphs show a snapshot of each days 'target' intake versus the 'actual' intake.

The Cumulative graphs show a running total of all days in the past 3 months added together to show a trend of what has been happening.

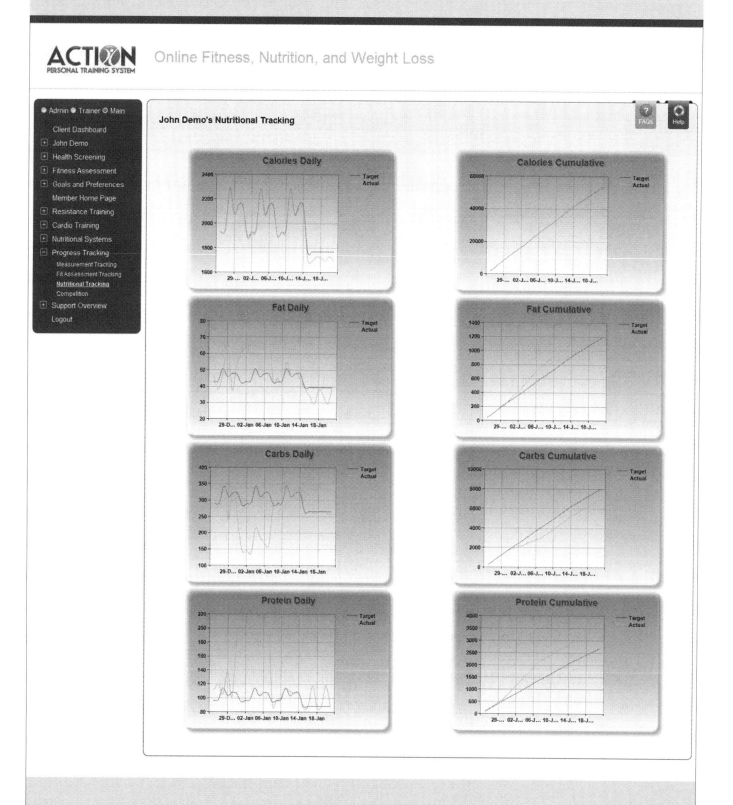

Competition Tracking

The Competition Tracking is used to display the current status or results of a competition that the client is involved in. The graph will show a visual representation of their ranking in the competition while the chart below displays the details of the current ranking and status. Depending on the 'Privacy' settings of the Competition (see Appendix: Trainer Menu: Advanced Features: Competitions) results will either be displayed showing the name of all participants, or only the clients name will be displayed with the remaining names displayed as 'Private'

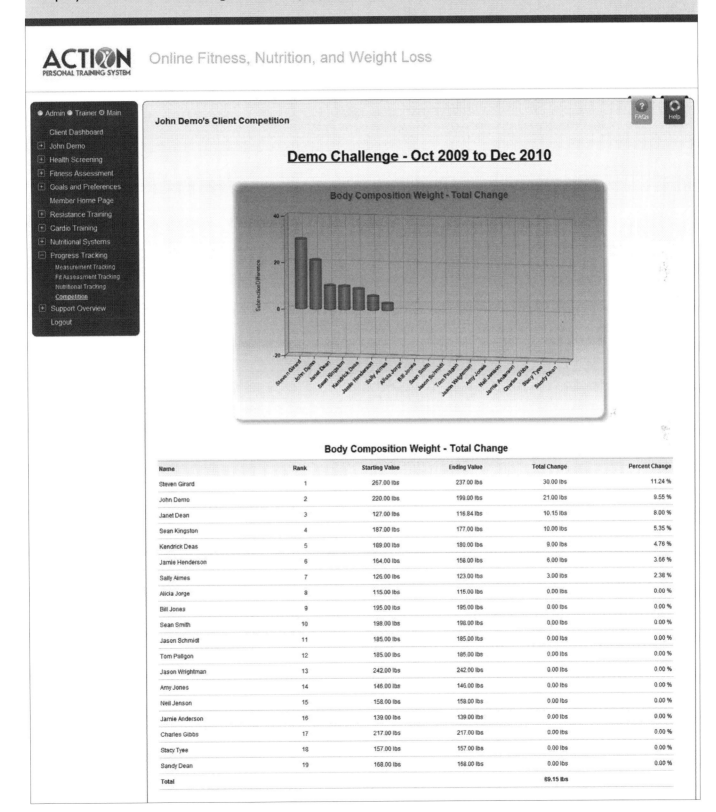

Body Composition Weight - Total Change

Name	Rank	Starting Value	Ending Value	Total Change	Percent Change
Steven Girard	1	267.00 lbs	237.00 lbs	30.00 lbs	11.24 %
John Demo	2	220.00 lbs	199.00 lbs	21.00 lbs	9.55 %
Janet Dean	3	127.00 lbs	116.84 lbs	10.15 lbs	8.00 %
Sean Kingston	4	187.00 lbs	177.00 lbs	10.00 lbs	5.35 %
Kendrick Deas	5	189.00 lbs	180.00 lbs	9.00 lbs	4.76 %
Jamie Henderson	6	164.00 lbs	158.00 lbs	6.00 lbs	3.66 %
Sally Aimes	7	126.00 lbs	123.00 lbs	3.00 lbs	2.38 %
Alicia Jorge	8	115.00 lbs	115.00 lbs	0.00 lbs	0.00 %
Bill Jones	9	195.00 lbs	195.00 lbs	0.00 lbs	0.00 %
Sean Smith	10	198.00 lbs	198.00 lbs	0.00 lbs	0.00 %
Jason Schmidt	11	185.00 lbs	185.00 lbs	0.00 lbs	0.00 %
Tom Paligon	12	185.00 lbs	185.00 lbs	0.00 lbs	0.00 %
Jason Wrightman	13	242.00 lbs	242.00 lbs	0.00 lbs	0.00 %
Amy Jones	14	146.00 lbs	146.00 lbs	0.00 lbs	0.00 %
Neil Jenson	15	158.00 lbs	158.00 lbs	0.00 lbs	0.00 %
Jamie Anderson	16	139.00 lbs	139.00 lbs	0.00 lbs	0.00 %
Charles Gibbs	17	217.00 lbs	217.00 lbs	0.00 lbs	0.00 %
Stacy Tyee	18	157.00 lbs	157.00 lbs	0.00 lbs	0.00 %
Sandy Dean	19	168.00 lbs	168.00 lbs	0.00 lbs	0.00 %
Total				89.15 lbs	

Summary

A fitness assessment is a useful tool for determining an exercise plan specific to the client; however, a trainer should avoid implementing an exercise routine that may cause the client injury or embarrassment, either physical or emotional. There are several components of a fitness assessment and some may be omitted or modified depending on the client's needs, conditions or goals. There are also several different tests that can be used to measure the same aspect of a fitness assessment (e.g., stretch test or sit & reach test). Some tests are designed for people who have high fitness levels and may be unsuitable for a beginning client. On the other hand, some tests may not be challenging enough for a very athletic client. It is best to schedule the initial and follow-up assessments according to what will best motivate and encourage the client. The order in which fitness assessments should be carried out is as follows: (1) Non-fatiguing tests, (2) Agility tests, (3) Maximal strength and power tests, (4) Sprint tests, (5) Muscular endurance tests, and (6) Flexibility tests. The specific type of test that is used for these categories should be chosen based on the client's current fitness level.

Although fitness assessments help personal trainers design effective exercise routines, in order for the regimen to be effective the trainer must take care in standardizing the conditions under which the assessments are performed. Certain factors may influence test results and will lead to an inaccurate assessment. A few of these factors include: ambient temperature, noise, humidity and the condition of the client being assessed. The amount of sleep the client had night before and the type of food and drink the client consumed can affect performance during the physical assessment. The time of day and the test environment may also affect the client's performance so the trainer should try to maintain these conditions by keeping them constant. Despite these factors, fitness assessments are still a great asset to a training program as they provide the personal trainer and the client with a lot of information. Once the client begins an exercise routine, progress can be used as a motivational tool to continue the program.

Review Questions

1. What is the purpose of the initial client assessment?

   a) To learn about the client

   b) To efficiently tailor the proper workout regimen

   c) To understand the likes and dislikes of the client

   d) All of the above

2. One of the many jobs a personal trainer has is to advise the client on how to handle any unresolved medical issues they may have. True or False?_____

3. In order to keep the client's medical information private the personal trainer should put a _____ in the assessment form.

4. All of the following are considered lifestyle categories: hobbies, physical activities, working in front of a computer and nutritional habits. True or False? _____

5. Knowing what medications the client is taking and possible side effects are important because:

   a) The trainer may need to borrow some if the medication runs out

   b) The client may be allergic to certain medications

   c) There may be conflicts between the recommended workout and the medication

   d) The trainer may need to refill the prescription

6. Small changes in one's daily routine like parking farther away from a building or taking the stairs can have a large impact on fitness goals. True or False?_____

7. Why do most people hire a personal trainer? _____

   _____

   _____

8. The optimum regimen that is specific to the client's needs can be best designed when the assessment is _____.

9. The best way to conduct an initial assessment is to:

   a) Give the client the form to take home so it is not filled out in a hurry

   b) Let the client fill the form out while demonstrating how to stretch

   c) Going over the form with the client personally

   d) E-mail it so the client will not be inconvenienced by having to write the answers

10. If the client has a condition such as lower back pain, the trainer should encourage the client to perform strength training for that region without prior approval from a health care physician. True or False?

Answers

1. d) All of the above.
2. False.
3. Confidentiality clause.
4. True.
5. c) There may be conflicts between the recommended workout and the medication.
6. True.
7. To add that special benefit that the client has been missing as a means of fulfilling weight-loss or fitness goals.
8. Thorough.
9. c) Going over the form with the client personally.
10. False.

References

Babette M, Pluim J, Staal B, Marks BL, Miller S, Miley D. Health benefits of tennis. *British Journal of Sports Medicine.* 2007;41:760-68.

Boreham CAG, Kennedy RA, Murphy MH, Tully M, Wallace WFM, Young I. Training effects of short bouts of stair climbing on cardiorespiratory fitness, blood lipids and homocysteine in sedentary young women. *British Journal of Sports Medicine.* 2005;39:590-93.

Frank J. Managing hypertension using combination therapy. *American Family Physician.* 2008;77(9):1279-86.

Hagberg LA, Lindholm L. Cost-effectiveness of healthcare-based interventions aimed at improving physical activity. *Scandinavian Journal of Public Health.* 2006;34(6):641-53.

Harris JR, Cross J, Hannon PA, Mahoney E, Ross-Viles S. Employer adoption of evidence based chronic disease prevention practice: a pilot study. *Preventing Chronic Disease.* 2008;5(3):A92.

Ruser CB, Federman DG, Kashaf SS. Whittling away at obesity and overweight. Small lifestyle changes can have the biggest impact. *Postgraduate Medicine.* 2005;117(1):31-34.

Chapter 4: Introduction to Designing Programs

Topics Covered

Introduction to Designing Programs

Program Design
Health Precautions to Consider when Designing a Program
Avoiding Overexertion and Injury
Signs of Dangerous Dysfunctional Breathing
Avoiding Discouragement

Aerobic Programs for Beginners

Physiological Factors to Consider in Designing Programs
Types of Muscle Actions
Energy Usage
The Kinetic Chain
Proper Positioning

Types of Training Used in Exercise Program Design

Principles of Exercise Training
Target Heart Rate
Measuring Exercise Intensity
Measuring Caloric Use
Principles of Resistance Training (RT)
Determining Resistance
Determining Rest Periods
Resistance Training Modalities
Periodization
Ways to Vary Volume and Intensity
Overtraining

Introduction to Designing Programs

To design a training program effectively, a personal trainer must have knowledge of anatomy and physiology, kinesiology and basic nutrition, as well as information about special populations like pregnant and post-natal women, adolescents, the elderly, and those with chronic medical conditions. Having this kind of background information will aid a trainer's awareness of the proper postural alignments for different exercises, the indications and contraindications for different populations, and the risks and precautions to be considered when designing the program.

Program success relies on the rapport and trust between the client and the trainer so it helps if the trainer develops both communication and active listening skills. Clients need to feel that they are in good hands and that they are working with a knowledgeable professional. They want to feel as if their trainer is personally interested in them and vested in their success.

It is helpful to have knowledge of motivating techniques and know the principles of causing behavior change. As the intensity of the program increases, client compliance usually falls off and it is up to the trainer to help keep the clients motivated, enthusiastic and committed to completing the program.

Client education plays a large role in the development of a training program and its success. Teaching the client about how the body works and what specific exercises accomplish is important for the client to trust in the program components, stay motivated and feel connected to the trainer. Education about the importance of resistance training is particularly important since many people still associate it with body building and many women fear building up muscle mass.

Clients can educate trainers too. Client feedback is crucial to the success of any training program, and the trainer must take client needs and feelings into account when developing and adjusting program components.

Continuing education is also important. Clients have many misconceptions about training due to faulty marketing campaigns. It helps if the trainer stays on top of current events and research in order to answer questions that may come up.

Trainers must educate clients about the types of physical contact that they will use. Explain the reasons behind any physical contact such as spotting techniques, assessments and assisted exercises. Be sure that the client is comfortable with these instances of physical contact.

The ACTION Personal Training System Goals and Preferences

The ACTION PTS Goals and Preferences tools are designed to let you record and save your clients experience level, goals, schedule, and preferences. This information can then be used when building a client's programming or by the ACTION PTS for the 'suggested' features such as suggested resistance programs and suggested nutritional programs.

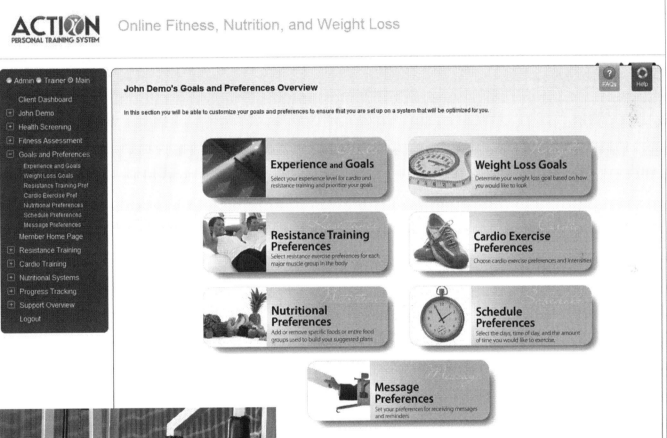

Experience and Goals

The Experience and Goals page will allow you to set an experience level for your client for resistance training and cardiovascular training. Experience ratings begin with 'No Experience' and go as high as 'Advanced' with detailed descriptions for each rating.

Below the Experience rating where you will rate your clients Goals based on priority. Up to 3 goals can be selected including 1st priority, 2nd priority, and 3rd priority goals. The goals may be chosen from overall wellness, to muscular or cardiovascular based, or even sport specific goals.

Key Features of the ACTION Experience and Goals Page

A. Select the experience level for resistance training and cardiovascular activities using the buttons

B. Select first, second, and third priority goals from the, list of options

Weight Loss Goals

The Weight Loss Goals page is designed to provide a visual representation of various body fat percentages. By selecting what the client's appearance goal is the system can determine the goal body fat percentage and therefore the goal weight. This system of determining a weight loss goal will help to prevent unrealistic expectations of goals.

Once a goal weight has been determined the next step is to calculate the Weight Loss Type. This will determine the amount of weekly fat loss the client can expect to see. There are various automatic safeguards built into this selection system. By default, the system will not allow a weekly weight loss that would require a deficit of more than 25% of total calories consumed. For example, a client that requires 2000 calories per day for their Basal Metabolic Rate would not have the option to select a weight loss type that would require more than 500 calories per day, which is equal to 1 pound per week. A client that is quite heavy and therefore has a much higher Basal Metabolic Rate would be able to select higher weekly weight loss goals.

In addition, clients that are very heavy and need to see accelerated weight loss will have additional options to not add calories required for exercise to their daily caloric goals. This will have the effect of increasing their daily caloric deficit and accelerating weight loss.

The weight loss safeguards and exercise calories have options to override them in the Master Preferences (see Appendix: Admin Menu: Settings and Tools: Master Preferences)

Once a Weight Loss Type has been selected the system will create a graph of the expected timeline to achieve the goal weight.

Key Features of the ACTION Weight Loss Goals page

A. Use the body fat percentage drawings to select a goals body fat percentage

B. The system will calculate Goal Weight, Goal Body Fat Percentage, and Goal Body Fat Weight

C. Choose from the available Weight Loss Types for the client

D. The Goal Timeline will be calculated and graphed

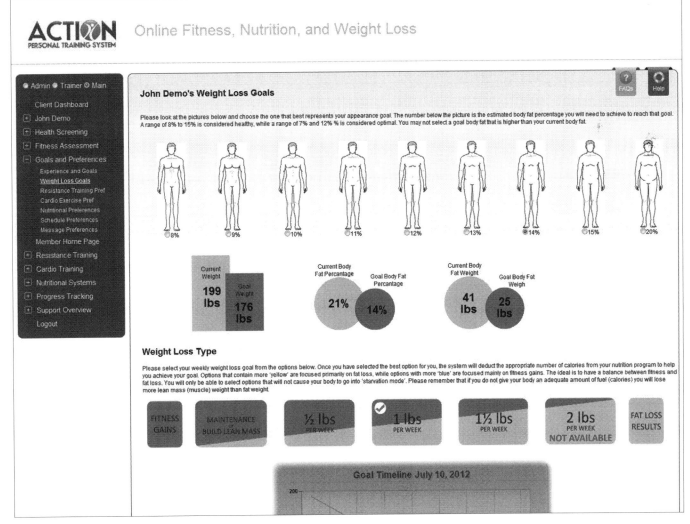

Resistance Training Preferences

The Resistance Training preferences is divided into 2 parts:

Equipment Availability is designed to allow you to remove entire resistance exercise groups based on the equipment type used. This is beneficial if you do not have a specific type of equipment in your facility or if you do not want the client to be using a particular type of equipment at this point. By un-checking an equipment type, the system will then remove any exercise using this equipment type from being used in a 'Suggested Program' for a client.

Trainers will always have the ability to manually select any exercise regardless of if it has been removed as a preference.

The Exclude Specific Exercises feature is designed to allow for the removal of any specific exercise in the system from being used in the Suggested Program feature. This is valuable if the client has a specific injury or contraindication that would require the exclusion of specific movements or exercises.

Clicking on 'View all [Muscle Group] Exercises' will open a detailed list of all exercises for that muscle group. Un-checking the box next to any exercise will then exclude that exercises from being suggested.

Changes that are made to the Resistance Training Preferences will not take effect until the next program is created.

Key Features of the ACTION Resistance Training Preferences page

A. Un-check specific equipment types to remove them from the 'Suggested Program' feature

B. Click on 'View all Exercises' to see a detailed list of all available exercises for that muscle group and un-check any exercises you want to remove from being suggested

---

ACTION PERSONAL TRAINING SYSTEM — Online Fitness, Nutrition, and Weight Loss

● Admin ● Trainer ● Main

Client Dashboard
⊞ John Demo
⊞ Health Screening
⊞ Fitness Assessment
⊟ Goals and Preferences
   Experience and Goals
   Weight Loss Goals
   Resistance Training Pref
   Cardio Exercise Pref
   Nutritional Preferences
   Schedule Preferences
   Message Preferences
   Member Home Page
⊞ Resistance Training
⊞ Cardio Training
⊞ Nutritional Systems
⊞ Progress Tracking
⊞ Support Overview
   Logout

John Demo's Resistance Training Preferences

☐ Click here if you will not be implementing a Resistance Training Program. All Resistance training in the system will be ignored.

Your resistance training exercises are chosen based on the equipment available, your exercise preferences, and your experience level as chosen in the Experience and Goals section.

Equipment Availability

Please select the equipment you have access to or would prefer to use in your resistance training programs. These choices may be updated at any time by returning to this page and changing selections.

☑ Body Weight ☑ Barbell ☑ Dumbbell ☑ Band ☑ Ball ☑ Disc ☑ Cables ☑ Functional ☑ Balance Board

Exclude Specific Exercises

You may also exclude specific exercises from selection for resistance training programs by clicking on the applicable muscle group(s) picture below, and un-checking the exercise.

View all Leg Exercises | View all Back Exercises | View all Chest Exercises | View all Core/Body Exercises | View all Shoulder Exercises | View all Tricep Exercises | View all Bicep Exercises

Cardio Preferences

The Cardio Preferences page allows the client or trainer to select specific types of cardiovascular activities they are willing to perform. Any activity selected will be available in the Schedule Preferences when selecting activities throughout the week and on the Cardio Program page. Cardiovascular activities are broken down into the following groups: Basic, Group Fitness, Racquet Sports, Specialty, Sports, and Water.

In many cases there is more than one 'intensity' option for a specific activity. Once an activity is selected the different intensity options will be displayed. More than one intensity may be selected.

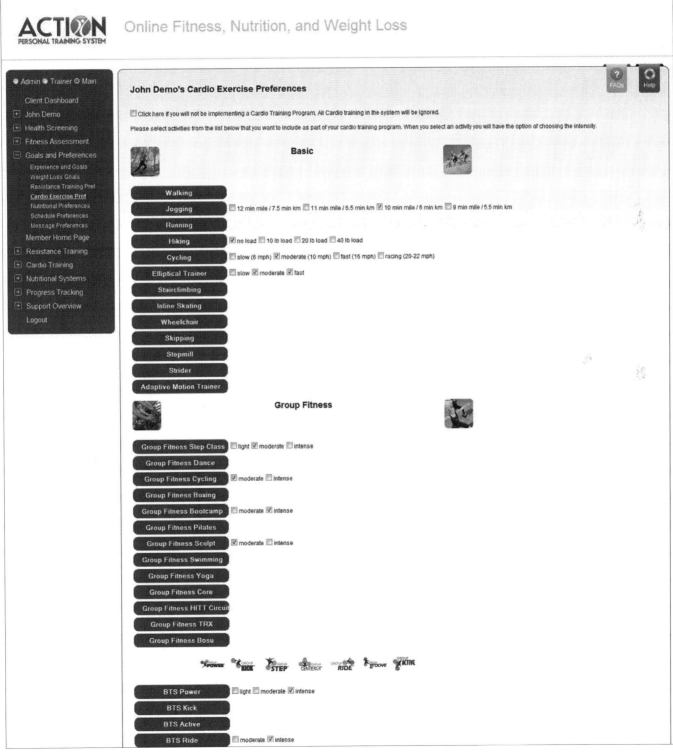

Schedule Preferences

The Schedule Preferences is designed to allow the client or trainer to set up their typical weekly schedule. The system will then use this information when building suggested resistance and cardio programs.

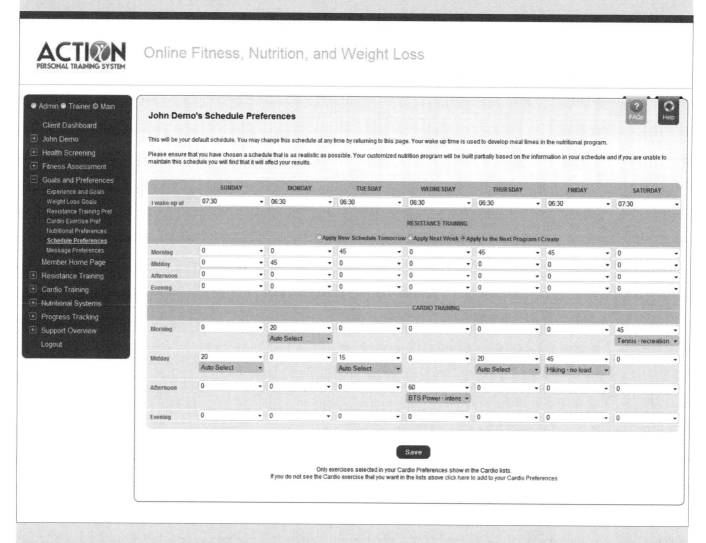

The 'Wake Up Time' is used to determine the first meal time of the day and set the remainder of the day's meal times.

In the Resistance Training area of the schedule, the days of the week that the client will be doing their resistance training program, the approximate time of day, and the amount of time they will spend doing the workout should be set. More than one workout per day may be selected. To prevent overtraining of muscle groups the system will suggest programs according to the following:

    1–3 workouts per week — Whole Body Program
    4–5 workouts per week — 2 Day Split Program
    6–7 workouts per week — 3 Day Split Program
    7–8 workouts per week — 4 Day Split Program
    9+ workouts per week — 5 Day Split Program

Although these programs are what will be suggested by the system, the trainer always has the ability to manually create a program of their choosing.

In the case of making changes to existing Resistance Training Schedule Preferences, the system will give 3 choices for when to apply these changes. They may be applied the next day, the following week, or when the next program is created. Changes applied the following day or week will re-schedule existing workouts in the current program.

The Cardio Training area of the schedule allows the day, time of day, duration, and activity to be selected. More than one activity may be selected per day. Activities set to 'Auto-Select' will be randomly chosen by the system based on the client's Cardio Preferences (see Cardio Preferences above). Suggested activities will then be added to the client's Cardio Program.

Nutritional Preferences

Please see 'Nutritional Programming with the ACTION Personal Training System' in Chapter 9

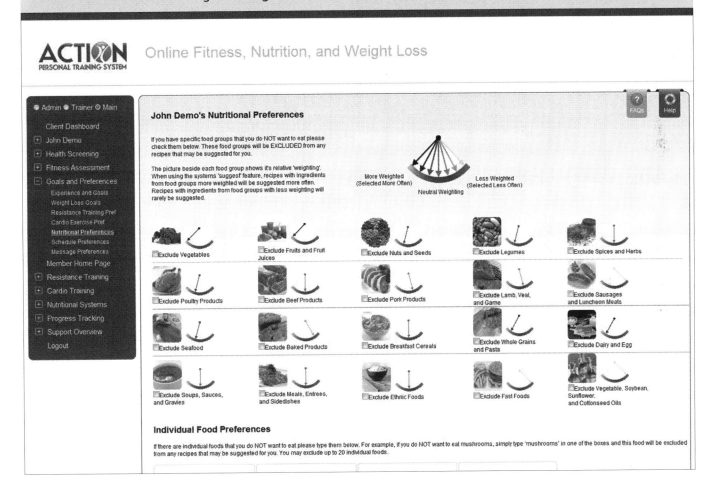

Program Design

Assessments are always the first step in designing a program. They help the trainer determine appropriate, customized goals to set as well as make them safe and attainable for the client. After the assessments have been done, an effective program can be developed. A program design will include types of exercise, their duration, frequency, intensity, total time spent training, short and long term goals and ways to maintain motivation. The design is an interactive endeavor between the trainer and the client. The trainer must measure the client's acceptance of the program components and define problems with motivation and other barriers to achieving goals. Proper goal development includes educating a client about realistic goals and time frames.

The most important factor to consider when designing a training program is the client's primary goal. No matter what the trainer may believe the client needs, the trainer is being paid to help the client attain this goal via healthy, safe methods. However, many clients come in with unrealistic expectations for their body potential or want too much progress for too little work.

Goals need to be realistic based on the client's existing level of fitness, age and time constraints. They should be aligned with the client's interests and ability and then reevaluated at regular intervals. Program design is never completely done. Training programs must continually change and evolve over time as the client's fitness and goals change.

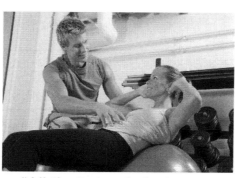

"All that stands between a good body and a great body is **someone to push you just a little further** than you would push yourself."

Training potential is the genetic potential of the client. If the client is unconditioned, the gains seen from beginning training will be great. If the client is highly fit, the gains will be less. As clients approach their genetic potential, which is the top level at which their bodies will perform, target goals must be changed. As less dramatic progress is seen, clients may become bored or unmotivated, which will pose an additional problem to take into account when designing a program.

Health Precautions to Consider when Designing a Program

Performance Enhancement & Personal Training (Abbreviated Sample):

Assessment Form (Medical/Health)

First Name _____

Last Name _____

☐ Male   ☐ Female

Date of Birth _____

Height _____

Weight _____

Occupation _____
_____

Have you ever suffered from any of the following: (Check all that apply)

□ High Blood Pressure   □ Heart Attack

□ Low Blood Pressure   □ Diabetes

□ High Cholesterol   □ Back/Knee Injury

□ Chest Pains   □ Seizures

Do you smoke?

□ Yes

How many cigarettes per day? _____

At what age did you start?_____

□ No, but I used to

□ No

Does your family have a history of the following: (Check all that apply)

□ Heart Attack

□ Heart Operations

□ High Blood Pressure

□ Diabetes

Muscular imbalances create postural misalignment and injury. They are caused by repetitive movement, poor posture or weak/tight muscles. Muscular imbalances cause imbalances on opposite sides of a joint and affect range of movement. The objective in treating imbalances is to strengthen weak muscles and stretch shorter muscles.

Arthritis is joint inflammation or damage. There are many different types of arthritis but osteoarthritis and rheumatoid arthritis are the most common. The goal in these cases is to restore joint function. This is best accomplished by having one or two sessions daily, extending warm-ups and decreasing intensity and duration in times of inflammation and increased pain. Anti-inflammatory medications may reduce the client's ability to evaluate pain during exercise so the trainer must be vigilant in watching and evaluating effort.

Osteoporosis is a disease that makes bones and joints fragile. Men over 80 and women over 65 may have undiagnosed osteoporosis so trainers must use caution in determining exercises and loads for older clients. In addition, replaced hips or formerly fractured hips cannot maintain a normal level of stress.

Aging populations have a decreased ability to regulate fluid balances in response to dehydration and thirst and therefore the sensations are compromised. It may be necessary to monitor fluid intake in the elderly as they exercise and educate them about the importance of regular hydration breaks.

> **Men over 80 and women over 65 may have undiagnosed osteoporosis.**

Avoiding Overexertion and Injury

Always listen to the client's feedback, both while designing the program and while working through it. If the program is too aggressive for the client's goals or current abilities, it should be scaled back. Learn to recognize physical danger signs of overexertion such as:

- Dizziness
- Lightheadedness
- Complexion changes
- Profuse sweating
- Facial expressions
- Muscle exhaustion
- Improper posture
- Labored breathing
- Faltering in movement

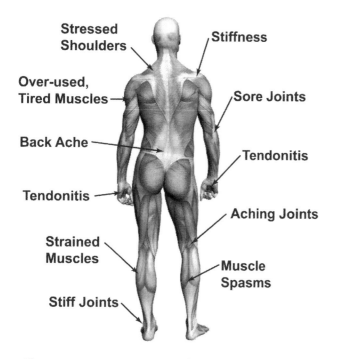

If exercises are properly explained before beginning them, clients are less likely to overexert themselves. When explaining an exercise to the client, always include an explanation of what muscle or muscle groups are being targeted. Teach them the difference between muscle fatigue and unintentional pain. If pain occurs in a non-targeted, non-supporting or stabilizer muscle, there may be a problem, but it is helpful

to remind the client that new and unfamiliar movement is typically uncomfortable at first.

Signs of Dangerous Dysfunctional Breathing

Dysfunctional breathing is very dangerous and can require medical attention. The trainer must watch a client's chest to determine where the breathing action is being generated and what muscles are being used. In dysfunctional breathing, the breathing pattern is shallow; it does not make use of the diaphragm and can develop into a long-term bad habit. The use of secondary muscles instead of primary muscles for breathing (e.g., the diaphragm) affects posture and tension. This can cause headaches, lightheadedness and dizziness. In addition, the spine and ribcage are used in normal breathing and inadequate motion of these joints restricts and stiffens them.

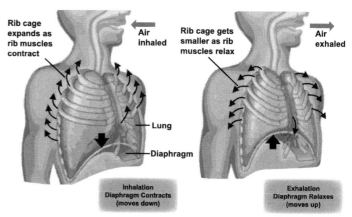

Excessive breathing leads to altered carbon dioxide and oxygen levels in the blood, which in turn triggers various physiological reactions.

One of these reactions is anxiety in the client. This ineffective breathing also results in lowered oxygen levels. The retention of metabolic waste in the muscles causes them to become stiff and fatigued.

Habitual dysfunctional breathing affects sleep patterns and circulation. The trainer can help correct and prevent dysfunctional breathing by watching the chest and teaching the client to breathe with the diaphragm.

Avoiding Discouragement

Educating the client about realistic goals and time frames will help a training program be successful. If the client has false expectations, discouragement and frustration, will quickly follow. Overloading is necessary for a client to make gains, but the trainer should be careful when increasing the load. If the load is increased too quickly, the client may become overwhelmed and/or discouraged. In addition, the client may begin to regress or, worse yet, become injured, necessitating time away from training. Keep in mind that compliance with the training program decreases as the intensity level increases. The

Aerobic exercise builds endurance by keeping the heart pumping for an extended period of time.

harder it gets, the less the client will want to do it.

Reassessment tests should be given often enough to encourage the client with regards to progress but not so frequently that not enough measurable progress has occurred. The reassessment can help the trainer track progress, note ineffective exercises and adjust the program accordingly.

Aerobic Programs for Beginners

Sometimes it is necessary to get clients ready to engage in more vigorous workouts by easing into aerobic activity. Walking is a great exercise for beginners, as it is relatively easy to maintain a constant intensity level and can be a group activity. If the client has had very low activity levels up until beginning training, walking frequently may help build up stamina so that other activities can be added slowly and without overexerting the body.

Swimming is a more difficult aerobic activity and some degree of skill is required, but the benefits of water exercise are tremendous. A study found that aerobic activities taking place in water have psychological benefits to clients. Being in the water hides physical defects and provides support. Water aerobics are useful for the disabled, obese, elderly and pregnant populations. The buoyancy and resistance of water requires higher energy expenditures than land exercises but without straining joints or causing pain.

It is recommended that aerobic activity sessions last 20 to 60 minutes each or be broken into a series of 10 minute segments. If the client has been sedentary, exercise must build up gradually. It is best to start with low intensity five minute bouts. If the client is deconditioned, the trainer should schedule multiple, short daily exercise sessions for that client's best results.

The aerobic component of the training program should strive to use 77% to 90% of the maximal heart rate or 60% to 80% of the heart rate reserve. It should burn 150-400 calories

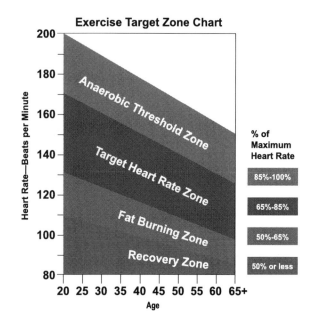

a day. If weight loss is the goal, 2000 calories or more a week should be used by scheduling activity five days a week for 45 minutes each session.

Judging the effectiveness of exercise by caloric use is difficult, as most sources of information on caloric use do not take into account coordination and skill level of the participant. An experienced swimmer spends less energy to go the same pace as an inexperienced swimmer will use with an inefficient stroke. This is why the heart rate measurement is the best way to judge how effective the aerobic exercise program is.

Physiological Factors to Consider in Designing Programs

Once the client has reached a level of fitness enabling the trainer to incorporate strength training, the trainer must create a well-rounded strength program that not only uses a variety of different muscle groups working in complementary ways but also uses different types of exercises. The various factors to be considered in designing specific workouts are described below.

Types of Muscle Actions

Exercises that include both concentric and eccentric muscle actions are the most effective in training programs. With concentric muscle actions, sufficient force is produced to overcome external load and shorten the muscle. Isometric muscle actions produce force but there is no change in muscle length. Eccentric muscle actions produce force while the muscle is lengthening—it is the resistance of the movement.

Energy Usage

ATP, adenosine triphosphate, is the typical storage and transfer unit of energy that the body uses. ATP is capable of storing large amounts

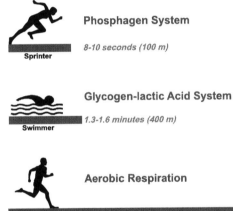

Phosphagen System
8-10 seconds (100 m)
Sprinter

Glycogen-lactic Acid System
1.3-1.6 minutes (400 m)
Swimmer

Aerobic Respiration
Marathon Runner *Unlimited Time (15 Km)*

of energy, but the supply in each cell is limited and the cell must have time to produce more in order to keep performing and to avoid damage to the body.

There are three bioenergetic pathways to produce ATP that should be taken into consideration when designing fitness programs:

1. ATP-creatine phosphate pathway (ATP-CP, also sometimes known as the Phosphagen system) is anaerobic. It does not require the use of oxygen.

2. The glycolic pathway is anaerobic.

3. The oxidative pathway is aerobic; it requires the presence of oxygen.

The Kinetic Chain

The kinetic chain consists of the muscular, articular and neural systems and refers to the

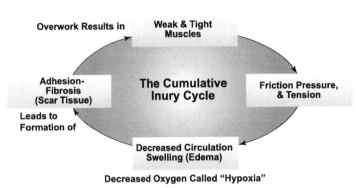

Overwork Results in **Weak & Tight Muscles**

Adhesion-Fibrosis (Scar Tissue)

The Cumulative Inury Cycle

Friction Pressure, & Tension

Leads to Formation of

Decreased Circulation Swelling (Edema)

Decreased Oxygen Called "Hypoxia"

sensorimotor integration of these systems for motor output; therefore, it includes all of the major systems of the body used in motion and their interaction with each other. Each system works interdependently with the others for structural and functional efficiency. If any one of the systems does not work efficiently, compensations and adaptations occur in the other systems. This can lead to tissue overload, decreased performance and predictable patterns of injury.

Proper Positioning

Proper positioning of the body during exercise is important to avoid injury and gain desired results. The trainer should look out for and educate the client about maintenance of a

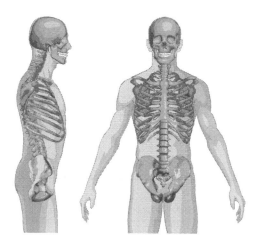

neutral spine position: curving slightly inward at the neck and lower back; curving slightly outward at the thoracic areas of the spine; keeping shoulders back and away from the ears; squaring hips; and avoiding hyperextention ("locking out") of a joint.

Types of Training Used in Exercise Program Design

Posture and Movement Training: Every movement requires a base from which to generate and accept force. This is the role of posture. Posture is the alignment and function of all components of the kinetic chain at any given moment, allowing all of the necessary body systems to work together for smooth, safe motion. It is controlled by the central nervous system.

Hypertonicity of the erector spinae, which leads to hyperlordosis

Hypertonicity of the abdominal muscles leads to ptosis.

Posture is not static and is not only measured when standing. The body goes through constant adjustments to maintain posture. Any deviations from proper posture changes the center of gravity for the body and affects the function and efficiency of the kinetic chain. Without proper posture, the body has a propensity for degeneration of the joints, tissue stress and injury.

The functional efficiency of the kinetic chain lies in the ability of the neuromuscular system to monitor and manipulate movement during functional tasks using the least amount of energy possible. Functional strength is the ability of the neuromuscular system to perform dynamic, eccentric, isometric and concentric muscle actions in all three planes of motion.

The body must maintain a "postural equilibrium" to maintain balance; this is the position from which all movement begins and ends. Proper muscle lengths and tensions in the relationships of force couples (muscles that work against each other or together) produce proper posture. Postural distortion patterns are predictable patterns of compensations made by the body due to muscle imbalances. If some core muscles are weaker than they ought to be, the body will compensate to regain postural equilibrium.

Balance/Stability Training: Balance is the ability to maintain a position for a given amount of time without moving. Work on core muscles increases balance and stability. People who play sports use many nontraditional movements that require good balance, such as squat hops and single leg hops. A number of exercises described in other sections (postural training, flexibility training) can also help with balance. Care should be taken to include plenty of exercises that require balance.

Flexibility Training: Flexibility is the degree to which a joint moves through a pain-free range of motion. Factors to consider when designing flexibility training are: joint structure, the condition of soft tissue around the joint and the length of muscles being stretched. These factors determine how well the joints help facilitate movement. There is a large section on types of flexibility training below.

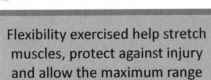

Flexibility exercised help stretch muscles, protect against injury and allow the maximum range of motion for joints

Resistance Training: The three primary resistance goals are hypertrophy, muscular strength and muscular endurance. Hypertrophy is the increase in

Resistance training builds strength of muscles, bones, and surrounding soft tissue; burns fat; and may lower cholesterol.

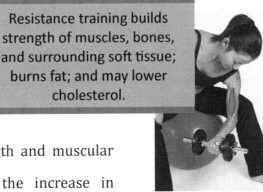

muscle mass or size. It is the increase of the size of muscle fibers. Once mass has accrued, strengthening and endurance training can make the most of the muscle.

Cardiovascular Training: Components of cardiovascular programs include mode of exercise, intensity of exercise, frequency of exercise and duration of each session. It is important to consider the sport, interest and common physical activity that the client employs. Training programs should include exercises that most closely mimic those activities and interests.

Functional Training: Functional training is custom designed for the client. It is the choosing or creating of activities and exercises that will best help the client perform better in daily life. Functional training can be those exercises that help an athlete perform better at a chosen sport or it can help the client with the physical activities done at work. Functional goals can be helping an elderly person have better balance to prevent falls.

Plyometrics: Plyometrics is used only with well-conditioned clients and athletes. These exercises are sports-specific and include training for speed, strength, power, endurance, flexibility and coordination for optimal sports performance. Plyometrics is based on using the elastic property of muscles to create a greater force. Its original use was as a jumping exercise for the lower extremities but is now used for the entire body.

Power Skipping

Repeated Tuck Jumps

Repeated Long Jumps

Diagonal Obstacle Jump

Alternate Leg Bounding

Squat Jump

Single Leg Hops

Plyometrics is the use of a strength-shortening cycle and begins with rapid stretching (eccentric muscle actions) which is followed by shortening of the same muscle (concentric muscle actions).

Principles of Exercise Training

Flexibility training can be helpful for all clients, including those interested mainly in building muscular strength. "Muscle-bound" bodybuilders do have compromised range of motion (ROM) and flexibility. The desire for mass and strength must be weighed against the loss of flexibility and ROM.

Cardiovascular health is central to overall health and may be one of your client's top concerns. If fat loss is one of the program goals, it is best to use a variety of modes of cardiovascular training. This is called cross-training. Mixing modes will increase fat loss and calorie-burning. As mentioned above, be sure to take your client's specific needs and likes into account when planning cardiovascular training.

Moderate intensity is the most recommended and used mode of aerobic activity. It is defined as the pace at which you break a sweat, have a slight increase in heart rate, and can still easily speak and hold a conversation. This intensity can be achieved by either mode of cardiovascular exercise: machine or non-machine.

A study found that moderate intensity activities were not understood by clients when verbally explained. Demonstrations of moderate intensity exercises greatly increased proper exercise procedures and success. Be sure that your client understands what is involved in an exercise before they attempt it.

Machine cardiovascular exercises include:

- Stair Master
- Treadmills
- Rowing machines
- Cycle ergometers
- Elliptical trainers

Non-Machine cardiovascular exercises include:

- Walking
- Jogging
- Running
- Swimming
- Aerobic dance

Target Heart Rate

What is your target heart rate range?

Intensity of Activity	% Maximal Heart Rate*
Very Light	<35
Light	35-54
Moderate	55-70
Hard	71-90
Very Hard	91-99
Maximal	100

*Maximal heart rate = 220 - age

Calculating your maximal target heart rate range using the percentage of maximal heart rate formula

For a moderately intense (55-70% maximum) activity level:
[220 - (your age)] x 0.55 to [220 - (your age)] x 0.70

Example:
Target heart rate range for a 54-year-old exercising at moderately intense activity:
[220 - 54] x 0.55 to [220 - 54] x 0.70 = 91 to 116 beats per minute

As mentioned above, heart rate is one of the easiest measures of how much and what intensity cardiovascular exercise the client is getting. There are a number of factors that influence heart rate besides level of exercise, and they are as follows: age, sex, fitness level, medications, body position, blood volume, heart disease, temperature and humidity. The maximum attainable heart rate decreases with age. Target heart rate should be between 60% and 80% of the maximum heart rate. There are formulas for calculating your client's targeted heart rate zones. The Karvonen formula, discussed in chapter 3, is more accurate because it takes into account the client's current fitness level (given the inclusion of the resting heart rate). Another method is the percentage of maximal heart rate, which is simpler and yields a more conservative target HR than the Karvonen method. There are two steps to the percentage of maximal heart rate formula:

To determine the client's maximum heart rate (HR) using the percentage of maximal heart rate formula:

220–Age of client = estimated maximum HR

To determine the lower limit of the client's training heart rate range:

Estimated maximum HR x percentage (60%)

To determine the upper limit of heart rate range that the client should work to achieve:

Estimated maximum HR x percentage (80%)

Resting heart rate is the number of heart beats in 60 seconds. Many factors can influence this so it is best to take it upon waking or, at the least, after five minutes of complete rest. To check heart rate, check the pulse at the wrist or the neck taking care not to apply too much pressure (that will distort the reading). The carotid artery can be found with the index and middle fingers at the side of the windpipe. The radial artery lies between the bone and tendon of the wrist, palm side and thumb side. Count the number of heart beats in 15 seconds and multiply by 4 to determine the heart rate per minute. When measuring heart rate during exercise, count the number of beats in 6 seconds and multiply by 10 or simply add a zero to the end of the number.

Stroke volume is the amount of blood pumped by the heart with each contraction of the ventricle. A trainer will not know what stroke volume a client has, but measuring heart rates gives a good indication of the work being done by the heart. A typical stroke volume is 75-80 mL per heart beat and the typical heart rate is 70-80 beats per minute.

> A trainer will not know what stroke volume a client has, but measuring heart rates gives a good indication of the work being done by the heart.

Cardiac output is the amount of blood pumped per minute through the arteries to all the tissues of the body, and it is calculated by multiplying the stroke volume by the heart rate.

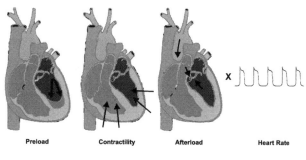

Preload **Contractility** **Afterload** **Heart Rate**

Stroke Volume X Heart Rate = Cardiac Output

Cardiac output = stroke volume (SV) x heart rate (HR).

Measuring Exercise Intensity

Exercise intensity measurement consists of the amount of oxygen consumed during exercise and the number of calories burned. It is important to determine individual ranges of target heart rates and to check heart rates frequently during the workout to be sure that the client is working within both a safe and effective range.

In order to see improvements in cardiovascular health, a certain level of oxygen consumption and/or heart rate reserve usage must be attained. Heart rate reserve is the difference between the client's resting heart rate and their maximum heart rate. In healthy adults, the aerobic level necessary to see improvement is between 50% and 80% of the heart rate reserve.

Maximal oxygen consumption or usage is generally accepted as the best measure of gauging cardio-respiratory fitness. The highest rate of oxygen transport and utilization is achieved at the point of maximum physical exertion. At rest, oxygen consumption is 3.5 mL of oxygen per kilogram of body weight per minute or 1 MET.

Measuring Caloric Use

(METs x 3.5 x bodyweight in kilograms)/

200 = calories used per minute.

Example: A client, who weighs 150 lbs or 68.2 kg (150 lbs/2.2 = 68.2 kg), using a treadmill at 0% intensity or grade level walks at 7 mph or 11.2 km/hr (7 mph/1.61 = 11.2 km/hr) for 45 minutes. This translates to 11.7 METs (taken from a standard MET table for jogging).

(11.7 x 3.5 x 68.2)/200 = 14 calories per minute.

14 x 45 = 630 calories per workout.

Typical oxygen consumption is 45 to 80 mL X kg X minutes or 11-23 METs. Maximal testing is not viable or feasible for the personal trainer to measure so submaximal testing is used to estimate it.

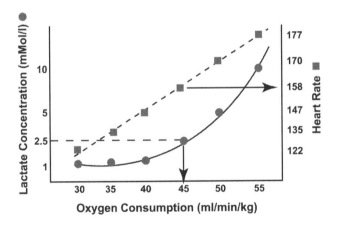

Submaximal tests exist that can give a sense of intensity of workouts. These include:

- Rockport Walk Test
- Step Test
- Field Protocols

These tests have errors of assumption built into them, meaning that they do not take individual differences into consideration but over time they can show trends.

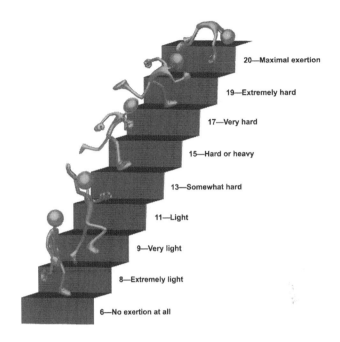

The Rate of Perceived Exertion (RPE) scale is a useful if subjective tool. The scale numbers are usually from 6 to 20 but other numbers are used as well. The RPE scale measures feelings of effort, strain, discomfort and fatigue during aerobic and resistance training.

It was developed by the Swedish psychologist Gunner Borg and is sometimes called the Borg Scale. You can ask your clients to rate how much exertion they are putting out on a scale of 6-20. No exertion at all is a rating of 6, 7 is extremely light exertion, 9 is very light exertion, 11 is light, 13 is somewhat hard, 15 is hard or heavy, 19 is extremely hard and 20 is maximal exertion.

Name: _____ Fitness Training Log (example)

Date:	Day of Week:		Weight:
Resting Heart Rate:		Aerobic Workout:	

Body Part:	# of Sets:	Body Part:	# of Sets:
Body Part:	# of Sets:	Body Part:	# of Sets:
Body Part:	# of Sets:	Body Part:	# of Sets:

Exercise Type	SETS	X	REPS	X	WEIGHT (lbs)

Level of Muscle Soreness (1-10 Scale):

Level of Fatigue (1-10 Scale):

Notes:

Training logs are a good way to monitor exercise intensity. They should include what exercises are in the program and the corresponding resistance or load, how fast repetitions are, how many sets and reps are performed, the distance and intensity of the activity, and the length of resting periods. The client should also record weight, resting heart rate, general health, general subjective experience of the workout, and muscle soreness and fatigue on a scale of 1 to 10.

Principles of Resistance Training (RT)

Resistance training (RT) was first created to help wounded soldiers recuperate. It later became popular with body builders and presently is used for general health and fitness. Resistance training can affect almost every system in the body and can greatly add to health benefits of any client population.

Resistance exercise and resistance training are not the same thing. Resistance exercise refers to the protocol for a single exercise or workout. Resistance training refers to the combination of many consecutive sessions. RT must target a specific muscle or muscle group.

Resistance Training: Split Routines (example)							
Program	Monday	Tuesday	Wednesday	Thursday	Friday	Saturday	Sunday
Total Body	Total Body	Rest	Rest	Total Body	Rest	Rest	Rest
Upper or Lower Body	Upper Body	Lower Body	Rest	Upper Body	Lower Body	Rest	Rest
Pull/Push	Chest & Triceps & Shoulders	Rest	Legs	Rest	Back & Biceps & Traps	Rest	Rest
Body Part Specific	Back & Chest	Legs	Arms & Shoulders	Rest	Back & Chest	Legs	Arms & Shoulders

The SAID principle is Specific Adaptations to Imposed Demands. An example of SAID is increasing the number of repetitions to increase muscle endurance.

The overload principle states that as adaptation of the muscle or muscles to a stimulus are made, an increased stimulus is required for further improvement. The overload principle is the idea that each workout should place a progressively higher demand on the muscle or muscles that are targeted in order to get results.

The degree of overload depends on the work load, the number of repetitions, the rest between sets and the frequency. It is important to remember to increase the demand of each workout. Overload increases can be created by increasing resistance or weight, increasing repetitions, increasing sets or decreasing rest periods.

Periodized training is the use of variation

> **Large muscle groups should be worked before small ones.**

in a training program to prevent boredom and optimize progress. Varying a program can be done by changing the choice of exercise, the order that exercises are done in, the resistance level, the number or reps, the number of sets in each exercise, or the duration or rest between sets.

Beginners should have multiple sets of exercises of simple techniques. Technique and technicality of activities should increase over the course of the program.

Some guidelines for resistance exercise choice are:

- Start out with multi-joint activities and progress to less complex, single-joint exercises to target muscles more specifically.
- The beginning of the program should produce the greatest amount of muscle mass and require the most energy. Studies show that these components are less effective at the end of a training program. A lessening in the amount

of reps leads to less fatigue in smaller muscle groups.

- Large muscle groups should be worked before small ones.
- Alternate pushing and pulling for the total body workout.
- Alternate upper and lower body exercises.
- Explosive/Power/Olympic type lifts should take place before basic strength and single-joint training.
- Exercise weak areas before strong areas.
- The exercise program should move from the most intense exercises to the least intense.

Determining Resistance

Resistance determination involves the use of repetition maximums (RMs). The repetition maximum is the maximal load that can be lifted for a certain number of repetitions or absolute resistance (a specific number of reps).

In a single training session, the RM target should be based on the goal of the training session (i.e., strength, hypertrophy or endurance).

Training Adaptation	Reps	Sets	Intensity
Strength	1-5	4-6	85-100%
Hypertrophy	8-12	3-4	75-85%
Endurance	12-25	2-3	40-70%

When working with a new client the personal trainer must assess the client's strength to identify the proper weight (or load) to utilize during subsequent workouts. A 10 rep max test is a safe way of predicting the client's maximal load. The personal trainer must first identify the weight that the client can lift using proper form for up to 10 reps (if the client surpasses 10 reps, the personal trainer should allow the client 2-5 minutes to rest before making another attempt with a higher weight). The trainer can then use the Brzycki Formula to predict the client's 1 rep max.

$$1 \text{ rep max} = \frac{\text{weight lifted}}{1.0278 - (0.0278 * \text{\# of reps})}$$

10 rep max tests should be included as part of the client's fitness assessment and should be reevaluated every 4-6 weeks.

Determining Rest Periods

ATP-creatine phosphate is the energy system and energy source used in resistance training. It is used up quickly and needs time to replenish itself. Resistance training that uses both glycolytic and ATP-creatine phosphate energy is best for enhancing muscle hypertrophy and muscle definition. Less rest is needed when both energy sources are used.

For advanced training that involves absolute power and strength, few repetitions near maximum resistance should be programmed with 3-5 minute rest periods in-between.

Beginner or intermediate clients should have a 2-3 minute rest period because they have a lower absolute resistance.

If the goal is strength and muscle mass, both long rest periods with heavy loading and short rest periods with moderate loading can work well. Short rest periods may increase anxiety and fatigue. The greater the discomfort and muscle fatigue, the more metabolic demand. Rest periods depend upon observation as well. The trainer should observe the client for loss of force, nausea, dizziness or fainting.

The trainer should consider that smaller muscle mass or single-joint exercises require shorter recovery periods, aging decreases toleration of resistance exercise (meaning longer and more frequent rests are necessary), and that the body's bicarbonate and phosphate levels buffer blood and muscle and are therefore improved by the gradual use of shorter rest periods.

Interval Training for Different Energy Systems

% of Maximum Anaerobic Power	Energy System Taxed	Time Interval	Work:Rest Ratio
90-100	Phosphogen	5-10 seconds	1:12 to 1:20
75-90	Fast Glycolysis	15-30 seconds	1:3 to 1:5
30-75	Fast Glycolysis & Oxidative	1-3 minutes	1:3 to 1:4
20-35	Oxidative	>3 minutes	1:1 to 1:3

A very short rest is 1 minute or less. A short rest is 1-2 minutes. A moderate rest is 2-3 minutes. A long rest is 3-4 minutes and a very long rest is 5 minutes or longer.

Resistance Training Modalities

Resistance training modalities include: variable resistance devices, static resistance devices, or isometrics and isokinetic devices.

Variable Resistance Devices

Variable resistance devices involve a pulley, lever arm or cam. They alter resistance through

range of movement in a continual contraction that matches a strength curve.

There are three kinds of curves relating to strength: bell-shaped, ascending and descending. An example of ascending strength curves is a squat. It uses only the top ½ or ¼ of the repetition. It is not the full ROM. An example of a descending strength curve is rowing. It uses only the bottom ½ of the repetition. An elbow curl is an example of a strength curve that is bell shaped. It is the middle of the ROM and leaves off the beginning and ending points of the repetition.

Static Resistance Devices or Isometrics

Static resistance devices involve pushing or pulling an immovable entity such as a wall,

an overloaded barbell or a maxed-out weight machine. Isometrics is a muscular movement in which muscle length is unchanged. Isometrics also pits a weak muscle against a strong one.

Isometrics or static resistance devices are rarely used as they only improve progress by 5%. Their success is related to the number of isometric actions, whether the action is maximal or sub-maximal and the duration of the action. Functional isometrics refers to their use when athletes or clients must overcome a sticking point in their progress.

Isokinetic Devices

Isokinetic devices use a variety of methods to provide maximum resistance and range of motion. Isokinetics are popular choices in rehabilitation facilities. They use either friction or compressed air to control the speed of movement in an exercise or activity. Isokinetic devices are often used to train at fast rates of speed like the type of velocities that occur in real-life sports.

With isokinetics, the muscular action is performed at a constant angular limb velocity. There is no set resistance and the action cannot be accelerated. The more you push, the more resistance you get from the device.

Hydraulic devices lack deceleration so there is no eccentric muscle activity employed. This halves efficiency because eccentric muscle is involved in injury protection. Pneumatic devices can be adjusted on both the concentric and eccentric muscle exercises. These are often used with older populations but lack balance and control components.

Isokinetics are used in "prehabilitation" presently. This refers to their injury prevention capabilities. They help clients to better resist injury, decrease recovery time from injury and lower the extent of damage.

Periodization

Periodization is the use of progressive cycles in resistance training. It is used to avoid overtraining, deter boredom, keep stimulus levels up and increase effectiveness of the training program. Periodic training is more effective than constant training exercises. It is the alternating of high loads of training with decreased loading phases. Variations in the training program are necessary to first build muscle mass and then strengthen that increased mass.

The time frames of periodization are microphases, mesophases and macrophases. Microphases are up to seven days and one should occur at least every four weeks. Mesophases are anywhere from two weeks to a few months. Four to six mesophases should occur in a year. The more mesophases that a training period includes, the more effective the training program will be. The sub-phases in mesophases are preparation, competition, peaking and transition. Macrophase refers to the whole training program and usually consists of a year.

Non-linear periodization programs are used when the client may have time constraints and a busy life.

Traditional periodization involves varying volume and intensity in a patterned way. The training program begins with a high volume of exercises that are low in intensity. Progressively,

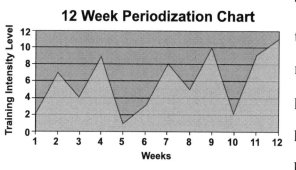

12 Week Periodization Chart

Training Intensity Level / Weeks

the volume is lowered over time as the intensity of exercises is increased. Small variations occur in each one to four week microcycle. A chart of the intensity is a rising diagonal line.

Stepwise periodization is the use of increasing intensity while decreasing volume of exercise during the training period. Repetitions generally decrease in the following manner: eight reps down to five reps and then down to three reps.

In undulating periodization, volume and intensity are increased and decreased but not in a traditional pattern.

Overreaching periodization consists of varying the volume or the intensity over a short period of time (one to two weeks) and then returning to the normal training program. Overreaching is generally done with well-conditioned clients and advanced athletes.

Ways to Vary Volume and Intensity

- Changing the choice of exercises
- Varying the order of exercises
- Adjusting resistance or load
- Adjusting number of sets of an exercise
- Changing the number of exercises for a specific muscle group
- Altering joint angles and positioning
- Changing an exercise from working a single joint to multiple joints or vice versa
- Changing exercises from primary to assisted exercise or vice versa
- Changing the repetition or range of exercise
- Changing the type of muscle contraction
- Adjusting speed of movement
- Altering rest periods between sets
- Adjusting nutrition

Overtraining

Overtraining syndrome is a neuro-endocrine disorder because it affects the nervous system and the hormonal system balance. Overtraining results in "burn out," "staleness" or "jet lag" and can compromise a training program for weeks or even months.

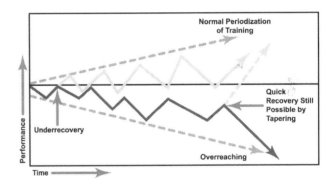

Rest periods are where physiologic improvement occurs. The period after working out is when the body reacts to the stressors put upon it and increases blood flow to the muscles, increases glycogen stores, increases enzyme systems and increases heart efficiency. When an athlete or client exercises intensely over a long period of time without proper rest periods, regeneration does not occur and performance will plateau and then decline.

Overtraining has emotional, behavioral and physical symptoms. An overtrained client may experience cumulative exhaustion that continues even after rest, like muscular soreness, fatigue, changes in sleep, loss of appetite, weight loss and weakened immune system. There may be serious mood effects, including irritability, moodiness, depression, loss of enthusiasm, loss of desire to compete, and an increase in illness and injuries. Physiologically, the body experiences increased cortisol levels (the hormone released when we are stressed), lowered testosterone levels and a high level of muscular waste byproducts. Other life stressors can exacerbate overtraining symptoms.

There are two forms of overtraining: sympathetic and parasympathetic. Sympathetic overtraining syndrome is common in sprint-type sports and is characterized by an elevated resting heart rate. Parasympathetic overtraining generally occurs in endurance sports. It is characterized by a decreased resting heart rate

Major problems resulting from overtraining

and a lowered heart rate for a given workload. It may result in hypoglycemia while exercising.

It is important to rule out hidden illnesses as the cause of symptoms before assuming overtraining has occurred. Rest is the cure for overtraining. If the overtraining has only happened over three to four weeks, the problem should be remedied by three to five days of rest. The normal training program must be corrected before resuming exercise. The athlete or client should begin exercising only on alternate days with decreased volume of exercise for a few weeks.

A training log can monitor the progress of the client and the success of the program. It can also prevent the occurrence of overtraining in the first place. A training log should include:

- Intensity of activity
- Resting heart rates
- Weight
- General health
- Subjective experience of the workout
- Levels of muscular soreness (on a 10 point scale)
- Fatigue (on a 10 point scale)

Resistance Program Design Using the ACTION Personal Training System

The Resistance Training area of the ACTION PTS will allow you to create, edit, and track client's programs. There are 2 key components of the Resistance Training area; the Resistance Program, and the Workout Tracking. Prior to building a program for a client you will want to make sure you have set their access level and that they have completed the necessary pre-requisites.

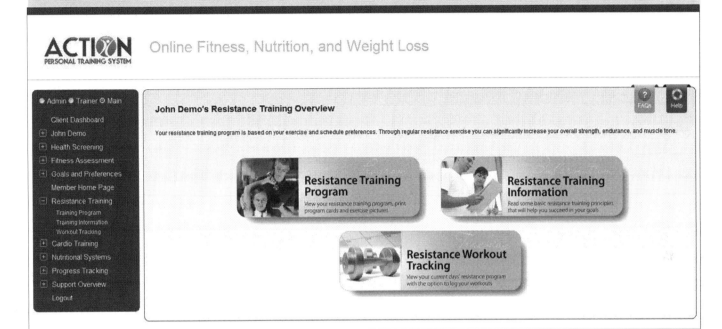

Setting and Understanding Client Access Levels

Using the 'Modules' display of your Client Management area you may choose between several options to control your client's access levels to their programs. These options are:

View — The View option will not allow client's to make any alterations to any locked or unlocked program. They have the ability to print workout cards and exercise description cards but may not make any alterations to the program itself. This setting is designed primarily to be used for trainers working with their clients in person.

Modify — The Modify option will allow clients to edit only the exercise selections of an unlocked program. Once the client or trainer has locked the program no more edits can be made by the client. Clients will also have the ability to have a new program suggested every 4 weeks, which they will then be able to edit only the exercise selections until the new program is locked. This setting is designed primarily for trainers working with clients online only.

No Restrictions — This option will allow clients the same level of access that a trainer has. They may add new programs and copy or edit existing locked or unlocked programs. This setting is designed for trainers working with advanced level clients where they want to offer a tool for the client to build their own workouts.

Prerequisites to Building a Program

There are several pre-requisites that must be completed prior to a program being built or suggested for a client. If any of these pre-requisites is incomplete when trying to build a client's Resistance Program the system will automatically re-direct the trainer to the Pre-Requisites page.

The four pre-requisites that must be complete are:

PAR-Q — The PAR-Q (see Health Screening) is required to ensure the client has completed at least a basic health screening prior to exercising

Body Composition — A Body Composition must be completed so the system has the necessary customized calorie information based on the client's lean mass values

Experience and Goals — These are required to ensure that the system has enough information about the client's experience level to suggest a safe and effective program

Schedule Preferences — The Schedule Preferences settings will determine what template program will be suggested for the clients based on the number of workouts per week they have scheduled. Additionally it will allow the system to be able to schedule the resistance program on the appropriate days each week

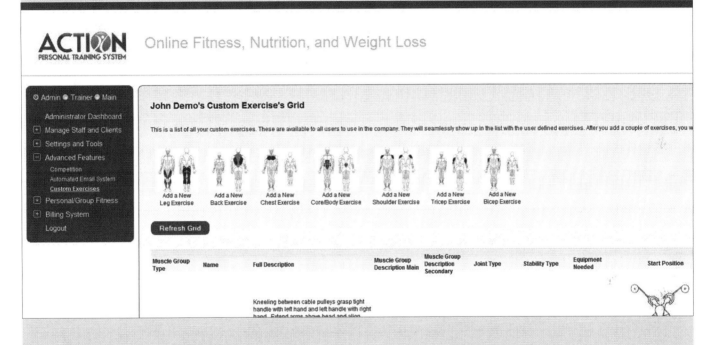

Creating Your Own Custom Exercises

There are a larger variety of exercises included in the ACTION Personal Training System. All of these exercises have both pictures and videos available.

You may add any custom exercises you wish to the system using the Custom Exercise page (Trainer Menu: Advanced Features: Custom Exercises)

To add a custom exercise, select the appropriate muscle group from the choices at the top of the page. If the exercise is compound, select the predominately used muscle group. The following fields may now be completed (all fields are optional):

Name — Give the exercise a name
Full Description — Provide a full description of the movement of the exercise
Main Muscle Group — Primary muscle group (agonist) used during this exercise
Secondary Muscle Group — Secondary muscle group (synergist) used during this exercise

Joint Type	— Isolation or Compound movement
Stability Type	— The higher the stability rating the more difficult the exercise is and the more stability required to complete the exercise correctly
Equipment Needed	— The type of equipment this exercise requires
Start Position	— Upload a picture or drawing of the initial position for the exercise
End Position	— Upload a picture or drawing of the finishing position for the exercise
Third Position	— Upload a picture or drawing of this exercise from a different angle
Muscle Group	— Upload a picture or drawing of the muscle groups used for the exercise
Video Link	— Insert a link to a video of the exercise

Program Design

The Resistance Program is one of the most powerful features of the ACTION PTS system. It will allow you to quickly and efficiently build effective resistance programs for your clients.

The drop down box at the top of the page will allow you to view any previous, current, or future program you have designed. Simply select the appropriate program from the drop down box. Below the drop down there are several options:

Add New Program — This will begin a completely new program. You will have 4 options for how you want to build the new program (see Program Design Options below)

Edit Program — Will allow you to makes changes to the currently selected program

Copy Program — Copies and reproduces the currently selected program as a new program

Delete Program — Will delete the currently selected program

Below this you will find a series of program tools:

Print Workout — If the program is a split routine you can select which day of the split you would like to print from the drop down and then select 'Exercise Full Descriptions', which will print detailed pictures and instructions for all exercises on that day, or 'Exercise Card', which will print a card to record weights, reps, and sets for up to 7 workouts. You may also use the 'Email' icon next to 'Exercise Card' to send an email link of the exercise card directly to your client

Status — The status will show whether a program is 'locked' or 'unlocked'. Locked programs have been scheduled with a start date and number of weeks to use the program and are not editable by clients who have 'View' or 'Modify' access levels (see Setting and Understanding Client Access Levels above) Unlocked programs are not yet scheduled and may be edited at any time by the trainer or client's with 'Modify' or 'No Restrictions' access levels

Periodization — This will display a graph outlining the timeline and program types selected

Stretches — Gives several options for printable stretching routines

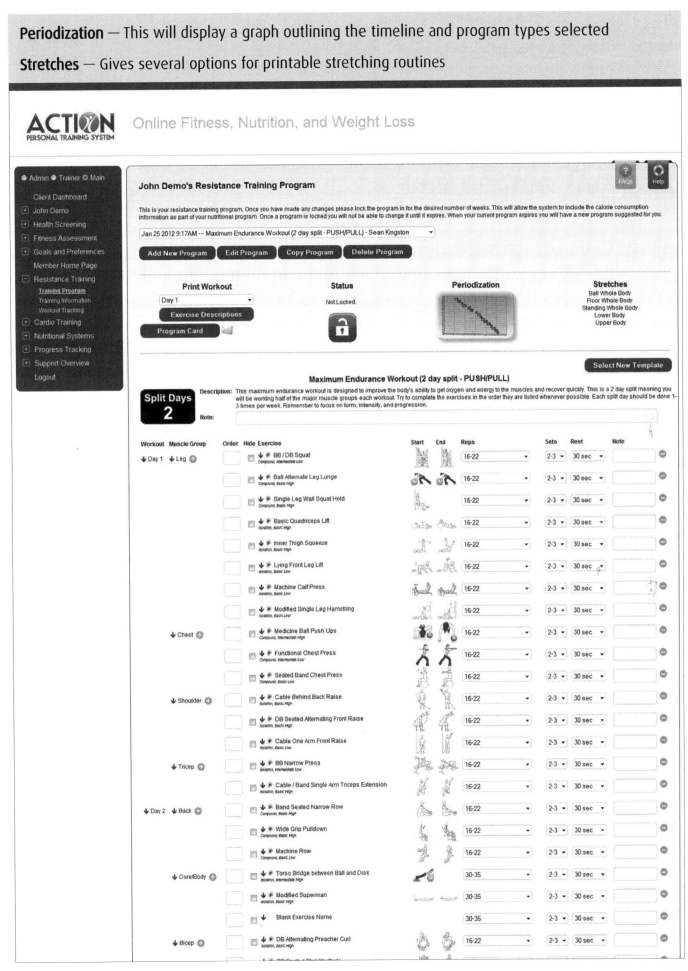

Program Design Options

There are 4 options for building a resistance program:

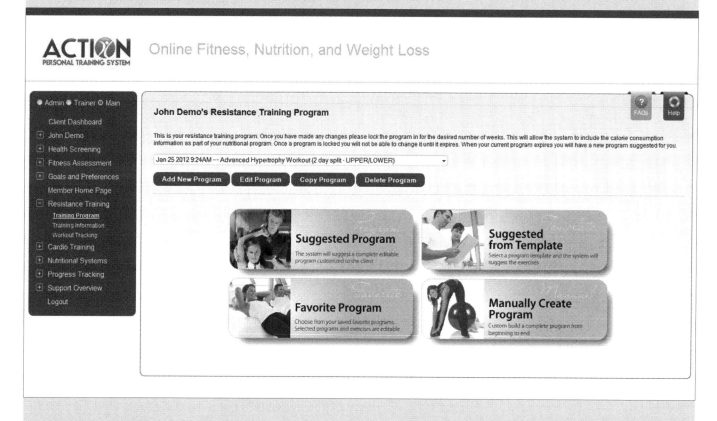

SUGGESTED PROGRAMS

The Suggested Program feature is the most quick and simple way to build a program for your client. The system will take into account the client's schedule and exercise preferences, experience level, goals, and previous programs to build a completely customized resistance program. The system will suggest the program template (e.g. whole body endurance, 2 day split hypertrophy, etc.) and all exercises including reps, sets, and rest. Once the program is suggested you will have full editing ability to make any changes desired (see Editing Programs below)

SUGGESTED FROM TEMPLATE PROGRAMS

The Suggested from Template feature will allow you to manually select the preferred program template for your client and the system will then suggest the appropriate exercises based on the clients preferences, goals and experience level. The completed program is fully editable.

FAVORITE PROGRAMS

The Favorite Program feature allows you to access any program that you have saved as a favorite and use it as a template for any other client. Near the bottom of the Resistance Training Program page there is a 'Program Favorite Name:' field where you can fill in a name to save this program as a favorite. The program will now be added to your list of favorites and be available to use with any other client. Once a favorite program is chosen it is fully editable.

MANUALLY CREATING PROGRAMS

Manually creating a program will allow you to select all of the criteria for the program manually, including the template, split type, and exercises.

Editing Programs

Regardless of the program design option chosen you have the ability to further customize any resistance program. Clicking the 'Edit Program' button near the top of the page will activate the editable fields in the resistance program. If you are editing a program that is 'Locked' you will be prompted with a warning that this will 'Unlock' any future programs you have scheduled.

ACTION PERSONAL TRAINING SYSTEM

Online Fitness, Nutrition, and Weight Loss

FAQs   Help

● Admin ● Trainer ● Main

Client Dashboard
⊞ John Demo
⊞ Health Screening
⊞ Fitness Assessment
⊞ Goals and Preferences
    Member Home Page
⊟ Resistance Training
    Training Program
    Training Information
    Workout Tracking
⊞ Cardio Training
⊞ Nutritional Systems
⊞ Progress Tracking
⊞ Support Overview
    Logout

John Demo's Resistance Training Program

This is your resistance training program. Once you have made any changes please lock the program in for the desired number of weeks. This will allow the system to include the calorie consumption information as part of your nutritional program. Once a program is locked you will not be able to change it until it expires. When your current program expires you will have a new program suggested for you.

Jan 25 2012 9:17AM --- Maximum Endurance Workout (2 day split - PUSH/PULL) - Sean Kingston ▾

[Add New Program] [Edit Program] [Copy Program] [Delete Program]

Print Workout	Status	Periodization	Stretches
Day 1 ▾	Not Locked.		Ball Whole Body
[Exercise Descriptions]			Floor Whole Body
[Program Card]	🔓		Standing Whole Body
			Lower Body
			Upper Body

[Select New Template]

Maximum Endurance Workout (2 day split - PUSH/PULL)

Split Days 2

Description: This maximum endurance workout is designed to improve the body's ability to get oxygen and energy to the muscles and recover quickly. This is a 2 day split meaning you will be working half of the major muscle groups each workout. Try to complete the exercises in the order they are listed whenever possible. Each split day should be done 1-3 times per week. Remember to focus on form, intensity, and progression.

Note:

Workout	Muscle Group	Order	Hide	Exercise	Start	End	Reps	Sets	Rest	Note	
⬇ Day 1	⬇ Leg ⊕		☐	⬇ ✳ BB / DB Squat *Compound, Intermediate Low*			16-22 ▾	2-3 ▾	30 sec ▾		⊖
			☐	⬇ ✳ Ball Alternate Leg Lunge *Compound, Basic High*			16-22 ▾	2-3 ▾	30 sec ▾		⊖
			☐	⬇ ✳ Single Leg Wall Squat Hold *Compound, Basic High*			16-22 ▾	2-3 ▾	30 sec ▾		⊖
			☐	⬇ ✳ Basic Quadriceps Lift *Isolation, Basic High*			16-22 ▾	2-3 ▾	30 sec ▾		⊖
			☐	⬇ ✳ Inner Thigh Squeeze *Isolation, Basic High*			16-22 ▾	2-3 ▾	30 sec ▾		⊖
			☐	⬇ ✳ Lying Front Leg Lift *Isolation, Basic Low*			16-22 ▾	2-3 ▾	30 sec ▾		⊖
			☐	⬇ ✳ Machine Calf Press *Isolation, Basic Low*			16-22 ▾	2-3 ▾	30 sec ▾		⊖
			☐	⬇ ✳ Modified Single Leg Hamstring *Isolation, Basic Low*			16-22 ▾	2-3 ▾	30 sec ▾		⊖
	⬇ Chest ⊕		☐	⬇ ✳ Medicine Ball Push Ups *Compound, Intermediate High*			16-22 ▾	2-3 ▾	30 sec ▾		⊖
			☐	⬇ ✳ Functional Chest Press *Compound, Intermediate Low*			16-22 ▾	2-3 ▾	30 sec ▾		⊖
			☐	⬇ ✳ Seated Band Chest Press *Compound, Basic Low*			16-22 ▾	2-3 ▾	30 sec ▾		⊖
	⬇ Shoulder ⊕		☐	⬇ ✳ Cable Behind Back Raise *Isolation, Basic High*			16-22 ▾	2-3 ▾	30 sec ▾		⊖
			☐	⬇ ✳ DB Seated Alternating Front Raise *Isolation, Basic High*			16-22 ▾	2-3 ▾	30 sec ▾		⊖
			☐	⬇ ✳ Cable One Arm Front Raise *Isolation, Basic Low*			16-22 ▾	2-3 ▾	30 sec ▾		⊖
	⬇ Tricep ⊕		☐	⬇ ✳ BB Narrow Press *Isolation, Intermediate Low*			16-22 ▾	2-3 ▾	30 sec ▾		⊖
			☐	⬇ ✳ Cable / Band Single Arm Triceps Extension *Isolation, Basic Low*			16-22 ▾	2-3 ▾	30 sec ▾		⊖
⬇ Day 2	⬇ Back ⊕		☐	⬇ ✳ Band Seated Narrow Row *Compound, Basic High*			16-22 ▾	2-3 ▾	30 sec ▾		⊖
			☐	⬇ ✳ Wide Grip Pulldown *Compound, Basic High*			16-22 ▾	2-3 ▾	30 sec ▾		⊖
			☐	⬇ ✳ Machine Row *Compound, Basic Low*			16-22 ▾	2-3 ▾	30 sec ▾		⊖
	⬇ Core/Body ⊕		☐	⬇ ✳ Torso Bridge between Ball and Disk *Isolation, Intermediate High*			30-35 ▾	2-3 ▾	30 sec ▾		⊖
			☐	⬇ ✳ Modified Superman *Isolation, Basic High*			30-35 ▾	2-3 ▾	30 sec ▾		⊖

Once you are in edit mode, you may make the following changes to programs (beginning from the left side of the page):

Program Note — Use the 'Note' field below the program description to add custom notes that will be printed on the program cards. You can also use the 'Note' field next to each exercise.

Select, Edit, or Remove Exercises for a Split Day — By clicking on the drop down arrow next to the 'Day' you will be taken to the Exercise Selection page where you can see exercises that have already been selected, add additional exercises, or remove exercises. Once you have completed any changes, clicking 'Save' at the bottom of the page will update your program with the selected exercises.

Select, Edit, or Remove Exercises for a Muscle Group — Clicking the drop down next to any muscle group will take you to the Exercise Selection page where you may select, add, or remove exercises for that muscle group.

Add an Exercise — Use the '+' symbol to add an addition exercise for the selected muscle group

Order — You may change the order that exercises will print on program cards by clicking the 'Order' link at the top of the exercise list. By changing the exercise number the system will alter the order the exercises are printed in on program cards to match the order in the boxes.

Change Exercise — Using the drop down arrow next to the exercise name will open a drop down list showing alternative exercises that may be selected. Click on the green check mark next to the exercise you want to select. You may also click the 'Add Custom Exercise' button at the top of the drop down to be taken to the Custom Exercises page where you can add your own custom exercises (see 'Creating Your Own Custom Exercises' above)

Exercise Video — by clicking on the 'Play' icon next to the exercise name you may watch a video of the exercise

Reps — Use the drop down to select the number or reps to be performed for the exercise. The system will default to the number of reps in the program template.

Sets — Use the drop down to select the number of set to be performed for the exercise. The system will default to number of sets allowed based on the schedule preference setting for time available for the workout.

Rest — Select the amount of rest time between sets using the drop down. The system will default to the rest time settings for the program template.

Note — You may add custom notes that will be displayed on the printable program cards.

Remove an Exercise — Use the '-' symbol to remove an exercise from the program.

You may fill in the text box a the bottom of the page to save the current program as a 'Favorite' and make it available to use with any other client. Any favorite program selected for a client is still fully editable.

Once you have finished editing the program you can click 'Save' which will save the program but not lock or schedule it, or you can 'Save, Lock and Schedule for the Defined Period' which schedules the program based on the days in the Schedule Preferences, from the start date, for number of weeks selected.

Workout Tracking

Once a program is locked and scheduled it will be available in the 'Workout Tracking'. The workout tracking page will allow for recording weight and reps completed for up to 5 sets per exercise. If the exercise has been done before, then the weight and reps completed in the previous workout with that exercise will be displayed beside each set.

Cardio Program

The ACTION PTS Cardio Program is used to log and track cardiovascular activities throughout the course of a week.

The system will use the information from the client's Schedule Preferences, Cardio Preferences, and Goals and Experience to develop a suggested week of activity. The suggested activities can be selected by the client by pre-selecting the activity of choice in the cardio component of their schedule preferences. Cardio activities left as 'Auto-Select' will be chosen by the system automatically.

The Cardio Program page can be used to view, edit, or delete planned activities, add additional activities, or log competed activities.

Once a week is planned it may be saved for the current week, or saved and set to repeat for up to 52 weeks.

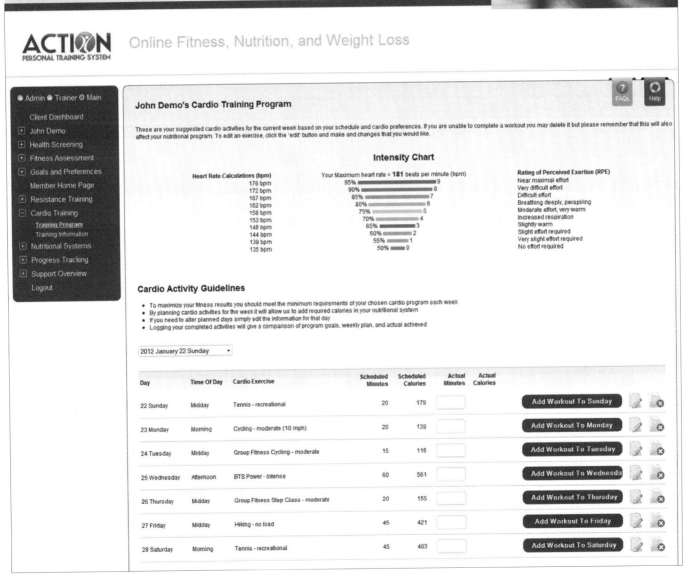

ACTION PERSONAL TRAINING SYSTEM — Online Fitness, Nutrition, and Weight Loss

John Demo's Cardio Training Program

These are your suggested cardio activities for the current week based on your schedule and cardio preferences. If you are unable to complete a workout you may delete it but please remember that this will also affect your nutritional program. To edit an exercise, click the 'edit' button and make and changes that you would like.

Intensity Chart

Your Maximum heart rate = **181** beats per minute (bpm)

Heart Rate Calculations (bpm)	%	RPE	Rating of Perceived Exertion (RPE)
176 bpm	95%	9	Near maximal effort
172 bpm	90%	8	Very difficult effort
167 bpm	85%	7	Difficult effort
162 bpm	80%	6	Breathing deeply, perspiring
158 bpm	75%	5	Moderate effort, very warm
153 bpm	70%	4	Increased respiration
148 bpm	65%	3	Slightly warm
144 bpm	60%	2	Slight effort required
139 bpm	55%	1	Very slight effort required
135 bpm	50%	0	No effort required

Cardio Activity Guidelines

- To maximize your fitness results you should meet the minimum requirements of your chosen cardio program each week
- By planning cardio activities for the week it will allow us to add required calories in your nutritional system
- If you need to alter planned days simply edit the information for that day
- Logging your completed activities will give a comparison of program goals, weekly plan, and actual achieved

2012 January 22 Sunday ▾

Day	Time Of Day	Cardio Exercise	Scheduled Minutes	Scheduled Calories	Actual Minutes	Actual Calories		
22 Sunday	Midday	Tennis - recreational	20	179			Add Workout To Sunday	
23 Monday	Morning	Cycling - moderate (10 mph)	20	139			Add Workout To Monday	
24 Tuesday	Midday	Group Fitness Cycling - moderate	15	116			Add Workout To Tuesday	
25 Wednesday	Afternoon	BTS Power - Intense	60	561			Add Workout To Wednesday	
26 Thursday	Midday	Group Fitness Step Class - moderate	20	155			Add Workout To Thursday	
27 Friday	Midday	Hiking - no load	45	421			Add Workout To Friday	
28 Saturday	Morning	Tennis - recreational	45	403			Add Workout To Saturday	

Summary

There is much to consider when designing a training program, but with time the personal trainer will gain an instinct about design components and creating programs will become easier and quicker.

Program design is individualized. It requires many assessments of the client before design can begin and then throughout the training program so that goals and exercises can be continually adjusted and updated. Designing a training program requires frequent, clear communication between a trainer and the client. The trainer must listen closely to client feedback and educate the client.

A successful training program is continually assessed and makes use of periodization techniques so that the improvement gains remain noticeable to the client and keep the client motivated.

Review Questions

1. What are some aspects of personal fitness that are included in program design? ____

   _____

   _____

2. Postural misalignment and injury can be created by muscular imbalances. True or False? _____

3. What are physiological factors that one should consider in designing a fitness program?

   a) Muscle action

   b) ATP usage

   c) Proper positioning

   d) All of the above

4. What are the three primary resistance training goals?_____

   _____

   _____

5. Plyometrics are used with exercise beginners. True or False?_____

6. Using a variety of modes of cardiovascular training is called _____.

7. How is exercise intensity measured?_____

   _____

   _____

8. Periodization is:

   a) Muscular action in which there is no change in muscle length

   b) The use of progressive cycling in resistance training

   c) The position from which all movement begins and ends

9. Name four ways that one can vary the volume and intensity of exercise._____

   _____

   _____

   _____

10. The two forms of overtraining are

_____ and

_____.

Answers

1. Anatomy, physiology, kinesiology, basic nutrition and knowledge of training special populations.
2. True.
3. d) All of the above.
4. Hypertrophy, muscular strength and muscular endurance.
5. False.
6. Cross-training.
7. By the amount of oxygen consumed during exercise and the number of calories burned
8. b) The use of progressive cycling in resistance training.
9. Any three of the following 1) Changing the choice of exercises; 2) Varying the order of exercises; 3) Adjusting resistance or load; 4) Adjusting number of sets of an exercise; 5) Changing the number of exercises for a specific muscle group; 6) Altering joint angles and positioning; 7) Changing an exercise from working a single joint to multiple joints or vice versa; 8) Changing exercises from primary to assisted exercise or vice versa; 9) Changing the repetition or range of exercise; 10) Changing the type of muscle contraction; 11) Adjusting speed of movement; 12) Altering rest periods between sets; or 13) Adjusting nutrition.
10. Sympathetic and parasympathetic.

References

Brzycki, M. Strength Testing: Predicting a One-Rep Max from Reps-to-Fatigue. *JOPERD*. 1993;-64(1):88-90.

Fowles JR, Sale DG, MacDougall JD. Reduced Strength After Passive Stretch of the Human Plantar Flexors. *Journal of Applied Physiology*. 2000;89(3):1179-88.

Kokkonen J, Nelson AG, Cornwell A. Acute Muscle Stretching Inhibits Maximal Strength Performance. *Resistance Quarterly: Exercise and Sport*. 1998;69(4):411-15.

Malliaropoulos N, Papalexandris S, Papalada A, Papacostas E. The Role of Stretching in Rehabilitation of Hamstring Injuries: 80 Athletes Follow-Up. *Medicine & Sciences in Sports & Exercise*. 2004;36(5):756-59.

Nelson AG, Kokkonen J, Arnall DA. Acute Muscle Stretching Inhibits Muscle Strength, Endurance and Performance. *Journal of Strength Conditioning and Resistance Training*. 2005;19(2):338-43.

Spernoga SG, Uhl TL, Arnold BL, Gansneder BM. Duration of Maintained Hamstring Flexibility After a One-Time Modified Hold-Relax Stretching Protocol. *Journal of Athletic Training*. 2001;36(1):44-48.

Thacker SB, Gilchrist J, Stroup DF, Kimsey CD Jr. The Impact of Stretching On Sports Injury Risk: A Systematic Review of the Literature. *Medicine & Science in Sports & Exercise*. 2004;36(3):371-78.

Witvrouw E, Mahieu N, Danneels L, McNair P. Stretching and Injury Prevention: An Obscure Relationship. *Sports Medicine*. 2004;34(7):443-49.

Chapter 5: Flexibility

Topics Covered

The Warm-Up
What is a Warm-Up?
Benefits of a Warm-Up
Warm-Up Considerations

Types of Warm-Ups
General Warm-Up
Activity-Specific Warm-Up
Passive Warm-Up

Warm-Ups and Stretching

Flexibility
What is Flexibility?
The Importance of Flexibility
The Science of Flexibility

Types of Flexibility
Corrective Flexibility
Active Flexibility
Functional Flexibility

Stretching Techniques
Static Stretching
Passive Stretching
Active and Active Assistive Stretching
Proprioceptive Neuromuscular Facilitation Stretching
Dynamic and Ballistic Stretching

Precautions and Safety
Types of Stretches

Developing the Program
Measuring Flexibility

The Warm-Up

What is a Warm-Up?

A warm-up is a short duration of activity preceding major exercise. A warm-up is necessary to increase muscle temperature and general core temperature of the body and should be designed to avoid fatigue or reduction of energy stores. A warm-up improves performance and personal well-being during exercise. Every training session should begin with a warm-up. If a warm-up is not conducted, heart rate can increase to dangerous levels to try to supply the necessary oxygen to the muscles. This can often lead to an increase in muscular injury. These kinds of injuries comprise greater than 30% of injuries seen in sports medicine clinics.

Benefits of a Warm-Up

- Increase in metabolic requirements
- Makes physical performance more effective and efficient
- Prevents blood lactic acid accumulation in the muscle (helps to prevent premature fatigue)
- Contributes to efficient removal of metabolic by-products (e.g., lactic acid, carbon dioxide, water)
- Slowly increases blood flow to muscles
- Makes muscle tissue more stretchable
- Reduces risk of tearing muscle fibers, tendons and muscle tissue
- Allows warmed muscles to move faster and to generate more force for greater mechanical efficiency
- Enhances neural transmission and motor-unit recruitment
- Allows nerve impulses to travel faster for quick reaction times
- Provides early alerts for potential musculoskeletal or cardiorespiratory problems

There are many benefits to a warm-up before exercise. First, a warm-up produces an increase in metabolic requirements. The short period of time used for a warm-up corresponds to the time necessary to allow the cardiorespiratory system to adjust blood flow effectively to the muscles, where the oxygen demand is great during exercise. This adjustment makes physical performance more effective and efficient. Secondly, a warm-up prevents blood lactic acid accumulation in the muscle, which can lead to premature fatigue. It also contributes to the efficient removal of metabolic by-products like lactic acid, carbon dioxide and water. A warm-up prevents the client from going from a state of inactivity to high intense activity too quickly by slowly increasing blood flow to the muscles. Third, muscle tissue becomes more stretchable in response to warm-ups. The risk of tearing muscle fibers, tendons and muscle tissue is reduced. Additionally, warmed-up muscles move faster and generate more force, allowing for greater mechanical efficiency due to low resistance within the muscle. A fourth benefit of a warm-up is that it enhances neural transmission and motor-unit recruitment. Nerve impulses travel faster in these cases and allow for quicker reaction times. Lastly, a warm-up provides an early alert for potential musculoskeletal or cardiorespiratory problems. These problems become apparent in a warm-up before they can cause serious injury during the higher intensities of exercise.

Warm-Up Considerations

During a warm-up, the amount, intensity and duration should be adjusted according to the individual's current fitness level. The intensity of the warm-up is important in effectively preparing the body for exercise. It is important to elevate the heart rate from the resting heart rate of 40-75 beats/minute to approximately 90-120 beats/minute. During the warm-up, the body temperature of the muscle tissue rises about 3.6 °F. The duration of the warm-up should be a minimum of 3-5 minutes; however, the actual length should be based on the exercise activity to follow. For elderly persons, pregnant women, overweight individuals or exercise beginners, the warm-up should be more gradual and for a longer duration, typically 10-15 minutes. In terms of activity, the warm-up should be controlled and go through an easy range of motion. It should never be beyond the range of motion, which might ultimately cause pain and discomfort.

> It is important to elevate the heart rate from the resting heart rate of 40-75 beats/minute to approximately 90-120 beats/minute.

There are three major types of activities that can accomplish efficient warm-up: general, activity-specific and passive warm-up. Often, however, warm-up exercises may be grouped as active and passive.

Types of Warm-Ups

General Warm-Up

A general warm-up involves rhythmic and continuous movement and callisthenic exercises. In this warm-up regimen, mostly large-muscle groups are engaged. Activities in a general warm-up include jogging, cycling and jumping rope. A general warm-up usually precedes an activity-specific warm-up and is more appropriate than a passive warm-up when a demanding physical activity is to follow. The aim of a general warm-up is to increase heart rate, blood flow, deep muscle temperature, respiration rate and perspiration. Additionally, decreasing viscosity of joint fluids is one of the main goals of a general warm-up.

Activity-Specific Warm-Up

An activity-specific warm-up includes movement that is actually a part of the main physical activity. For example, an activity-specific warm-up can include swinging a tennis racket before playing tennis or conducting light resistance training movements before

weight lifting. This method of warming-up is more desirable because it increases the temperature of the same muscle groups that will be used in the specific activity as well as serve as a mental rehearsal. An activity-specific warm-up usually includes 8-12 minutes of dynamic stretching, focusing on movements that work through the range of motion.

Passive Warm-Up

A passive warm-up includes things like a hot shower, a massage and heat applications. This can have a positive effect and does not cause fatigue in a person prior to the exercise session. However, a passive warm-up is less likely to warm deep muscles and may even be counterproductive. The increased surface temperature of the skin often leads blood vessels that are close to the surface of the skin to dilate. Blood then moves to the surface of the skin and away from working muscles.

Warm-Ups and Stretching

A misconception is that a warm-up and stretching are the same thing—they are not. A warm-up raises the body and muscle temperature while stretching improves flexibility. In some instances, however, a warm-up can, increase flexibility by increasing muscle elasticity. Due to these considerations, flexibility stretching should occur only after a warm-up.

Some warm-up routines do not include flexibility training. However, the addition of flexibility exercises are often part of a warm-up routine and are often matched to the demands of the activity that will be conducted. It usually depends on the nature of the exercise that will follow. If the activity will be of great intensity (e.g., basketball), then flexibility training would be necessary. However, if the activity is more static (e.g., stationary biking), then flexibility training may be needed or the warm-up may only consist of static stretching.

Warm-up Exercises

Back/Hamstrings

Neck/Shoulders

Quads/Hip Flexors

Lowerback

Back/Hamstrings

Flexibility

What is Flexibility?

Flexibility is the ability of your joints to move through a full range of motion. It is the capacity to move freely in every direction and, at times, beyond the normal range of motion. Flexibility ultimately measures the tightness of the muscles.

The Importance of Flexibility

Flexibility is often a neglected part of physical fitness. A high level of flexibility can be gained quickly but can also be lost quickly through inactivity. Also, levels of flexibility decrease with age. Lack of flexibility can cause lower back and hamstring muscle pain and weak abdominal muscles. In theory, the risk of injury to the muscle-tendon unit is based on the fact that tight muscles are more likely to be strained compared to more flexible muscles. An increase in the interaction of actin and myosin filaments of the muscle occurs when a person is more flexible and this ultimately improves performance. This highlights the importance of a consistent flexibility training program.

Improving flexibility can also lead to good posture by realigning the skeletal structure that has adapted to poor posture and exercise habits. The more unrestricted the movement is, the more flexible the body will be. Because of this, flexibility enhances safety and efficiency in conducting not only exercise regimens but also daily tasks. Too much flexibility or overly restricted movement in the body can lead to problems. This is often due to compromising joint stability. Forcing the body to a point of pain is never encouraged.

Another important aspect of designing an effective flexibility training program is that the correct performance and correct positioning of the exercises are conducted no matter which training method is utilized. Stretching exercises and techniques are often used in designing a program to gain flexibility. Programs may include a variety of techniques for the joints with periodic repetitions to chart progress.

The Science of Flexibility

One factor affecting flexibility is joint structure. Flexibility is joint specific. This is one of the primary limiting factors for the range of motion since the structure determines how much movement is available. Flexibility also varies between joints of the body due to construction. One joint may have above-average range of motion and another joint have below-average range. Hinge-type joints, including the joints of the knee and elbow, conduct only backward and forward movement so they have less range of motion compared to ball and socket joints, like that of the hip and shoulder. Movement is allowed in all anatomical planes in this area, which has

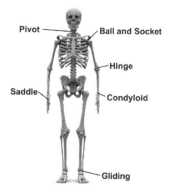

Females are typically more flexible than males.

the greatest range of motion compared to other joints.

Another factor is age. People become less flexible with age and never again reach levels seen during early childhood due to a loss of muscle elasticity. Early childhood is the best time to start flexibility programs.

Females are typically more flexible than males. This is thought to exist from childhood through adult life. It is attributed to the anatomical variation in joint structure seen in the trunk, hips and ankles. At puberty, boys have increased muscle size, stature and muscle strength that ultimately hinders flexibility. It has been proposed that increases in growth rates in different parts of life may result in rigidity of bones composing a joint and therefore lead to decreased flexibility.

The composition of connective tissue is another factor. This includes cartilage, which lies between bones to provide protection at the contact points and offer padding and shock-absorbing capabilities. Ligaments, which connect bones, offer stability and integrity to joint structures, while tendons, which connect bone to muscle, lead to efficient bodily movement and play a role in flexibility. The three layers that wrap the muscle, the muscle fascia, play an even greater role. Muscle can be stretched to 150% of its length if relaxed and unrestricted without any injurious effects. Ligaments and tendons, though important to flexibility as a whole, are hard to stretch because of their roles in stabilization and muscle force protection. Muscle fascia is relatively easy to stretch.

Types of Flexibility

Flexibility Training System (Integrated)

Flexibility training programs involve increasing flexibility through a progression of three phases. The three phases, known as the flexibility continuum, are corrective, active and functional flexibility.

Corrective Flexibility

- Static Stretching
- Neuromuscular Stretching
- Neurodynamic Stretching
- Self-Myofascial Release

Active Flexibility

- Neuromuscular Stretching
- Active Isolated Stretching

Functional Flexibility

- Dynamic Stretching

Corrective Flexibility

Corrective flexibility was designed to correct muscle imbalances and improve joint ailments.

It involves two main concepts known as static stretching and self myofascial release (SMFR). Static stretching refers to stretching an antagonist muscle to its maximum limit and holding the position for a period of time. An antagonist muscle stretches during a contraction while working against agonist and synergist muscles. Agonist muscles initiate muscle contractions and synergist muscles provide additional support the body needs to perform a particular action. This type of static stretching strengthens muscles and prevents injuries or tearing of soft tissue.

SMFR is a technique used to remove knots from muscles; these knots can form during vigorous exercises or stressful activities. This technique incorporates the use of a foam roll or cylindrical object and body pressure to massage muscles and decrease micro-adhesions that lead to the formation of muscle knots. Micro-adhesions that form during a workout stimulate the release of healing proteins, which lead to an increase in muscle density and metabolism. Unfortunately, the release of proteins causes the development of knots within the muscle. Knots that are left untreated make muscles inflexible and tight and decrease a muscle's ability to function and contract properly. Knots can also cause chronic muscle tension, joint pain and poor posture. All these complications can be avoided by simply massaging muscles with a foam roll after a workout. In other words, SMFR is a cool-down technique that leaves the muscle free of knots and in better shape by the start of the next workout regimen.

Areas of the body that should be focused on when performing SMFR include: the gastrocnemius (calf muscle), tensor fascia latae/iliotibial tract band (hip and leg muscle), adductor muscle (hip muscle), piriformis (gluteal) muscle and the latissimus dorsi (triangular back muscle). Static stretching followed by SMFR begins to improve flexibility and enhances the body's ability to heal its muscles after a workout. This is the first part of the flexibility continuum.

Active Flexibility

Active flexibility, the second phase of the continuum, entails the use of SMFR and active-isolated stretching to improve the efficiency of neuromuscular (nerve and muscular) interactions. In addition, an increase in soft tissue extensibility can be noticed by the end of this phase. Active-

isolated stretching utilizes agonist and synergist muscles to perform the entire movement of a specific action while allowing the antagonist muscle to stretch. For example, when performing straight leg raises in a supine position, the hip flexor and quadriceps cause the leg to raise and allow the hamstring (antagonist) to be stretched. Active-isolated stretching techniques are held for approximately 2 seconds and allow muscles to easily repair themselves and enhance daily performance activity. This form of stretching also increases joint elasticity and improves circulation. Overall, the active flexibility phase increases clients' level of strength and prepares them for the final functional flexibility phase.

Functional Flexibility

The functional flexibility phase allows individuals to achieve maximum extensibility of soft tissue and neuromuscular control through dynamic stretching and SMFR. Dynamic stretching involves the combination of active muscle exertion, speed of movement and momentum to stretch a particular muscle or group of muscles. This form of stretching is most often conducted before a competition and bouncing or jerking movements are avoided. Dynamic stretching reduces muscle tightness, which is associated with the occurrence of musculotendinous (muscle and tendon) tears. The results of recent studies also suggest that dynamic stretches before a competition are more beneficial than static stretches. This final phase of the flexibility continuum increases power in addition to strength. An important point to remember in regards to the flexibility continuum is that, for each phase, SMFR should be performed after stretching.

Stretching Techniques

We will discuss in further detail the following different forms of stretching: static, active, proprioceptive neuromuscular facilitation, dynamic and ballistic.

Static Stretching

Static stretching is slow and sustained stretching to increase movement at the corresponding joint. It can be performed to cool down muscles after a workout by holding specific stretches for 10 seconds or to increase range of movement and mobility by holding the stretches for 30 seconds. The benefits come from simultaneously relaxing and lengthening the stretched muscle. This type of stretch does not activate the stretch reflex because of the slow speed of stretch. Static stretching requires no voluntary muscular activity. Static stretching is known to prevent overstretching and exceeding the normal range of motion while requiring a lower energy requirement. Lower instances of muscle soreness are also associated with static stretching. Aspects of static stretching may also be included in the other forms of stretching. Static stretching techniques include the following:

Gastrocnemius stretch:

Stand upright facing a wall and place the left leg in front of the right leg. Hands should be raised to shoulder level and placed against the wall. Slowly move the right leg away from the wall, keep it straight and firmly press the heel into

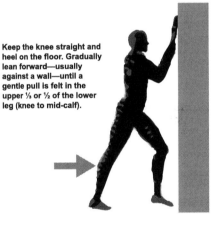

Keep the knee straight and heel on the floor. Gradually lean forward—usually against a wall—until a gentle pull is felt in the upper ⅓ or ½ of the lower leg (knee to mid-calf).

the floor. Hold the stretch for 20-30 seconds. The calf muscle will be stretched. Repeat this stretch with the left leg.

Static standing adductor stretch:

Stand upright with the feet placed approximately two shoulder lengths apart. Lift the right leg by bending at the knee and then lower the body, leaning into the bent right leg.

151

Keep the back straight and use the arms to maintain balance while holding for 20-30

Start   Finish

seconds. The left leg adductor will be stretched. Repeat the stretch with the opposite leg.

Static standing psoas stretch:

Stand upright with one leg bent and slightly forward and the other leg back. Rotate toes of back foot inward. Pull stomach inward. Squeeze butt muscles and, while

Start   Finish

rotating pelvis to the back, shift body forward and straighten the back leg. A mild tension should be felt in the front of the hip. Raise the arm (same side as the back leg) up and over to the opposite side of the body while holding the pelvis position. Continue to hold this position and rotate backwards at a slow rate. Hold for 20-30 seconds. Repeat on the opposite side.

Static kneeling hip flexor stretch:

Kneel down on one leg with the back leg being bent at a 90° angle. Keep posture tall. Internally rotate your back hip. Place same sided hand on

Start   Finish

front thigh to help you balance. Hold other arm straight up with hand in air. Pull navel inward, squeeze butt muscles and rotate pelvis toward the front of the body. Move body forward slowly until mild tension can be felt in the front of the hip/leg that is supporting your weight. Hold for 20-30 seconds. Repeat on other side, switching legs and arms.

Static pectoral wall stretch:

Stand perpendicular to a wall (or door opening) with right foot forward and toes pointing forward. Form a 90° angle with your arms, palms of hand flat against the wall/door jam. Pull navel inward. Slowly lean forward until a mild stretch is felt in the front shoulder and chest region. Hold for 20-30 seconds and repeat 3 times.

Start   Finish

Static latissimus dorsi ball stretch:

Stand in front of a stability ball. Place the bottom side of right hand on the ball with the thumb pointing upward. Roll the

ball to the left and kept the hips square keeping the right fist on the ball. Draw in your core tightly and prevent hips from moving to get the best stretch. Hold this position for 3-5 breaths and then switch to left hand and roll ball to the right.

Static upper trapezius/scalene stretch:

Stand upright with a proper posture position and place the left arm behind the body. Pull the navel inward then retract and depress the

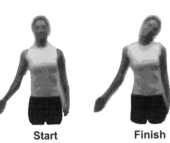

Start   Finish

scapula on the left side. Tuck in the chin and tilt the head from left side toward right side. Hold this position for 20-30 seconds, then repeat on the right side.

Passive Stretching

Passive stretching is a form of static stretching and is so named because it requires assistance, which is needed from an external force to reposition parts of the body. This force can be from gravity, which weighs the body down or from another person like a personal trainer. To maximize results from passive stretching, one should remain relaxed and stop any reflexive movement.

Active and Active Assistive Stretching

In active stretching, the person who is stretching supplies the force of the stretch. The stretched muscle is being actively engaged and moved through the range of motion. This requires energy greater than what is used for static stretching. Active assistive stretching is sometimes considered a partner stretch. It is the same as active stretching but the muscle being stretched

may also require some assistance to go through the range of motion. This is most likely because of muscular weakness.

Active stretch techniques strengthen agonistic muscles while increasing active flexibility. Most active stretches do not need to be held for more than 15 seconds and holding an active stretch position for more than 10 seconds is usually difficult. A variety of yoga exercises are active stretches. Active stretch techniques include:

Active Gastrocnemius stretch with Pronation and Supination:

Stand facing a wall in the lunge position and lean against the wall, using the upper body for support. The leg closest to the wall should be bent and the leg behind the body should be

153

straight. Pull the navel inward, lift the bent leg and rotate the body from left to right. The stretch should be held for 2 seconds and performed 5-10 times on both sides of the body.

Start **Movement** **Finish**

Active supine biceps femoris stretch:

Lie on the back with both legs extended straight. Lift the right leg and bend the knee.

Start **Movement** **Finish**

Place the right hand behind the right knee for support. Pull the navel inward and extend the leg towards the ceiling. Hold this stretch for 2 seconds and repeat 5-10 times. Repeat with the left leg.

Active standing psoas stretch:

Stand upright with one leg bent and slightly forward. Rotate the back leg inward. Draw the navel inward while raising the arm overhead. Squeeze butt muscles and rotate backwards. Lean forward on the front leg, controlling the movement, until slight

Start **Movement** **Finish**

tension can be felt in front of the hip being stretched. Bend to the side and rotate toward the back. Hold for 2 seconds for 5-10 repetitions.

Active kneeling hip flexor stretch:

Kneel down on one leg with the back leg bent at a 90° angle. Keep posture tall. Internally rotate your back hip. Place same sided hand on front thigh to help you balance. Hold other arm straight

Start **Movement** **Finish**

up and down with hand in air overhead. Pull navel inward, squeeze butt muscles and rotate pelvis toward the back of the body. Move body forward slowly until mild tension can be felt in the front of the hip/leg that is supporting your weight. Bend to the side and rotate toward the back. Hold for 2 seconds for 5-10 repetitions. Repeat on other side switching legs and arms.

Active standing adductor stretch:

Stand upright in a proper posture position with the feet placed two shoulder lengths apart. Lift the right leg, bend the knee and slowly lower the body. Use the arms to balance and keep the back straight. Hold the stretch for 2 seconds, repeat 5-10 times then repeat with the left leg.

Start **Movement** **Finish**

Proprioceptive Neuromuscular Facilitation Stretching

Proprioceptive neuromuscular facilitation (PNF) stretching was initially developed as a technique to relax muscle with increased activity but has been expanded to improve the range of motion. It is thought to be superior to other stretching methods because  it also assists in muscular relaxation. PNF makes use of both passive and active stretching. The type utilized depends on what is the best response to the stretch stimulus. It includes contract-relax (hold-relax), which involves the muscle contracting and then relaxing. The muscle is then further stretched into its available range of motion during the relax phase. In another type of PNF, contract-relax-contract (hold-relax-hold), the same procedure is conducted but the contraction of the antagonist muscle gains slightly more range of motion.

Dynamic and Ballistic Stretching

Dynamic stretching is often confused with ballistic stretching. Ballistic stretching entails quick jerking and bounce-like movements on the resistant tissue. This stretching is performed at high speeds and therefore is often

uncontrolled because of the high rate and degree of stretch as well as force applied to induce the stretch. The disadvantages of this stretching technique include the predisposition of the muscle to injury. This may outweigh any benefit from this type of stretching. Ballistic stretching also has a higher energy requirement, which may cause fatigue and hinder performance in the main exercise activity. Additionally, though it has a greater range of motion than the static range of motion, some do not consider this an acceptable method for increasing the range of motion.

Dynamic stretching techniques involve controlled arm and leg exercises that gradually increase speed of movement, range of motion and extensibility. They usually comprise 8-12 repetitions or less and are a good warm-up routine for aerobic workouts. Dynamic stretching techniques include the following:

Prisoner squat:

Stand upright with the feet shoulder length apart and point the toes slightly outward in an

Start   **Movement**   **Finish**

angle. Place the hands behind the head and hold the chest and shoulders in an upright position during the exercise. Bend at the hip and knees and slowly lower the body. Balance on the heels, do not lean forward and make sure the knees do not pass over the toes. Repeat 8-12 times.

Multiplanar lunge:

This lunge involves three parts: the front lunge, the side lunge and the turning lunge. For the front lunge, stand upright with the legs together and the hands placed on the hips. Step forward with the right leg and bend the right leg at a 90° angle. Make sure not to extend the

Start   Movement   Finish

knee over the toes and keep the upper body upright. Return to the start position and repeat the lunge with the left leg. To perform the side lunge, stand in the same starting position and step to the side with the right leg. Bend at the hips towards the right leg, keeping the torso upright and the hips facing forward. Return to the starting position and repeat with the left leg. To perform the turning lunge, stand in the same starting position and step to the side with the right foot at a 45° angle. Pivot the left foot while slowly lowering the body into a lunge position.

When coming out of the lunge position, pivot back to the starting position, then repeat on the other side. Repeat the entire series 6-8 times.

Single-leg squat touchdown:

Balance on one leg while keeping the corresponding shoulder in line with the knee and hip. Squat as far as possible with the opposite leg elevated and extended forward. Do not allow the knee of the balance leg to go over the toes. Return to the starting position and repeat with the other leg.

Tube walking/side-to-side:

Stand upright with the feet shoulder width apart and pointed forward. Pull in the belly and slightly bend the knees. Tighten the glutes and step toward the left with the left foot, then step toward the left with the right foot. Take 5-10 steps to the left, then 5-10 steps to the right in the same manner. Perform this stretching exercise 1-5 times.

Medicine ball chop and lift:

Stand upright with the feet two shoulder-lengths apart and slightly bend the knees. Hold a medium-sized medicine ball with both hands above the head and bring the ball down in front of the torso in a chopping motion. The ball can

be brought down to the knee level or to the floor for a greater challenge. While continuing to hold the ball, reverse directions and bring the ball back to the starting position over the head. Repeat 8-12 times and maintain a consistent pace throughout the exercise.

Precautions and Safety

No two individuals are the same so each client interested in beginning a flexibility training program should have an effective regimen specific to that client's needs. The ease at which flexibility can be increased is normally limited by muscle fascia (connective tissue), which causes the most resistance to improving range of movement. Trainers and their clients enrolled in a training program should pay close attention to making sure range of movement can be altered without causing joint injuries or increasing the risk of serious injuries. Trainers should closely monitor their clients while stretching exercises are being performed, and clients should clearly understand how to perform movements and concentrate while performing stretches.

Types of Stretches

Static Stretching:

- Safest option for beginners
- Most effective form of flexibility techniques
- Lowest incidence of rate of injuries
- First phase of flexibility continuum

Active Stretching:

- Tedious and difficult for average person
- Agonist muscle strength and mental concentration is needed to perform properly
- If increase in range of movement is not noticed, passive or combination of passive and active stretching can be performed
- Second phase of flexibility continuum

Dynamic Stretching:

- Can be performed as active and/or passive stretching
- Dynamic active stretching utilizes momentum to increase range of movement
- Safety is dependent on one's flexibility level, speed at which performed and range of motion necessary
- High injury risk

- Typically performed by athletes for a specific event
- No substantial evidence that it is better than other types of stretches
- Third phase of flexibility continuum

By following concepts such as these, the trainer and client can be reassured that flexibility training will be conducted in a safe manner. Static stretching is the safest option to start for individuals who are inactive or who simply want to become more flexible. Static stretching belongs to the first part of the flexibility continuum and is typically labeled as the safest and most effective form. Long-duration, low-force static stretching exercises produce much more muscle extensibility than active and dynamic stretches. Static stretching also offers the lowest incidence rate of injuries.

Active stretching, unlike static stretching, is usually tedious and difficult for average individuals to perform. One common problem is that most people do not have the agonist muscle strength and mental concentration needed to properly perform active stretching techniques. Individuals who fall under this category typically do not notice an increase in their range of movement. One way to overcome this problem is by performing passive stretching or a combination of passive and active stretching. Passive stretching allows individuals to gradually stretch the agonist muscle of interest and puts less strain on the agonist muscle. Combining passive and active stretches makes the transition into the second phase of the flexibility continuum less stressful.

Dynamic stretching, the third part of the flexibility continuum, can also be performed in an active and/or passive manner. Dynamic stretching differs from active stretching, however, by utilizing momentum to increase range of movement. The safety of dynamic stretches depends on the individual's flexibility level, the speed at which the movement is performed and the range of motion necessary to perform the stretch.

Dynamic stretching is typically performed by athletes needing to prepare for a specific sports routine or aggressive sporting event. Dancers, divers and professional gymnasts extensively use dynamic stretching. A high injury risk is associated with this form of stretching and, although many athletes prefer to use dynamic stretches to warm-up, there is no substantial scientific evidence that suggests dynamic stretching is better than any other form of stretching. However, if an individual who has been physically inactive for an extended

> **Static stretching is the safest option to start for individuals who are inactive or who simply want to become more flexible.**

period of time needs to prepare for a vigorous sporting event, (e.g., marathon) implementing dynamic stretches in the beginning of the training program may be justified. In every case, safety precautions such as drinking and eating properly before training, maintaining proper posture while training and concentrating should be taken seriously.

Individuals who suffer from a disease that limits or increases their range of motion or who have had previous surgeries/injuries that reduced or increased their flexibility must be cautious when stretching. Ailments such as arthritis cause a lot of pain for sufferers due to inflamed joints. Putting unnecessary pressure on affected joints or stretching a muscle beyond its range of motion can leave the individual in more pain and discomfort than before starting the training program.

> Knowing what type of surgeries or injuries an individual has had will allow the trainer to suggest stretching techniques that will not re-injure or further injure the client

Knowing what type of surgeries or injuries an individual has had will allow the trainer to suggest stretching techniques that will not re-injure or further injure the client. Sometimes clients choose to take part in a training program in order to regain strength or flexibility they may have lost due to an accident. If proper care is not taken when the training program is designed or if the client is not closely monitored when stretching, the recovery process may be delayed. When requesting medical history information, the trainer must impress upon the client the importance of thoroughly informing the trainer about every procedure had and any ailments currently causing issues.

Developing the Program

Designing the right training program depends on factors such as age, gender and the client's current and previous physical activity level. Young children are usually more flexible than adults so exercises that may be easy for children to perform might cause extreme difficulty for older individuals. Gender also plays a role in levels of strength and flexibility. Men tend to be stronger than women, but women tend to be more flexible in the hip region. These factors may affect the client's ability to properly carry out certain techniques and may also affect the outcome of the stretch exercises. In addition to gender, a client's physical activity level is one of the most important factors to consider when designing a training program. A person who practiced karate on a weekly basis for several years and then took a break may be more flexible and stronger than an individual who has not performed any form of physical activity for years. Knowing details such as these ensure that each individual achieves the desired results without pushing beyond the body's limits.

Goals such as improving range of movement in specific joints and increasing endurance should also play a role in how the training program is structured. If a client needs to simply become more active and wishes to do so by first increasing the level of flexibility, the training program may be comprised of mainly static stretching exercises. If a fairly active individual needs to increase strength and flexibility in the next two months for an upcoming event, the training program may start off with static and active exercises and then quickly shift to dynamic exercises. A training program may also alternate between phases as the trainer and/or client see fit.

Three factors for Workout Design

1. Warming up
2. Proper breathing
3. Maintaining posture

Three important factors that should also be included in the workout design include: warming up, proper breathing and maintaining proper posture. Warm-up exercises have been shown to reduce the body's resistance to stretching by increasing muscle temperature, which in turn leads to an increase in elasticity (the muscle's ability to extend). Warm muscle tissue is less stiff than cold muscle tissue and responds better during stretch exercises. Warm-up exercises include running on a treadmill or stationary cycling.

Breathing properly allows the client to relax and smoothly progress into each stretching exercise. Proper breathing also ensures that only the muscles of interest are being stretched and strengthened. Breathing properly relieves muscle tension, which can cause unwanted muscle pain during and after the workout. The trainer should clearly describe how to breathe during a stretch routine so the client can get the most out of the workout regimen. In order to properly breathe throughout the routine, the client must concentrate.

Maintaining a proper posture while working out also involves concentration. Bad posture can lead to muscle knots and chronic muscle pain, which cause the stretch exercises to be ineffective. Maintaining correct posture also means properly extending the limbs during the workout. Overextending can cause serious injuries and under-extending will lead to a lack of results. Only proper posture held throughout the exercise will lead to an increase in strength, flexibility and range of motion.

Measuring Flexibility

There is no single test that can be administered to test the flexibility of the whole body. However, separate tests can measure the flexibility at certain joint areas. Flexibility assessments include 3-5 minutes of warm-up and stretching to avoid injury or muscle strain. This test is often repeated every 4-6 weeks to monitor progress and help reach a higher level of flexibility.

The typical devices for measuring flexibility include manual and electric goniometers to measure joint angles and the sit-and-reach test. These tests evaluate combined flexibility of the lower back and hips. Goniometry is the measurement of joint range of motion measured in either linear units like inches and centimeters or angular units like the degrees of an arc.

Summary

Prior to starting a flexibility training program, clients should have a good understanding of their current level of strength, flexibility, mobility and range of motion. Previous injuries, ailments and surgeries should also be considered prior to beginning a training program. Once an individual makes a decision to start a training program, a discussion with a trainer needs to follow and the client needs to fully define medical history, physical activity history and goals. The trainer must then use the information obtained to create a specific program that enhances the client's speed of movement, mobility, endurance, strength and flexibility without causing injury or discomfort. If the client is relaxed while working out and notices positive results, the training program will be more successful.

Individuals who are suffering from a debilitating ailment (e.g., arthritis, muscle imbalance, osteoporosis) or a recovering from surgery or an injury need to start with the corrective flexibility phase of the flexibility continuum. Individuals who are active and possess high levels of flexibility may be able to start at the functional flexibility phase, but they may also need to regress to the corrective and active phases during their training program. Every individual, regardless of the strength and flexibility level, should perform SMFR after working out. Warming up before exercising and performing SMFR afterwards prevents muscle ailments and serious injuries, helps remove unwanted muscle knots and allows muscles to be in better shape prior to the next workout.

Warming up softens muscles and improves muscle elasticity and SMFR is a simple massage technique that enhances muscle healing, strength and extensibility.

Breathing properly and maintaining proper posture while performing stretches is also of the utmost importance. An individual can cause more damage to the body or delay healing if stretches are not performed properly. The client needs to ask questions when a particular movement of a stretch routine is not completely understood and make sure to concentrate at all times. By following these guidelines, strength, endurance and flexibility can be improved with ease.

Review Questions

1. More than 30% of sports injuries seen are due to a lack of a warm-up. True or False?

   _____

2. Which of the following is NOT a type of passive warm-up?

   a) Heat application

   b) Hot shower

   c) Massage

   d) Stretching

3. Because a warm-up can improve flexibility, stretching should be done after the warm-up. True or False? _____

   _____

4. What are the three types of flexibility? ___

   _____

   _____

5. Where should a client with arthritis start on the flexibility continuum? _____

   _____

   _____

6. Which of the three phases belong to the flexibility continuum?

   a) Functional flexibility

   b) Ballistic flexibility

   c) Active flexibility

   d) Corrective flexibility

7. What is SMFR and what does the acronym stand for? _____

   _____

   _____

8. Which three factors should be included in the design of a training program?

   a) Breathing

   b) Running

   c) Posture

   d) Warming up

9. What is the purpose of the corrective flexibility phase? _____

   _____

   _____

Answers

1. True.
2. d) Stretching.
3. True
4. Corrective, active and functional flexibility.
5. At the corrective flexibility phase of the flexibility continuum.
6. a) Functional flexibility, c) active flexibility and d) corrective flexibility.
7. It stands for Static stretching and self myofascial release and is the technique involved in corrective flexibility.
8. a) Breathing, c) posture and d) warming up.
9. To correct muscle imbalances and improve joint ailments.

References

Cramer JT, Housh TJ, Weir JP, Johnson GO, Coburn JW, Beck TW. The acute effects of static stretching on peak torque, mean power output, electromyography and mechanomyography. *European Journal of Applied Physiology.* 2005;93(5-6):530-39.

Gleim GW, McHugh MP. Flexibility and its effects on sports injury and performance. *Sports Medicine.* 1997;24(5): 289-99.

Halbertsma JP, van Bolhuis AI, Göeken LN. Sport stretching: effect on passive muscle stiffness of short hamstrings. *Archives of Physical Medicine and Rehabilitation.* 1996;77(7):688-92.

Krivickas LS, Feinberg JH. Lower extremity injuries in college athletes: relation between ligamentous laxity and lower extremity muscle tightness. *Archives of Physical Medicine and Rehabilitation.* 1996;77(11):1139-43.

Sady SP, Wortman M, Blanke D. Flexibility training: ballistic, static or proprioceptive neuromuscular facilitation? *Archives of Physical Medicine and Rehabilitation.* 1982;63(6):261-63.

Shrier I. Stretching before exercise does not reduce the risk of local muscle injury: A critical review of the clinical and basic science literature. *Clinical Journal of Sports Medicine.* 1999;9:221-27.

Smith CA. The warm-up procedure: to stretch or not to stretch. A brief review. *Journal of Orthopedic Sports Physical Therapy.* 1994;19(1):12-17.

Witvrouw E, Danneels L, Asselman P, D'Have T, Cambier D. Muscle flexibility as a risk factor for developing muscle injuries in male professional soccer players. A prospective study. *American Journal of Sports Medicine.* 2003;31(1):41-46.

Witvrouw E, Mahieu N, Danneels L, McNair P. Stretching and injury prevention: an obscure relationship. *Sports Medicine.* 2004;34(7):443-49.

Woods K, Bishop P, Jones E. Warm-up and stretching in the prevention of muscular injury. *Sports Medicine.* 2007;37(12):1089-99.

Yamaguchi T, Ishii K. Effects of static stretching for 30 seconds and dynamic stretching on leg extension power. *The Journal of Strength Conditioning and Research.* 2005;19(3):677-83.

Chapter 6: Program Design Elements

Topics Covered

Cardiorespiratory Conditioning
The Importance of Cardiorespiratory Fitness

Training Design

Postural Considerations

Smart Progression
Interval Training

Interval Training Model

Stage Training

Circuit Training
Fat Burning

Muscular Strength
Endurance Conditioning
The Adaptation of Strength Training

Flexibility Training
Types of Stretching

Things to Avoid
Postural Muscle Imbalance

Balance, Agility, Speed
Balance
Balance Training
Coordination and Speed
Sensory Function
Speed

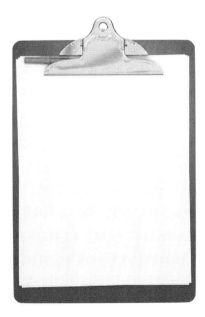

Cardiorespiratory Conditioning

Cardiorespiratory conditioning is an activity used to improve the body's ability to process and deliver oxygen, which produces the energy required to complete a desired activity. It involves intense movements and activities that stimulate the cardiovascular system. This typically involves specific muscular endurance training of the large muscles of the hips, thighs and buttocks and a focus on a client's ability to perform repetitive, moderate-to-high intensity training routines. Cardiorespiratory training is often used to burn more calories than other areas of training and involves sport actions that are high energy and nonstop. Common cardiorespiratory conditioning exercises include running, cycling and swimming. The body will adapt to the level of stress put upon it and in turn require more energy. Ultimately, selecting the right training exercises is important in obtaining maximal benefits.

The Importance of Cardiorespiratory Fitness

As the respiratory system gathers oxygen, the cardiovascular system processes and distributes the oxygen. During cardiorespiratory conditioning, it is important to apply the correct overload (increase in heart rate and return of blood to the heart) to properly strengthen the heart. The ultimate goal is to increase heart rate and respiration in order to place appropriate stress on the cardiorespiratory system. The overload must be progressive and can be measured by increases in maximal oxygen consumption (VO_2 max). Sustaining a large volume of blood returning to the heart is necessary to see the positive effects of exercise. For example, lifting weights will increase heart rate but will not increase VO_2 max and will not lead to a large volume of blood returning to the heart. Thus, increasing heart rate alone does not always correlate with work being done to train the cardiovascular system.

Since fitness of the cardiorespiratory system is improved by enhanced heart function and use of oxygen by the working muscle to produce energy, it should be added to any exercise routine. Cardiorespiratory fitness also includes a decrease in the risk of death from heart disease and other causes, as well as an increase in the performance of daily activities. Cardiorespiratory conditioning reduces resting heart rate and normalizes resting blood

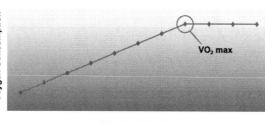

Oxygen Consumption Relative to Exercise Intensity

Ocygen Consumption

VO_2 max

Exercise Intensity

pressure. Additional benefits of cardiovascular conditioning include reduced stress levels and fatigue along with improved self-confidence.

Training Design

In designing a cardiorespiratory training program, it is important to begin with a warm-up. This is usually a 5-10 minute low intensity muscle activity, which may include stretching. It is at the lower end of the intensity progression of the target exercise and represents the transition from rest to the main workout. The warm-up is followed by the endurance or exercise phase. This is the target of the workout and carries the main cardiorespiratory benefits.

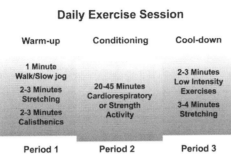

Daily Exercise Session

Warm-up	Conditioning	Cool-down
1 Minute Walk/Slow jog	20-45 Minutes Cardiorespiratory or Strength Activity	2-3 Minutes Low Intensity Exercises
2-3 Minutes Stretching		3-4 Minutes Stretching
2-3 Minutes Calisthenics		
Period 1	Period 2	Period 3

Total Time is Generally 30-60 Minutes

Some exercises in this phase are weight-dependent. The intensity is maintained throughout the exercise and a relatively constant amount of energy is expended. Examples of weight-dependent exercises include walking and running. Other exercises do not factor in body weight due to the support of the body during the routine (e.g., cycling and swimming). An appropriate cool-down period of approximately 10 minutes of low intensity activity should follow the endurance phase; this represents the transition from higher intensity exercise back to rest. The heart rate, blood pressure and respiration rate is shifted downward and back to rest. This gradual decrease will help in the removal of lactate from the muscle and aid in the dissipation of body heat.

There are a few considerations to keep in mind when determining the rest of the exercise intensity or the rate of work being performed that is described as a speed or load of the body. The intensity should be recommended within a range that would allow for increased cardiovascular health and oxygen consumption. Intensity should be considered in conjunction with duration. Exercise intensity cannot be accurately chosen without taking duration into consideration since they are inversely related. Frequency, the number of times the cardiorespiratory system is stressed, also plays a pivotal role. There may be an advantage to more frequent training. Training two days a week or less does not really lead to an improvement in oxygen consumption. The optimal frequency for training is three to five days a week, with exercise occurring every other day when possible, rather than consecutively, to allow for proper rest.

In the design of a conditioning program, other factors should be taken into account, including individual differences, physical limitations and beginning fitness level. Age and health status of the individual will also help to determine an appropriate cardiovascular training program. Furthermore, the choice of the type of exercise should be based upon interest, availability and should lower the risk of injury.

Postural Considerations

Cardiorespiratory conditioning training follows the same kinetic parameters as flexibility and resistance training. There are postural considerations in selecting the appropriate form of cardiorespiratory training for the beginner. Some people possess a rounded shoulder, forward head posture, an anteriorly rotated pelvis causing low back arches, feet that turn out or knees that move in. These factors can affect their performance on workout equipment, such as steppers and treadmills, as well as stationary bicycles.

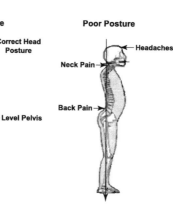

Smart Progression

Example: Progressive Walking Routine

Week	Walks (Week)	Distance (Miles)	Warm-Up (Minutes)	Walking (Minutes)	Cool-Down (Minutes)
1	4	1.25	5	25	5
2	3-4	1.25	5	25	5
3	4	1.50	5	30	5
4	4	1.75	5	32	5
5	4-5	2.0	5	34	5
6	4-5	2.25	5	36	5
7	4-5	2.50	5	38	5
8	5	2.75	5	42	5
9	5	3.0	5	46	5
10	5	3.25	5	50	5

Adaptation to a particular exercise routine can occur easily. When this happens, the same amount of work is done in less time and it is associated with less psychological disruption; in addition, it results in lower levels of fatigue or exertion. The workload must then be increased if benefits from training are to be seen. Smart progression involves the progression from a lower intensity level to a higher intensity level, longer duration, and/or increased frequency of the exercise session. An effective guideline is to keep the increase in activity to no more than 5% for each progression and the adaption to this increase spread over a period of a week or two. Additionally, change only one element (e.g., frequency, duration) at a time. Initial progression is from discontinuous to continuous activity, which leads to a relatively rapid initial progression.

Interval Training

The body adapts whenever possible so that it uses less energy to do the same processes. Therefore, interval training, involving both aerobic and anaerobic processes, can maximize the amount of calories burned to ensure that the body can maximize the energy used by the body. This also involves maximizing the excess post exercise oxygen consumption (EPOC). The body's metabolism is elevated after exercise since fat burning is often greater following exercise. The higher the intensity of the exercise, the greater the magnitude of EPOC. Splitting the training sessions into intervals also enhances the effects of EPOC.

Classic interval training principles are key to cardiovascular training and can be applied to beginners, less fit individuals and trained athletes. This is because interval training is the best choice of conditioning to optimize aerobic benefits. Interval training is different from the comfortable level of effort, where there is a balance between energy demands by the muscle and aerobic metabolism. This comfortable level is different for everyone and depends on their varying abilities to deliver and use oxygen. Interval training involves periods called intensity training, with an intermediate effort that is above the comfortable level. This is often followed by cardio activity that is at the comfortable level or lower. It is important to be aware of the difference in effort exerted during the comfort zone versus the intensity training zone.

In interval training, any switch in the intensity or duration leads to a switch in the particular energy system. There are many aspects to interval training that are important to gain maximal benefits. An increase in cardiorespiratory fitness or aerobic endurance can increase a person's ability to exercise for prolonged periods of time at the limits of aerobic metabolism. Even individuals that are not physically fit can use interval training to raise their anaerobic threshold. This change in anaerobic threshold can allow for increasingly intense paces and longer durations, leading to increased work efforts in manageable doses. The more work that is performed, the more total calories and fat that are burned. More total

<figure>
O2 Deficit
4
3
Alactacid
2
EPOC
1
Lactacid
0 2 4 6 8 10 12 14
Rest   Exercise   Recovery (minutes)
</figure>

exercise effort is accumulated during interval workouts, especially if there is a limited amount of time set aside for exercise. This allows for a more effective use of time, no matter the fitness level. Additionally, training in intervals increases exercise compliance. Interval training also offers exercise variety and enjoyment and is also mentally engaging. It is used to avoid monotonous exercise intensities and provide positive motivation. Interval training also decreases overuse injury potential.

Interval Training Using Optimum Running Times Based on Best 10-km Time*

Best 10-km time (min:sec)	200 m Intervals (anaerobic) (min:sec)	400 m Intervals (aerobic) (min:sec)	400 m Intervals (aerobic-anaerobic) (min:sec)
46:00	00:46	2:00	1:51
43:00	00:43	1:52	1:44
40:00	00:40	1:45	1:37
37:00	00:38	1:37	1:29
34:00	00:36	1:30	1:16

Example: A runner with 40 min. 10k best time should train 200 m intervals (half a lap on a track) at 40 secs per interval (mainly using anaerobic system); if preferred interval workout is f 400 m (1 lap), but desire is to still remain in aerobic zone (so as to not build lactic acid), the runner would complete interval in 1:45; final column is for the runner wanting interval workouts consisting of 400 m in which they would build speed in order to get faster—they would cover 400 m in 1:37 (for the runner who runs a 40 min 10k, a 1:37 would be very challenging and would require both anaerobic and aerobic systems for energy).

Heart monitors should be used for interval training to assess the efforts of the training program. A heart monitor provides more information than using time over distance measurements since it allows for the influence of external factors (e.g., weather and surfaces) on training.

Interval Training Model

Example: Work to Rest Ratios for Various Exercises

% of Maximum Power	Energy System Stressed	Exercise Duration	Exercise:Rest Ratios
90-100	Phosphagen	5-10 sec	1:12 to 1:20
75-90	Glycolytic	15-30 sec	1:3 to 1:5
30-75	Glycolytic & Oxidative	1-3 min	1:2 to 1:4
20-35	Oxidative	>3 min	1:1 to 1:3

Concepts of the interval training model include the idea of speed play. Speed play is used in many instances and represents an easy-to-use model for training. In speed play, there are increases in cardiovascular efforts and then an adequate recovery period follows. In terms of recovery, anaerobic conditioning is usually performed at the expense of lactic acid buildup in the muscles and blood. The length of time to recover depends on the effort to recovery ratio used in training. In the case of speed play, recovery is usually three times as much rest as intense training. For example, 5 minutes of hard pedaling on a stationary bike is followed by about 15 minutes of rest. This is done as many times as is appropriate or according to the physical capabilities of the client. Speed play works regardless of the physical fitness level since the training intensity can be kept to a specific fitness level.

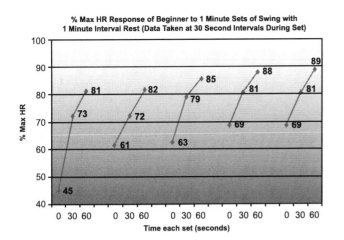

% Max HR Response of Beginner to 1 Minute Sets of Swing with 1 Minute Interval Rest (Data Taken at 30 Second Intervals During Set)

Health and fitness interval training is more structured than speed play. It can be performed using the aerobic and anaerobic model. The effort in this interval usually has a 1:1 effort to recovery ratio. Excellent training techniques are used to enhance cardiovascular performance and variables, such as intensity, duration and frequency, are often fixed according to goals. Since fitness interval training is the most structured type of interval training and is associated with high intensity performance, it is usually reserved for more highly conditioned persons.

Stage Training

Aspects of interval training can be broken down into three stages that use three different heart training zones. These zones are organized to maximize cardiorespiratory training benefits. The goal of zone one is to increase blood supply to tissue and is often used for beginners to improve the delivery of oxygen throughout the body and remove waste. The first zone is also

called the stabilizing phase and is characterized by a heart rate of 65-75% of the maximal heart rate. Zone two has an increased heart rate of about 80-85% of the maximal heart rate and is

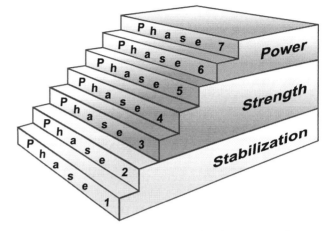

near the point at which the body can no longer produce energy for the muscle. This is often known as the anaerobic threshold and results in more calories being burned, much of which comes from fat. Importantly, this does not lead to the huge production of lactic acid. The third and last zone is a true, high intensity workout over a short amount of time. In this zone, the heart rate is 86-90% of the max. Zone three is often used in conjunction with the other two zones to try and avoid a plateau in exercise. Zone three is the power level.

Circuit Training

Circuit training is one of the most beneficial forms of cardiorespiratory training and, more specifically, interval training. Combining aspects of both cardiovascular and strength training, it involves a series of resistance training exercises back to back with very little rest or recovery period. The purpose is to keep the client constantly moving and allow for major exercise benefits without spending prolonged periods of time. Circuit training also differs from training programs that only target one or more specific muscle groups. It is effective because it keeps pushing the body aerobically and challenges the strength of the body simultaneously.

The term "circuit" refers to a group of activities that are performed one after the other to form

the workout regime. The activities that compose a circuit can include squats, lunges, jumping rope and back extensions. Once all these exercises are finished, you have completed one circuit. As with other forms of training, it is important to warm up with light cardio and cool down with stretching.

Fat Burning

Respiratory Exchange Ratio (RER)		
RER	Fat %	Carb %
1.00	0	100
.98	6	94
.96	12	88
.94	18	81
.92	26	74
.90	32	68
.88	38	62
.86	47	53
.84	53	47
.82	62	38
RER	Fat %	Carb %
.80	68	32
.78	74	26
.76	81	18
.74	88	12
.72	94	6
.70	100	0

The primary reason for exercise is usually to reduce total body fat. It is a common myth that fat burning can only occur through extreme cardiovascular exercise. There is no special fat burning zone that needs to be reached in order to cause the body to mainly use fat as fuel. Conversely, as long as there is more energy being burned then being consumed, fat is being burned. This plays into the law of thermodynamics.

Besides glucose, fat is a major source of fuel for exercise. The oxygen that enters the body allows for fat or carbohydrates to be burned. Fat and carbohydrates differ in the amount of oxygen use. The body uses the most fat when the respiratory exchange ratio (RER), the ratio of carbon dioxide produced to the volume of oxygen consumed, is approximately 0.71. The body uses respiratory gasses to estimate caloric expenditure. For instance, at complete rest, the amount of energy used is minimal so there is no overall loss of weight.

Muscular Strength

Example: Guidelines for a Hypertrophy Weight Training Program	
Load	67-85% IRM
# of Exercises	6-9
# of Reps per Set	6-12
# of Sets per Exercise	3-6
Rest	3-5 Minutes
Speed	Slow-Medium
Times per Week	2-4

Muscular strength is defined as the maximum amount of weight any one muscle can endure without strain. The idea of developing muscular strength focuses on increasing muscle fibers that will lead to hypertrophy (enlargement) of the muscle. This happens over time with good strength training without damaging the muscle from overexertion. The job of a personal trainer is to provide gradual intensity that leads to gradual hypertrophy of the muscles. A client trying to obtain muscular strength overnight

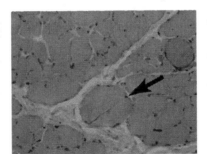

Muscle fiber hypertrophy and splitting are found here. Arrow marks split fiber. Also, see how easy it is to appreciate endomysium in this illustration. Whenever it is this prominent, it is too thick.

has unrealistic expectations and the personal trainer needs to address those expectations at the beginning of the program; otherwise, both parties will feel they failed. Another important aspect of developing muscular strength is rest between workouts. Muscles become fatigued and need rest to overcome this physiological phenomenon. Slow oxidative fibers fatigue slower than fast oxidative fibers but take twice as long to recover. The majority of muscles contain both kinds of fibers. Working out many muscle groups at one time can minimize the amount of fatigue a client will experience.

There are various levels of working out a muscle. First is the mechanical force being used, which involves the energy directly expended to produce the work necessary for the workout. Secondly, there is the neuromuscular aspect, which involves the motor units of the nerves and the muscles they innervate. Motor units are important because they allow movement and relaying of messages to the central nervous system to produce the desired movement.

The last is the metabolic activity involved. The body needs energy to produce any desired voluntary movement. If a client is not properly hydrated or does not have the proper nutrients, that client's desire is of little use. Remember, part of the trainer's job is to make sure the client is eating a diet conducive to the workout. If a client is mainly focusing on cardio, the trainer should propose eating more carbohydrates and, for a focus on strength training, a good combination of carbohydrates and protein. The trainer should suggest an increase of 5-10% of lean proteins for resistance training. Resistance training that leads to muscular strength and hypertrophy is very individual and is one of the most important aspects of personal training.

Developing a cardiovascular workout is a very general process. Once a client moves into muscular strength training, the personal trainer must develop a workout that is tailored to the client by taking a very thorough initial assessment. If a client's expectations are going to be met, the personal trainer must pay attention to what is going to work for that individual client. Trainers should find out from clients what has worked and what has not worked for them in the past. If a client has never done any resistance training, the trainer needs to make sure realistic expectations are discussed. The number one reason for failure of any workout is unrealistic expectations. Muscular strength development is

a gradual process and overworking muscles will not help clients achieve their goals any faster. Pacing is very important when building muscle and it is easy to overdo workouts because soreness, feeling out of breath and fatigue are not immediate responses to these types of training.

Example: Relationship Between Volume & Training		
Objective for Training	# of Repetitions	# of Sets
Strength	<6	2-6
Power	3-5	3-5
Hypertrophy	6-2	3-6
Endurance (Strength)	>12	2-3

Resistance training can involve several ways to strengthen muscle. Free weights, weight machines, the client's own body weight or elastic resistance are all examples of ways

to gain muscular strength via resistance. Variance helps to keep the workout fresh and keeps clients on their toes. Varying the type of resistance also gives clients a more well-rounded workout because each type of resistance mechanism will use different groups of muscles.

Another important issue of developing muscular strength is working a muscle to fatigue. This simply means that clients must do enough repetitions until they cannot do anymore, which is usually between 6-10 repetitions (depending on the strength of the client). The personal trainer must take great care to work the client's muscles to fatigue but not to exhaustion. Remember, every client is different so great attention to detail, as well as individualization of the client's workout, is very important. As a client's muscular strength increases, the trainer will have to adjust the number of repetitions. Sets are the number of times clients do their prescribed number of repetitions.

When clients start resistance training regimens, they should only work out muscles two times per week with at least a day of rest in between. There should also be proper rest between sets as well. Clients' muscles require a recovery period before being fatigued again with another set. This is why a high carbohydrate meal/snack is important before workouts and an increased protein meal after a workout and possibly even the next day is beneficial as well.

> The personal trainer must take great care to work the client's muscles to fatigue but not to exhaustion.

Endurance Conditioning

Example: Types of Aerobic Endurance Training

Types of Exercise	# of Times per Week	Length of Session	Intensity
Long, Slow Distance	1-2	30-120 Minutes (Distance of Race)	70% VO$_2$ Max
Pace/Tempo	1-2	20-30 Minutes	Lactate Threshold
Interval	1-2	3-5 Minutes (Work:Rest Ratio 1:1)	VO$_2$ Max
Repetition (Interval)	1	30-90 Seconds (Work:Rest Ratio 1:5)	VO$_2$ Max
Fartlek	1	20-60 Minutes	Variable: 70% VO$_2$ Max + bouts $\geq$ Lactate Threshold

When clients first start resistance training, their endurance will be low, meaning the amount of time they can sustain their workout will be short. As they perform their workout over time, their endurance will increase and their muscles can be worked for a longer period of time. As their endurance increases, a muscular strength workout can quickly become a cardiovascular workout and, if the client wants resistance training, this aspect needs to be carefully monitored. If this happens to a client, resistance must be increased by increasing repetitions and/or sets or the amount of weight. Endurance is important when allowing sustained movements with a load attached over a prolonged period of time.

At the beginning of a new workout regimen, a client will experience a lot of soreness due to the buildup of lactic acid that is released in the muscles from energy expenditure. As a client gains endurance, the soreness will subside because the muscles will better utilize oxygen and less lactic acid will buildup, which in turn will result in less soreness. Some clients may view this lack of soreness as an inefficient workout, which is not the case. As muscles develop, they will become less and less sore. Remember, endurance conditioning is something that should be addressed once the client is comfortable with the regimen that the trainer and client have established together.

In the beginning, the most important thing to teach a client is technique. Lack of proper technique in resistance training can lead to undue stress as well as injuries. Before endurance can begin to improve, proper technique must be obtained. If a trainer is not familiar with a particular technique of a specific type of resistance training, such as those that use elastic bands, then the trainer should not recommend the exercise until the trainer has been educated on proper form. Also, it is important to keep good records of the training the client is doing. Having individual records for each client is the best way to achieve this and will help the trainer in the future when designing different programs for the client to achieve endurance conditioning. Initial assessments are important to get started but follow-ups are more important to keep trainers and clients on track.

Endurance conditioning is important for maintaining the length-tension relationship between muscles. Instead of being over extended the muscles need to be kept in proper contraction for maximal gain. The length-tension relationship is also important to keep

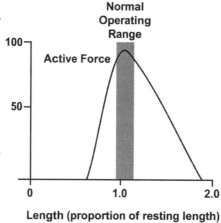

balance in order to reduce the chance of injuring joints. Stabilization is another important aspect and can be achieved with proper posture (even in non-training movements) and involves ensuring the least amount of stress is put on the joints. Muscular endurance is important in stabilization because it helps recruit muscles that are involved in prime movements, which decreases stress on the joints. If the client's muscles cannot sustain the training over an extended period of time, the client is likely to experience joint problems. The prime movers are responsible for providing force throughout the majority of the training, so they are the most important muscles that need endurance conditioning.

Endurance conditioning is a progressive process that is achieved by slowly working all muscle groups targeted and increasing load and longevity endurance over time. One positive aspect about endurance training is the finding that it does not disappear if the client misses some time from training. Cardiovascular conditioning is much faster to "lose" than muscular strength and conditioning. This makes sense because muscular conditioning takes much longer to achieve than cardiovascular conditioning. If a

176

client misses some sessions, the trainer should offer encouragement by explaining all is not lost because of the absence. Very little muscular strength and conditioning is lost over the first few months of stopping resistance training. The personal trainer should keep calling the client to reiterate the fact that little has been lost in terms of strength and conditioning.

Another interesting aspect to muscular strength and endurance conditioning is that it is much easier to maintain than cardiovascular conditioning. One report showed that, once the client's goal is met, the client only needs to resistance train every 10 to 14 days to maintain the same level of effort as long as the intensity remains the same as when the training was more frequent.

The Adaptation of Strength Training

The principle of the adaptation of strength training lies in the physiology of the human body. The body wants to remain in equilibrium so it will do what it needs to do in order to be physiologically content. During resistance training, stress is put on the body to achieve a desired look, feeling or strength. By adding this stress, the body is conditioned to want to be able to

adapt, with the end result being hypertrophy of the muscles. In cardiovascular training, the heart is a highly adaptable muscle, so cardiovascular adaptation to walking or running occurs quite fast. On the other hand, skeletal muscles are not highly adaptable and are challenged when "asked" to do things, such as lifting a heavy object. It takes much longer for these muscles to adapt to a frequent stimulus such as resistance training because, physiologically speaking, muscles do not know the difference between "training" and a transient need to take a heavy box from downstairs to upstairs. This is why achieving skeletal muscle adaptation takes much longer than achieving cardiovascular adaptation. Any hope for achieving muscular hypertrophy must be approached with patience and encouragement from the personal trainer and the client. No one can perform resistance training for a month and expect to see significant changes. Muscles need time and stimuli for adaptation to occur. The body can "instruct" the muscles to enlarge because the stimulus is not going away and the muscles will then need to adapt.

The body's need to adapt in order to maintain proper homeostasis is termed the general

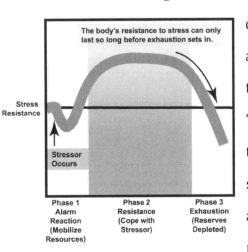

The body's resistance to stress can only last so long before exhaustion sets in.

Stress Resistance

Stressor Occurs

Phase 1
Alarm Reaction
(Mobilize Resources)

Phase 2
Resistance
(Cope with Stressor)

Phase 3
Exhaustion
(Reserves Depleted)

adaptation syndrome. According to Hans Selye, a medical doctor in the early 20th century, the body responds to stress in three different stages. The first is the alarm reaction, and it begins when the body is initially put under stress it must respond to, such as lifting weight or resistance training. In order to respond, the body needs more oxygen to produce more strength so that it can keep up with the demand. In the beginning of any new workout regimen, it can be challenging to achieve the number of repetitions and sets that are being expected. As time passes, the stress being put on the body lessens, not because the 50 pound weight is any less, but because the body is adapting over time.

The next stage is resistance development, when the body is quite efficient at recruiting muscle fibers needed to lift a load and distribute oxygen efficiently to the needed areas. At this time, resistance training can feel like a "breeze," so something needs to change to prevent a loss of hypertrophy in the muscles. The load needs to be increased and/or more repetitions added in order to add more stress that will prompt the body to move toward adaptation. The last stage is exhaustion, which the personal trainer should strive to avoid.

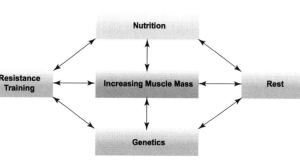

Physiologically, the body will start to shut down, which will leave your client feeling tired as well as frustrated. This is why careful individualization of a client's workout is important. Not everyone can do 3 sets of 15 repetitions lifting a 20 lb. barbell. The initial workout is the time when the personal trainer needs to discover and record the client's training limits.

In order for adaptation to occur, the body must "think" there is a reason for adaptation. This requires an interaction of three primary specificities: mechanical, neuromuscular and metabolic. Mechanical specificity involves the movements made to accommodate the specific load. Each muscle group, from the legs to the arms to the chest, has differing mechanical specificities. One person may need heavier weights being lifted at slower speeds to produce maximal results. Another person may need lighter weights at faster repetitions to achieve the best results. As a personal trainer, it is important to be educated regarding the mechanical specificities of the muscle groups.

Neuromuscular specificity has to do with the intensity of the contraction being elicited by the specific movement. The stronger the contraction, the more motor units need to be recruited.

Over time, the neuromuscular specificity will lead to hypertrophy due to the higher intensity contraction required to lift the load. The last specificity is the metabolic specificity, which has to do with the amount of energy required to sustain each workout and how that energy is utilized. It is important to understand that most resistance training uses anaerobic respiration to obtain its metabolic needs. A personal trainer must be familiar with the concepts of anaerobic respiration versus aerobic and which exercises typically use one or the other. Nutrition is very important for any person undergoing a new workout routine, especially resistance training. Stress on muscle fibers needs to be alleviated and this is accomplished through proper protein intake. Protein provides the muscles with the necessary amount of amino acids for repairs to be made.

Flexibility Training

Example of Recommendations for Flexibility Training:

- Frequency
  - 3 Days a Week—Daily
- Intensity
  - Stretch all major muscle groups and joints

- Mild discomfort may occur but not pain
- Duration
  - Hold each stretch 10-30 seconds
  - 3-5 repetitions for each stretch
  - 15-30 minutes per session
  - Can combine with other exercises: aerobic, resistance, etc.

Flexibility is the extent to which a joint passes through a normal range of motion comfortably. Flexibility training has become an important topic in maintaining a healthy lifestyle in a sedentary society. It is an organized, regular program of stretching used to elongate soft tissues without resulting in injury. Some advantages to integrating flexibility training into training programs include relieving joint stress, improving function and neuromuscular efficiency. It can also help in maintaining the normal functional length of all muscles.

In developing a flexibility training program, several instructions should be integrated. Stretching, which can occur at any time during a workout, should follow a warm-up. The increase in muscle tissue temperature decreases stiffness and encourages flexibility. It can help a client's performance so more is gained from the training. Properly executed breathing exercises reduce stress and tension in muscle tissue. It is essential that proper posture is maintained during stretches to prevent injury.

The acronym FIDM stands for frequency, intensity, duration and mode, all of which are important factors to remember when preparing flexibility programs for clients. Clients should be advised to stretch two to three times a week; however, little information reports any disadvantages to stretching every day. Intensity can be achieved by placing a client in a position of slight discomfort before maintaining stretches. The duration of stretching varies depending on which type of stretch is used, and the mode of flexibility should improve general stretching.

Types of Stretching

There is a set of guidelines that will ensure safe flexibility. The main muscle groups should be stretched to achieve balance and should be held for 10 to 60 seconds, which should be the range to achieve mild intensity. Stretches should be conducted after a proper warm-up and the range of motion should be increased steadily.

Stretches for Various Body Parts	
Neck & Head	• Flexors, extensors
Shoulder	• Forward flexion, extension, abduction, adduction • External & internal rotators • Scapular retractors & depressors
Elbow	• Extensors, flexors
Wrist & Forearm	• Supinators, pronators • Flexors, wrist extension
Hand	• Extensors, finger flexors • Abductors, thumb adductors
Lower Back, Trunk	• Forward flexion, extension, side bending, rotations hips • Forward flexion, abduction, adduction, extension • External rotation, internal rotation
Knee	• Flexors, extensors
Foot & Ankle	• Plantar flexors, dorsiflexors • Everter, inverters • Extensors, toe flexors

There are a variety of stretches that a trainer can have a client use in a flexibility training program. It is important to consider the client's individual composition and goals in the program before choosing which stretches to incorporate. This can help determine when to conduct the exercises and the intensity of the stretches to be used. Passive stretching involves outside forces to help stretches. In static stretching, flexibility is achieved with a low chance of potential injury. The muscle of interest should be held in a stretch for at least 20 seconds. Static stretching is one of the most popular stretches used in fitness training today. It is an example of corrective flexibility and uses autogenic inhibition to achieve its results. Active

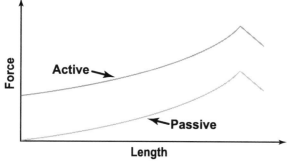

Active vs. Passive Stretching

stretching can increase the tendency of soft tissue to elongate and improve neuromuscular efficiency. Active stretching may be difficult for clients because of the mental and physical endurance needed. Passive stretching is preferred as stretches are eased. A combination of both active and passive stretching may satisfy some clients.

Ballistic Stretch   **Dynamic Stretch**

There are similarities in using ballistic and dynamic stretching. Because of the intensity of the stretches, safety should be taken into consideration when performing them. Ballistic stretching results in elongating a certain area of the body, which limits the available range of motion. Momentum plays a major role in accomplishing this action. There are certain disadvantages, which include muscle soreness and the absence of tissue adaptation. In dynamic stretching, a type of functional flexibility, momentum is used to increase the range of motion. This type of stretching can be carried out actively, passively or as an arrangement of

both. The speed of the range of motion should be controlled to prevent injury. Both of these types of stretching can be used for clients who are athletes and preparing for sporting activities. However, caution should be practiced in using them for the general population.

Proprioceptive neuromuscular facilitation (PNF) seeks to increase the range of motion at joints by incorporating both active and passive stretching. Three main methods are used: contract-relax (CR), contract-relax with agnostic contraction (CRAC) and contract-relax with a passive stretch (CRAC-P). In CR, clients experience little tension when increasing the degree of the contraction over a given period of time. After the contraction is maximized, passive force is used. CRAC is like CR, but it uses an active stretch rather than passive forces after maximum contraction is used. CRAC-P is similar to CRAC but incorporates a passive force to complete the technique. PNF can work best for clients who are somewhat fit and willing to challenge themselves with this intense training; however, any client can engage in this vigorous training if the trainer is knowledgeable in the subject area. The trainer should also consider the client's limits.

Active-isolated stretching integrates an active stretch that then uses passive force followed by static stretching. The opposite muscle to the targeted muscle is contracted to isolate the targeted one, then the targeted muscle is relaxed. Afterward, a passive force, like the trainer, is used to assist clients in finishing the stretching.

Things to Avoid

Flexibility training is also important in promoting neuromuscular efficiency. To achieve this efficiency, correct flexibility in all planes of motion—sagittal, frontal and transverse—is needed. Flexibility training must be an integrated program that incorporates a variety of flexibility techniques. In developing a useful program, the muscular, nervous and skeletal system can be thought of as a kinetic chain. Each system works together to ensure balance.

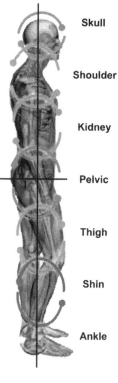

Skull
Shoulder
Kidney
Pelvic
Thigh
Shin
Ankle

Any misalignment or damage to one system can impact the effectiveness of the other systems. This can lead to decreased neuromuscular efficiency and overuse type of injuries. Muscle imbalances may result from improper posture or technique or injury. Pattern overload, where the same pattern of motion is repeated, may also contribute to muscle imbalance, which leads to interferences within the kinetic chain.

When injury occurs in the body, it can lead to inflammation and reduced elasticity of soft tissue. This idea is based on Davis's law, which proposes that soft tissue rebuilds itself along the lines of stress. The soft tissue is rebuilt with inelastic collagen, usually inconsistent with the direction of muscle fibers. This tissue can later prevent the muscle fibers from elongating properly and results in reduced flexibility.

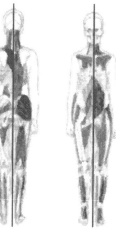

Tight Muscles   Weak Muscles

The reduced inelasticity of soft tissue leads to altered length-tension relationships and altered force-couple relationships. It can also result in arthokinetic dysfunction, which changes joint motion. All of these alterations lead to muscle imbalances.

Postural Muscle Imbalances

Arthritis affects approximately 66 million Americans and contributes to inflammation and damage of joints. The two most prevalent types are osteoarthritis and rheumatoid arthritis; however, more than 100 types exist. Osteoarthritis damages the cartilage of bones overtime, while the immune system tears down joint surfaces in rheumatoid arthritis. People

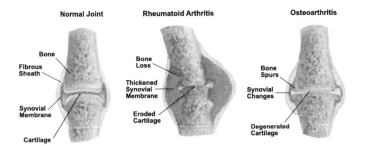

Normal Joint — Bone, Fibrous Sheath, Synovial Membrane, Cartilage

Rheumatoid Arthritis — Bone Loss, Thickened Synovial Membrane, Eroded Cartilage

Osteoarthritis — Bone Spurs, Synovial Changes, Degenerated Cartilage

with this condition are advised to conduct flexibility techniques one to two times a day. Warm-ups should be extended to ensure that joints are not stiff. Those who are on current anti-inflammatory medications should be monitored for stress levels.

Clients with osteoporosis and osteopenia are losing bone density and are at a higher risk for bone fractures. In performing flexibility training, clients should steer clear of repetitive exercises that use spinal twisting. Exercises that encourage proper posture and spinal alignment should be practiced. For those clients who have had a hip fracture or replacement, exercises should include internal rotation of the hip, hip adduction and hip flexion.

There are times when clients should be advised not to stretch, such as during the first day to three days after a muscular or tendonous trauma. Training should not take place after any muscle or ligament sprains have occurred or if joints or muscles are infected. Stop training if any discomfort is felt or if there is pain in the joint or muscle when exercising.

Distal Biceps Tendon Rupture

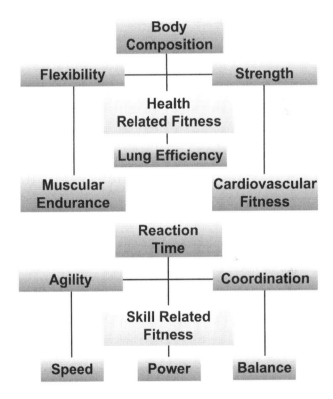

Balance, Agility, Speed

Everyday activities and sporting activities require balance, stabilization and coordination. For the body to master skills of movement, there is a constant need to change direction and movement. Also known as skill-related components of fitness, these factors are key in athletic endeavors and allow individuals to move accurately, quickly and efficiently. Skill-related

Body Composition

Flexibility — Strength

Health Related Fitness

Lung Efficiency

Muscular Endurance

Cardiovascular Fitness

Reaction Time

Agility — Coordination

Skill Related Fitness

Speed — Power — Balance

Health and Skill Related Fitness

fitness components are therefore stressed when performance enhancement is the primary goal. When used appropriately, balance, agility and speed can create a synergy of muscle responses.

In turn, this can lead to a decreased risk of injury due to an increased ability to react to changes in the environment. Persons engaging in activities that require skill-related fitness components will benefit greatly from a warm-up.

Balance

Balance, the first and most fundamental component of biomechanical function, is one of the major factors in sports performance. Balance is defined as the ability to maintain a certain position for a given amount of time without a change in movement. It involves being able to maintain stability, even through motion, environmental changes and gravity. Many activities rely on the maintenance of balance to successfully complete the exercise, which involves a constant interplay between losing and regaining balance. This is important not only in activities that require standing positions but also in sitting positions.

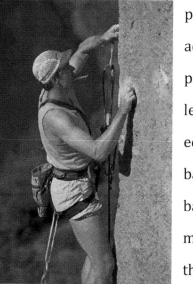

Balance is affected by three major principles: center of gravity, base support, and the relationship between center of gravity and base support. The lower the center of gravity and the larger the base support, the smaller the amount of balance that is needed. Furthermore, the closer a person's center of gravity is to their base support, the smaller the amount of balance needed.

Static, Peripheral and Dynamic Balance

The most basic aspect of balance is static balance. It is the ability to maintain central balance, or equilibrium, while balancing on one foot. Static balance is essential for activities that require prolonged periods of static positioning (e.g., rock climbing). The ability to balance and reach away from the center of gravity is called peripheral balance. This is usually accomplished with reaching some part of the body, such as the arms, legs or torso, while maintaining equilibrium. Conversely, dynamic balance is the ability to maintain balance while in motion. While in motion, the body gains feedback through visual stimuli, kinesthetic awareness and changes made by the nervous system. Even standing still is an exercise in dynamic balance since the body is constantly swaying to all sides and balance is maintained through alternate contraction and relaxation of the leg muscles.

Balance Training

Balance training prepares athletes to perform when the center of mass moves outside of the base support. It has also been adopted to try and prevent injuries to the ankles and knee joints during sports and other activities. Balance can be trained during an exercise by constantly standing, walking or sitting on an uneven or unstable surface. Appropriate balance training should then stress an individual's limits of stability, which in turn increases the awareness of the limit of stability by creating instability. Within balance training, the use of balance equipment can be used to create balance challenges in multiple planes of motion. Equipment can improve reaction times and dynamic functional use of core muscles.

Patients can balance on one foot on a wobble board to enhance dynamic ankle stability for training or ankle sprain rehabilitation.

Traditional training does not challenge the sensory mechanisms of the kinetic chain and balance training fills the gaps. It improves dynamic joint stabilization or, in other words, the ability of the kinetic chain to stabilize a joint during movement. There are three levels of balance training that are similar to the three levels of traditional training programs. The first one is stabilization, which comprises exercises involving joint motions aimed at improving stability of the joints. In this level, exercises are all based around positions where the body is unstable, such as when standing on one leg. The second level is strength. Balance exercises for strength are dynamic eccentric and concentric movements through a full range of motion. This ultimately improves the neuromuscular efficiency of the entire kinetic chain. The third and last level is power. Power exercises increase endurance, reactive joint stabilization, neuromuscular efficiency and eccentric strength.

Balance training is especially important for older adults. This group of individuals tends to lose lean body mass and is therefore more prone to injury from falling. Initially, a trainer should identify a client's current balance threshold before starting an activity-specific program. There are specific tests to determine balance deficiencies. The simplest of these is the Romberg test in which a client stands with the feet together and eyes closed. The loss of balance is then checked. For a more difficult test, a client conducts this test while standing on only one leg, which is referred to as a stork stand.

Another test that measures balance in elderly persons is the functional reach test. As shown in the diagram, a client rests one fist on a wall while leaning as far forward

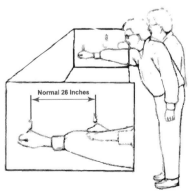

Normal 26 Inches

as possible. The client then moves the fist along the wall as far as possible without taking a step or off-balancing, and the distance that the fist moved is measured. A movement of less than six inches means that there is a lack of balance and thus a higher risk of falling.

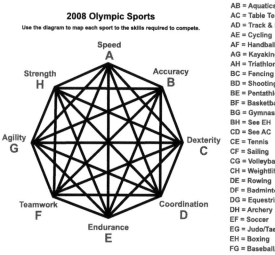

2008 Olympic Sports
Use the diagram to map each sport to the skills required to compete.

AB = Aquatics
AC = Table Tennis
AD = Track & Field
AE = Cycling
AF = Handball
AG = Kayaking
AH = Triathlon
BC = Fencing
BD = Shooting
BE = Pentathlon
BF = Basketball
BG = Gymnastics
BH = See EH
CD = See AC
CE = Tennis
CF = Sailing
CG = Volleyball
CH = Weightlifing
DE = Rowing
DF = Badminton
DG = Equestrian
DH = Archery
EF = Soccer
EG = Judo/Taekwondo
EH = Boxing
FG = Baseball/Softball
FH = Hockey
GH = Wrestling

Coordination and Speed

There is a direct relationship between coordination and speed. Movements at varying speeds produce differential demands for the control of ongoing movements. Often, these ongoing movements need to be precise and coordinated in order to conduct the desired motion. To understand how each skill-related fitness component relates to each other, it is essential to be aware of importance of coordination and speed in human activity.

"Strength and speed are useful, son, but coordination is crucial!"

Coordination

Nearly all human movement occurs through multiple joints and muscle groups. When the body undergoes a new movement, the neuromuscular system limits the ability of the body to conduct a specific activity. This leads to awkward and clumsy movement. It therefore takes many tries to become familiar with the activity. Coordination is the ability to use multiple areas of the muscles and joints at the same time while accurately performing motor functions. Coordination complements other skills like speed, agility and balance.

Specific requirements of coordinated movement include several factors. Activity perception is the basic element of coordination and is the awareness of volitional muscle activity or joint positioning. Any activity performed is evaluated by the central nervous system. The learning process involved in the development of coordinated movement is considered feedback. Likewise, the activity becomes more accurate with repetition and adjustments. Repetition thus allows the performance to become more consistent. This is a major requirement for development of total coordination, which is when activity becomes automatic and is no longer a conscious process.

During athletic performance, coordination allows for some muscles to be stimulated to provide activity while allowing other muscle groups to be inhibited to permit the activity. If a muscle is too weak to provide a necessary response, activity will be uncoordinated. Lastly, inhibition is important since it is necessary for undesired muscle activity or unwanted muscle responses to be cut down for coordinated activity.

There are two major types of coordination: intramuscular coordination and intermuscular coordination. Intramuscular coordination is the ability of the neuromuscular system to allow for an optimal level of motor function. Muscles of the core-stabilization system need sustained contraction to improve intramuscular coordination. Intermuscular coordination is the ability of the neuromuscular system to allow muscles to work together. Muscles of the core-movement system (e.g., hamstrings, adductors) must work synergistically with the stabilization system to ensure optimal coordination.

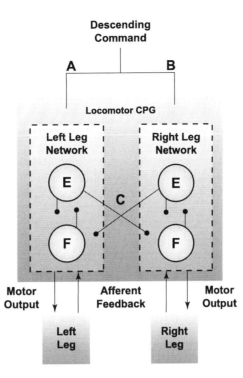

Agility

Agility is the ability to rapidly change body position with speed and accuracy. Believed to be influenced by heredity, this skill is integral to explosively start, accelerate, decelerate and change direction while maintaining control of the body and speed. Though there is a lack of agreement with the precise definition of agility, agility has relationships with trainable physical qualities such as strength, power and technique and it has cognitive components such as anticipation. Agility is related to coordination since it is often referred to as the ability to coordinate several sports-specific activities at once (e.g., dribbling a basketball while running). Agility is also aligned with balance in that it requires the body to regulate shifts in the body's center of gravity. Activities such as climbing, skiing and snowboarding all require large amounts of agility. These sports especially require agility of the lower extremities. Upper-extremity agility is required for activities that require accurate movement of the fingers and hands.

Agility Training

Agility training can be very intense and it places stress on joints, connective tissues and tendons. Aerobic conditioning and regular exercise in a balance and strengthening program should be performed before starting a strenuous agility program. If a client is interested in improved agility for a specific sport, activities that test the client's agility should closely resemble that activity. The primary effect of training is to increase body control. It is focused on controlling motor control in the neck, shoulder, back, hip, knee and ankle joints. Agility tests are similar to conditioning and practice drills used in various sports (e.g., zigzag runs, hexagonal jump).

Sensory Function

Agility, balance and coordination are controlled by proprioceptors of the sensory system. Proprioception is the ability to transmit position sense, interpret sensory information and respond to it, all in order to execute conscious or unconscious movement. This is fundamental to accurate performance and plays an important role in motor skills and the ability to master specific tasks.

Proprioceptors are the specific afferent nerves that receive and send impulses throughout the body and are thus responsible for the neuromuscular control, or proprioception. Found in the skin, joints, muscles, tendons and ligaments, these nerves maintain posture and balance, awareness of joint position and movement. They create the ability to change direction of movement and contribute to coordination to produce activity. Receptors within the skin are known as cutaneous receptors and are either considered fast-adapting receptors or slow-adapting receptors. Fast-adapting receptors are responsible for vibration sense and sudden changes in speed and movement. Slow-adapting receptors are responsible for sensory perceptions like skin stretching as well as joint and limb position. Cutaneous receptors are not thought to play a major role in proprioception but rather to provide cues regarding small sensory perception.

Proprioceptors of the joints lie within the connective tissue of a joint's capsule. Joint receptors respond to high velocity changes when the joint accelerates or decelerates and they identify joint compression. Muscle spindles and Golgi tendon organs are the major receptors

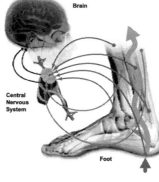

188

of the muscles and tendons used to detect tension within the muscles. These receptors respond to muscle contraction, which can then result in muscle relaxation. Muscle spindles respond to the stretch of a muscle and then act to contract it. Proprioceptors are also found in the knee and are generally not active in the middle ranges of movement, but they are activated when ligaments are stressed. This produces an inhibitory response to the agonistic muscles.

Speed

Precision of speed is fundamental to coordination. Increasing the speed of athletic performance is a way to advance the difficulty of coordination exercises. In other words, in order to be effective, speed must be accomplished by coordination. Speed implies acceleration from a starting position. Speed of the muscles is also limited by neuromuscular coordination. The neuronal system has a specific range of speed within which the body is allowed to move.

Reactive training improves the range of speed. It is comprised of quick and powerful movements, involving eccentric contraction and then concentric contraction. It begins with less demanding exercises. As the body adapts, training progresses to more demanding exercises, which increase the reaction time of muscle actions. This is similar to other forms of training. Short runs are often used to evaluate speed.

Summary

Balance, agility, speed and coordination are all skill-related fitness components that, if improved, can lead to enhanced athletic performance. Balance is the body's ability to maintain equilibrium by controlling the body's center of gravity over its base support and is necessary for both static and dynamic activities. Coordination is a complex process in which motion of the body is conducted through a combination of muscle groups working together with appropriate timing. Coordination often requires agility, which is the ability to control the direction of the body or body parts during movement. Proprioception encompasses the

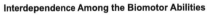

Interdependence Among the Biomotor Abilities

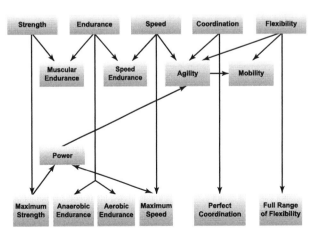

body's sensory function and is important to sustain proper agility, balance and coordination. Proprioception is the body's ability to transmit afferent information regarding position sense, to interpret this information and to respond to it accordingly. To varying degrees, receptors of the skin, muscle, tendons, joints and ligaments all influence proprioception.

Review Questions

1. What is cardiorespiratory conditioning?__

   _____

   _____

2. The progression from a lower intensity level to a higher intensity level, longer duration, and/or increased frequency of exercise is known as _____

   _____

   _____

3. Fat burning can only occur through extreme cardiovascular exercise. True or False? ___

   _____

4. What form of strength training leads to muscle hypertrophy? _____

   _____

   _____

5. A short duration of activity that precedes major exercise is:

   a) Cool-down

   b) Stretching

   c) Warm-up

6. Flexibility is how far and how easily one can move the joints. True or False? _____

   _____

7. What are some physical benefits to improving flexibility? _____

   _____

   _____

8. Passive stretching requires additional mental and physical endurance compared to active stretching. True or False? _____

   _____

9. What is the first and most fundamental component of biomechanical function in sports performance?_____

   _____

   _____

10. Speed play only works with individuals who are at an optimal level of physical fitness. True or False? _____

Answers

1. Cardiorespiratory conditioning is an activity used to improve the body's ability to process and deliver oxygen by using intense movements and activities that stimulate the cardiovascular system.

2. Smart progression.

3. False.

4. Resistance training.

5. c) Warm-up.

6. False.

7. Relieving joint stress, improving function and neuromuscular efficiency, and maintaining the normal functional length of all muscles.

8. False.

9. Balance.

10. False.

References

Carson RG. Changes in muscle coordination with training. *Journal of Applied Physiology*. 2006;101(5):1506-13.

Chatara M et al. Effect of concurrent endurance and circuit resistance training sequence on muscular strength and power development. *Journal of Strength and Conditioning Research*. 2008;22(4):1037-45.

Davis WJ, Wood DT, Andrews RG, Elkind LM, Davis WB. Concurrent training enhances athletes' cardiovascular and cardiorespiratory measures. *Journal of Strength and Conditioning Research*. 2008;22(5):1503-14.

Hawkins MN, Raven PB, Snell PG, Stray-Gundersen J, Levine BD. Maximal oxygen uptake as a parametric measure of cardiorespiratory capacity. *Medicine and Science in Sports and Exercise*. 2007;39(1):103-07.

Henatsch HD, Langer HH. Basic neurophysiology of motor skills in sport: a review. *International Journal of Sports Medicine*. 1985;6(1):2-14.

Hrysomallis C. Relationship between balance ability, training and sports injury risk. *Sports Medicine*. 2007;37(6):547-56.

Kallinen M, Markku A. Aging, physical activity and sports injuries. An overview of common sports injuries in the elderly. *Sports Medicine*. 1995;20(1):41-52.

Lephart SM, Henry TJ. Functional rehabilitation for the upper and lower extremity. *The Orthopedic Clinics of North America*. 1995;26(3):579-92.

McNeal JR, Sands WA. Stretching for performance enhancement. *Current Sports Medicine Reports*. 2006;5(3):141-46.

Rubini EC, Costa AL, Gomes PS. The effects of stretching on strength performance. *Sports Medicine*. 2007;37(3):213-24.

Sheppard JM, Young WB. Agility literature review: classifications, training and testing. *Journal of Sports Science*. 2006;24(9):919-32.

Woods K, Bishop P, Jones E. Warm-up and stretching in the prevention of muscular injury. *Sports Medicine*. 2007;37(12):1089-99.

Chapter 7: Warning Signs

Topics Covered

The Warning Signs that Can Mean Trouble

Muscle Cramps
Dehydration
Heat Exhaustion
Heat Stroke

How to Respond to Various Events

Dehydration that Leads to a Loss of Performance and Energy
Dehydration and Muscle Cramps
Heat Exhaustion that Causes Light-headedness, Dizziness and Cold, Clammy Skin
Heat Exhaustion that Causes Nausea and Headaches
Heat Stroke, High Body Temperature and Dry Skin
Heat Stroke that Causes Confusion and Unconsciousness

The Warning Signs that Can Mean Trouble

There are general warning signs that indicate when the body needs a break or that an individual may be training too hard. The early warning signs can be put into three groups: life signs, training signs and health signs. Life signs include loss of interest in activities that the individual normally enjoys, increased irritability, tension, anger and sleeping problems. Training signs that may appear are deterioration in performance, cutting sessions short, abnormal muscle soreness after training, fatigue that lasts during the workout and remains throughout the day, and loss of motivation to train. Health signs include aches and pains throughout the body, increased resting heart rate and/or blood pressure, loss of appetite, nausea and head colds.

Warning Signs that the Body Needs a Break or the Individual is Training Too Hard

Life Signs	Training Signs	Health Signs
Loss of interest in normally enjoyable activities	Deterioration in performance	Aches and pains throughout the body
Increased irritability	Cutting sessions short	Increased resting heart rate and/or blood pressure

Warning Signs that the Body Needs a Break or the Individual is Training Too Hard

Life Signs	Training Signs	Health Signs
Increased tension	Abnormal muscle soreness after training	Loss of appetite
Increased anger	Fatigue during the workout which remains throughout the day	Nausea
Increased sleeping problems	Loss of motivation	Head colds
May indicate an unregulated/undiagnosed mood disorder	May indicate undiagnosed neuromuscular disorder	May indicate undiagnosed neuromuscular disorder

If these warning signs are not properly heeded, the individual may develop muscle cramps, dehydration, heat exhaustion or heat stroke. Severe complications like these can be avoided by ensuring the exercise regimen does not cause the individual to over train and allows for a recovery period, which is the time for muscles to rest and rejuvenate. While it is important to be observant and watch for these signs, it is also important to keep the client motivated. When starting any new training program, the trainer should tell the client to expect some level of discomfort until getting used to the exercise regimen. Life signs are important because they can be indicative of an unregulated or undiagnosed mood disorder. Training and health signs may be an indication that there is a neuromuscular disorder that has not been checked by a physician. If the personal trainer notices any of the signs above, the trainer should strongly recommend that the client make an appointment with a clinician.

If warning signs are not properly heeded, individual may experience:

- Muscle cramps
- Dehydration
- Heat exhaustion
- Heat stroke

Do the following to help the individual:

- Make sure exercise regimen does not cause overtraining
- Exercise regimen should allow for a recovery period (muscle to rest and rejuvenate)
- Keep the client motivated
- Tell the client to expect some level of discomfort when starting a new program
- If any of the three warning signs are seen, personal trainer should recommend client see a clinician

Muscle Cramps

During exercise, the muscles needed to perform particular movements contract and relax. Even muscles that support the head, neck and back contract to maintain proper posture during exercise. A muscle spasm is caused when a muscle or a few of its muscle fibers contracts involuntarily when it should not be contracting. If the spasm persists for an extended period of time and increases in intensity, it becomes a muscle cramp. In other words, a muscle cramp

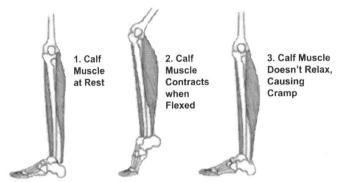

1. Calf Muscle at Rest

2. Calf Muscle Contracts when Flexed

3. Calf Muscle Doesn't Relax, Causing Cramp

occurs when a muscle involuntarily contracts with an intense force and does not relax right away. Muscle cramps can last for a few seconds, up to 15 minutes or even longer in some cases. Such involuntary contractions cause palpable and visible hardening of the muscles that are cramping. Cramps sometimes cause no pain or can be felt as mild twitching within the muscle, or they can be so bad that they cause extreme pain. Cramps that occur during or after training usually produce abrupt and severe pain.

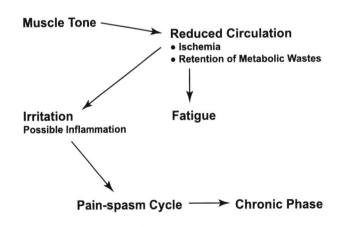

Muscle Tone → Reduced Circulation
- Ischemia
- Retention of Metabolic Wastes

Irritation
Possible Inflammation

Fatigue

Pain-spasm Cycle → Chronic Phase

Cramps typically occur in the skeletal muscles of the hands, legs, feet, thighs, the arch of the foot and, most often, in the calves (commonly referred to as a charley horse). Each of these muscles can be controlled voluntarily. Involuntary muscles that make up organs such as the uterus, intestinal tract, urine and bile passages, bronchial tubes and blood vessel walls can also cramp. Cramps develop during several conditions, which include improper stretching before exercising, muscle fatigue, exercising in extremely warm temperatures, and electrolyte imbalances of phosphate, sodium, chloride, potassium or calcium.

Hydration is important in reducing muscle cramping because, as we sweat, we lose electrolytes, such as sodium and potassium, along with water, which creates an imbalance that can then lead to cramping. Pickle juice is sometimes given to athletes who are experiencing cramping for the simple reason that it contains so much sodium that it can help restore some of the lost sodium and relieve cramping. Gatorade is also used for this reason. Athletes who sweat a lot can replenish the sodium and potassium they have lost through sweating by drinking Gatorade or any other electrolyte-based drink. Electrolyte

Pickle juice is sometimes given to athletes who are experiencing cramping.

imbalances lead to muscle cramping because sodium and potassium are the main electrolytes utilized during exertion. For every two sodium molecules pumped out of your muscle cells, three are pumped back in—it is this mechanism that keeps the muscles contracting properly and not over-contracting, which can lead to muscle cramps.

Dehydration

Even when the temperature is not very hot, many people get dehydrated because they rely on their thirst to signal when they should drink water during a workout. A large amount of bodily fluid is lost during exercise and this fluid must be replaced by drinking water periodically. Sweating is the body's main cooling mechanism, but overexertion, coupled with neglecting to supply the body with an adequate amount of liquid, can lead to dehydration. Dehydration causes a deterioration of both mental and physical performance during a workout. The symptoms of dehydration include a decrease in sweating, an increase in body temperature, heat distress, severe fatigue, unconsciousness and, in some cases, death. If athletes exercising only stop for water breaks when they feel thirsty, they will more than likely become dehydrated. By the time they feel thirsty, they may have already lost one to two liters (a quarter to half gallon) of bodily fluid and by this point it may take more than a few water breaks to replenish the body.

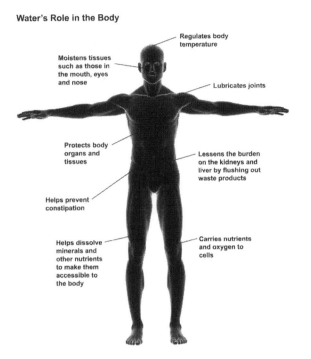

Water's Role in the Body

Regulates body temperature

Moistens tissues such as those in the mouth, eyes and nose

Lubricates joints

Protects body organs and tissues

Lessens the burden on the kidneys and liver by flushing out waste products

Helps prevent constipation

Helps dissolve minerals and other nutrients to make them accessible to the body

Carries nutrients and oxygen to cells

Exercising produces heat in the body. Overheating can be avoided when the body properly transfers heat to the surface of the skin in water droplets that form sweat and evaporate when they come in contact with the air. If fluids are not replaced during exercise, the body will lose its ability to remove heat through water evaporation. In addition, if an individual who is exercising and not drinking liquid continues to sweat, the level of water in the blood decreases and the blood thickens. This thickening of the blood places a strain on the heart by causing it to pump more rapidly in order to maintain adequate blood flow to muscles and organs

that are being utilized during the workout. The thickening of blood also means a decrease in blood volume and blood flow to the skin. As a result, water and heat cannot be transported to the skin and removed by sweating, and this condition causes the body temperature to rise. This form of heat stress can lead to severe dehydration, unconsciousness and, in some cases, death.

Dehydration
serious effects

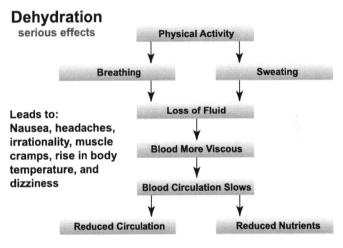

Leads to:
Nausea, headaches, irrationality, muscle cramps, rise in body temperature, and dizziness

Physical Activity

Breathing

Sweating

Loss of Fluid

Blood More Viscous

Blood Circulation Slows

Reduced Circulation

Reduced Nutrients

Performing high intensity exercises in hot, humid areas often leads to dehydration, but exercising for prolonged periods of time in cool areas can also cause significant fluid loss.

Effects of Increasing Dehydration on Physical Performance	
Body Water Loss	Effects
0.5%	Increased strain on the heart
1%	Reduced aerobic endurance
3%	Reduced muscular endurance
4%	Reduced muscle strength; reduced fine motor skills; heat cramps
5%	Heat exhaustion; cramping; fatigue; reduced mental capacity
6%	Physical exhaustion; heatstroke; coma

Brief bouts of dehydration have been shown to decrease mental and physical performance while prolonged dehydration can cause problems with judgment, reaction time, making decisions and concentration. When exercising in cooler climates or during the winter months, people need to be conscious of the fact that the cooler weather does not mean dehydration cannot occur. People often associate profuse sweating with dehydration, but in cooler climates sweating can be more insidious. Also, in colder climates people tend to layer on clothing to work out—this can lead to more sweating and, because the extra clothing can absorb more sweat, this can lead to inconspicuous dehydration.

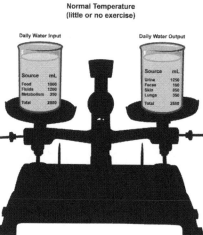

Normal Temperature (little or no exercise)

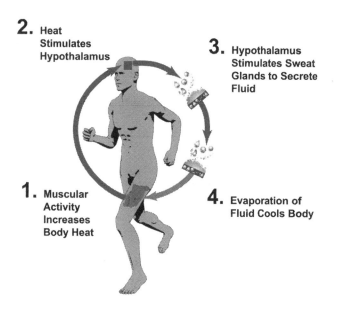

2. Heat Stimulates Hypothalamus

3. Hypothalamus Stimulates Sweat Glands to Secrete Fluid

1. Muscular Activity Increases Body Heat

4. Evaporation of Fluid Cools Body

The thirst center in the hypothalamus of the brain sends signals of thirst when the body has lost a significant amount of fluid; therefore, when clients feel thirsty, they are already on their way to dehydration. The best way to prevent dehydration is to drink water all day long. Simply drinking water right before a workout or even during a workout is not the best scenario to avoid dehydration. Staying hydrated throughout the day is the best advice a personal trainer can give their clients. Drinking electrolyte-based drinks (e.g., Gatorade) after a workout is a good way to replenish the fluids a client has lost. It is not a good idea to recommend electrolyte-based drink consumption during the day because most clients are not likely to be losing electrolytes and may end up with an over-abundance of sodium and potassium, which is not desired either.

There are other sources of water loss that are termed senseless, meaning that the person losing water is unaware of the water loss. The greatest senseless water loss comes from the respiratory system. Air is breathed in, warmed and moistened in the upper respiratory tract and then makes its way to the lungs to supply the body with oxygen. When we breathe out, our breath is humidified, meaning there is water in the air, so we lose water. Obviously, when we exercise, we breathe more frequently; therefore, more water is lost. This additional water loss can also contribute to dehydration. It is important to remind clients of all aspects of water loss as many people do not realize they can become dehydrated even if they are not sweating.

Heat Exhaustion

Heat exhaustion normally occurs when an individual is playing, working or exercising in a hot and humid area that causes extensive sweating and overheating. The individual's body temperature may be noticeably elevated but usually does not rise above 104°F. The normal

Heat Index Table													
Relative Humidity (%)													
Temp °F	40	45	50	55	60	65	70	75	80	85	90	95	100
110	136												
108	130	137											
106	124	130	137										
104	119	124	131	137									
102	114	119	124	130	137								
100	109	114	118	124	129	136							
98	105	109	113	117	123	128	134						
96	101	104	108	112	116	121	126	132					
94	97	100	102	106	110	114	119	124	129	135			
92	94	96	99	101	105	108	112	116	121	126	131		
90	91	93	95	97	100	103	106	109	113	117	122	127	132
88	88	89	91	93	95	98	100	103	106	110	113	117	121
86	85	87	88	89	91	93	95	97	100	102	105	108	112
84	83	84	85	86	88	89	90	92	94	96	98	100	103
82	81	82	83	84	84	85	86	88	89	90	91	93	95
80	80	80	81	81	82	82	83	84	84	85	86	86	87

With Prolonged Exposure and/or Physical Activity	Extreme Danger: Heat Stroke or Sunstroke Likely	Caution: Fatigue Possible
	Extreme Caution: Sunstroke, Muscle Cramps, and/or Heat Exhaustion Possible	Danger: Sunstroke, Muscle Cramps, and/or Heat Exhaustion Likely

body temperature is 98.6°F. An individual's body temperature slightly increases with activity. Performing exercise in a hot and humid area causes the body temperature to rise too quickly. In this case, the amount of water lost through sweating cannot be replaced quickly enough to keep the body temperature from rising. When exercising in a humid area, the body not only loses water through sweating but also loses electrolytes such as sodium.

Signs of Heat Exhaustion:

- Individual looks pale
- Moist skin
- Sweats profusely
- Increased pulse
- May have a headache
- May feel dizzy
- May be nauseous
- May have weakness
- May experience muscle cramps
- Body will be able to self-regulate its temperature

When fluid and electrolytes are not replaced quickly, the body's circulatory system works inadequately and the body undergoes a mild form of shock. An individual who is suffering from heat exhaustion will start to look pale, develop moist skin, begin to sweat profusely and have an increased pulse rate. The individual may get a headache, experience muscle cramps, and feel dizzy, nauseous, and/or weak. The main difference between heat exhaustion and heat stroke is the temperature of the body. When a person is suffering from heat exhaustion, they are still able to cool down if they are taken into a cool place and are able to relax long enough to let the body self regulate its temperature. During heat stroke, the body is beyond self-regulation. Heat stroke is a very dangerous condition.

Heat Stroke

Signs of Heat Stroke:

- Body can no longer control its temperature
- Body can no longer sweat
- Brain damage can occur
- Damage to vital organs can occur
- Body temperature is 105°F or higher
- Deterioration in mental performance
- Confusion
- Dizziness
- Hallucinations
- Unconsciousness
- Coma is even possible
- Skin is flushed, hot and dry
- Individual may hyperventilate
- May have high blood pressure and then have it drop dramatically

A heat stroke is a life-threatening medical condition/medical emergency. A heat stroke occurs when an individual's body is no longer able to control its temperature. The brain

regulates the body's ability to sweat but, during a heat stroke, the cooling system stops working. A heat stroke usually occurs when an individual is performing strenuous activity under extremely hot conditions. The inability of the body to control an elevated temperature can lead to brain damage and damage to vital organs. When a heat stroke occurs, an individual's body temperature can be 105°F or higher.

Heat strokes often develop rapidly; however, there are several indicators, including deterioration in mental performance, confusion, dizziness, hallucinations, unconsciousness, and/or coma. In addition, the skin becomes flushed, hot and dry. The person may also hyperventilate and have high blood pressure that then drops dramatically after a short period of time. Medical problems and medication that inhibit a person from sweating properly can predispose them to heat strokes. Infants and elderly persons have a higher heat stroke risk than children and adults but, regardless of age, individuals who are training under strenuous conditions should be closely monitored.

When living in a hot or humid environment, as well as during the summer months, personal trainers need to monitor their clients very carefully and avoid putting them in situations that would cause heat exhaustion and, most importantly, heat stroke. When taking the client's initial assessment, the personal trainer should take great care to ensure the client provides an accurate description of medications since some medications may elicit or predispose the client to heat stroke. For example, antihistamines are commonly used to control allergies and are a fairly frequent over-the-counter or prescription medication taken for seasonal allergies or an allergic reaction. Antihistamines lessen and/or prevent an allergic reaction by blocking the body's anti-inflammatory response. In part this is accomplished by decreasing bodily secretions (many people taking antihistamines complain of a dry mouth). A side effect of this response is that people taking antihistamines may sweat less. As previously noted, sweating is the body's way of getting rid of excess heat and maintaining a body temperature below 104°F. Therefore, the side effect of decreased sweating with antihistamines can leave clients prone to overheating. Typically, allergies are a problem in warmer weather, so it is more likely that a client will be taking an antihistamine during the warmer months. The most common over-the-counter antihistamine is Benadryl, and many of the prescription medications given for allergies are antihistamines.

Sweating leads to a loss of electrolytes and fluids and then to dehydration.

Education on the part of the personal trainer regarding common medications is important for this very reason. As stated previously, it is not the job of the personal trainer to provide medical advice on medications; however, it is important to recognize medications that may influence the client's workout regimen. Other common medications a client may be taking are those used to regulate hypertension, also known as high blood pressure. Many times, hypertension medications are classified as diuretics, which cause the person to sweat more frequently. Remember, sweating leads to a loss of electrolytes and fluids and then to dehydration. If a client is taking any medication for hypertension, the personal trainer should know the type of medication and become educated on the mechanism of the medicine's action. If the medicine is a diuretic, the client needs to be educated about the importance of staying hydrated throughout the day, especially on workout days and, more importantly, during the summer months.

How to Respond to Various Events

Dehydration that Leads to a Loss of Performance and Energy

If a client or the trainer notices a loss of energy, decreased performance, and/or dehydration during the client's workout, the client should drink liquids that contain electrolytes and carbohydrates. Carbonated beverages (e.g., soda) should be avoided as they may cause gastrointestinal  problems, flatulence and abdominal cramps. Sports drinks usually contain 6% carbohydrates that the body can easily absorb. Carbohydrates prevent flatulence that can be caused by carbonated drinks. Water transports nutrients to cells and removes waste from cells. Water also acts as a skin lubricant (sweat) that helps maintain an optimal body temperature by removing heat from the body during a workout.

Water accounts for 60% of the total body weight. Muscles and organs consist of approximately 70% water, so adequate water levels in the body should be maintained at all times. The body loses water in several ways. For example, water is lost through breathing because exhaled breath is moist. It is also lost through the skin, even when an individual is not sweating, and it is removed from the body through waste and urine. Drinking sufficient amounts of water daily ensures that the body is always properly hydrated and that its water reserves are full. Unfortunately, most people drink when they are feeling thirsty, not realizing that thirst is an indicator that dehydration has already occurred. Drinking fixed amounts of liquids periodically can prevent the development of dehydration.

Dehydration and Muscle Cramps

When a cramp develops during an exercise regimen and the individual is also dehydrated, the individual should immediately stop exercising and massage the muscle that is cramping. Gently stretching the muscle that

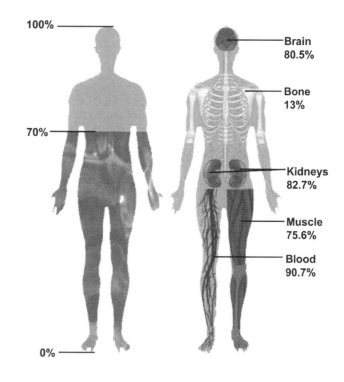

is cramping until it stops cramping is another solution. If an individual's leg begins to cramp while lying down, putting weight on the leg and walking around may relieve the cramp. Sometimes, consuming a sports drink that contains sodium helps relieve muscle cramps by restoring electrolyte levels. The sports drink also begins to rehydrate the body. Properly warming up and stretching before working out, particularly focusing on muscles that normally cramp, can help to avoid muscle cramps and the recurrence of cramps. Staying hydrated before and during a workout can also prevent muscle cramps.

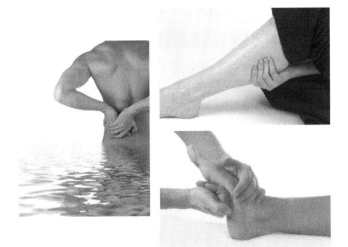

Dehydration is an important aspect in muscle cramps, but muscle fatigue is also a common cause of muscle cramps. If a client is experiencing muscle cramps, this can be a clear indication of dehydration or overexertion. Again, it cannot stressed enough how important it is to understand that clients are individuals and taking good notes on clients can prevent a lot of these issues from occurring.

At the initial assessment, the personal trainer should ask if the client has a history of muscle cramping and what were the conditions of those cramps. For example, was the client performing cardiovascular training or resistance training when they experienced the cramping and did the cramping go away after the person became more acclimated to the workout? If a client does experience a cramp, the best thing to do to is stop the activity and have the client rub out the cramp. If the trainer and client feel comfortable, the trainer can offer to rub out the cramp, especially if it is in a hard to reach area. Also, give the client something to drink to replenish any 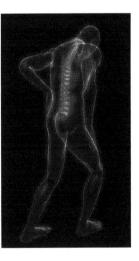 fluids lost, as this may be a contributing factor to the cramping. Another important question to pose is how long into a workout did the cramp present itself, as this may give the trainer an idea of how long to plan the workout. Remember, clients experiencing too much discomfort will not want to continue with their workouts.

Heat Exhaustion that Causes Light-Headedness, Dizziness and Cold, Clammy Skin

Individuals experiencing heat exhaustion should immediately relocate to a cool area, drink cold liquids and rest until their dizzy spell passes. Lying down and elevating the legs, increases blood flow to the brain and helps alleviate dizziness. Gently stretching can also help the individual improve blood circulation and prevent fainting. Wetting the skin and then sitting in front of a fan (or simply fanning the skin) will also lower body temperature.

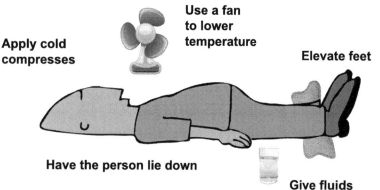

Apply cold compresses

Use a fan to lower temperature

Elevate feet

Have the person lie down

Give fluids

The personal trainer should take great care of a client if the trainer suspects the client is experiencing heat exhaustion. Upon standing, the client may experience brief fainting, so the personal trainer should support the client during relocation. The personal trainer should check to see if the client is sweating profusely, also called diaphoresis. This is a good indication that the client is experiencing heat exhaustion

and the condition has not worsened to heat stroke, which presents with a loss of sweating because the internal body is no longer able to regulate the temperature via sweating.

Heat Exhaustion that Causes Nausea and Headaches

When an individual is experiencing nausea and a headache in addition to heat exhaustion, rehydrating quickly is of the utmost importance. Sports drinks and salty snacks are recommended because they replace the salt the body has lost. The individual should rest in a cool area and lie down to help alleviate the headache. Removing or loosening the individual's clothes and applying water to the skin are also helpful. A person that has suffered from heat exhaustion should avoid strenuous activities for a few days to ensure proper rehydration.

Heat Stroke, High Body Temperature and Dry Skin

If an individual begins to complain about having chills, has goose bumps on the skin, and is feeling pins and needles in the arms, blood circulation to the skin is deteriorating and the individual is beginning to have a heat stroke.

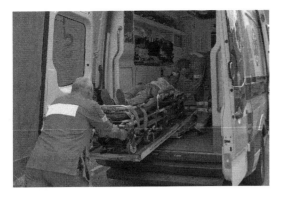

Heat stroke is a serious medical condition that should be treated immediately. Individuals who are having a heat stroke typically have a high body temperature and dry skin. At the first sign of a heat stroke, an emergency medical technician (EMT) should be contacted. The individual should be relocated to a cool location and measures, such as the use of cold packs, should be taken to lower body temperature.

Normally, when a person is exercising or just in the heat, the body generates internal heat from metabolism, but during heat stroke the external temperature becomes so hot that the body cannot keep up with its own internal temperature. The body becomes less efficient at dissipating the heat to the external environment via sweating. As a result, more heat is retained internally and the person's temperature begins to rise. Any body temperature over 40°C or 104°F is classified as heat stroke. A person suffering from this condition will need aid in cooling off the external temperature via ice packs—this action enables the blood

circulating from the skin's surface to cool and assist in bringing the internal blood to a lower temperature and thereby eventually lowering the core body temperature back to normal. Heat stroke is usually a problem in hotter, more humid climates, although it can occur during winter months.

Heat Stroke that Causes Confusion and Unconsciousness

Confusion followed by unconsciousness means the individual has had a heat stroke. This is a medical emergency that can lead to death if it is not swiftly and properly treated. While waiting for medical professionals, the trainer should place the individual in an ice bath or use any

other means to lower the body temperature as fast as possible. Moistening the skin with lukewarm water and using a fan to blow cool air on the skin also helps lower body temperature. Sufficient amounts of cool liquids can be given periodically to individuals that are awake and alert. People who have had a heat stroke may need to be hospitalized and monitored in order to determine if any damage has occurred to the brain or vital organs.

Anytime vital signs, such as temperature, are out of the normal range, the brain or central nervous system is always going to be affected. The brain is usually one of the first organs affected, so personal trainers should look for signs and symptoms that may be altered via

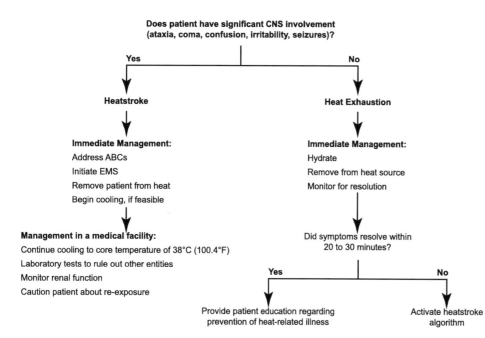

Does patient have significant CNS involvement (ataxia, coma, confusion, irritability, seizures)?

Yes → **Heatstroke**

Immediate Management:
Address ABCs
Initiate EMS
Remove patient from heat
Begin cooling, if feasible

Management in a medical facility:
Continue cooling to core temperature of 38°C (100.4°F)
Laboratory tests to rule out other entities
Monitor renal function
Caution patient about re-exposure

No → **Heat Exhaustion**

Immediate Management:
Hydrate
Remove from heat source
Monitor for resolution

Did symptoms resolve within 20 to 30 minutes?

Yes → Provide patient education regarding prevention of heat-related illness

No → Activate heatstroke algorithm

the central nervous system if they suspect their client may be suffering from heat exhaustion or heat stroke. Remember, confusion will usually precede unconsciousness, so trainers must pay close attention to clients' mannerisms and speech on hot days. Do not bombard them with questions throughout the workout, but it is a good idea to ask questions periodically, mainly to check their current mental status. Simple one answer questions can be a good indicator of how their mental status is without overexerting them.

In order to avoid developing such severe complications while exercising, an individual can follow these guidelines:

- Drink approximately three liters of liquid every day, especially the day before a workout.

- Drink at least two cups of liquid two to three hours before working out.

- Replace sweat that is lost by drinking ½ cup or more of liquid every 10 to 20 minutes.

- Monitor fluid loss and do not rely on thirst to signal the next water break.

- Re-hydrate within two hours after exercising.

Research has shown that drinking liquids with 6% carbohydrates (e.g., energy drinks) aids intestinal absorption and gastric emptying, enhances the desire to drink during exercise, reduces physical and mental fatigue, and thereby increases workout performance. It is also important to consider the type of exercise that is being performed when deciding how much and how often fluid

should be consumed. Canoeists and runners usually drink approximately 500 milliliters of liquid per hour, while cyclists can drink up to 1.2 liters of liquid per hour. This difference may be due to discomfort that runners and canoeists experience when they drink large amounts of water during exercising. They may also feel that drinking more than 500 milliliters of liquid in an hour could slow them down. In such cases, runners and canoeists have extended rehydration periods in order to fully replace the water their bodies lost during exercise.

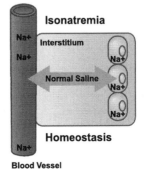

Hydration is good, but must be matched by the correct sodium intake.

Another important aspect of hydration is over-hydration, also known as water intoxication or water excess. Although this concept may seem bizarre, it is increasingly becoming a problem for people. Guidelines exist that indicate how much people should drink and how often, but once again, personal trainers need to understand and stress to clients the notion of individuality. Some people can drink copious amounts of water and be physically okay, while others cannot. Clients need to develop their own balance between feeling thirsty and having to void too frequently.

Surprisingly, this is a challenge for the majority of people.

The importance of not becoming dehydrated is often stressed over the fact that a person can become overhydrated, although this can be as big of a problem as dehydration. The majority of time this is not a problem as long as a client does not have heart or kidney trouble. As previously stated, every client is different and a good initial assessment is so important for this reason. Past and present medical histories are important sections to bear in mind.

Water intoxication, also called hyponatremia, occurs when a person drinks so much water that the water dilutes the sodium in the body. When this happens, the electrolyte imbalance leads to the person becoming confused or disoriented. The brain is the primary organ affected by over-hydration, so a change in personality is the first sign of water intoxication. Treatment for water intoxication requires a doctor's care.

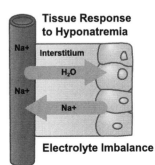

Typically, diuretics are administered to rid the body of excess fluid. During this time, careful monitoring by a physician is best. Although water intoxication is rare and personal trainers will see more dehydration-related problems, it is important to be aware of this condition and how to react if over-hydration is suspected. Also, personal trainers need to educate clients on both aspects of water balance.

Summary

Trainers and individuals who are exercising should pay close attention to the type and quantity of liquids consumed the day before working out. Liquid should also be periodically consumed during the workout. When possible, training should be performed in cool, well-ventilated areas. If training requires that the individual exercise in a hot and humid area, sufficient amounts of cool liquids should be consumed frequently. If ailments such as severe muscle cramps, dehydration, heat exhaustion and heat stroke occur, even when necessary precautions are taken, the individual should refrain from exercising for several days following the incident.

Review Questions

1. Muscle cramps can be caused by the following:
   a) Electrolyte imbalances
   b) Muscle fatigue
   c) Dehydration
   d) All of the above

2. If a person feels _____, dehydration has already started.

3. Dehydration can be avoided if a client drinks a lot of water right before training. True or False? _____

4. Water is lost through
   a) Skin and respiratory tract
   b) Urination and feces
   c) Skin
   d) Both a and b

5. If a person is suffering from _____, he should be relocated to a cool area where he can lie down and drink plenty of fluids.

6. If a person is suffering from _____, he needs medical attention in addition to being relocated to a cool area and given fluids.

7. Over-hydration is a common problem that can be treated with rest and fluid restriction. True or False? _____

8. If a person is dehydrated, the best way to overcome this is to consume:

    a) Water

    b) Electrolyte based drinks (e.g., Gatorade)

9. Water intoxication causes thickening of the blood and hypernatremia (too much sodium). True or False?_____

10. A person suffering from heat exhaustion will have _____ skin, while a person suffering from heat stroke will have _____ skin.

Answers

1. d) All of the above.
2. Thirsty.
3. False.
4. d) Both a & b.
5. Heat exhaustion.
6. Heat stroke.
7. False.
8. b) Electrolyte based drinks (e.g. Gatorade).
9. False.
10. Moist and flushed; hot and dry

References

Bentley S. Exercise-induced muscle cramps. Proposed mechanisms and management. *Sports Medicine.* 1996;21(6):409-20.

Casa DJ, Armstrong LE, Hilman SK, Montain SJ, Reiff RV, Rich BS, Roberts WO, Stone JA. National Athletic Trainer's Association Position Statement: Fluid Replacement of Athletes. *Journal of Athletic Training.* 2005;35(2):212-24.

Coyle EF. Fluid and carbohydrate replacement during exercise: how much and why? *Sports Science Exchange.* 1994;50(7):3.

Maughan L, Leiper JB, Shirreffs SM. Rehydration and recovery after exercise. *Sports Science Exchange.* 1996;62(9):3.

Ryan AJ, Lambert GP, Shi X, Chang RT, Summers RW, Gisolfi CV. Effect of hypohydration on gastric emptying and intestinal absorption during exercise. *Journal of Applied Physiology.* 1998;84(5):1581-88.

Schwellnus MP, Drew N, Collins M. Muscle cramping in athletes—risk factors, clinical assessment and management. *Clinical Sports Medicine.* 2008;27(1):183-94.

Von Duvillard SP, Arciero PJ, Tietjen-Smith T, Alford K. Sports drinks, exercise training and competition. *Current Sports Medicine Reports.* 2008;7(4):202-08.

Chapter 8: Special Populations

Topics Covered

Introduction to Special Populations

Pregnant Women

Designing a Safe Exercise Plan During Pregnancy
Exercises to Perform and Avoid
Safety Precautions

Seniors

Exercises to Perform and Avoid
Safety Precautions

Youths

Training Programs and Supervision
Preventing and Controlling Childhood Obesity
Safety Precautions

Injured Persons

Exercising with an Injury
Exercising after an Injury
Exercises to Perform and Avoid
Safety Precautions

Persons with Specific Medical Conditions

Arthritis
Asthma
Preparing for Exercise
Diabetes Mellitus

Hypertension

Monitoring Blood Pressure
Types of Exercises for Persons with Hypertension

Introduction to Special Populations

As we know, exercise is necessary to maintain our health. Some people have the misconception that, in order to be healthy, they must engage in strenuous exercise. Personal trainers should educate people regarding the difference between maintaining health and modifying body weight. Most physicians will suggest 30 minutes of continuous exercise per day in order to maintain health. The 30 minutes, however do not have to be continuous—they can be broken up into shorter time periods throughout the day. A person's attitude is important and the personal trainer should encourage any exercise during the day. There is plethora of evidence stating that exercise can stave off chronic illnesses such as heart disease and diabetes mellitus.

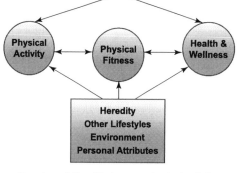

Complex relationships among physical activity, physical fitness, health, wellness and other factors (Adapted from Bouchard, et al., 1990)

Pregnant Women

When a woman becomes pregnant, she may think that eating healthy foods and getting a lot of rest are the top priorities in order to stay fit throughout the pregnancy and have a healthy baby. However, exercising throughout pregnancy is also of great importance. While a pregnant woman may not be able to perform the same exercise regimen as before her pregnancy, there are several recommended exercises that can be performed during pregnancy that not only promote the proper circulation of fluid and nutrients to the baby but also keep the mother in top physical condition. Exercising during pregnancy can also shorten the length of time a mother needs to lose baby fat after the baby is born. When a woman becomes pregnant, she should speak with her doctor before beginning a workout regimen and speak with a trainer to make sure the appropriate exercises are performed. The level and type of exercise that a doctor and trainer recommend usually depends on a woman's fitness level prior to becoming pregnant.

Although exercising while pregnant normally helps both the mother and baby, there are certain cases, such as high-risk pregnancies or complications that arise during the pregnancy, which can prevent a pregnant woman from exercising. However, under normal circumstances, exercising provides many benefits to the mother and her growing baby.

When a pregnant woman's body begins to change, she may feel increasingly fatigued and stressed about aches and pains or other symptoms the pregnancy may be causing. Exercise has been shown to increase energy levels and lead to the release of endorphins, which are chemicals produced naturally in the brain that lead to a decreased sensitivity to stress and pain. This can help relieve tension and help a pregnant mother sleep comfortably. Exercise relieves back pain and improves posture by toning and strengthening muscles in the thighs, buttocks and back. Exercise also prevents joint damage by stimulating the release of relaxin, a hormone that increases the flexibility of joints and ligaments.

Exercise improves circulation within the intestines, which in turn reduces constipation. It also increases the circulation of blood to the skin, which produces a healthy glow. One of the most important benefits of exercising during pregnancy is that it strengthens the heart and body muscles. This plays a role in the ease at which a mother goes into labor and the event of giving birth. For example, breathing exercises help manage pain during labor, and

Active Mums-To-Be
Specific Exercise Class for Pregnancy

Benefits from exercising during pregnancy

- Improves mood swings
- Improves your self-image
- Less physical discomfort
- Control weight gain
- Prevents low-back pain
- Improves circulation
- Sleep better
- Improve transfer of oxygen (gas exchange) at the placenta.
- Research has shown that women who exercise don't have low birth weight babies, but they do have more lighter babies and fewer big babies.
- Increases your chances of having easier, shorter, and less complicated labours

performing exercises throughout the pregnancy that increase endurance can help a woman get through long hours of labor. Another essential benefit is that less fat will be gained if the mother was properly exercising before she became pregnant and continued to do so throughout the pregnancy. In addition, the mother will regain her normal size after the baby is born more quickly than if she did not exercise during pregnancy. Currently, studies are investigating the notion that exercising while pregnant can decrease the risk of developing complications such as gestational diabetes and preeclampsia (pregnancy-induced high blood pressure).

Designing a Safe Exercise Plan During Pregnancy

Designing a safe exercise program during pregnancy depends on whether or not the woman was exercising before she came pregnant, the stage of pregnancy at which she wants to start and whether or not complications arise during the pregnancy. If a woman was exercising prior to her pregnancy, she can more than likely continue her program by making a few modifications. For example, if a woman was in a weight lifting program before she became pregnant, she may be able to continue by lifting lighter weights. She should not continue lifting the same weights because the pregnancy already puts more strain on joints and could lead to avoidable joint injuries. The stage at which a pregnant woman wants to begin exercising also plays a role because the type and level of exercise that can be done changes as the pregnancy progresses. During the first trimester, exercises can be performed in the supine (lying on the back) position, but this is not recommended after the first trimester.

According to the U.S. Department of Health and Human Services, women should be exercising at least 2.5 hours a week to maintain their health. However, even if a woman was not exercising before she became pregnant, she can start performing slow, easy and short exercises. Exercise intensity and speed can be increased as the expectant mother begins to feel stronger. If the pregnancy is free of complications, the risks of exercising at a moderate level are low and do not increase the risk of early miscarriages, preterm deliveries or low birth weights. In every case, a woman who becomes pregnant should have a discussion with her doctor regarding plans to continue or begin exercising. Complications that usually limit a woman's ability to exercise during her pregnancy include:

- Early contractions
- Vaginal bleeding
- Dizziness
- Chest pain
- Headache
- Muscle weakness
- Decreased fetal movement
- Dyspnea (shortness of breath) before exercising
- High blood pressure that is pregnancy induced
- Premature rupture of the amniotic sac (water breaking early)
- Calf swelling and pain

Exercises to Perform and Avoid

Safe Exercises to Perform When Pregnant

Low Impact Exercises:

- Dancing
- Yoga
- Pilates

Water Exercises:

- Swimming
- Water Aerobics

Aerobic Exercises:

- Walking
- Bicycling
- Light/Low Impact Aerobics
- Running (if a runner prior to pregnancy— modify routine)

Weight Lifting (Less weight than prior to pregnancy):

- Maintain health (not increase muscle)

Dancing, yoga and Pilates are all fantastic forms of low impact exercises that help stretch muscles. Swimming and water aerobics are

also good exercises for an expectant mother. The water provides a pregnant woman with the ability to easily move around and stretch almost all muscle groups. Swimming and water aerobics are especially beneficial because they give a pregnant woman the feeling of buoyancy (weightlessness) at a time when she may feel pressure from her growing baby and increasing weight. Walking and biking are additional exercises that can be performed during pregnancy, but walking is recommended more often than biking. It is very easy to change the pace during a walking routine. When walking short distances is not a satisfying workout, the distance can be increased or hills can be added to the walk to increase the intensity. A pregnant woman who is not used to walking should start out by walking one mile or less, three times a week. A warm-up and cool-down of at least five minutes should be included in this workout routine.

As previously stated, expectant mothers can continue to lift weights but should decrease the weight they have been previously lifting. Expectant mothers should also consult their doctor before continuing a weight lifting program to make sure this will not cause joint problems or complicate the pregnancy. If a mother decides to continue lifting weights after consulting her doctor, she should make sure to use less weight as the pregnancy progresses. Jumping and jerking movements should be avoided during the pregnancy and an expectant mother, as well as her trainer, should focus on using exercise to maintain the mother's health, not increase muscle tone or mass.

Many pregnant women who were runners before becoming pregnant can continue running by modifying their routine. However, an expectant mother must remember that exercises, such as running, should be performed in moderation and do not have to be performed on a daily basis. In addition, listening to the body and its warning signs is of the utmost importance. For example, as a baby grows, the mother's center of gravity changes, making it easier for an expectant mother to become dizzy or lose her balance. This occurs especially during the last trimester. A growing baby also puts more pressure on the lungs, which decreases her ability to breathe properly when she is exercising. Furthermore, energy levels can change daily—if a pregnant woman feels extremely tired on the day she is supposed to exercise, she should shift the workout to the next day, assuming she will be feeling better the following day.

Safety Precautions

There are several safety precautions that a pregnant woman, as well as her trainer, should not ignore. A pregnant woman's pulse rate should not rise above 140 beats per

Safe Pregnancy Exercise

minute during exercise. If a heart monitor is not available, a talk test can be used. This test determines whether or not a pregnant woman can have a conversation while she is exercising or if she appears to be gasping for air when she tries to speak. When this occurs, the expectant mother should stop exercising or avoid the exercise that is causing the overexertion. Exercising outside when it is hot and humid should be avoided as well. When a pregnant woman begins to overheat, this can be very dangerous for her baby. Body temperatures higher than 102.6°F can harm a growing baby and cause birth defects. This is especially critical during the first trimester. Swimming is a good option on hot, humid days because it keeps the body cool. If swimming is not an option on that day, exercising in an air-conditioned facility is recommended. As opposed to typical sportswear that clings to the skin, pregnant women should wear comfortable, loose-fitting clothes while exercising. Finally, as with any exercise routine, adequate amounts of water should be consumed before, during and after exercising.

If any of the following symptoms occur during exercise, the expectant mother should immediately stop and contact her doctor:

- Dizziness
- Severe fatigue

- Shortness of breath
- Heart palpitations (strong and rapid heartbeats)
- Headaches
- Pain in the pelvis and/or back
- Bleeding

Seniors

As people age, people often think that exercising is too tedious and may cause them unwanted injuries. However, exercising at any age can improve an individual's quality of life. Elderly persons can also exercise for short periods of time and still notice an increase in muscle strength and tone. Similar to other individuals, elderly persons need to focus on strength training, 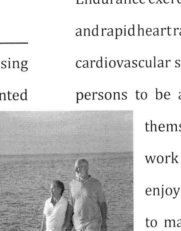 flexibility training and cardiovascular training to maintain as much mobility and strength as their body allows. Ailments, such as arthritis, often hinder their ability to move around, but recent studies have shown that exercising can reduce inflammation and pain that is caused by arthritis. Strength training has also been shown to improve muscle strength in elderly persons who have suffered from a hip fracture. These are just a few of the many benefits that exercise provides to elderly persons.

Exercises to Perform and Avoid

Endurance Exercises

In elderly persons, endurance exercises increase the maximum amount of oxygen the body and muscles can uptake and transport. Endurance exercises reduce high blood pressure and rapid heart rate as well. Endurance, especially cardiovascular strength, is necessary for elderly persons to be able to shop and take care of themselves, perform housework, work outdoors (e.g., in a garden) and enjoy recreational activities. In order to maintain their strength and level of endurance, exercises that increase their heart rate and breathing for extended periods of time without causing complications should be performed. Beneficial exercises for the elderly include walking, swimming and dancing, while

high-impact exercises such as running, cycling and jumping rope should be avoided because they put a lot of strain on joints and muscles.

Low impact exercises should be performed for 20 to 40 minutes at least 3 times a week.

Strengthening Exercises

Elderly persons can strengthen their upper and lower body by lifting weights or using weight lifting machines. In the beginning of a weight lifting regimen, weights that can be effortlessly lifted five times should be used. When this routine becomes too easy, the same set of weights should be lifted five times for two sets. The routine can be increased periodically until the individual can do 15 continuous repetitions. When the individual can lift the weight 5 times for 15 repetitions, the size of the weights can be increased. This type of strength training can be performed for 30 to 40 minutes, 2 or 3 times a week.

There are several strengthening exercises that can be performed at home. Plantar flexion is an exercise that strengthens ankle and calf muscles. To perform this exercise the individual slowly raises their body so that they are standing on their tiptoes and holds this position for one second. This exercise can be repeated 8 to 15 times and if the individual begins to feel stronger after some time, they can alternate legs while performing this exercise. Arm raises strengthen shoulder muscles and can be performed by sitting in a chair with the arms facing the side of the body and raising both arms to the shoulder height. This position is held for one second and then the arms are lowered back down to the individual's side. Arm raises can be repeated 8 to 15 times.

Lower back strength is also important for elderly persons because back pain is a symptom that often occurs when people begin to age. Having a strong back makes it easier for the elderly to stand up from a sitting position, get into and out of a car, pick up objects, move around and work in the yard. Back muscles can be strengthened by sitting upright in a seat with the feet placed flat on the floor, arms bent and relaxed, then pulling the shoulders back as far as possible. Another exercise that strengthens back muscles can be performed by lying on the floor and placing a pillow or cushion under the hips. The arms are placed at the sides and the legs are straight. The head and feet are slightly lifted off of the floor at the same time and held for one second. The individual can relax for a moment and then repeat the exercise.

Stretching Exercises

The muscles and joints of elderly persons are often inflexible, stiff and inflamed. In order to avoid unnecessary injuries and lessen the

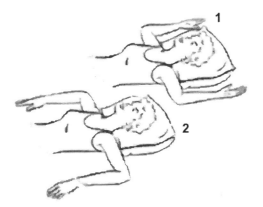

pain that is caused by inflammation, stretching exercises should be performed throughout the week, especially before strength training. In fact, warm-ups and cool-downs should involve 5 to 15 minutes of stretching before strength exercises are performed. Elderly persons should make sure they stretch their arms, shoulders, back, chest, stomach, thighs and calves. Shoulder rotations are easy to perform and are often recommended. First, the individual lies flat on the floor with their head placed on a pillow. The palms are placed face down and the elbows are bent so that the arms are forming an angle. This position is held for 10 to 30 seconds and then the arms are rotated so that the palms are facing

upward and held again for 10 to 30 seconds. This exercise can be repeated three to five times.

Calves and ankles can also be easily stretched by standing in front of a wall, fully extending the hands and then placing them on the wall. The individual then moves one of their legs

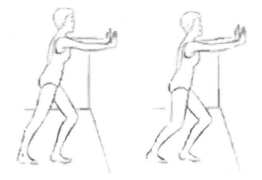

backwards while keeping their foot and heel pressed against the floor. This position is held for 10 to 30 seconds, then the knee is bent and the leg is brought back to its original position. This stretch is performed again with the opposite leg and the entire exercise is repeated three to five times. Elderly persons should work closely with a personal trainer to make sure stretches are performed correctly and that posture is maintained throughout the stretch.

Balance Exercises

By helping older individuals maintain posture and mobility, balance exercises have been shown to prevent injuries that are typically caused from falling. In addition, elderly persons who can maintain their balance also retain their independence by reducing their need for a walker, wheelchair or assistance when it comes to moving around. In order to enhance an elderly person's ability to maintain their balance, trainers usually focus on increasing the individual's core muscle strength.

One commonly used method of improving balance involves the use of a Bosu balance trainer. This is an exercise ball that has been cut in half (half-ball) that engages small stabilizer muscles in the upper and lower parts of the body that are normally not active. After a period of time, the individual learns how to stabilize their body and maintain

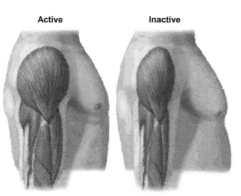

their balance on top of the half-ball. This form of exercise also improves agility (needed to avoid falling), increases the ease at which an elderly person can move and enhances their reaction time in case of an emergency. Simple balance training on a Bosu can greatly improve an elderly individual's quality of life by increasing their mobility and reducing injuries typically caused from falling down. In every case, it is important for elderly persons to remember that the best way to reduce the symptoms of aging

Active   Inactive

is by staying active, even if they cannot exercise two or three times a week.

Safety Precautions

Sarcopenia, a loss of muscle mass and strength and a decline of muscle tissue, also occurs in people as they age. Experts suggest that muscle mass decreases approximately 4% each decade from ages 25 to 50. Aerobic fitness, which normally increases the amount of oxygen that is delivered to muscles, is also hindered as people age. This may reduce one's mobility and alter daily activities. Joints become stiffer, which often leads to a higher risk of injuries. Each year, more than 300,000 people are hospitalized for broken hips caused by falls.

Recently, more and more scientists claim that the complications of aging can be avoided or become less severe if people remain active as they age. Older adults, regardless of age, should make sure time is devoted to exercising on a regular basis. Even exercising one or two times a week is more healthy and beneficial than being inactive. However, elderly persons should constantly be aware of their level of physical fitness by periodically undergoing a medical examination and working under a trainer's supervision. The doctor will ensure the patient is not putting too much strain on the body and the trainer will ensure the exercises performed accommodate the client's current level of fitness. In addition, elderly persons who have chronic conditions should consider the role their condition plays in their ability to exercise safely in order to avoid unnecessary injuries. These persons should be sure to consult regularly with their doctor and personal trainer. If the individual begins to experience chest pain, shortness of breath or lightheadedness while exercising, they should stop and contact their doctor.

Youths

Children, teenagers and adolescents may often think they do not really need physical education classes or aerobic exercises to keep in shape, but inactive young people are just as susceptible to health problems as adults who are inactive. In fact, a large number of children and youths are at risk for developing coronary artery disease (heart disease), type 2 diabetes, high blood pressure, high cholesterol and even heart attacks because of inactivity and consuming unhealthy

foods. Overweight persons increase their chances of developing such conditions when their weight continues to increase, so it is good advice for even young people to manage their weight and physical activity.

Surveys performed over recent years suggest that the majority of obese children and youths are overweight due to an absence of physical activities in their daily routine and an unhealthy diet. Years ago, children, youths and adults alike used to walk or cycle to school or work and play sports regularly. Nowadays, people travel mainly by car and children are transported to school by their parents or by school buses. In the afternoons when kids return from school, they typically sit in front of the television or computer for several hours before going to bed. According to a U.S. National Diet and Nutrition Survey, 6 out

of 10 girls and 4 out of 10 boys are not engaging in physical activity for a minimum of one hour a day, which is recommended by health care professionals. Training programs and classes that educate children and young people about how to get into shape or stay in shape will begin to lower the currently increasing obesity rates.

Training Programs and Supervision

Training programs are beneficial tools that can be used to combat obesity. They are sometimes conducted in school for students or information is given to parents seeking ways to help their child reach their ideal weight and optimal physical fitness level. Training programs for parents should include ways that their child's activity level and eating habits can be monitored and improved. Training programs and supervision also entail physical education, which means making sure children are engaging regularly in

recreational activities. It is also important that children and youths are supervised while they are exercising or playing sports, since a lack of concentration or playing during training can lead to unnecessary accidents and injuries.

Training programs should offer students a variety of options. Children and youths have different personalities and will often prefer various types of exercises and sports. Parents, teachers and trainers should pay close attention to behavioral patterns when a child or youth is engaging in recreational activities. When individuals are performing an activity or sport they do not like or find difficult, they may become less motivated and will not reap the health

benefits that performing a sport they are enthusiastic

about can provide them. Allow youths to try a number of activities to find the exercise or sport that is right for them and encourage them to engage in this activity on a regular basis.

Preventing and Controlling Childhood Obesity

Preventing and controlling obesity involves introducing a healthy and well-balanced diet to an obese child or youth that is overweight. Fatty foods like chips, hotdogs and hamburgers should be replaced with fruits, vegetables and starchy foods such as potatoes, pasta and rice. In addition, sodas and other carbonated drinks should be replaced with fruit juice, milk and water. Controlling obesity also involves improving

eating habits. For example, if a parent and their child are used to eating meals at random times during the day, regular eating intervals can be implemented with healthy snack foods between meals. Eating while watching television should also be avoided because the child will, more than likely, not move around once they have finished eating. If consuming fast food during the week is the normal routine, try to encourage the parents to implement a family night when the whole family cooks healthy foods together.

Safety Precautions

For children and youths who were previously inactive, doctors recommend that an easy exercise be chosen and the intensity of physical activity be gradually increased. Walking for approximately one hour a day is one of the easiest approaches to becoming physically active. If a child's school or the shopping center is not very far from home, parents should encourage walking instead of going by car. Taking children to a park regularly and playing sports with them also encourages children to become more active and shows that physical fitness is important to their parents. Parents can also make recreational activities fun by going to amusement parks, riding bikes, swimming, etc. Avoid inactivity by reducing the amount of time the child or youth is allowed to watch television or play on

the computer. Inactivity can also be avoided by making sure children engage in activities that are appealing to them and give them a sense of satisfaction. One may also consider rewarding children and youths for maintaining healthy eating habits and being active during the week by buying them a small gift, taking them to the cinema or by another means that shows them you are proud of the progress they have made.

Injured Persons

Physically active people who have recently been injured may think they have to stop exercising until they have fully recovered, but this is not always true. According to the type of injury you have, performing certain exercises under the supervision of a medical professional or physical therapist can speed up the recovery time. However, it is important to only perform exercises that a doctor recommends and do so under close supervision to avoid further injury. This is particularly good news for people who have recently torn a ligament or strained a muscle and thought they would have to sit at home or at their desk all day for the next couple of weeks. An injured individual should speak with their doctor about whether they can exercise and what kind of exercise can be performed while they are recovering. In most cases, people who were already active only need to change certain parts of their normal exercise regimen.

Exercising with an Injury

Exercising with an injury should only be considered if the injured part of the body has been given some time to begin healing and if a doctor recommends that a person do so. Putting weight on injured parts of the body (e.g., a sprained ankle or broken bone) directly after an accident can lead to a chronic condition or chronic pain. However, after a certain amount of time a doctor may suggest specific exercises to strengthen the injured area. In fact, not doing these exercises could prolong the recovery period. When individuals begin performing exercises that involve injured body parts, they should pay close attention to body warning signs. Some people tend to push themselves when they are exercising—for example, forcing one's self to do just one more sit-up even if they are beginning to feel pain. For injured individuals, this can be quite harmful. When individuals start to feel increased pain in an injured region or in other parts of the body, they should try a

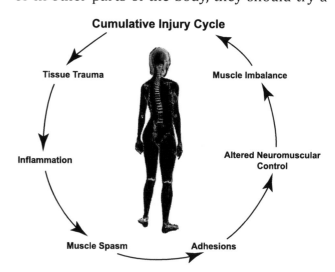

Cumulative Injury Cycle

Tissue Trauma

Muscle Imbalance

Inflammation

Altered Neuromuscular Control

Muscle Spasm

Adhesions

different exercise or stop exercising. This will prevent further damage to the injured region. Following a doctor's instructions is important but listening to individual body signals also aids the recovery process.

Exercising after an Injury

Once a person has fully recovered from an injury, they should educate themselves about how to avoid further injuries or re-injuring the same area. One of the best ways to prevent future  injuries is by learning to maintain balance and flexibility. This can be done at home or under the supervision of a trained professional. It is important to make sure the personal trainer or physical therapist has been informed about the recent injury or previous injuries before beginning a new workout regimen. Tight muscles can lead to imbalances in the body and this can cause accidents and injuries. Injuries can also be prevented if a person avoids overtraining. If muscles and joints are overworked, they are more susceptible to becoming damaged and less able to protect their connective tissues, which increases the risk of damaging cartilage, bones, ligaments and tendons. Training should be performed throughout the week and at regular intervals with recovery periods in between workouts. In addition, focusing on strengthening all of the body's muscle groups will avoid muscle imbalances by reducing the need for overworked muscles to compensate for weaker inactive muscles.

Exercises to Perform and Avoid

Exercises that put direct pressure on the injured area should be avoided for some time. For example, if a person has a knee or foot injury, they should avoid running or riding a bike. Instead, this person can concentrate on upper body strength while recuperating. Their workout regimen can be modified to include exercises that can be performed while sitting or lying down. The same idea should be applied when the person has an injury in the upper part of the body, such as an elbow or shoulder, by concentrating on the body's lower regions. Yoga and Pilates are often recommended for people who are recovering from an injury. These exercises are easy on muscles and joints (e.g., in the hands and feet) and typically improve balance, flexibility and posture. Before starting one of these courses, the instructor should be informed about the injury. If these exercises will be carried out at home, the individual should speak with a doctor or physical therapist before beginning the exercise. Swimming and water aerobics are typically good workouts for people who have strained muscles or broken bones in their legs or feet. The use of a pull-buoy is especially helpful, as placing this device between the thighs allows the lower part of the body to float and forces the upper regions to do all of the work. In every case, an injured person should speak with a doctor or physical therapist about the best time and types of exercises that should be performed.

Safety Precautions

It is very important to know as much as possible about a client's injury and to work closely with the doctor on developing a workout regimen. The exact precautions a trainer needs to take will depend on the specific type of injury. It is better to take things too slow than to risk re-injury or create a chronic condition.

Persons with Specific Medical Conditions

Arthritis

Arthritis is an inflammatory condition affecting the joints of the body and afflicts a majority of older persons. Aging is often associated with degeneration of the functional ability of the body. However, arthritis does not just occur in the aging. Collectively affecting about 15% of the general population, arthritis is one of the most prevalent chronic conditions in the U.S.

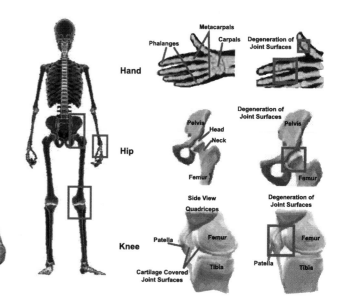

Arthritis
(Degenerative Joint Disease/Osteoarthritis)
Three Examples

Arthritis is separated into two major groups—osteoarthritis and rheumatoid arthritis. Osteoarthritis is due to the degeneration of cartilage in the joints. This ultimately creates a wearing of the bone surfaces where they come

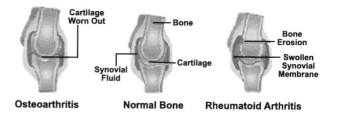

Osteoarthritis   Normal Bone   Rheumatoid Arthritis

in contact and leads to inflammation and pain. The most common areas where people develop osteoarthritis are in the hands, knees, hips and spine. The second major type of arthritis is rheumatoid arthritis, an autoimmune joint disease. In this case, the immune system attacks the tissues of the joints or organs. This too leads to pain and stiffness and the loss of joint integrity in multiple joint areas, most commonly in the hands, feet, wrists and knees.

Managing Arthritis

The major ways people with arthritis manage their arthritis is proper rest, exercise, a good diet and medication. Splints or braces can also help to lower arthritic pain. In cases of chronic arthritis, when other methods do not prove effective, surgery could be necessary.

In terms of exercise training, fitness professionals should always be aware of the major types of arthritis and determine whether their client is arthritic. The progress of arthritic clients in exercise training programs should be closely monitored. Any movement that leads to persistent pain for more than an hour following exercise should be noted. A good way to manage arthritis is to be aware of what types of activities lead to joint aggravation. These exercises should be modified or eliminated from the routine. They often involve high intensity exercises or ones that involve a high number of repetitions. People with osteoarthritis usually have a decrease in strength and proprioception, which leads to postural alignment issues and decreased ability to balance while standing.

Other training considerations include morning stiffness and lowering of the maximal oxygen uptake due to decreased exercise ability.

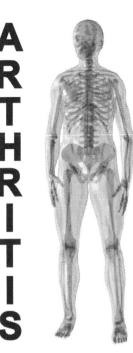

ARTHRITIS

Understanding Arthritis Facts

If a client is under the supervision of a fitness professional for exercise training, both parties should be aware of medications being taken (e.g., acetaminophen, NSAIDs, corticosteroids) as pain relievers to manage this condition. For example, corticosteroids can lead to osteoporosis, a condition characterized by a decrease in bone density. This condition can hinder certain training routines because it causes arthritic flare-ups and therefore affects the client's exercise tolerance.

Also, this medication is known to increase body mass, anemia and gastrointestinal bleeding.

Types of Exercise for Arthritis

It used to be a common practice to avoid any type of strenuous exercise if the individual suffered from arthritis. The reason for this former misconception is that a lack of activity and complete rest was thought to have the most benefit in managing arthritis. However, research studies show that this is not the case. Joint pain and stiffness associated with arthritis can actually be heightened through inactivity due to muscle atrophy and lack of flexibility of the joint tissue. Therefore, inactivity is often

227

associated with the perpetuation of the chronic pain cycle. Rather, there should be a balance of activity and rest. Consistent exercise can have some great benefits for clients with arthritis. Research in sports medicine reports have demonstrated that long-term strength training, including proprioceptive training, can provide some immediate and prolonged relief to arthritic patients. The decrease in the symptoms of arthritis is primarily due to the increase in muscle strength gained from exercise training. Literature also supports the benefits of isometric strength training because strength can be developed in joints with little to no movement, so it is less likely to inflame joints. People with arthritis are advised to participate in structured exercise routines and work with their trainer in the design of a personalized program to help restore their functional mobility. If a trainer cannot be consulted, then a strong increase in daily activities can also be beneficial.

Three types of exercises that are best for arthritic people include range of motion exercises (e.g., stretching and dance) to maintain normal joint movement and relieve stiffness; strengthening (e.g., weight training and water exercises) to increase muscle strength, which helps support and protect joints; and endurance exercises (e.g., swimming and cycling) to improve cardiovascular fitness, control weight and improve overall bodily function. Range of motion exercises (E.G., dance, aerobics and rowing), which decrease risk of orthopedic complications, can be enjoyable and therefore, increase exercise compliance. Exercise programs with range of motion focus can include anything from walking around the block, taking a yoga class or playing a low-key game like golf. However, it is important to work only the pain-free range of motion that one can exhibit. In the case of strength training, weight training can be conducted with small free weights, exercise machines or elastic bands to create resistance.

Correct body position when using weights is crucial to avoid muscle tear and more joint swelling. Low impact, water-based exercise works well because the body's buoyancy reduces stress on hips, knees and spine, areas primarily affected by arthritis. The water should be about 83-88°F to be soothing to the joints. Some beneficial modes of basic endurance exercises that should be conducted include

Strengthening

Aerobics/Heart and Lung Health

Range of Motion

Pyramid diagram:
- Recreation
- Aerobic Exercise
- Muscle Strengthening
- Range of Motion and Stretching

228

stationary cycling and distance swimming. They should be preceded by extended warm-ups and include special considerations to exercise intensity and duration.

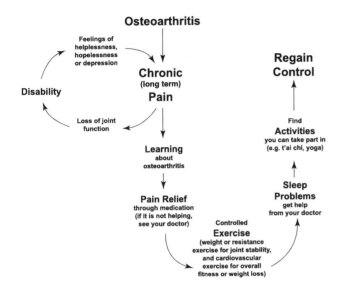

In rheumatoid arthritis, the joint structure of the body is damaged through the wearing away of cartilage as a result of autoimmune degeneration. Improving muscle strength and flexibility through a properly designed training routine can complement the use of medication, rest and diet to manage this type of arthritis.

Asthma

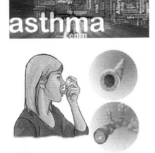

There are more than 10 million Americans that suffer from asthma or asthma-like symptoms, such as shortness of breath, coughing, headaches and abdominal pain. Exercising correctly can be helpful for asthmatic clients by reducing their vulnerability to asthma triggers such as pollutants, allergies and cold/dry air. Exercise can also reduce shortness of breath or dyspnea, which is common among this population. Therefore, it is important that personal trainers understand how to deal with people affected by asthma in order to avoid complications.

Preparing for Exercise

Before setting up an exercise program, the client should finish an asthma screening form which can be used to figure out the appropriate

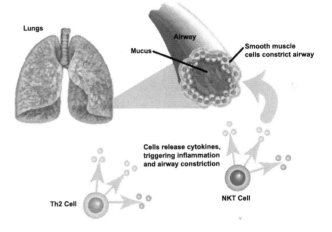

kind, duration and frequency of the exercise to be performed. It can also establish when and where the client will exercise. It might be advantageous to work with the client's doctor to learn more about the client's condition. An asthma management team can help determine the most beneficial training program for the client.

It is very important that a client have the asthma under control. This can be accomplished mainly by using inhaled or oral drugs. Some clients may use inhalers that can decrease the chance of having an attack up to 2 hours after doing so if this action is taken approximately 15 to 30 minutes before exercise. Clients should also try to prevent interaction with variables that contribute to asthmatic symptoms.

Proper warm-up and cool-down may prevent or reduce the incidence of exercise-induced asthma.

The client may also consider exercising to try and induce an asthma attack with mild symptoms. This may be especially advantageous if the client is an athlete. After the first attack, there is a lower chance of another one occurring and this period is referred to as the refractory period. Depending on the individual, this period can occur from half an hour to three hours after the initial asthma attack.

If this technique is used, the following steps can be taken:

1. The technique should be discussed with the client's physician.
2. The client should take the normal medication.
3. Warm up for 10-15 minutes by having the client's heart rate at 50-60 percent of the normal rate.
4. Cool down or stretch for 10-15 minutes and have the client stay hydrated.
5. The client should work to 70-85% of the normal heart rate.

When to Avoid Exercise

All exercise should stop when the client experiences an asthma attack. The following steps should be taken:

1. Place the client in an upright position.
2. Unfasten any tight or restraining clothing.
3. Ask the client where their medication is and allow the client to self-administer. It is important to note that the personal trainer should have the knowledge or permission to administer the medicine or should not do it at all.
4. Should symptoms persist for half an hour or more, medical assistance should be requested immediately.

An asthma attack can be brought on during exercise and this is known as exercise-induced asthma (EIA). It is present in children, adolescents and young adults who frequently work out. This condition can be induced if the client exercises constantly at 70% of aerobic capacity for a minimum of five minutes. It can happen either in the first 6 to 12 minutes or last 5 to 10 minutes of exercise. Therefore, longer periods of exercise consistent with certain sports should be limited or avoided.

EIA can also be avoided by exercising in the proper weather conditions or locations. Clients should exercise caution when the air is cold or dry. They should also limit exercise when they have a cold or viral infection. Clients who suffer from asthma allergies should not exercise in outdoor locations where these allergies can be activated by certain triggers. There are certain medications that can bring about EIA, and clients should speak to their doctor about which medications can do this. They should learn more about the side effects to medicine they are currently taking and how it can be influenced by exercise.

Diabetes Mellitus

Exercise can potentially reduce the risk of diabetes mellitus and help manage diabetes. There are two types of diabetes mellitus (type 1 and type 2) and personal trainers should familiarize themselves with the different types. Diabetes mellitus is a condition in which a person has high glucose in their blood. Glucose is the primary fuel for our bodies and the process of converting glucose into energy occurs within a cell. This process is regulated by the hormone insulin, which is secreted by the pancreas. The difference between type 1 and type 2 diabetes mellitus is seen at the molecular level.

In type 1 diabetes mellitus, a person's pancreas malfunctions and starts to lose the ability to secrete insulin. When a person with type 1 diabetes mellitus eats a meal, the pancreas does not secrete enough or any insulin. Without insulin, glucose cannot gain entry into the cells and thus glucose accumulates in the blood, which can elicit many dangerous outcomes.

People with type 1 diabetes mellitus can inject insulin that mimics their own insulin, which is lacking, so that they can lead a mostly normal life. People with type 2 diabetes mellitus have a different malfunction. These people typically have normal insulin levels; however, for a reason yet to be understood, their cells stop responding to the insulin. This essentially blocks glucose from entering the cell, thus causing the person to have high blood glucose levels.

Some research has shown that chronic overeating, which can lead to being overweight, along with a sedentary lifestyle, can increase the risk of developing type 2 diabetes mellitus. As with many chronic illnesses, being active and maintaining health is believed to help decrease the risk of developing type 2 diabetes mellitus, along with good eating habits. Exercise is beneficial for people with either type 1 or type 2 diabetes mellitus. Some people with type 2 diabetes mellitus can manage their own diabetes with exercise and eating without needing medication. In the next section, we will discuss the benefits of exercising in terms of reducing the risk for diabetes or how it can manage diabetes.

Benefits and Risks of Exercising

The majority of evidence from current research suggests that there is a positive effect of exercise on diabetes mellitus, especially

cardiovascular exercise. Exercise is beneficial to those individuals with diabetes mellitus because it burns calories and can therefore help lower blood glucose. Burning extra calories can come from many different sources, such as taking stairs or parking further away at work or the store. A cardiorespiratory workout of walking briskly or a mild jog is a great way to manage diabetes or to help reduce the risk of getting type 2 diabetes mellitus. Studies have shown that as little as a 5% reduction in weight is enough to prevent type 2 diabetes mellitus. Along with keeping diabetes in check or reducing the risk of developing it, exercising also helps to stave off other chronic diseases, such as high blood pressure or cardiovascular disease.

Benefits & Risks of Exercising with Diabetes in the Elderly	
Benefits	**Risks**
Increased exercise tolerance	Sudden cardiac death
Increased glucose tolerance	Injuries to the feet and joints
Increased maximal O_2 consumption	Hypoglycemia
Increased muscle strength	
Increased muscle mass	
Improved lipid profile	
Improved sense of well-being	
Decreased blood pressure	
Decreased body fat	

There are some risks that personal trainers must be aware of if a client has diabetes. Taking a good initial assessment should reveal this chronic condition, along with the medications a diabetic client is taking. The trainer will also need to know if the diabetic is trying to use the workout being designed as a means to manage the diabetes. Fulfilling clients' goals is important, but trainers also need to be aware of any associated risks and be sure to ask if their doctors advised them that it was acceptable to try to manage their diabetes without medication. One symptom of diabetes is called neuropathy—this condition occurs when diabetes has damaged nerves in the extremities and it renders the client unable to feel pain. For example, if a diabetic client with neuropathy gets a blister, it will go unnoticed, and this could lead to an undetected and unmanaged infection, which will often lead to amputation. Trainers must be very careful and knowledgeable when it comes to diabetic clients. For these clients, you may recommend water exercises, since walking or running may put too much strain on their feet and legs. Also, heavy weight lifting is not recommended for a client with diabetes, as they already have a lot of pressure on the vessels within the eyes. That is why exercise-induced lower blood pressure helps with diabetes, as it aids in decreasing vessel pressure. Another important consideration is to be mindful of

> **Heavy weight lifting is not recommended for a client with diabetes, as they already have a lot of pressure on the vessels within the eyes.**

medications they are taking, which are designed to lower blood glucose. When they exercise, they are further lowering their blood glucose—this could lead to hypoglycemia (low blood glucose) and can result in fainting. Some medications can also cause hypoglycemia on their own; therefore, it is important to know what medications clients are taking and the mechanism of those medications. Also, ensure a glucose meter is handy and keep a sugary snack on hand in case of this problem. Do not give a diabetic client any food prior to checking glucose levels because, if the glucose level is already high, the situation will worsen.

Exercise Can Help Control Diabetes

Exercise helps to control diabetes mellitus by burning more calories, which utilizes more glucose than if a person were sedentary.

Dietary Management

Physical Activity

Blood Pressure Control

Blood Sugar Check

Diabetes Control

Foot Care Practices

Stress Management

Dental Care & Hygiene

Proper Medication Use

Additionally, exercise has been shown to increase the cells' ability to utilize glucose as well as increase the function of insulin. Increasing cardiovascular output also reduces blood pressure and, as stated earlier, one effect of diabetes mellitus is that it can cause blood vessels to constrict (especially in the eye). Exercising can also lower LDL (bad cholesterol) and raise HDL (good cholesterol). Lowering cholesterol has been shown to help control diabetes mellitus. Lowering triglycerides is also important in maintaining a healthy weight, as excess glucose is stored in fat tissue as triglycerides. As little as a 5-10% weight loss can eliminate type 2 diabetes mellitus in some people. Unfortunately, people who suffer from type 1 diabetes mellitus will always be insulin dependent, but a good exercise program can aid in their longevity and quality of life. Again, exercise has a beneficial and broad-spectrum effect on overall health.

Vigorous

Moderate

Light

Types of Exercises for Diabetics

There are several safe exercises for diabetics. The only exercises unsafe for diabetics are heavy weight lifting and any other exercise that would cause a lot of straining. Most diabetics will suffer from blood vessel constriction in the eye and trainers want to minimize this side effect as much as possible. Walking and light jogging are great exercises for healthy diabetics. If the client is experiencing numbing or tingling in the extremities, the trainer should recommend a swimming regimen or water aerobic type exercise. They can also do stretching, yoga or mild weight lifting and, if they feel capable, a stationary bike may also be an option.

Precautions

Personal trainers should know if clients' physicians have approved them for a workout regimen. Trainer should ask what medications they are taking and if they have type 1 or type 2 diabetes mellitus. In addition, the trainer should determine if the client has neuropathy, as this will be important in determining the workout regimen. No straining exercises, such as heavy lifting or high resistance bands, should be used. Strength training is acceptable and building muscle is an excellent way to burn more calories at rest; however, ensure it is not overdone. It may be wise to purchase a glucose meter and keep glucose strips, prickers and gloves readily available to test blood glucose levels if necessary.

Personal trainers will frequently encounter clients with many different chronic illnesses.

Before
- Include 5 minute warm up
- Check blood sugar

After
- Include 5 minute cool down
- Check blood sugar

Diabetes mellitus is quite prevalent and it is likely that a trainer will eventually have a client with this disorder. It is therefore important that trainers be aware of the general precautions and details of type 1 versus type 2 diabetes mellitus and the types of exercises appropriate for this demographic of client.

Hypertension

High blood pressure (hypertension) or a dramatic increase in blood pressure occasionally occurs during exercise. A study involving athletes with mild hypertension, whose ages ranged from 55 to 75, showed a correlation between exercise-induced hypertension and an inhibited ability of blood vessels to increase in size while exercises were being performed. Normally, when people exercise, blood flow increases and blood vessels dilate. The inability of blood vessels to dilate places more pressure on the heart and, as a result, increases blood pressure. Exercise-induced hypertension usually leads to a systolic pressure of 250 mmHg (millimeters of mercury) or higher. Systolic pressure is produced when the heart is contracting. Systolic blood pressure that rises to 200 mmHg during exercise is normal, but if blood pressure rises above 220 mmHg, it needs to be monitored by a doctor and probably controlled with medication. Diastolic pressure, which occurs when the heart is dilating (expanding) and relaxing, typically remains constant or drops slightly during exercise due to increased blood flow. Some individuals exhibit an increase of diastolic pressure that is approximately 10 mmHg or higher.

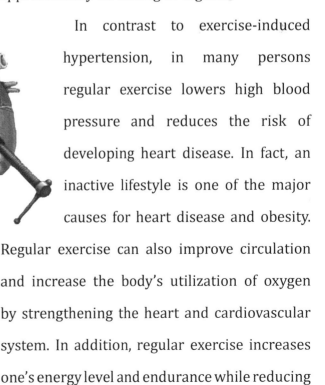

In contrast to exercise-induced hypertension, in many persons regular exercise lowers high blood pressure and reduces the risk of developing heart disease. In fact, an inactive lifestyle is one of the major causes for heart disease and obesity. Regular exercise can also improve circulation and increase the body's utilization of oxygen by strengthening the heart and cardiovascular system. In addition, regular exercise increases one's energy level and endurance while reducing

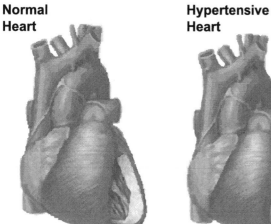

Normal Heart

Hypertensive Heart

Thickening in Walls of Ventricles

fatigue, shortness of breath and heart failure symptoms.

Monitoring Blood Pressure

People who have a history of hypertension, or know the condition runs in their family, should

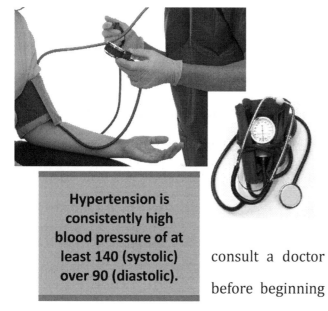

Hypertension is consistently high blood pressure of at least 140 (systolic) over 90 (diastolic).

consult a doctor before beginning an exercise regimen. Once the individual starts a routine, that individual should review the exercise plan with a doctor on a regular basis. Factors that should be discussed with a doctor include: how much exercise can be performed daily, the types of exercises that should be

performed, activities that should be avoided, when to take medication (e.g., before or after exercising) and how often one's pulse should be measured during exercise. Typically, doctors and trainers recommend that hypertension patients gradually increase the amount of aerobic exercise that is performed to approximately 20 or 30 minutes, at least 3 times a week. The use of a portable heart monitor while exercising is also recommended for people with hypertension. This allows these individuals to determine if they are pushing themselves too hard or if the activity needs to be changed. If a rapid or irregular heartbeat (heart palpitations) develops during exercise, the individual should rest by sitting for a few minutes and then check the pulse again. If the pulse remains higher than 100 beats per minute or the heartbeat is still irregular, a doctor should be contacted. When the individual is not exercising, lifting and pushing heavy objects should be avoided, as well as household activities such as mowing, scrubbing, shoveling or raking.

Types of Exercises for Persons with Hypertension

Exercises for Persons with Hypertension

- Stretching exercises
  - Slowly lengthen muscles
    - Yoga (include warm-up and cool-down)

- Cardiovascular/aerobic exercises
  - Benefits the heart
    - Jogging/walking, cycling, golf, swimming, etc.
- Strengthening exercises
  - Improves muscle tone and mass, endurance
    - Walking, taking stairs, etc.

Exercises for persons with hypertension are divided into three groups: stretching, cardiovascular/aerobic exercise and strengthening exercises. Stretching involves slowly lengthening the body's muscles. Performing specific stretch routines for the arms and legs before and after exercising prepares muscles for the activity while reducing the risk of injuries and muscle strains. A warm-up and cool-down of 5 to 10 minutes is normally recommended. The cool-down is especially important because blood pressure medication often causes a significant decrease in blood pressure after exercise or if an activity is abruptly interrupted. To avoid this, the cool-down period should be at least 10 minutes but longer if possible. Stretching also increases an individual's flexibility and range of motion. Yoga is a good form of stretching.

Cardiovascular/aerobic exercise is physical activity that incorporates the use of large muscle groups and provides many benefits for the heart.

Cardiovascular exercise improves circulation and the use of oxygen by strengthening the heart and lungs. When performed on a regular basis, cardiovascular exercise leads to improved breathing during exercise, decreases the heart rate and reduces high blood pressure. Recommended cardiovascular exercises include: jumping rope, jogging, walking, cycling (e.g., outdoors or stationary), rowing or canoeing, cross-country skiing, skating, water aerobics, golf, fishing and swimming. Strengthening exercises involve repetitive muscle contractions which improve muscle tone and increase muscle mass. Strong muscles also increase one's endurance, allowing individuals to perform more challenging exercise routines for extended periods of time. Taking the stairs instead of the elevator is a form of strength training, as well as, getting off the bus one or two stops early and walking the remainder of the way. For individuals who drive to work daily, parking at the far end of the lot and walking to the building also builds strength.

Stretching involves slowly lengthening the body's muscles.

Exercise should be interrupted or avoided if the following symptoms occur:

- Dizziness
- Lightheadedness
- Chest pain
- Weakness

- Irregular swelling or weight gain
- Pressure in the jaw, neck, chest or shoulders

If any of these symptoms persist for more than a couple minutes after the activity is discontinued, a doctor or emergency medical team should be contacted immediately.

Summary

In general, special consideration needs to be given to individuals within these special populations. Depending on clients' unique situations, workout regimens need to be tailored to both protect them from further complications and help them become stronger. Pregnant women need to be aware of the impact of exercise not only on themselves but also on their growing baby. Elderly persons should use light weights and not overexert themselves. Youths will benefit from exercise and enjoy the process more if they are given several options from which to choose. People with recent injuries need to protect their injury but work to strengthen it at the same time. And those people with specific medical conditions need to work closely with their doctor when developing a workout regimen. Trainers need to listen to clients to gather as much information as possible about their specific situations and be prepared to consult with their doctors on which exercises are appropriate and which exercises should be avoided.

Review Questions

1. Pregnant women in their second trimester should avoid lying on their backs while performing exercises. True or False? _____

   _____

2. Which of the following activities is NOT recommended for a pregnant woman?
   a) Pilates
   b) Light/low impact aerobics
   c) Long distance running
   d) Swimming

3. List three types of exercises that are beneficial for elderly persons. _____

   _____

   _____

4. What are some reasons for the current increase in childhood obesity?_____

   _____

   _____

5. When can exercise-induced asthma (EIA) occur during exercise?
   a) During the first 6-12 minutes of exercise
   b) During the last 5-10 minutes of exercise
   c) It can only happen after exercising for more than 30 minutes
   d) Both A and B

6. Which part of the body is typically NOT affected when an individual suffers from osteoarthritis?

    a) Knees

    b) Back

    c) Hips

    d) Spine

7. Type 1 diabetes mellitus is caused by a failure of what organ? _____

8. Type 2 diabetes mellitus can be managed with diet and exercise. True or False? ____

    _____

9. High blood pressure is referred to as ____

    _____.

10. Name three types of exercises that are beneficial for persons with high blood pressure._____

    _____

    _____

Answers

1. True.

2. c) Long distance running.

3. Walking, dancing, swimming, light-to-moderate weight training.

4. There is the absence of physical activity in the daily routine of today's youth and they are participating in an unhealthy diet.

5. d) Both a & b.

6. b) Back.

7. Pancreas.

8. True.

9. Hypertension.

10. Any three of these—yoga, jogging, taking the stairs, walking, cycling, golf and swimming.

References

Bell R, Palma S. Antenatal exercise and birth weight. *Australian and New Zealand Journal of Obstetrics and Gynecology*. 2000;40(1):70-73.

Berger L, Klein C, Commandeur M. Evaluation of the immediate and midterm effects of mobilization in hot spa water on static and dynamic balance in elderly subjects. *Ann Readapt Med Phys*. 2008;51(2):84-95.

Blackham J, Garry JP, Cummings DM, Russell RG, Dealleaume L. Does regular exercise reduce the pain and stiffness of osteoarthritis? *Journal of Family Practice*. 2008;57(7):476-77.

Bowman AJ, Clayton RH, Murray A, Reed JW, Subhan MF, Ford GA. Baroreflex function in sedentary and endurance-trained elderly people. *Age Ageing*. 1997;26(4):289-94.

Christiansen CL. The effects of hip and ankle stretching on gait function of older people. *Archives of Physical Medical Rehabilitation*. 2008;89(8):1421-28.

Clark SL, Cotton DB, Pivarnik JM, Lee W, Hankins GD, Benedetti TJ, Phelan JP. Position change and central hemodynamic profile during normal third-trimester pregnancy and postpartum. *American Journal of Obstetrics and Gynecology*. 1991;164:883-87.

Gaudin P, Leguen-Guegan S, Allenat B, Baillet A, Grange L, Juvin R. Is dynamic exercise beneficial in patients with rheumatoid arthritis? *Joint Bone Spine*. 2008;75(1):11-17.

Klaus D. Management of Hypertension in Actively Exercising Patients: Implications for Drug Selection. *Drugs*. 1989;37(2):212-18.

Ning Y, Williams MA, Dempsey JC, Sorensen TK, Frederick IO, Luthy DA. Correlates of recreational physical activity in early pregnancy. *Journal of Maternal Fetal Neonatal Medicine*. 2003;13(6):385-93.

Plasqui G. The role of physical activity in rheumatoid arthritis. *Physiology and Behavior*. 2008;94(2):270-75.

Portegijs E, Kallinen M, Rantanen T, Heinonen A, Sihvonen S, Alen M, Kiviranta I, Sipilä S. Effects of resistance training on lower-extremity impairments in older people with hip fracture. *Archives of Physical and Medical Rehabilitation*. 2008;(9):1667-74.

Qi L, Hu FB, Hu G. Genes, environment and interactions in prevention of type 2 diabetes: A focus on physical activity and lifestyle changes. *Current Molecular Medicine*. 2008;8(6): 519-32.

Simonsick EM, Newman AB, Visser M, Goodpaster B, Kritchevsky SB, Rubin S, Nevitt MC, Harris TB. Mobility limitation in self-described well-functioning older adults: importance of endurance walk testing. *The Journals of Gerontology. Series A, Biological Sciences and Medical Sciences*. 2008;63(8):841-47.

Snapp CA, Donaldson SK. Gestational diabetes mellitus: physical exercise and health outcomes. *Biological Research for Nursing*. 2008;10(2):145-55.

Stathi A, Simey P. Quality of life in the Fourth Age: exercise experiences of nursing home residents. *Journal of Aging and Physical Activity*. 2007;15(3):272-86.

Stewart KJ, Sung J, Silber HA, Fleg JL, Kelemen MD, Turner KL, Bacher AC, Dobrosielski DA, DeRegis JR, Shapiro EP, Ouyang P. Exaggerated Exercise Blood Pressure is Related to Impaired Endothelial Vasodilatory Function. *American Journal of Hypertension*. 2004;17(4):314-20.

Wang TJ, Belza B, Elaine Thompson F, Whitney JD, Bennett K. Effects of aquatic exercise on flexibility, strength and aerobic fitness in adults with osteoarthritis of the hip or knee. *Journal of Advanced Nursing*. 2007;57(2):141-52.

Weker H. Simple obesity in children: A study on the role of nutritional factors. *Med Wieku Rozwoj*. 2006;10(1):3-191.

Chapter 9: Nutrition

Topics Covered

Introduction to Nutrition
Recommended Caloric Intake
Nutrition for Working Out

Carbohydrates
Recommended Carbohydrate Intake
Types of Carbohydrates
Carbohydrates for Working Out
Alcohol as a Carbohydrate?

Fats
The Role of Fats in the Body
Types of Fats
Triglycerides
Unsaturated Fats
Trans Fats
Saturated Fats
Cholesterol
Problems with Fats
Metabolic Syndrome
Obesity
Insulin Resistance
Heart Disease
Fat Requirements

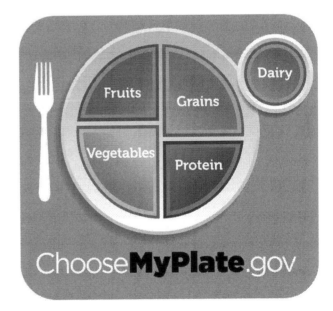

Protein
Protein Digestion
Factors that Affect Protein Requirements

Proper Hydration
Sports Drinks vs. Water
Signs of Dehydration
Hydration to Maximize Training

Supplements
Types of Supplements

Introduction to Nutrition

One of the most important aspects of designing a complete personal program for a client is advice on proper nutrition. Regardless of a client's goals for personal fitness and training, the fundamentals of a proper diet do not change. In fact, a training regimen combined with proper nutrition will enhance the client's health and performance, help fight disease and infection, increase energy and reduce total body fat. It is the job of the personal trainer to be armed with information on proper nutrition as a means of counteracting the popularity of fad diets and the "lose weight quickly" mentality.

The relationship between physical activity and caloric intake is a simple one: eat fewer calories than you burn and you will lose weight; eat more calories than what you expend and you will gain weight. All of life's processes require the energy provided by food and exercise only increases these requirements. However, knowing when to eat and what to eat at each meal is the key to the client achieving fitness and training goals. Keep in mind, however, that exercise increases the rate at which calories are burned; however, only 40% of the potential energy in food is converted into energy; the other 60% is lost as heat. The rate of sweating increases in the body's attempt to lower its temperature. Because of this, frequent hydration is an important component of proper nutrition in order to maintain the body's water content and replace any fluid lost as sweat.

For athletes and physically active adults, each meal should consist of 65% of the calories from carbohydrates, specifically complex carbohydrates, 15–20% from lean protein and 15–20% from fat. Carbohydrates, which are converted to the forms glucose and glycogen, are the body's primary source of instant energy and longer term energy storage, respectively. Additionally, carbohydrates are required to burn fat; without a sufficient quantity of carbohydrates, a person will not effectively lose body fat. Protein is required to build and repair body tissues and structures. It is also used in the process of synthesizing hormones and hemoglobin, and is the body's alternative source of energy if there is an insufficient source of carbohydrates. Fats are also an important aspect of a proper nutrition regimen and should not be feared. Fats are needed for the proper absorption of many vitamins, minerals and supplements, and they

Weight Maintenance

Weight Gain

Weight Loss

Food Intake

Energy Expenditure

function as the long-term energy storage for the body.

Recommended Caloric Intake

Although a client should not become obsessive over daily calorie intake, it is helpful to establish caloric intake requirements. There are two simple ways to do this: determine a client's resting metabolic rate (RMR) and lean body weight (LBW). The resting metabolic rate is the amount of energy needed to sustain the body at rest and is determined by multiplying the body weight by 10. For example, if a client weighs 150 pounds, the RMR is 1,500, meaning that the client requires at least 1,500 calories per day. Next, estimate the calories expended for scheduled exercise and training. For easy activities, a person will expend around 3-5 calories per minute. For moderate activity, assign 6-10 calories per minute and, for strenuous activity, estimate 11-15 calories per minute. To calculate the calories used for scheduled training, multiply the number of minutes spent in that activity (do not count time spent resting and recovering) by the assigned calories burned per minute for that level of intensity.

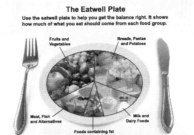

The Eatwell Plate
Use the eatwell plate to help you get the balance right. It shows how much of what you eat should come from each food group.

Fruits and Vegetables
Breads, Pastas and Potatoes
Meat, Fish and Alternatives
Milk and Dairy Foods
Foods containing fat and foods containing sugar

For example, if a client participated in a normal 40-minute strength training session, then the trainer calculates that the client expended approximately 240 calories [because (6.8 METs x 3.5 x 50 kg)/200=6 calories/minute] for that session. Next the trainer estimates the time spent in activity outside of scheduled exercise. For a sedentary person, add 20-40% of the RMR; for a moderately active person, add 40-60% of the RMR; and for a very active person add 60-80% of the RMR. A moderately active client weighing 150 pounds requires 750 calories for daily activity:

(150 lbs x 10 = 1500 RMR) x

50% moderate activity =

750 moderate daily activity calories

To determine the total calorie requirement per day, add the RMR plus the formal exercise plus the daily activity:

1,500 RMR calories + 240 formal exercise calories

750 activity calories = 2,490 total

calories required per day

The other method to determine daily calorie requirements for a client is to estimate the client's lean body weight (LBW). To use this method, a trainer must know the client's body fat percentage, which is multiplied by the client's weight to determine the body fat weight.

For example, a client weighing 150 pounds with a 22% body fat percentage has a body fat weight of 33 pounds of body fat.

150 lbs x 22% body fat = 33 lbs body fat

Next, the trainer determines the client's lean body weight by subtracting the body fat from the total weight. For this client, the lean body weight would be 117 pounds, indicating that the client's bones, muscle and soft tissue weigh 117 pounds.

150 lbs – 33 lbs body fat = 117 lbs LBW

(lean body fat weight)

To determine the lower range of your client's calorie intake, multiply her LBW by 16. This client requires at least 1,872 calories per day. To find the upper limit of the calorie intake, add 500 calories, which for this client would equal 2,372 calories per day.

117 LBW x 16 = 1872

lower range of calorie intake

(117 LBW x 16) + 500 = 2372

upper limit of calorie intake

Notice that there is a slight difference in daily calorie requirements between the two methods. The RMR determination can be higher by up to 1,000 calories since it takes into account scheduled and nonscheduled training. Regardless of the method used, however, it is important to remember that this is an estimate. If a client

begins to gain fat and the goal is to lose fat, it may be necessary to adjust calorie intake. Additionally, many factors can influence daily energy requirements. The resting metabolic rate and daily activity will use most of the available energy per day. The rest of the energy that is used is determined by such factors as sex, activity level, weight, body composition and age.

Many clients will be interested in how to put on muscle while simultaneously reducing body fat—unfortunately, they often turn to diets where they dramatically lower total energy intake. This practice is actually counterproductive because they will burn into their lean body mass. This will reduce their total muscle mass and decrease their metabolic rate, the rate at which they burn calories. The result of a lower metabolic rate is usually an increase in body weight (from an increase in body fat) due to the body's inability to effectively burn the calories that are consumed. Conversely, many people will turn to eating a high amount of protein;

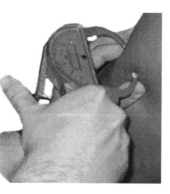

however, a high-protein diet does not amount to more muscle mass because muscles are unable to store excess protein. Additionally, a client may want to consume high calorie shakes or other dietary supplements, wrongly thinking that the calories will be turned into muscle. Unfortunately, all extra energy that is not used, regardless of the form, is stored as fat.

The goal for nutrition is to have a client in an energy balance, consuming and burning an equal amount of calories. Many studies now suggest that the best way to achieve energy balance is to spread the intake of calories evenly over the course of the day by eating small, frequent meals, rather than three large meals separated by long time gaps. This practice has been shown to have many benefits, including maintaining metabolic rate and blood sugar level, decreasing body fat and increasing lean body mass, and improving performance. Additionally, energy deficits can be better managed or possibly eliminated by spreading calorie intake evenly over the entire day. Problems caused by energy deficits, which can be most evident early in the day or after intense training, include the following: an inability to maintain energy stores (affecting endurance), an inability to maintain lean muscle mass and metabolic rate, and an increased risk of injury due to both muscle and mental fatigue.

> The goal for nutrition is to have a client in an energy balance, consuming and burning an equal amount of calories.

Nutrition for Working Out

Not only is it important for a client to eat small frequent meals throughout the day that contain the correct proportion of carbohydrates, protein and fats, it is also important to determine what a client will eat before, during and after the workout. Although the timing and type of nutrition to suggest to a client has been determined by science, all people are different and this regimen may take experimentation to determine what works for each individual client.

Although eating before a workout or competition can cause stomach discomfort and diarrhea, it is important that a client eat before participating in physical activity to maintain constant blood sugar levels and prevent early fatigue. Following a few guidelines can help eliminate any possible discomfort. First, a client should be consuming a low-fat, high carbohydrate diet daily. This will help ensure that there are adequate energy stores (in the form of glycogen) in the muscles and liver. A client should avoid meals high in fat and protein immediately prior to activity. If the planned activity will be shorter than an hour, eating foods such as breads and pasta should be sufficient. However, if the activity will last longer than an hour, foods with lower glycemic indexes, such as bananas and oatmeal, are recommended because they provide sustained energy.

For short workouts (less than 30 minutes), it is usually unnecessary for a client to eat during the activity. However, for light to moderate intensity exercise, most people can tolerate small amounts of plain food and this may increase their performance. For activities lasting longer than 60 minutes, maintaining a sufficient fluid and carbohydrate supply becomes a challenge. For fluids, a client's sweat loss should match their fluid intake. To determine if fluids are being adequately replenished, weigh the client before, during and after long, vigorous workouts. Ingesting enough carbohydrates is also important to maintain blood sugar levels and ensure endurance for long workouts. Every hour of endurance exercise requires approximately 100-300 carbohydrate calories or about 0.5-0.8 grams of carbohydrate per pound of body weight.

The recovery diet is an often overlooked but extremely important component of the client's performance on days following training. The priorities are carbohydrate and fluid replacement. After exercise, a client should begin to immediately replace fluid loss by drinking water (possibly sports drinks if severely dehydrated) and by eating food with high water content. After stopping the activity, the first major intake of food should be approximately no less than 15 minutes and no

more than 2 hours. It should consist of about 300 calories of carbohydrate-rich foods such as bananas. It is also recommended that protein, such as that provided by lean meats and low-fat milk, be a part of the recovery meal. Protein helps shuttle blood glucose to muscles to replenish glycogen stores and is needed for cell and tissue repair following a workout.

Proper nutrition is extremely important for a person's health and performance. Although the trainer and client should both be aware of what the client is eating, the process does not have to be complex. The trainer can monitor the client's eating habits for several weeks by having the client keep a food journal. Additionally, trainers can help clients learn to read food labels to determine how many grams of carbohydrate, fat and protein they are consuming per day. It may also be helpful to suggest that clients buy a food scale so they can accurately measure serving sizes. After the trainer and client have determined a regimen for exercise nutrition, it will still require periodic adjustments to ensure that the client is performing as well as possible.

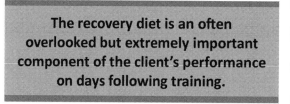

The recovery diet is an often overlooked but extremely important component of the client's performance on days following training.

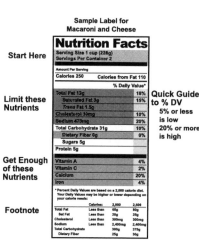

There are six essential classes of nutrients the body needs to function properly. The first is carbohydrates, the body's primary fuel sources. Fat is the second—despite popular belief, the body does need fat to transport vitamins A, D, E and K. The third class of nutrients is proteins, which help to keep our bodies supplied with the eight essential amino acids. The next is vitamins. Vitamins work as coenzymes to aid the many enzymatic processes occurring in the body at any given moment. The fifth is minerals, such as zinc and iron, which function as cofactors for many biological processes. Without iron, the body could not transport oxygen to any tissues. The last but not least is water. The body needs water, plain and simple.

Carbohydrates

Carbohydrates are chains of sugars held together by chemical bonds. Sugars are also known as saccharides. There are five monosaccharides, or single sugars, that are the building blocks for carbohydrates. Three of the best-known monosaccharides are: glucose, fructose and galactose (milk sugar). The body can absorb several different types of monosaccharides and disaccharides (simple sugars made up of two monosaccharides, like sucrose and lactose);

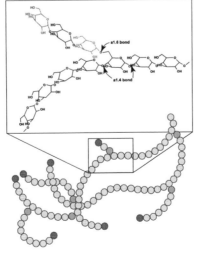

however, it can only use glucose as a form of energy. When someone drinks milk, for instance, the galactose is absorbed and transported to the liver where enzymes in the liver convert galactose (or any other carbohydrate) into glucose for the body to use. Any excess glucose is converted into glycogen, which is the storage molecule made from glucose. Glycogen is stored in the liver. When the body needs it, the liver converts the glycogen back to glucose for use. For any active person, carbohydrates are the number one source of energy because they are metabolized the fastest. Fat is the slowest to be metabolized and protein is somewhere in the middle; therefore a good balance of all three is necessary.

Carbohydrates have received a bad reputation in recent years due to diets such as the Atkins and South Beach Diet. However, not all carbohydrates are bad, and a good understanding of this is key to any client who is trying to improve overall health. Carbohydrates are more than just sugar. Complex carbohydrates like the fiber found in fruits, vegetables, cereals and whole grains are important energy sources for the body. Fiber is also important for maintaining the health and function of the digestive system as well as for weight control. Trainers should make sure clients fully understand food groups and classifications before they start omitting food items from their diets. A good understanding of food labels is important.

So what is the difference between simple carbohydrates and complex carbohydrates? The term complex carbohydrate simply means that the source is primarily made from monosaccharides, disaccharides or polysaccharides. In general, monosaccharides and disaccharides are considered simple. An example of a simple carbohydrate would be a soda, which is made from high fructose corn syrup (fructose is a monosaccharide). Breads made from bleached flour are also considered simple carbohydrates. Care should be taken with wheat bread: if the labeling does not state 100% whole wheat or other whole grains, it is not a complex carbohydrate and therefore no better than white bread. An apple is also a complex carbohydrate. It has fructose (or fruit sugar), but it is plant material that contains cellulose, which is a polysaccharide. Vegetables are polysaccharides and thus considered complex.

Recommended Carbohydrate Intake

A food pyramid shows that the suggested foundation for any dietary plan is carbohydrates.

In general, the abundance of calories should come from carbohydrates. Dietary guidelines currently recommend that 40-60% of daily calories come from carbohydrates—for an active person, 60-65% is probably best. Carbohydrates are the main fuel of muscles. Many people think that increasing the amount of protein will increase their muscle size. Protein is important after a strenuous workout because the amino acids in protein are used to help repair and renew muscles; however, during a workout, the body is using carbohydrates for fuel.

Of course, exercise physiology is not that simple, as fat is also being used at low levels during training. In reality, a combination of fat and carbohydrates are used during any workout. While carbohydrates are used to fuel the body when the body is at work, fat is the main source of fuel when the body is at rest or during low levels of exercise. The problem is that most American diets contain an overabundance of fat. A person should be eating 200-300 grams of carbohydrates based on a 2000 calories/day diet. There are 4 calories in every gram of carbohydrate or protein, and there are 9 calories per every gram of fat.

Types of Carbohydrates

Not surprisingly, a candy bar, which is mostly sugar and fat, is not the same as an apple or an orange. The fruit is more nutritionally dense because, while it also has sugar, it has fiber and vitamins that are also good for the body. If an individual is just counting calories, some candy bars may seem similar to some fruits. A banana, for example, is a high carbohydrate fruit and may have the same calories as a candy bar, but the banana is more nutritious. Vegetables contain very little sugar but can still be high in carbohydrates. Potatoes, for example, are considered more of a starch (carbohydrate) than a vegetable. Broccoli is another vegetable, but its carbohydrates come from its high content of cellulose. The body lacks the enzyme to break down cellulose, making broccoli a good source of fiber and low in calories. We cannot digest the majority of the vegetable, but we get many nutrients in the form of vitamins and minerals; therefore, broccoli is a high-density food for this reason.

The body lacks the enzyme to break down cellulose.

While it is not bad to occasionally eat a candy bar, the majority of carbohydrate calories should come from foods that are nutritionally dense. A personal trainer will be asked all sorts of questions regarding health, fitness and nutrition, so it is important to have an understanding of the basics of nutrition. Most people trying to lose weight want to omit food groups or extremely limit an entire nutrient class. The advice should be that fad diets do not work in the long run. Instead, clients should educate themselves on the six classes of nutrients the body needs for proper function. It is very important when trying to achieve or maintain a healthy standard of living to include maintaining proper weight and muscle mass.

Classification	GI Range	Examples
Low GI	55 or less	most fruit and vegetables (except potatoes, watermelon), grainy breads, pasta, legumes/pulses, milk, products extremely low in carbohydrates (fish, eggs, meat, nuts, oils)
Medium GI	56-69	whole wheat products, brown rice, basmati rice, orange sweet potato, table sugar
High GI	70-99	corn flakes, baked potato, watermelon, some white rices (e.g., jasmine), croissant, white bread, candy, cereal
	100	straight glucose

Most people have heard about the glycemic index and personal trainers are undoubtedly going to be asked about it by clients. The glycemic index is a ranking of carbohydrates based on their simplicity; simple carbohydrates have a higher GI and vice versa. When a person consumes a carbohydrate-rich meal, digestive enzymes break down the carbohydrates starting in the mouth. Digestion continues in the stomach; however, the majority of carbohydrate digestion occurs in the small intestines.

The simpler the sugar, the easier and faster the breakdown of that carbohydrate is going to occur. The idea behind simple sugars being "bad" derives from studies showing a "crash" after a meal of mostly simple carbohydrates. This is believed to happen because digestion occurs so fast that the result is a huge spike in insulin, which is responsible for transporting glucose into the cells. A huge sugar spike means a "crash" will follow, leaving the individual feeling sluggish. This is also believed to be one of the leading causes in type II diabetes. A person eating in this fashion is constantly cycling between this spiked insulin and then a huge drop. The cells stop responding to the insulin stimulus and stop letting the glucose from the high carbohydrate meals into the cells. The result is high glucose in the blood, also known as diabetes. Type II diabetes is different than type I because, in type I, there is a defect in the production of insulin—this is usually a genetic defect and has nothing to do with how the person eats. This is also why type II diabetes is a gradual process: it takes time for the cells to finally stop responding.

The glycemic index was designed to help reduce type II diabetes by giving people a means to label a food as either a good or bad carbohydrate. The lower the GI for a particular food, the better it is because the insulin released will be gradual since the body will take longer to break down a complex carbohydrate than a simple carbohydrate. A personal trainer should also advise a client that no foods need to be totally eliminated. Once a food is omitted, it becomes that much more alluring. Clients should allow themselves to still enjoy an occasional ice cream or candy, just not every day. A dietary plan followed 60-70% of the time is still successful. Many clients will think if they "cheat" on their diet one day, there is no use working out or following the plan for the rest of the day. This is not the case so trainers should advise them to forget the slip-up and keep moving forward. One Friday night binge or skipped workout is not failure. Trainers need to keep clients, as well as themselves, positive.

> A huge sugar spike means a "crash" will follow, leaving the individual feeling sluggish.

Carbohydrates for Working Out

As already stated, an extremely athletic person should be consuming 60% of calories from carbohydrates. Fluids are also important in order to stay hydrated throughout the day; however, clients should try to not drink copious amount of water a few hours before or during their workout. They should try to avoid caffeinated and carbonated drinks on workout days. Studies have shown that for every hour of endurance workout (cardio), a person needs 100-300 carbohydrate calories. Trainers should recommend that, approximately three hours before clients work out, they should eat a high carbohydrate meal equivalent to what will be needed for their workout. They can have a small snack right before, such as crackers and juice, if they like. Preferably, some of the meal should come from foods with a low glycemic index, which will keep them feeling fuller longer and help to avoid any "crashing" due to insulin spiking. After their workout, trainers may want to suggest a slightly higher protein meal to help repair any muscle damage from their session. On non-workout days, they should try to stay within their recommended caloric intake; 40-60% of their daily calories should be coming from carbohydrates.

Alcohol as a Carbohydrate?

Many people enjoy a beer or wine at the end of their day to help them relax. Clients may wonder if this is hurting or slowing their progress or how alcohol factors into their daily caloric intake and overall nutrition. Contrary to popular belief, alcohol is not a carbohydrate. It contains carbohydrates because it is generated from various grains which are themselves carbohydrates. However, there are very few residual carbohydrates left over from the processes of making alcohol. To be more specific, beer and wine are made through a process of fermentation so these types of alcohol contain a small amount of carbohydrates. However, liquor such as whiskey or vodka is made from a distillation process which leaves nothing but the ethanol. Another important aspect of alcohol is that despite what most people hear, the breakdown products are not sugar. When alcohol of any sort is consumed, it is metabolized in the liver by an enzyme called alcohol dehydrogenase, and that enzyme breaks alcohol down into a chemical called acetate. Acetate is not a sugar and thus not a carbohydrate.

Alcohol does have a lot of calories. Next to fat, it has the most: 7 calories for every gram of alcohol. If a person is trying to lose weight, it is important to decrease the amount of alcohol because it is very calorie dense but provides virtually no nutritional value. This is why beer companies have tried decreasing the amount of carbohydrates in beer in order to lower calories without lowering alcohol content. The focus on lowering carbohydrates has given the general public the impression that alcohol is a carbohydrate, while in actuality it

If a person is trying to lose weight, it is important to decrease the amount of alcohol.

253

has more calories than carbohydrates and is not a carbohydrate. If trainers are asked this question, the response to give is that alcohol is not a carbohydrate nor is it converted into a carbohydrate, and it has more calories than a carbohydrate. Another important fact about alcohol is that it is a diuretic, which means that it blocks the hormone responsible for keeping water in the body and will cause the person to excrete more urine than normal. Also, alcoholic drinks are often laden with sugary mixtures, such as margaritas and daiquiris, that are high in simple sugars and that are essentially empty calories. Beer or wine is a much better alternative.

Fats

Fats, or lipids as they are commonly referred to in nutritional circles, are an important part of the diet. It is essential that personal trainers and clients understand the role of particular fats in the body in order to include them in the diet in the most beneficial way. Many people have either a fear of eating fat and avoid it altogether or a misguided belief that athletes can benefit from a high-fat diet for increased performance. It is generally accepted that neither a very low fat nor a very high fat diet is ultimately beneficial for active individuals. A balanced diet with between 25-

30% of a person's daily calories coming from fat is ideal for maintaining a healthy weight, keeping up bodily energy levels and maintaining metabolic functions. Those who aim to lose body fat as part of their workout goals may restrict fats to as low as about 10% of their daily calories; however, limiting one's intake to lower than this is not advisable due to the important role of fats in the body.

The Role of Fats in the Body

Most athletes understand that the body relies primarily on carbohydrates as an immediate source of energy. Fats, however, are also very important in the release of energy to the muscles of the body. They are the most concentrated energy source in the body and provide over double the amount of calories per gram than protein or carbohydrates; 9 calories versus 4 calories. Because fats are so energy dense, they should be eaten wisely. When calorie requirements for a person increase, as they do during a training schedule, their fat requirement also increases. It is advisable to make sure that when food consumption is increased in order to increase calories, fat intake stays in the same ratio. High-fat, low-carbohydrate diets, which are very popular among people currently, are generally thought to be inappropriate for athletes seeking

Fats are very important in the release of energy to the muscles of the body.

to increase their energy output because of the potential to starve the body of energy from carbohydrates.

It is important to understand the role of fats in the transportation of vitamins around the body. Many essential vitamins cannot be utilized by the body without the fats that provide the medium for them to enter the body's cells. Physically active adults will often gain benefits from carefully supplementing with fat-soluble vitamins (A, D, E and K) and essential fatty acids. These vitamins act as anti-oxidants, helping to repair the damaged cells and tissue in the body that are a normal result of working out. Healthy fats in the diet ensure that these vitamins are of the most benefit to clients.

Hormones are extremely important chemicals in the body. They regulate many different body systems and have a large effect on energy levels and the building of muscle tissue. In order for the body to manufacture these important regulatory hormones, it must have fats. Fats form the precursors, or first steps, that allow the body to make what it needs.

Nerve fibers in the body transmit messages to muscles and organs via electrical impulses. Fats are used by the body to compose a myelin sheath which coats these nerve fibers and allows the messages to move around the body without difficulty.

Hormones regulate many different body systems and have a large effect on energy levels and the building of muscle tissue.

Many people who make the loss of body fat a goal of their exercise program may complain that they do not feel full or satisfied after a well-balanced meal. Fats play a role in helping to provide this feeling. They stay in the stomach longer and therefore create the sense of feeling fuller for a longer period of time. The ability of the fat molecule to require a longer time to break down can also help prevent people from overeating.

The cells that make up all of the body's organs and tissues, including the muscles, require fats to help send and receive signals from other cells. This is especially important in the brain, where fatty acid chains assist messages to cross synapses as the neurons fire. New studies also stress the importance of "brown fat" in signaling cells to create muscle tissue, which is essential for the human body and especially those of athletes.

A complex mixture of nutrients, minerals and vitamins must pass in and out of cells through the cell membranes in order to be used by the body. Lipid molecules are able to control this process, ensuring the body is able to extract what it needs for optimal functioning from the foods eaten.

Fats not only act as a physical buffer for the organs, protecting them if the body suffers a blow or a fall, but more importantly, they form a kind of barrier around the organs, protecting them from disease organisms and toxins until they can be removed from the body.

Types of Fats

Fat molecules are referred to as fatty acids. They are essentially long chains of hydrocarbons (longer than a typical acid) with a carboxyl group on the end. There are many different kinds of fatty acids that vary slightly in the numbers and composition of their hydrocarbons.

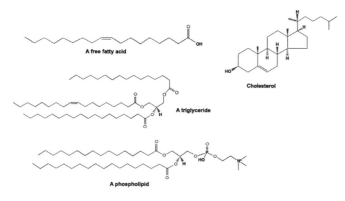

Some of the most beneficial types of fats are known collectively as omega-3 fatty acids. These fatty acids assist in brain function and are important for the health of the heart and the joints. There are three main types of omega-3 fatty acids: Docosahexaenoic acid (DHA), Eicosapentaenoic acid (EPA) and Alpha-linolenic acid (ALA).

EPA and DHA are found primarily in fatty fish like sardines and salmon, while ALA is commonly found in vegetable oils, avocados and walnuts. The body converts ALA to EPA and DHA in order to use it for cellular functions. Fish oil supplements are readily available for those who find it difficult or unpalatable to eat fish once or twice a week as recommended to meet the body's need for EPA and DHA omega-3 fatty acids.

Triglycerides

The "normal" fats that we eat are composed of three fatty acid chains bonded together with glycerol. These are known as triglycerides and an excess of these molecules can cause fatty build up around the body. The types of fatty acids that make up these molecules determine the properties of the particular fats. For example, whether a fat is a solid or a liquid at room temperature or whether or not it saturates, is determined by the particular acid chains that make up the triglycerides. Some studies show that an increased intake of medium-chain triglycerides (MCT) may be a good way for athletes to positively increase their caloric intake, but these studies are not conclusive.

Unsaturated Fats

These fats have certain hydrogen atoms missing from their carbon/hydrogen chains, forcing the carbons to make a double bond. For this reason, these fats are liquid at room temperature. Those with one double bond are referred to as mono-unsaturated fats. Examples are olive oil and canola oil. Fats with double carbon bonds are referred to as poly-unsaturated. Many researchers and nutritionists recommend that mono-unsaturates should make up a large proportion of the fats consumed by a healthy, active person. It should be noted, however, that current research shows that unsaturated fats should not be heated, as this changes the properties of the oil and makes them act more like a trans fat in the body.

Trans Fats

Trans fats refer to a group of unsaturated fats that are normally liquid at room temperature but have been "hydrogenated" in order to make them solid. This process is used, for example, to turn vegetable oils into margarine. The fat is heated to a high temperature to break the double bonds and attach hydrogen to them. Trans fats are difficult for the body to metabolize and are associated with health problems like high cholesterol and heart disease. Most studies conclude that eating less hydrogenated fats will likely decrease LDL levels. Many prepared foods, like cakes and chips, are made with trans fats because they are inexpensive to use in the processing of foods.

> Trans fats are difficult for the body to metabolize and are associated with health problems like high cholesterol and heart disease.

Saturated Fats

These fats have every bond filled with a hydrogen atom and are, therefore, termed "saturated" or "filled up." They are solid at room temperature and have received considerable negative attention because of the link between their consumption and increased blood cholesterol levels and heart disease. Because they are both saturated and solid, they are more likely to deposit in the walls of the arteries, creating blockages. Recent studies have shown, however, that because of their chemical composition, these fats may not be as bad for the body as originally thought and cooking with butter, a saturated fat, is now preferred over margarine among many nutrition scientists. Although eating butter and other saturated fats, such as those found in red meats, should be limited, these fats are currently preferred by health professionals over trans fats. Part of the reason is that the molecules that form a saturated fat are more easily recognized and processed by the body than the physically-altered molecules of trans fats.

Cholesterol

The amount of cholesterol and fat found in people's diets is directly related to the amount of cholesterol circulating in their blood. Studies

	Saturated g/100g	Monounsaturated g/100g	Polyunsaturated g/100g	Cholesterol mg/100g	Vitamin E mg/100g
Animal fats					
Lard	40.8	43.8	9.6	93	0.00
Butter	54.0	19.8	2.6	230	2.00
Vegetable fats					
Coconut oil	85.2	6.6	1.7	0	.66
Palm oil	45.3	41.6	8.3	0	33.12
Cottonseed oil	25.5	21.3	48.1	0	42.77
Wheat germ oil	18.8	15.9	60.7	0	136.65
Soya oil	14.5	23.2	56.5	0	16.29
Olive oil	14.0	69.7	11.2	0	5.10
Corn oil	12.7	24.7	57.8	0	17.24
Sunflower oil	11.9	20.2	63.0	0	49.0
Safflower oil	10.2	12.6	72.1	0	40.68
Rapeseed/Canola Oil	5.3	64.3	24.8	0	22.21

have shown that eating foods high in saturated fats (e.g., butter) or trans fats (e.g., margarine) increase the amount of "bad" cholesterol, or LDL, in the blood. High LDL cholesterol levels have been linked to heart disease in many individuals. Raising levels of "good" cholesterol, or HDL, in the blood can help to lower the LDL. Foods that raise HDL cholesterol include those high in omega-3 fatty acids, high-fiber foods like oat bran and lentils, and oils like olive oil and canola oil.

Problems with Fats

Metabolic Syndrome

This is a group of symptoms that includes obesity, insulin resistance and cardiovascular problems. Overeating in general and eating a diet high in saturated or trans fats can contribute to this syndrome. A simple way to help protect against this combination of health problems is to keep the polyunsaturated/saturated fat ratio of the diet in a healthy range. Balancing fats with carbohydrates and protein, as well as eating plenty of fiber, can also protect against developing this deadly combination.

Obesity

Fat molecules in excess of what is needed by the body form large droplets, or globules, that clump together and form adipose tissue, or white fat. This fat collects in the body's "problem areas" and it is difficult for the body to burn these fatty deposits because they are not well supplied with blood, which carries the hormones that assist in the process of burning white fat.

Consuming more than 30% of calories from fat slows metabolism and contributes to the depositing of dietary fat in stores in the body. Obesity is not simply a result of the overconsumption of fat. There are many environmental, physical and social factors that contribute to a person's likelihood of becoming obese. Understanding that these factors all play a role in storing excess fat in the body is important when making dietary and exercise recommendations.

Insulin Resistance

Insulin resistance is a condition that increases a person's risk of developing diabetes or heart disease. Storing excess fat increases a person's risk of developing insulin resistance because fat in the body interferes with the ability of the muscles to use insulin properly. Studies suggest that there is a clear connection between excess fat and the inability to use insulin properly.

Heart Disease

Saturated fats have long been connected to problems with heart muscle function. Arteries that supply the heart with blood become hardened and clogged from the build-up of fats, which negatively affects their ability to function properly. High LDL cholesterol levels, as well as the stress on the heart from supplying excess body tissue with blood, can also contribute to problems with proper heart functioning.

Fat Requirements

Different people have different fat requirements. Those who have high cholesterol, who are obese or who are suffering from other conditions, such as high blood pressure or heart disease, will need to pay very careful attention to the types of fats they eat to best control their conditions. Most people can benefit from a diet lower in saturated fat and higher in unsaturated fat, with care taken to avoid partially hydrogenated oils or trans fats and attention given to include good sources of omega-3 fatty acids. A good way to avoid the consumption of "bad" and unwanted fats is to avoid processed and prepared foods. If clients prepare their own foods, they will be better able to control the type and amount of fats they ingest. Fats are an important component of a healthy diet and essential to an active and optimally-functioning metabolism. It is not necessary to be obsessed with fat consumption but understanding the functions of fat in the body will help personal trainers better advise clients about their individual dietary needs.

> Consuming more than 30% of calories from fat slows metabolism and contributes to the depositing of dietary fat in stores in the body.

Protein

Proteins are large molecules made up of individual amino acids linked together by a peptide bond, similar to pearls on a necklace.

The amino acids are arranged in a specific sequence that folds into particular 3-dimensional structures to yield a specific functional protein. Proteins have a number of functions in the body, including building and repairing tissue, synthesizing hormones and other enzymes and functioning as an energy source for the body in the event of insufficient carbohydrate levels. Good sources of protein include meats, eggs, legumes, nuts and dairy products such as low-fat milk and cheese.

There are 20 different amino acids and they can be divided into two main classes: essential and non-essential. Essential amino acids are those that cannot be synthesized by the body and must be obtained by food or supplements. These include leucine, isoleucine, valine, lysine, threonine, tryptophan, methionine, phenylalanine, histidine and arginine. The last two amino acids are termed semi-essential as they are produced at levels too low to sustain growth, especially in children. The non-essential amino acids are alanine, asparagine, aspartic acid, cysteine, glutamic acid, glycine, proline, serine and tyrosine. These amino acids are synthesized by the body in sufficient amounts using fats and carbohydrates as building block precursors.

Protein Digestion

In order to build protein in the body, the ingested protein must first be broken down into its individual amino acids through the process of digestion. Where the amino acids end up after digestion will depend on the needs of the body. If too little protein is consumed, the body will begin to burn lean muscle mass. Excess protein is not stored in the muscles for muscle building; it is instead converted to fat or carbohydrate and then stored, or it is excreted in urine.

Digestion of proteins begins in the stomach where harsh hydrochloric acid causes the protein to denature or unfold. This unfolding allows proteases (enzymes that cut proteins) such as pepsin to begin to break the peptide bonds between the amino acids, releasing short polypeptide (protein) chains and individual amino acids. In the small intestines, the polypeptides are further broken into chains of two to three amino acids. The resulting dipeptides and tripeptides are absorbed through the cells lining the small intestines and are further cut into individual amino acids which then enter the bloodstream. They then travel to the liver and other tissues for protein synthesis.

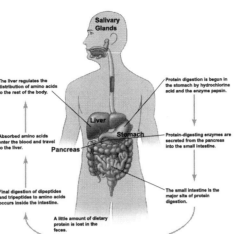

Not all protein-rich foods are able to equally satisfy the body's need for amino acids. When determining the quality of a protein, physiologists examine the amino acid content, the digestibility of the protein and its bioavailability, as well as the ability of the body to incorporate that protein's amino acids into its own tissues. There are several methods to determine these values, such as the protein efficiency ratio (PER), which examines the ability of the amino acids to be incorporated into tissues by measuring muscle growth. However, the values were determined for lab rats, which may have different amino acid requirements than humans.

Historically, protein quality was determined by measuring the biological value (BV), which measures nitrogen incorporation from digested proteins. Proteins with a higher BV score contain a ratio of different amino acids that are most suited for the needs of the human body.

For example, a chicken egg has a BV of 94 while beef has a BV of 76. Unfortunately, BV content is an idea that is often misused, especially by marketers of protein supplements. They try to sell the idea that if someone who is already consuming adequate protein takes a high-BV supplement, then that person will build muscle to a greater degree than someone who is not taking the supplement. However, excess protein is not stored for later use in the muscles; any unused amino acids are stored as fat or are excreted from the body. One advantage, though, of consuming foods with a high BV is that a

Biological Value of Some Protein-Rich Foods

	Ile	Leu	Val	Thr	Met + Cys	Trp	Lys	Phe + Tyr	His	Biological Value
Egg, chicken	1,0	1,0	1,0	1,0	1,0	1,0	1,0	1,0	1,0	0,94
Milk, human	1,1	1,4	1,0	1,0	1,1	1,6	1,0	1,0	0,9	0,95
Milk, cow	1,1	1,3	1,0	0,9	0,7	1,3	1,3	0,9	1,1	0,90
Muscle, beef	0,8	0,9	0,7	0,9	0,9	0,9	1,4	0,7	1,6	0,76
Soybeans	1,0	0,9	0,8	0,8	0,6	1,3	1,1	1,0	1,4	0,75
Rice	0,8	0,9	0,9	0,8	0,9	1,2	0,5	1,2	0,8	0,75
Wheat	0,6	0,8	0,6	0,7	0,8	1,1	0,4	0,8	1,0	0,67
Potatoes	0,6	1,1	0,8	1,3	0,6	1,9	1,4	0,8	1,1	0,67
Oats	0,8	0,8	0,8	0,7	0,6	1,2	0,6	1,0	1,1	0,66
Corn	1,0	1,7	0,8	0,7	1,1	0,5	0,4	1,0	1,0	0,60

Source: McGilvery, Biochemistry, 1970

person's amino acid requirement can be met with less total protein, thus a person may be able to cut calories from his diet if the goal is to lose weight. Conversely, if one consumes low-BV foods, more protein will be needed to satisfy the amino acid requirement. The shortcomings of using BV is that it does not include factors that affect digestion of protein and it measures the maximum potential of amino acid incorporation and not an actual value.

The current preferred method to determine protein quality is referred to as the protein digestibility corrected amino acid score, or PDCAAS. This method determines the content of amino acids of certain proteins based on the actual amino acid needs of children between the ages of two and five (an age group that is considered to be the most nutritionally-demanding). This method is not without its flaws. PDCAAS measures the amount of protein present in feces and compares that to what is eaten. The result is the amount of protein utilized by the body. However, most of the protein that reaches the colon is consumed by bacteria and would not be present in the feces. According to measures by the PDCAAS method, it would appear that protein has been digested and used by the body, when in fact it has not.

Factors that Affect Protein Requirements

The primary uses for amino acids in the body are the anabolic processes, such as building muscle mass. Therefore, it is not surprising that athletes have a higher requirement for protein than a sedentary population. Having a sufficient supply of amino acids enhances protein synthesis for muscle building during anaerobic activities and for muscle recovery and repair afterwards. Endurance athletes also have a need for increased protein intake. For example, marathoners may not want to "bulk up," but having extra protein prevents lean muscle mass from being consumed for energy during long runs, which will have an overall detrimental effect on endurance abilities. Protein requirements increase as total energy or calorie intake decreases overall. When there is an insufficient supply of carbohydrates available for energy, the body will instead use amino acids as its primary energy source. Additionally, children, pregnant and breastfeeding mothers and those recovering from trauma or surgery have an increased need for protein in their diets.

However, consuming too much protein if part of a high-calorie diet will cause the excess protein to be stored as fat rather than used for muscle

> The primary uses for amino acids in the body are the anabolic processes, such as building muscle mass.

building. High-protein fad diets that propose cutting down or eliminating carbohydrates as a way to lose weight can lead to the development of metabolic ketosis that, if severe enough, can lead to coma and death. High protein diets have also been thought to increase blood lipid levels and blood pressure, which can increase the risk for cardiovascular disease. High protein diets may stress the kidneys and, in extreme cases, this can lead to kidney failure. Additionally, high protein diets can lead to calcium loss from bones, which can be extremely dangerous for older, female clients because it increases their risk of osteoporosis. Although athletes and those individuals who regularly exercise need a slight increase in protein over the rest of the population, it is important to stress a balanced diet when advising clients on nutrition. Too much of anything is not a good idea and that also goes for protein.

Proper Hydration

The function of water in the human body is extensive and should be repeatedly emphasized to any athlete. Water makes up about 50% of a woman's total body weight and about 60% in men. Water is responsible for digestion, sweating to maintain temperature regulation, lubricating tissues and joints and is especially important for the elimination of waste. When adding extra physical activity such as moderate exercise, the need for water grows.

When we exercise we use many different muscles. Each muscle generates heat when in motion and that heat translates into an overall higher body temperature. The body starts to perspire to regulate temperature. When we sweat our body loses valuable nutrients that can increase the chance of muscle cramps and injury. Replacing fluids throughout exercise is vital to productive training and overall health. Sweat is mostly water but the other mineral content proportions can vary from individual to individual. The minerals present in sweat are: calcium, sodium, potassium, magnesium, and trace amounts of copper, iron, chromium, nickel, zinc and lead. The amount of each is tied to how often the individual exercises and to that individual's ability to dissipate heat, which can depend on individual acclimation to climate.

The process of sweating is actually controlled in the brain. The skin is one receptor that sends information to the brain

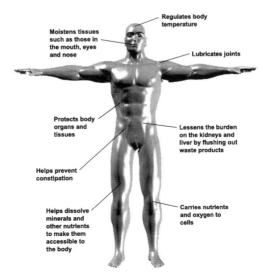

Regulates body temperature

Moistens tissues such as those in the mouth, eyes and nose

Lubricates joints

Protects body organs and tissues

Lessens the burden on the kidneys and liver by flushing out waste products

Helps prevent constipation

Helps dissolve minerals and other nutrients to make them accessible to the body

Carries nutrients and oxygen to cells

but the core temperature is the main catalyst that stimulates sweating. Sweating is actually a twofold process. The sweat on skin evaporates, cooling the skin, but the actual act of sweating cools the core temperature in the body.

Replacing fluid lost through sweating is one of the most important elements of effective training. It is important that hydration happens before, during and after exercise. If a client begins exercising in a dehydrated state, it is impossible to catch up. To help avoid dehydration and its many complications, drink 15 fluid ounces of water or sports drinks 2 to 3 hours before exercising and then 10 fluid ounces again 10-15 minutes prior to the activity.

Electrolytes are positively and negatively charged ions. A common electrolyte is known as sodium chloride, which is table salt. Other electrolytes are potassium, calcium, magnesium, phosphate and sulfate. Electrolytes have a vital function throughout the body. They carry electrical impulses, such as muscle contractions and nerve impulses, to other cells. This function is most important to the heart, nerves and muscles. The kidneys are responsible for maintaining concentrations of electrolytes in the blood. When training, the electrolyte level begins to change because of loss via sweating.

Each drop of sweat takes water and electrolytes out of the body. Replacing electrolytes is vital to hydration during exercise so that the body has all the necessary tools to communicate and regulate temperature. Sports drinks often contain electrolytes such as potassium or sodium chloride and have become a popular water replacement, especially for elite athletes. Are sports drinks a more effective means of hydration?

Sports Drinks vs. Water

Looking at the differences between sports drinks and water can aid clients in the decision as to which is a better choice for their hydration. Water is often free or low-cost, which makes it a more cost-effective means of hydrating, but the lack of flavor can make it a bit boring. This can be easily altered by adding lemon to water or purchasing flavored water Sports drinks come in a variety of flavors that may tend to prompt more drinking because the taste is more enjoyable. The real difference between sports drinks and water is the electrolyte content. Sports drinks are formulated with sodium, potassium and a healthy dose of carbohydrates to enhance energy supply. The sodium can also lift and maintain the sodium balance in the blood, which will keep more fluid

> Electrolytes carry electrical impulses, such as muscle contractions and nerve impulses, to other cells.

in the system, whereas water will stimulate the kidneys to turn on urine production.

For a variety of reasons the sugar content in sports drinks can be an issue for some athletes. Luckily, manufacturers have begun to produce sugar free or low sugar sports drinks. Often the choice between sports drinks and water depends on the individual and the type of exercise or training being performed. Someone taking a brisk 30 minute walk will do fine with a bottle of water, while an elite athlete vigorously training over a period of hours will need the extra ingredients found in sports drinks to regulate electrolytes and enable necessary hydration without overdoing it. For these intensely training athletes, often the best course of action is a combination of sports drinks and water before, during and after their workout.

> If an athlete is even moderately dehydrated it can take many hours for them to consume enough fluid to safely continue their training.

Signs of Dehydration

When individuals are not getting enough to drink, their body will begin to tell them through a variety of symptoms. If these symptoms are ignored, they can grow worse and, in the worst case scenario dehydration, they can lead to death. At the first sign of dehydration, it is vital that any athlete stop, hydrate and then gauge if activity should be continued. It can be difficult to get enough fluid in or for the body to hydrate quickly enough for an athlete to continue. If an athlete is even moderately dehydrated it can take many hours for them to consume enough fluid to safely continue their training. The first signs of mild to moderate dehydration are:

- Sticky, dry mouth
- Fatigue
- Headache
- Lightheadedness or dizziness
- Muscle weakness

At the first sign of these mild to moderate dehydration symptoms, athletes should stop, drink a sports drink and some water and discontinue exercise. It is unlikely they will be able to "catch up" their hydration level to safely continue training. Children have higher metabolic rates and require more fluid than an adult, regardless of their smaller size. Their kidneys are not able to conserve fluid as well as their adult counterparts so they must be closely monitored to avoid dehydration.

Severe dehydration symptoms include:

- Very dry mouth
- Extreme thirst
- Rapid heartbeat
- Confusion and irritability
- Sunken eyes
- Cessation of sweating
- Fever

In the most extreme, cases dehydration can cause fainting and unconsciousness. One of the best indicators of dehydration is urine color. Amber colored or dark yellow urine is a sign of dehydration. Clear or light colored urine demonstrates adequate hydration.

Thirst is a natural indicator to hydrate the body but unfortunately it is not always the best indicator. During normal daily activities people can trust thirst to remind them when they need to drink water, but during exercise it cannot be relied upon as an adequate reminder. Hydration must occur before, during and after physical needs during training. In addition, there is a condition called hyponatremia, which is water intoxication. This condition results in a dilution of salt or sodium in the body. Athletes may experience this if they drink too much water without also drinking a sports drink with necessary electrolytes. This is the primary reason why sports drinks are an important addition to any training program. A U.S. Army study found that "dehydration in excess of 2% of body weight consistently impairs aerobic exercise performance" but effects can begin to be seen at only 0.5%. This study goes on to warn of the dangers of hyponatremia from hyper-hydrating before, during or after exercise. Only elite athletes with access to qualified health professionals to monitor them should experiment with hydration levels at any kind of extreme.

> A U.S. Army study found that "dehydration in excess of 2% of body weight consistently impairs aerobic exercise performance."

Hydration to Maximize Training

Athletes who know how to fuel their bodies with nutrition and hydration are able to do more for longer periods of time. They will begin to understand the level of hydration they need throughout their training. But a personal trainer must emphasize the need for hydration on a daily basis and not just during exercise. Everyone benefits from adequate hydration but an athlete who begins training with any kind of hydration deficit will quickly learn that it is difficult if not impossible to recover from that deficit.

The optimum level of hydration is the same for every human being. Athletes, however, are unique: their ultimate level depends on the intensity of exercise or training, climate, altitude and the conditioning of the athlete. The American College of Sports Medicine recommends that athletes who exercise for 60 minutes or more at high intensity include sports drinks in their regimen. The drink should include approximately 100 calories per 8 ounces to meet athletes' calorie needs. General recommendations for athletes performing a moderate training or exercise session include drinking 20 fluid ounces about 3 hours before exercise, 8 fluid ounces every 15 minutes throughout exercise and, if exercising for an hour or more, 8 fluid ounces of a sports drink every 15 minutes. The carbohydrate content of sports drinks should be no more than 8% carbohydrate solution. In other words, the level of glucose should be less than 8%. A simple way to re-hydrate after exercise is to weigh before and after training and then drink 20 fluid ounces for every pound lost. Athletes need to replenish glycogen stores by ingesting a 4-1 ratio of carbohydrates to protein within 2 hours of training.

> The carbohydrate content of sports drinks should be no more than 8% carbohydrate solution.

A 2008 University of Connecticut study looked at the effects of hydration and its connection to muscle damage. Studying different levels of hydration in physically compatible study participants showed that the optimal state of hydration to protect athletes from injury is an euhydrated state, or normal state of body water content. They found that this allowed athletes to "maximize endogenous hormonal, mechanical and metabolic benefits."

While there is a school of thought that elite athletes can "hyper-hydrate" before working out, most sports science experts are coming to agree that an average athlete should start out at a normal hydration level, maintain it throughout, and hydrate adequately to recover for optimum results and safety.

Supplements

In an attempt to gain a competitive edge in sports performance or to ensure the maximum effect of sports training, people often resort to supplements. Supplementation is a legal and popular way to support physically active individuals. Athletes seek means to improve their performance beyond training alone. Often, supplements are used to obtain adequate calorie intake, resynthesize energy and increase tolerance in training. Other major goals in using supplements are the use of energy efficiently with quick recovery and the enhancement of physical power or the ability to produce energy specifically for athletic performance. Additionally, noncompetitive athletes and fitness enthusiasts are turning to supplements to lose weight, add muscle mass, prevent injury, relieve pain and alleviate stress.

Hundreds of dietary supplements have been marketed in the form of protein shakes, powders, energy bars and sports drinks. Certain supplements are beneficial to certain people under certain circumstances so it is important to determine the extent of exercise and training that will be performed to adequately choose the supplements that will give the best results.

Types of Supplements

Creatine

Creatine is a nitrogenous amine and natural dietary constituent of animal foods. It is normally found in animal flesh, especially those animals that are physically active. Primary food sources of creatine are fish and red meat; thus, vegetarians may have lower serum concentrations of creatine. Creatine absorption is highest after carbohydrate intake. Creatine is not an essential nutrient since adequate amounts can be synthesized by the body. Normally, creatine is synthesized from the amino acids methionine, glycine and arginine by the liver, kidney and pancreas to be used anaerobically as a fuel. Since only approximately 2 grams are needed for daily activities, it must be constantly resynthesized for use because only a limited amount of creatine is stored for several seconds for activity.

Creatine participates in the production and maintenance of ATP and therefore plays an important role in cellular energy production. Creatine regenerates ATP in skeletal muscle in the form of phosphocreatine (PCr). PCr gives up its phosphate to facilitate ATP synthesis.

Normally, the amount of ATP available for use by the muscle is very small so it must be made continuously. Creatine phosphate (CP) is one of the three pathways used for the production of ATP by muscle fibers. The high-energy phosphate from CP is transferred to re-phosphorylate ATP from ADP by creatine kinase. This rapid reaction is conducted in one enzymatic step but is limited by the amount of stored creatine or PCr in free muscle.

Creatine is one of the most popular and well-known supplements used by athletes. Many professional sports teams actually supply creatine to their athletes. Supplementation is thought to elevate muscle creatine stores. Additionally, creatine increases the amount of water that each muscle cells hold—thus it increases the size of the muscle and therefore power outputs.

> Benefits of creatine may also be due to the person's ability to increase strength from harder training.

Research has shown that creatine monohydrate supplementation may improve athletic performance in activities that are marked with high intensity. Benefits of creatine may also be due to the person's ability to increase strength from harder training and maintain strength and power for repeated short-duration movements. If this is the case, creatine may not be beneficial for sedentary persons. Creatine supplements are used extensively in resistance-exercise training and are marketed as a body-building and strength-boosting aid. Resistance training is known to stress the ATP-CP energy system and it is the primary energy system for this type of training.

The most common regimen for supplementation follows a 2 phase cycle. The first phase, or loading phase, consists of taking about 20-25g/day for 5-10 days. After the loading phase, the maintenance phase is utilized to sustain a beneficial amount in the body. The maintenance phase is of variable length and usually consists of taking 2-5g/day. Intake of supplemental creatine can increase muscle creatine levels for several weeks. Only longer periods of supplementation help in training and shorter periods do not enhance exercise performance. It is important to note that creatine has not been thoroughly tested for safety so it may be wise to avoid usage of creatine supplementation if energy consumption is adequate. Creatine supplements can be associated with weight gain so anyone taking them should be advised.

Glutamine is the most common amino acid in muscle and plasma.

Amino Acid Supplements

The 20 amino acids are the basic building blocks for protein and therefore build cellular tissue. Each of these amino acids has unique metabolic properties in human physiology. Amino acid supplements containing one or more amino acids are popular as sports enhancers. These amino acid supplements have been promoted on the market with claims that these products are more rapidly digested and absorbed than protein obtained from food. The claim is that amino acid supplements can inhibit muscle loss, maintain immune system function and promote glucose/glycogen metabolism. However, evidence for the athletic benefits of isolated amino acids is mixed. It has been found that large intakes of some single amino acids may interfere with absorption and lead to imbalances in metabolism, so it is wise to monitor usage of amino acid supplements.

Glutamine

Glutamine is a 5-carbon compound with two nitrogen groups. An amide derivative of the amino acid, glutamine, is converted to its natural form in tissues of the liver, brain, kidney, skeletal muscle and intestine. Food sources include foods rich in protein, such as milk and meat, and plant foods, such as spinach, parsley and cabbage.

Glutamine is the most common amino acid in muscle and plasma. It accounts for about 10% of the amino acid content in muscle protein and upwards of 50% of the amino acids released from muscle during exercise stress. Glutamine provides nitrogen and carbon molecules for synthesis of macromolecules and energy production. It also neutralizes cortisol, a steroid hormone that induces catabolism and accompanies strenuous exercise. Under certain physiological conditions (e.g., injuries, infections and extreme stress), glutamine stores in the muscles can be depleted and supplementation becomes necessary to maintain adequate concentrations in the body. Lasting fatigue is often also associated with low plasma glutamine levels. Glutamine is also important for athletes in terms of recovery and healing, and thus glutamine is considered an indispensable amino acid during stress.

> Besides oral supplements, athletes often inject large amounts of arginine, which may cause a temporary rise in growth hormone levels.

Glutamine supplements are currently available as L-glutamine and are in the form of individual supplements or protein supplements. Usually, supplements are taken several hours before or after food to prevent interaction with regular dietary amino acids.

Arginine

Arginine is a conditionally essential amino acid and one of the most commonly used amino acid supplements for sports training due to its postulated stimulatory effects on human growth hormone (HGH) production. Others hypothesize that arginine stimulates the release of HGH by increasing upstream hormones that act on this endocrine pathway. It is well-known that this growth hormone produces anabolic effects, including the stimulation of protein and nucleic acid synthesis in the skeletal muscle. This also leads to an increase in muscle mass and a decrease in body fat. Arginine is also thought to be involved in several other physiological areas of interest to athletes, including creatine synthesis, release of insulin and removal of toxic ammonia. Besides oral supplements, athletes often inject large amounts of arginine, which may cause a temporary rise in growth hormone levels.

Branched-Chain Amino Acids (BCAA)

Branched-chain amino acids (BCAA) include leucine, isoleucine and valine. These amino acids have been hypothesized to help in resistance-training by improving endurance exercise performance. BCAAs are important nitrogen sources for alanine, which is converted to glucose as a fuel source. Importantly, BCAAs compete with tryptophan for entry into the brain and can thus prevent fatigue. The central fatigue hypothesis suggests that an increase of serotonin in the brain impairs the function of the central nervous system during bouts of prolonged exercise and can then hinder sports performance. This increase in serotonin synthesis is ultimately due to the elevated levels of tryptophan, which is a precursor of serotonin. Thus, hindering levels of tryptophan by BCAA is thought to prevent the onset of fatigue.

Caffeine

Caffeine is the most widely consumed psychoactive drug used worldwide. Caffeine is a central nervous system stimulant and often increases both adrenaline and noradrenaline concentration after ingestion. The main sources of caffeine are coffee, tea and cocoa products. Additionally, it is contained in many energy drinks.

The benefits of using caffeine as an ergogenic aid is that it is inexpensive and has little to no adverse health effects. A high rate of tolerance is associated with caffeine usage, which then leads to reduced dose effects. More caffeine is then needed to get the same benefits as before. At high doses, caffeine can be used as a diuretic, which also increases the chance for dehydration. One should never increase the consumption of caffeine before exercise for this reason and because caffeine can increase heart rate. But if caffeine is consumed normally, the same amount can be ingested since adaptation of caffeine occurs. If heart measurements are being taken as a part of training, one should not consume caffeine or other stimulants for at least 30 minutes prior to exercise. Overstimulation with caffeine can cause insomnia, restlessness, anxiety, high blood pressure and headaches.

> The benefits of using caffeine as an ergogenic aid is that it is inexpensive and has little to no adverse health effects.

Caffeine is believed to be useful in improving endurance by increasing effective fat metabolism during exercise. It may also work by enhancing exercise capacity and recovery from fatigue if exhaustion normally ensues after 30-60 minutes, since this is when there is a peak plasma concentration. This is especially true for exercises like cycling and swimming. Caffeine can improve aerobic endurance during short-term, extreme exercise, increase fat oxidation and decrease the perception of pain, all which can allow for more intensity in athletic performance. Recently, caffeine has been shown to decrease plasma potassium levels. This is important because during exercise, potassium is transported out of muscle cells, leading to a decrease in muscular force output. For supplementation, caffeine can also be obtained from herbal sources with high content, like guarana and kola nut.

Conjugated Linoleic Acid (CLA)

Conjugated linoleic acid (CLA) is the collective name given to a group of linoleic acids, the parent compound of the omega-6 group of unsaturated fatty acids. An isomer of linoleic acid, CLA is an essential fatty acid and must be provided in consumed food. It is mostly found in corn, sunflower, peanut and soy oils. The CLA used for supplements are from these oils but can also be found naturally in dairy products and beef.

CLA is primarily marketed as a weight-loss and muscle-building supplement. However, there is no real clinical evidence to support CLA supplementation. Because of these effects, CLA is thought to prevent muscle wasting and improves body composition. The typical recommended dosage is 3-6 g/day.

Medium Chain Triglycerides (MCT Oil)

Medium chain triglycerides or MCT oils, are a class of lipids made from saturated fatty acids 6-12 carbons in length. MCT oils are synthetically derived dietary fats processed from coconut oil. These oils were initially formulated for people who were unable to digest regular fat since they are less viscous. Instead of long carbon chains like regular fats, MCT oils have much shorter carbon chains and can therefore be digested, transported and metabolized quicker and easier. Medium chain triglycerides are also not stored like traditional fats but are directly used for energy through oxidation by the liver or in peripheral tissue. Additionally, MCT oils are metabolized more as a carbohydrate than as a fat, but have a higher energy density.

Supplements with MCT oils are used as muscle builders and as an energy source. MCT oils are used to increase total intake of calories in athletes who need high energy for sports performance. They are thought to improve athletic performance because these oils can enter the mitochondria without carnitine, unlike other fats and they also help conserve muscle stores of carbohydrates. Improvement in muscular development and increases in the loss of body fat from enhanced metabolic rate are other benefits of MCT oils. Also hypothetically MCT can aid in recovery from injury by adding more calories that spare lean muscle without becoming body fat if excess fat is ingested. If taken, doses should be monitored because large amounts may be associated with gastrointestinal disturbances like intestinal cramping.

> MCT oils are synthetically derived dietary fats processed from coconut oil.

Nutritional Programming with the ACTION Personal Training System

The Nutritional Program component of the ACTION PTS will allow you to create completely customized nutritional systems for your clients. All programs are based on the client's lean mass values (from the Body Composition) and nutritional preferences. The system can be used as a simple tracking tool where clients can record the foods they eat and receive feedback on their nutritional content, or can be used as a full functional program including the ability to have meals suggested that will meet their nutritional needs.

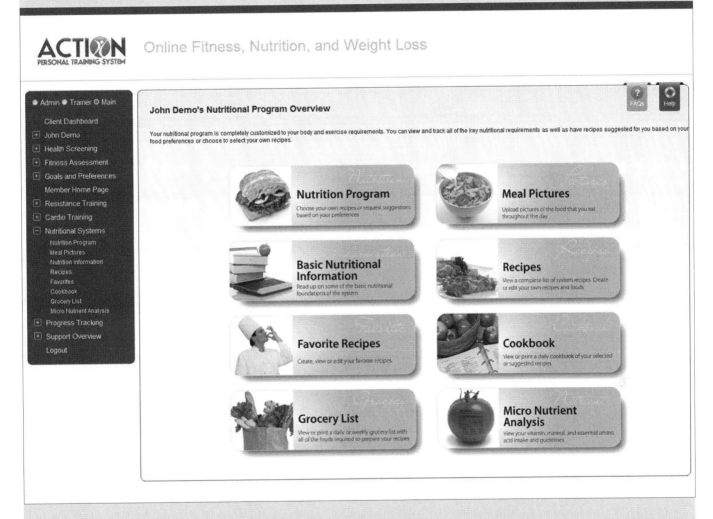

The client ALWAYS has complete control over their nutritional systems and may make any changes they desire. This is done to ensure that the ACTION PTS falls within the scope of practice of a Personal Trainer. There is no food or meal prescriptions, simply suggestions that your client may choose to follow that will help guide them to a well balanced diet.

Setting Client Nutritional Preferences
Prior to building a nutritional program you may want to ensure that the client has set any nutritional preferences they may have. The Nutritional Preferences area is located in the Main menu, under Goals and Preferences. Clients can exclude food groups they prefer not to eat, or may even exclude specific foods by entering the name of the food in the spaces provided. The system will then disregard any foods or recipes that contain items from the food groups or individual foods that have been excluded.

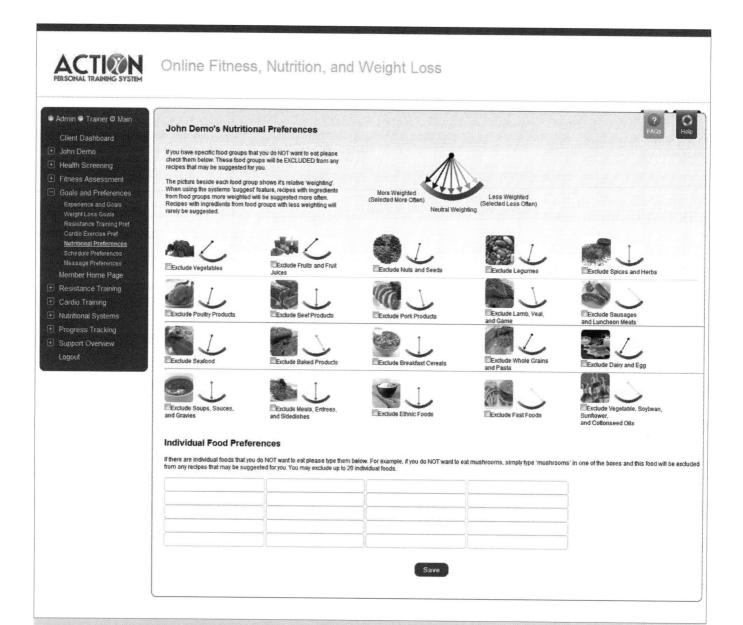

Prerequisites to Building a Nutritional Program

Prior to be able to use the 'Suggested' features of the nutritional system the ACTION PTS system must have the Lean Mass value for the client as determined in the Body Composition. If you try to access the Nutritional Program prior to completing the client's Body Composition the system will default to the 'Prerequisites' page and indicate that the Body Composition must be completed prior to continuing.

The Lean Mass value is used to determine the client's Basal Metabolic Rate which will allow for a more accurate estimate of the client's caloric needs.

Adding Custom Foods and Recipes

You can add an unlimited number of custom foods or recipes to the ACTION PTS system. In the Main menu, under Nutritional Systems, in the Recipes section you will find the 'Add Custom Recipes' and 'View or Add Custom Foods' buttons.

ADDING CUSTOM RECIPES

To add a Custom Recipe simply click on the 'Add Custom Recipe' button and you will be taken to the custom recipe builder page where you can add the following information:

John Demo's Custom Recipes

Add your own recipes.

Recipe Name

Description and Preparation

Makes How Many Servings   1

Prep Time in Minutes

Cook Time in Minutes

Marinate Time in Hours

Recipe can be Served as a   ☐ Breakfast ☐ Lunch ☐ Dinner ☐ Snack

Serve Recipe with a Side Dish of ☐ Vegetables ☐ Soup ☐ Potato ☐ Rice ☐ Salad ☐ Fruit

Ingredient (start typing and a list will appear) [Add Custom Food if not found in List]   Unit of Measure   Amount

whole wheat

Bread, pita, whole-wheat
Bread, whole-wheat, commercially prepared
Bread, whole-wheat, commercially prepared, toasted
Bread, whole-wheat, prepared from recipe
Bread, whole-wheat, prepared from recipe, toasted
Buckwheat flour, whole-groat
Cereals ready-to-eat, corn, whole wheat, rolled oats, presweetened, single brand
Cereals ready-to-eat, corn, whole wheat, rolled oats, presweetened, with almonds
Cereals ready-to-eat, MALT-O-MEAL, Cinnamon Sweet Whole Wheat and Rice C
Cereals ready-to-eat, MALT-O-MEAL, Frosted Whole Wheat Cereal
Cereals ready-to-eat, WEETABIX WHOLE WHEAT CEREAL
Cereals ready-to-eat, whole wheat, rolled oats, presweetened, with nuts and fruit, s

[Save and Calculate] [Save and Add Another Recipe] [Save and Copy this Recipe] [Return To Recipe List]

- Recipe Name

- Description and Preparation Instructions

- Number of Servings the Recipe Makes

- Preparation Time

- Cooking Time

- Marinating Time (if applicable)

- What Meal Type the Recipe is Suitable for

- Option to Add a Side Dish to the Recipe

- Recipe Ingredients

To add recipe ingredients, click on a blank field and start typing the name of the ingredient. The system will automatically refine the search for the ingredient based on what you type. If you find the ingredient in the list then click on the name of the ingredient and the system will add it to the recipe. You can now adjust the Unit of Measure and Amount of the ingredient. If you do not find the ingredient in the list you can add the ingredient as a Custom Food if you wish (see Add Custom Foods below).

Once you have added all of the ingredients to the recipe you have several options:

- **Save and Calculate** — this will save the recipe and calculate the nutritional content based on the ingredients you have added. You will remain on the Recipe Builder page

- **Save and Add Another Recipe** — will save the recipe and open a new blank recipe for you to create

- **Save and Copy this Recipe** — will save the current recipe and open a copy of the recipe that you can then make changes to and save as a new recipe. This is helpful if you are adding recipes that are similar or are the same but use different side dishes

- **Return to Recipe List** — will save the current recipe and take you back to the recipe search page

- **Make this recipe available for all users** — This option is available for Administrators and Trainers ONLY and will add the current recipe to a master list that will be available for all users.

ADD CUSTOM FOODS

You can add Custom Foods in two ways. On the recipe builder page you can click the 'Add Custom Food if not found in list' button, or from the Recipes main page you can click the 'Add Custom Food' button. Selecting either of these will take you to the Custom Food builder (shown at right). Here you can enter any nutritional info you have for your Custom Food.

Building a Nutrition Program

There are multiple options for building a Nutritional Program using the System. They range from a basic 'food log' to a completely suggested week customized completely to the individual user.

PRE-DEFINED WEEKS, PREP AND COOK TIMES, AND MAX INGREDIENTS

Pre-defined weeks can be set up to allow you to have clients only be able to select from limited recipe or food choices. Once a pre-defined week is set up, it will be available to be selected in the drop down list.

Prep and cook time maximums may be selected from the drop down list and the system will then limited recipes suggestions to those parameters that fall within the selected range. For example,

Nutrition Facts

Food Group
Vegetables ▾

Name of Food
Enter Name Here

| Serving Size | 1.00 | Enter | 0 | g |
| Example | 4 | Crackers | 17 | g |

Amount Per Serving

Calories 0   kcal

Total Fat 0   g

   Saturated Fat 0   g

   Monounsaturated Fat 0   g

   Polyunsaturated Fat 0   g

   Trans Fat 0   g

Cholesterol 0   mg

Sodium 0   mg

Potassium 0   mg

Total Carbohydrate 0   g

   Dietary Fiber 0   g

   Total Sugars 0   g

     Sucrose 0   g

     Fructose 0   g

if a user were to select a max prep time of 10 minutes, the system will not suggest any recipes with a prep time over 10 minutes.

Max ingredients works very similar to the prep and cook time limits. The user can select the maximum number of ingredients they want their suggested recipes to contain and the system will ignore any recipes with a higher number of ingredients.

SUGGESTED PROGRAMS

There are 2 types of Suggested Weeks:

Suggest My Favorites will only use recipes that the user has set as a 'Favorite' to build their week's nutritional program. There must be a minimum of 5 favorite recipes saved for each meal type for the 'Suggest My Favorites' option to appear. The system will aim to balance calories, macronutrients, micronutrients, and food guidelines (e.g. MyPlate) as closely as possible through an advanced algorithm.

Suggest My Week will use all system and custom recipes that are not excluded based on client preferences (see Setting Client Nutritional Preferences above) to build a suggested weeks program. The system will aim to balance calories, macronutrients, micronutrients, and food guidelines (e.g. MyPlate) as closely as possible through an advanced algorithm.

USING A PREVIOUS WEEK

The Use a Previous Week option will become available as soon as at least one week has been suggested for a client. The using a previous week option will allow a client to view and edit any previously suggested weekly nutritional program. Any recipes 'unchecked' in the previous week viewer will automatically be re-suggested by the system.

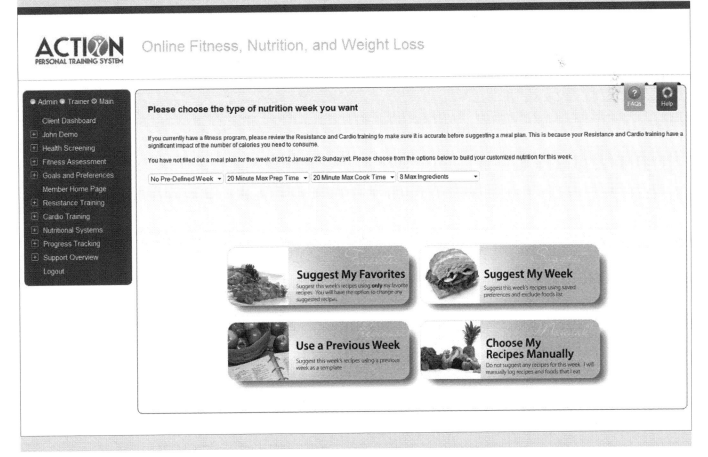

CHOOSING RECIPES MANUALLY

The 'Choose Recipes Manually option will create a blank template week that has no foods or recipes suggested. Users can then either manually add foods or recipes using the 'Add a Food' or 'Choose a Recipe' options for each meal, or they can have suggestions made one meal at a time by using the 'Favorite Recipes' or 'Suggest Recipes' options. These 2 options will display a list of applicable recipes that may be used for that meal that fall within 10% of their caloric goals for that meal.

Using the Nutrition Program

BASIC INFORMATION

At the top of the 'Nutritional Program' page you will find the basic information for using the program. The day highlighted in red is the currently selected day. Any other day of the week may be chosen by simply clicking on the appropriate button. In addition previous weeks may be viewed or future weeks planned by using the drop down and selecting a date in the past or future.

The left side of the page contains to applicable 'food guide' information for the country or residence. The options are the 'Canada Food Guide' for Canadian residents, the Australian Food Pyramid' for Australian residents, and the MyPlate for the United States and all other countries. The food guide list the goal and target values for the applicable system.

The center of the page contains the Caloric Goals for the currently selected day. This includes the BMI/BMR (Body's Basic Requirement) calories, the number of calories required for planned cardiovascular training on that day (Cardiovascular Training), the average number of calories used for resistance training throughout the current week (Resistance Training), the caloric deficit required to meet the weight loss goals (Weight Loss Deficit), and the target number of calories for the selected day (Target)

The right side of the page contain the Micro-Nutrient information for the currently selected day. This includes the target and actual values for calories, fats, carbs, and protein. The actual values are updated every time a change is made to the program itself (e.g. switching a recipe)

Listed vertically down the left side of the page is the ideal meal time for each meal and snack of the day and amount of water that should be consumed throughout the day.

At the bottom of the page there are options to:

'Re-Suggest My Week' which will delete the currently planned week and allow the option of rebuilding the weekly nutritional program using the options outlined above in the 'Suggested Programs' section.

'Copy Day' which will copy the currently selected days recipes and foods to any day within a 2 week period.

Once a nutritional program is built there are many different options available to further customize or change the program. These features are outlined in the sections below:

Basic Features

To get more detailed information about any food or recipe simply click on the name of the food or recipe and the system will open a separate window with detailed information.

There are buttons on each meal of the day to perform the following tasks:

Online Fitness, Nutrition, and Weight Loss

John Demo's Nutritional Program | Print Week |

- Admin - Trainer - Main
  - Client Dashboard
  - [+] John Demo
  - [+] Health Screening
  - [+] Fitness Assessment
  - [+] Goals and Preferences
    - Member Home Page
  - [+] Resistance Training
  - [+] Cardio Training
  - [-] Nutritional Systems
    - **Nutrition Program**
    - Meal Pictures
    - Nutrition Information
    - Recipes
    - Favorites
    - Cookbook
    - Grocery List
    - Micro Nutrient Analysis
  - [+] Progress Tracking
  - [+] Support Overview
  - Logout

2012 January 22 Sunday ▾ | Sunday | Monday | Tuesday | Wednesday | Thursday | Friday | Saturday |

MyPlate

7 [3.5]	Grains	6.5 [3.5]
3	Vegetables	13.5
2	Fruit	7.5
3	Dairy	1.5
6	Protein	8
6	Oils	6

Daily Caloric Goals for January 25

Body's Basic Requirement	2,212
Cardiovascular Training	+ 561
Resistance Training	+ 58
Weight Loss Deficit	- 500
Target	2,331

MacroNutrient Goals

Target		Actual
2,331	Calories	2,338
52g	Fats	52g
350g	Carbs	381g
117g	Protein	110g

6:30-7:30 AM | **Breakfast** | 🔒 Favorite Recipes | Suggest Recipes | Choose a Recipe | Add a Food |

Fav	Edit	Recipe	Servings	Calories	Fat	Carbs	Protein	Brain	
☑	✎	Blue Hawaii Smoothie	2.00 +−	563	3	138	5	2	⊗

Goal: 23% of caloric requirement = **543 Kcal**   Running Total: Goal=543 Actual=563 **Diff=20**

9:30-10:30 AM | **Morning Snack** | 🔒 Favorite Recipes | Suggest Recipes | Choose a Recipe | Add a Food |

Fav	Edit	Recipe	Servings	Calories	Fat	Carbs	Protein	Brain	
☑	✎	Tropical Carrots	1.00 +−	110	0	27	2	0	⊗
	✎	Side Rice	1.00 +−	114	0	23	4	0	⊗
		Total for Meal		223	1	50	6	0	

Goal: 10% of caloric requirement = **233 Kcal**   Running Total: Goal=776 Actual=786 **Diff=10**

12:30-1:30 PM | **Lunch** | 🔒 Favorite Recipes | Suggest Recipes | Choose a Recipe | Add a Food |

Fav	Edit	Recipe	Servings	Calories	Fat	Carbs	Protein	Brain	
☑	✎	Basic Asian Beef Stir Fry with Rice	2.00 +−	733	36	29	70	12	⊗

Goal: 23% of caloric requirement = **543 Kcal**   Running Total: Goal=1319 Actual=1519 **Diff=200**

3:30-4:30 PM | **Afternoon Snack** | 🔒 Favorite Recipes | Suggest Recipes | Choose a Recipe | Add a Food |

Fav	Edit	Recipe	Servings	Calories	Fat	Carbs	Protein	Brain	
☑	✎	Smoothie, strawberry, dairy	1.00 +−	246	2	51	8	3	⊗

Goal: 10% of caloric requirement = **233 Kcal**   Running Total: Goal=1552 Actual=1765 **Diff=213**

6:30-7:30 PM | **Dinner** | 🔒 Favorite Recipes | Suggest Recipes | Choose a Recipe | Add a Food |

Fav	Edit	Recipe	Servings	Calories	Fat	Carbs	Protein	Brain	
☑	✎	Spanish Vegetable Stew With Eggplant	2.00 +−	335	9	63	11	9	⊗
	✎	Side Salad	1.00 +−	51	1	11	1	6	⊗
		Total for Meal		386	9	75	12	15	

Goal: 23% of caloric requirement = **543 Kcal**   Running Total: Goal=2095 Actual=2151 **Diff=56**

9:30-10:30 PM | **Evening Snack** | 🔒 Favorite Recipes | Suggest Recipes | Choose a Recipe | Add a Food |

Fav	Edit	Recipe	Servings	Calories	Fat	Carbs	Protein	Brain	
☑	✎	Blackberry Smoothie	1.00 +−	188	1	37	10	0	⊗

Goal: 10% of caloric requirement = **233 Kcal**   Running Total: Goal=2328 Actual=2339 **Diff=11**

Re-Suggest My Week
Delete the current week's suggested foods and recipes and re-suggest a new week

Copy Day
Copy the current day to the selected day

2012 January 15 Sunday ▾

Daily Guidelines

- Each meal or snack should be no larger than 650 calories
- You must eat at least 5 times per day
- There should be no more than 3 hours between meals and snacks
- Try to keep your meals and snacks similar in size
- Aim to be no more than 150 calories above or below your daily goal
- Fat, Carbs, and Protein goals are guidelines. You may be slightly over or under these goals

'**Favorite Recipes**' will display a list of suggested recipes that are categorized as favorite recipes (see Favorite Recipes below) and are within 10% of the nutritional goals for that meal. Any recipe may be selected and added to the current meal by clicking on the green check mark.

'**Suggest Recipes**' will display a list of suggested recipes that are within 10% of the nutritional goals for that meal. The suggested recipes will be from all system and custom recipes, excluding and recipes that do not fall into the clients Nutritional Preferences (see above). Any recipe may be selected and added to the current meal by clicking on the green check mark.

'**Choose a Recipe**' will allow for manually selecting any system or custom recipe to be added to the current meal.

'**Add a Food**' will allow for an individual food to be added to the current meal. This may be a system or custom food or a custom food may be created.

Clicking the 'Remove' icon on the far right of the page next to each recipe or food will remove that food or recipes from the meal.

With any of the above options, all calorie, and macronutrient and micronutrient total are automatically added to the meal total and the 'Actual' value at the top of the page.

Advanced Features

Some of the more advanced features available for each meal are:

The icon in the 'Fav' column may be clicked to automatically add a meal to the favorites list. This will turn the icon green. Clicking the icon a second time will add the recipes to the excluded list and the icon will turn red. Clicking it for a third time will remove the recipe from both the favorite and excluded lists and the icon will return to the default grey color.

Clicking the 'Edit' icon will open a copy of any system recipe where changes can be made to the recipe and it can then be re-named and saved as a custom recipe. This works well for making small changes to system recipes such as substituting one or two foods.

Clicking the 'Lock' icon will lock the currently selected recipe in for the selected meal until it is unlocked. This is particularly effective for clients who may eat the same meal every day. Regardless of how a nutritional week is built in the future, any locked recipe will be suggested for the selected meal until the recipe is unlocked.

Searching Recipes

The 'Recipes' link (Main: Nutritional Systems) may be used to add new custom foods or recipes and to search for existing recipes. A search may be done using any combination of the following fields:

Search for — type in all or part of any food or recipe to refine the search results

Meal Type — searches may be conducted for recipes only of a certain meal type

Include Recipe Types — System recipes (default recipes provided in the system), Custom recipes (recipes that have been added by the user), or All recipes

Number of Results — the smaller the number of results to display the faster the search will load

Max Prep Time (min) — The maximum preparation time, in minutes, that the recipe should be

Max Cook Time (min) — The maximum cooking time, in minutes, that the recipes should be

● Admin ● Trainer ◉ Main

Client Dashboard
⊞ John Demo
⊞ Health Screening
⊞ Fitness Assessment
⊞ Goals and Preferences
   Member Home Page
⊞ Resistance Training
⊞ Cardio Training
⊟ Nutritional Systems
   Nutrition Program
   Meal Pictures
   Nutrition Information
   Recipes
   Favorites
   Cookbook
   Grocery List
   Micro Nutrient Analysis
⊞ Progress Tracking
⊞ Support Overview
   Logout

John Demo's Recipe Selection

Use the search criteria to select a food or recipe. Or add a customer recipe or food.

Search for

Meal Type   ☐ Breakfast ☐ Lunch ☐ Dinner ☐ Snack

Include Recipe Types   ◉ All ○ System Only ○ Custom Only

Number of Results   50

Max Prep Time (min)

Max Cook Time (min)

Sort Results By   Recipe Name

Search Recipes

Add
Custom Recipes
Custom Recipes use a list of individual foods and preparation instructions

View or Add
Custom Foods
Custom Foods are individual items or pre-packaged meals that can be used to build recipes or as meals.

Sort Results By — Results may be sorted by name, or various calorie or macronutrient information

Favorite Recipes

Favorite recipes will be suggested based on nutritional preferences and the ease of preparation. When visiting this page the system will display suggested favorites with grey checkmark icons. Clicking on the grey icons will lock the recipe in as a favorite. (It will turn green)

At any time you can remove a recipe from your favorites list by clicking on the green icon (✓). A red icon (✓) means that the recipes will be excluded from any future suggestions, and a grey icon (✓) means that the recipe can still be suggested but is no longer in your favorites.

You can also add recipes to your favorites list from your 'Nutritional Program' and the 'Recipes' area by simply clicking on the checkmark icon until it turns green.

● Admin ● Trainer ◉ Main

Client Dashboard
⊞ John Demo
⊞ Health Screening
⊞ Fitness Assessment
⊞ Goals and Preferences
   Member Home Page
⊞ Resistance Training
⊞ Cardio Training
⊟ Nutritional Systems
   Nutrition Program
   Meal Pictures
   Nutrition Information
   Recipes
   Favorites
   Cookbook

John Demo's Nutrition Favorites and Exclusions

Favorite recipes will be suggested for you based on your nutritional preferences and the ease of preparation. When you visit this page possible favorites are in Grey.

Click on the grey check boxes to lock the recipe in as a favorite. (it will turn green)

You can also add recipes to your favorites list from your 'Nutritional Program' and the 'Recipes' area by simply clicking on the checkmark until it turns green, or you can exclude any recipe by clicking until it turns red.

✓ – saved as a favorite
✓ – suggested as a favorite (not saved unless you click to turn green)
✓ – excluded from being suggested

Breakfast Favorites			
✓ Apple and a Banana	✓ Bagel and Peanut Butter	✓ Banana and Toast	✓ Banana and Toast with Milk
✓ Banana and Toast with OJ	✓ Egg, Toast and OJ	✓ Morning Fruit Salad	✓ Oatmeal with Milk and Banana
✓ Oatmeal with Milk and Banana and strawberries	✓ Peanut Butter and Banana Sandwich	✓ Scrambled Eggs and Blueberries	✓ Blackberry Smoothie
✓ Egg Sandwich	✓ Ham and Cheese Omelette	✓ Ham, Mushroom, and Cheese Omelette	✓ Oatmeal with OJ and Banana
✓ Peanut Butter and Jam Sandwich	✓ Refreshing Summer Shake	✓ Rice Cakes with Cottage Cheese and a Banana	✓ Scrambled Eggs and an Orange
✓ Scrambled Eggs and Kiwi	✓ Sweet Potato Scrambled Eggs	✓ Walking Apple Salad	

Cookbooks and Grocery Lists
COOKBOOK

The Cookbook link will open a separate window with a printable version of the current day's recipes. At the top of the page a different day of the week may be selected for printing or the drop down may be used to select different weeks.

By default, all of the calorie, macronutrient and food guide information will be displayed and printed. The 'card view' checkbox may be selected to remove all of the nutritional information and only display and print the basic recipe information.

To get more detailed information about any individual food, click on the food name and the system will open a separate window with detailed micronutrient information about that food item.

The 'Print' button may be used to print the cookbook. Some browsers block this type of control button from working, in which case the page may be printed by selecting File: Print from the main browser bar.

ACTION
PERSONAL TRAINING SYSTEM

John Demo's Cookbook

2012 January 22 Sunday ▾ | Sun | Mon | Tue | Wed | Thu | Fri | Sat | ☐ Card View | **Print**

Breakfast: Blue Hawaii Smoothie
Description: Blend ingredients in blender. Enjoy! Recipe courtesy of the Michigan Blueberry Growers Association Prep Time = 5 min.

Makes 2 Serving(s). Eat 2.00 Serving(s).

	Amount Unit	Calories	Fat	Carbs	Protein	Grains	Veg	Fruits	Dairy	Protein	Oils	Brain
Blueberries, frozen, unsweetened	2 1/2 cup, unthawed	197.6	2.5	47.2	1.6	0	0	2.5	0	0	0	3
Water, municipal	3 (3.00) ice cube (3/4 f	0	0	0	0	0	0	0	0	0	0	0
Pineapple juice, frozen concentrate, unsweetened.	2 cup	255	0.2	63.4	2	0	0	2	0	0	0	-3
Bananas, raw	1 medium (7" to 7	105	0.4	27	1.3	0	0	0.5	0	0	0	2
Total for entire recipe (Micro Nutrients for entire recipe)		557.6	3	137.5	4.9	0	0	5	0	0	0	2
Total per serving		278.8	1.5	68.7	2.5	0	0	2.5	0	0	0	2

Morning Snack: Tropical Carrots
Description: Place carrots in a saucepan. Add water to cover; bring to a boil. Cover, reduce heat, and simmer 12 minutes or until crisp-tender; drain. Combine pineapple, cornstarch, and ginger in a medium saucepan; bring to a boil. Reduce heat to low, and cook, stirring constantly, until thickened. Add carrots, and cook 1 minute or until thoroughly heated, stirring occasionally. Prep Time = 15 min. Cook Time = 15 min. Served with a side dish: Rice

Makes 1 Serving(s). Eat 1.00 Serving(s).

	Amount Unit	Calories	Fat	Carbs	Protein	Grains	Veg	Fruits	Dairy	Protein	Oils	Brain
Carrots, raw	1 cup, strips or	50	0.3	11.7	1.1	0	1	0	0	0	0	3
Pineapple, canned, juice pack, drained	1/2 cup, crushed	58.5	0.1	15.2	0.5	0	0	0.5	0	0	0	-3
Cornstarch	1 dash	0.5	0	0.1	0	0	0	0	0	0	0	0
Spices, ginger, ground	1/8 tsp	0.8	0	0.2	0	0	0	0	0	0	0	0
Total for entire recipe (Micro Nutrients for entire recipe)		109.8	0.4	27.1	1.7	0	1	0.5	0	0	0	0

Morning Snack: Side Rice
Description: Place equal amounts of water and rice into pot, bring to boil, cover and simmer to desired tenderness. Add soy sauce and serve. Brown or wild rice may be substituted. Prep Time = 5 min. Cook Time = 25 min.

Makes 1 Serving(s). Eat 1.00 Serving(s).

	Amount Unit	Calories	Fat	Carbs	Protein	Grains	Veg	Fruits	Dairy	Protein	Oils	Brain
Soy sauce made from soy (tamari)	1 tbsp	10.8	0	1	1.9	0	0	0	0	0	0	0
Rice, white, long-grain, regular, cooked	1/2 cup	102.7	0.2	22.3	2.1	2.8	0	0	0	0	0	0
Total for entire recipe (Micro Nutrients for entire recipe)		113.5	0.2	23.3	4	2.8	0	0	0	0	0	0

Lunch: Basic Asian Beef Stir Fry with Rice
Description: Combine cornstarch and beef stock and blend well. Prepare all ingredients. Heat oil over medium heat in a wok of heavy skillet. Cook onion for one minute, stirring constantly. Add beef stock mixture. Increase heat to medium high and add bok choy, and salt and pepper to taste. Cook for 2-3 minutes, stirring constantly. Add beef, cover, and reduce heat to low. Cook until beef is thoroughly heated. Serve over hot cooked rice. Prep Time = 10 min. Cook Time = 15 min.

Makes 4 Serving(s). Eat 2.00 Serving(s).

	Amount Unit	Calories	Fat	Carbs	Protein	Grains	Veg	Fruits	Dairy	Protein	Oils	Brain
Cornstarch	2 dash	1	0	0.2	0	0	0	0	0	0	0	0
Soup, stock, beef, home-prepared	1 cup	31.2	0.2	2.9	4.7	0	0	0	0	0	0	0
Oil, olive, salad or cooking	1 tbsp	119.3	13.5	0	0	0	0	0	0	0	3	3
Onions, raw	1/2 cup, chopped	32	0.1	7.5	0.9	0	0.5	0	0	0	0	3
Cabbage, chinese (pak-choi), raw	2 cup, shredded	18.2	0.3	3.1	2.1	0	2	0	0	0	0	3
Beef, tenderloin, separable lean and fat, trimmed	16 oz	1047.8	56.2	0	126.9	0	0	0	0	16	0	0
Rice, brown, long-grain, cooked	1 cup	216.4	1.8	44.8	5	6.9 [6.9]	0	0	0	0	0	3
Total for entire recipe (Micro Nutrients for entire recipe)		1466	72.1	58.4	139.6	6.9 [6.9]	2.5	0	0	16	3	12
Total per serving		366.5	18	14.6	34.9	1.7 [1.7]	0.6	0	0	4	0.8	12

Afternoon Snack: Smoothie, strawberry, dairy
Description: Combine all ingredients in blender and blend until smooth. Prep Time = 5 min.

Makes 1 Serving(s). Eat 1.00 Serving(s).

	Amount Unit	Calories	Fat	Carbs	Protein	Grains	Veg	Fruits	Dairy	Protein	Oils	Brain
Yogurt, vanilla, low fat, 11 grams protein per 8 o	1/2 cup (8 fl oz)	104.1	1.5	16.9	6	0	0	0	0.5	0	0	3
Orange juice, frozen concentrate, unsweetened, dil	1 cup	112	0.1	26.8	1.7	0	0	1	0	0	0	-3
Strawberries, frozen, unsweetened	8 berry	29.7	0.1	7.7	0.4	0	0	0.4	0	0	0	3
Water, municipal	8 (3.00) ice cube (3/4 f	0	0	0	0	0	0	0	0	0	0	0
Total for entire recipe (Micro Nutrients for entire recipe)		245.9	1.8	51.5	8.1	0	0	1.4	0.5	0	0	3

Dinner: Spanish Vegetable Stew With Eggplant
Description: In a heavy skillet, heat oil & sauté onions. Add other ingredients, stirring well so that they are coated with the oil. Cover & simmer for 15 minutes or till the peppers are cooked but firm. Add water if the casserole is too dry. Prep Time = 15 min. Cook Time = 15 min. Served with a side dish: Salad

Makes 4 Serving(s). Eat 2.00 Serving(s).

	Amount Unit	Calories	Fat	Carbs	Protein	Grains	Veg	Fruits	Dairy	Protein	Oils	Brain
Oil, olive, salad or cooking	1 tbsp	119.3	13.5	0	0	0	0	0	0	0	3	3
Onions, raw	4 medium (2-1/2"	176	0.4	41.1	4.8	0	2.8	0	0	0	0	3
Peppers, sweet, green, raw	4 large (2-1/4 pe	131.2	1.1	30.4	5.6	0	4.4	0	0	0	0	0
Tomatoes, red, ripe, raw, year round average	4 large whole (3"	131	1.5	28.3	6.4	0	4.9	0	0	0	0	3
Eggplant, raw	1 eggplant, peele	109.9	0.9	26.1	4.6	0	5.6	0	0	0	0	0
Spices, pepper, red or cayenne	1/8 tsp	0.7	0	0.1	0	0	0	0	0	0	0	0
Spices, paprika	1/4 tsp	1.6	0.1	0.3	0.1	0	0	0	0	0	0	0
Salt, table	1 dash	0	0	0	0	0	0	0	0	0	0	0
Total for entire recipe (Micro Nutrients for entire recipe)		669.8	17.5	126.4	21.6	0	17.6	0	0	0	3	9
Total per serving		167.5	4.4	31.6	5.4	0	4.4	0	0	0	0.8	9

GROCERY LIST

The Grocery List link will open a separate window with a printable grocery list. The default is to display all foods for every recipe for the entire week. The checkboxes at the top of the page may be used to select specific days of the week to print and the drop down may be used to select a different week.

Foods are categorized into groups that are typically found together in the grocery store.

The 'Print' button may be used to print the grocery list. Some browsers block this type of control button from working, in which case the page may be printed by selecting File: Print from the main browser bar.

ACTION
PERSONAL TRAINING SYSTEM

John Demo's Grocery List

[2012 January 22 Sunday ▼] ☑ Sunday ☑ Monday ☑ Tuesday ☑ Wednesday ☑ Thursday ☑ Friday ☑ Saturday

Print

Fruits and Vegetables

1 oz - Alfalfa Seeds	3 oz - Broccoli	1 head - Cabbage, Chinese Pak-Choi
6 medium - Carrots	1 package (10 oz) - Corn, Sweet Yellow, frozen	5 cucumber (8-1/4") - Cucumber
2 eggplant, unpeeled (approx 1-1/4 lb) - Eggplant	2 clove - Garlic	1 head - Lettuce, Romaine or Cos
1 package (10 oz) - Mixed Vegetables, frozen	9 large - Onions	10 medium (4-1/8" long) - Onions, Green, Spring, or Scallion
10 sprigs - Parsley	2 oz - Peas, Green	8 large (2-1/4 per lb, approx 3-3/4" long, 3" dia) - Peppers, Sweet Green
2 large (2-1/4 per lb, approx 3-3/4" long, 3" dia) - Peppers, Sweet Red	1 Potato medium (2-1/4" to 3-1/4" dia) - Potatoes	8 oz - Snap Beans, Green
2 package (10 oz) - Spinach	8 large whole (3" dia) - Tomatoes, Red Ripe	1 large (3-1/4" dia) (approx 2 per lb) - Apples
5 medium (7" to 7-7/8" long) - Bananas	1 package (18 oz) - Blackberries, frozen	1 package (20 oz) - Blueberries, frozen, unsweetened
1 cup - Cherries, dried	2 oz - Cranberries, dried, sweetened	1 oz - Grapes, red or green (european type varieties, such as, Thompson seedless), raw
1 fl oz - Lemon juice, canned or bottled	1 melon, large (about 6-1/2" dia) - Melons, cantaloupe, raw	1 can (6 fl oz) - Orange juice, frozen concentrate
7 large (3-1/16" dia) - Oranges	2 pear, large (approx 2 per lb) - Pears, raw	1 can (6 fl oz) - Pineapple juice, frozen concentrate
9 oz - Pineapple, canned	6 oz - Raisins, golden seedless	1 package (10 oz) - Strawberries, frozen
24 extra large (1-5/8" dia) - Strawberries, raw	2 oz - Nuts, coconut meat, dried (desiccated), sweetened, shredded	1 oz - Miso
3 oz - Soy sauce made from soy (tamari)	1 oz - Soy sauce made from soy and wheat (shoyu)	7 oz - Soybeans

Baked Products

3 slice - Bread, whole wheat

Meats and Seafood

48 oz - Chicken, thigh, meat only	26 oz - Beef, tenderloin	9 slice (3-1/2" square; 8 per 6 oz package) - Turkey breast meat
64 medium - Shrimp		

Dairy and Egg

1 cup - Butter, salted	39 oz - Cheese, cottage	4 oz - Cheese, parmesan, grated
5 large - Egg, whole, raw, fresh	34 oz - Milk, lowfat, 1% milkfat	46 fl oz - Milk, nonfat (skim)
8 fl oz - Milk, reduced fat, 2% milkfat	3 container (6 oz) - Yogurt, fruit	5 oz - Yogurt, vanilla

Fats and Sweets

3 oz - Oil, olive, salad or cooking	1 oz - Oil, vegetable	12 oz - Salad dressing, italian dressing, reduced calorie
3 oz - Salad dressing, ranch dressing, fat-free	1 cup - Candies, M&M MARS, "M&M's" Milk Chocolate Candies	2 oz - Honey
1 oz - Sugars, granulated		

Breakfast Cereals

3 oz - Cereals ready-to-eat, corn flakes, plain, single brand	1 oz - Cereals ready-to-eat, GENERAL MILLS, HONEY NUT CHEERIOS	4 oz - Cereals ready-to-eat KELLOGG, KELLOGG'S FROSTED MINI-WHEATS, bite size
4 oz - Cereals, oats		

Whole Grains and Pasta

1 oz - Cornstarch	25 oz - Rice, brown	5 oz - Rice, white
7 oz - Wheat Flour, white		

Spices and Herbs

2 tbsp - Italian Seasoning	1 oz - Salt, table	1 oz - Spices, dill weed, dried
1 oz - Spices, garlic powder	1 oz - Spices, ginger, ground	1 oz - Spices, onion powder
1 oz - Spices, paprika	1 oz - Spices, pepper, black	1 oz - Spices, pepper, red or cayenne

---

Micronutrient Analysis

The Micro Nutrient Analysis link will open a separate window with a detailed micronutrient analysis. This includes a full Vitamin, Mineral and Essential Amino Acid list, as well as some other key nutrients. The list contains the Recommended Intake (where applicable), the actual Intake, and the Percentage of Recommended intake achieved (where applicable).

The default analysis is for the entire current week's foods and recipes but any individual day may be selected by clicking on the buttons at the top of the page.

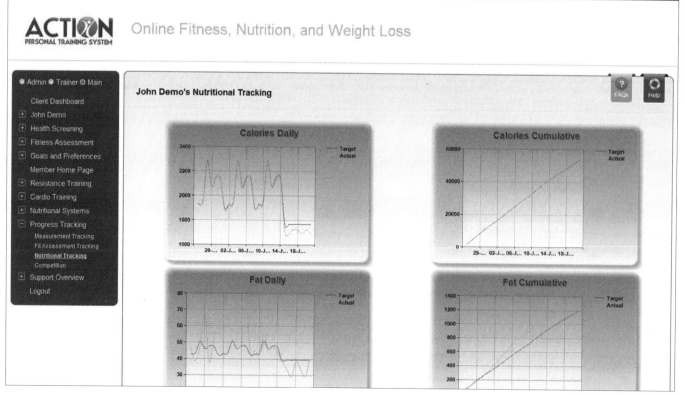

John Demo's Micro Nutrient Totals

This is a detailed Micro Nutrient Analysis.

2012 January 22 Sunday ▾ | Sunday | Monday | Tuesday | Wednesday | Thursday | Friday | Saturday

Macro	Recommended Intake	Intake	Percentage of Recommended
Fat (g)		326.56	
TransFat (g)		0.44	
Saturated Fat (g)		106.73	
Monounsaturated Fat (g)		117.79	
Polyunsaturated Fat (g)		63.25	
Cholesterol (mg)		2257.01	
Carbohydrates (g)		2203.18	
Fiber (g)	266.00	281.74	105.92%
Sugars (g)		1064.85	
Sucrose (g)		134.83	
Fructose (g)		221.98	
Glucose (g)		176.58	
Lactose (g)		101.35	
Galactose (g)		2.67	
Maltose (g)		2.68	
Protein (g)		753.04	
Caffeine (g)		1.82	
Starch (g)		157.66	

Vitamins	Recommended Intake	Intake	Percentage of Recommended
Vitamin A (IU)	21000.00	146603.46	698.11%
VitaminB6 (mg)	9.10	21.61	237.48%
VitaminB12 (mcg)	16.80	38.52	229.29%

To see a breakdown of the source of any individual micronutrients the name of the micronutrient may be clicked on and a separate window will open with a complete list of all foods and recipes for the selected day(s) and the amount of the selected micronutrient contained within these foods.

Nutritional Tracking

Nutritional Tracking is part of the Progress Tracking section in the Main Menu. The Nutritional Tracking will provide graphs of daily and cumulative totals for both target and actual values for calories, fats, carbs, and protein. These graphs serve to show trends in nutritional habits.

John Demo's Nutritional Tracking

Summary

In summary, the majority of a person's calories should come from carbohydrates. Your client should be aware that the best sources of carbohydrates are fruits and vegetables, which also contain vitamins and minerals. Simple sugars, such as table sugar or high fructose corn syrup, should be avoided. Clients should eat a high-carbohydrate meal with a good variety of complex carbohydrates approximately 3 hours prior to a workout and then consume an additional small snack of crackers right before the workout. A follow-up meal higher in protein after the workout is important to provide the necessary amino acids to help repair and refresh the muscles. The glycemic index is a good reference for those concerned with eating too many carbohydrates. Personal trainers should never recommend that clients omit carbohydrates from their diet, not even for a couple of weeks. The muscles rely on carbohydrates to get the necessary glucose as their fuel. Moderation is also good advice to give a client. Candy, ice cream or beer/wine/liquor is okay, as long as it is not the bulk of their calories and not consumed on a daily basis.

Fats are also an important part of the daily diet. They serve many functions in the body, including allowing vitamins to move throughout the cells, protecting nerve fibers, providing the building blocks for hormones and supplying a concentrated source of energy. About 25-30% of a healthy person's daily calories should come from fat. Following a fat-restricted diet (less than 10% of daily calories) can lead to problems with the body's metabolic functioning. Too much fat in the diet (more than 35% of daily calories) can also cause problems, such as increasing the chances of obesity and heart disease. Lipids are composed of long acid-chain molecules bonded together to form different kinds of fats. Unsaturated fats, like olive oil, are generally better for the body's health. Saturated fats, like butter, should be limited because of their links with heart disease. Some fats, like omega-3 fatty acids found in oily fish, can help the body function more optimally and reduce cholesterol and the chances of heart disease. Other fats, like partially-hydrogenated oils or trans fats, are detrimental to health because they raise cholesterol levels. Depending on their current health status and their weight loss goals, people have different fat requirements. However, too little or too much fat—i.e., any extreme—is not advisable for most people.

The proper addition of protein to the diet is yet another aspect of good nutrition. Ingestion of protein provides the body with the amino acids it needs to perform several bodily functions. Lean meats, eggs, nuts, dairy products and legumes are all good sources of protein and should be incorporated into every meal. However, clients should be informed that if too much protein is ingested, it will not be stored as protein and instead will be stored as fat. This fact is often unknown to clients who are attempting to follow the popular high-protein, low-carbohydrate diets.

Hydration is a crucial aspect of nutrition and must be maintained during workouts by the intake of plenty of water. Sports drinks are usually an unnecessary source of calories and sugar, which is fine for athletes training for hours vigorously but may inhibit weight loss in clients trying to lose weight. If sports drinks are preferred for hydrating clients that want to lose weight, sugar free ones are the best option.

When clients feel their diet is not providing enough nutrients, they may turn to supplements. While it is always best to attempt to get nutrition from food, it is sometimes difficult and supplements can help fill in the gaps. There are several types of supplements available and great care should be taken to discuss the risks and benefits of the specific supplement a client is considering.

Nutrition is very important for any active person. It is the body's source of fuel—it is what keeps people going, what supplies the energy for everything they do. Good nutrition will maintain bodily functions, such as breathing, and internal processes, such as maintaining heart and brain function, all of which require energy. Just to stay alive, the body is equipped with a certain amount of calories it needs and this is dictated by hormones released from the thyroid gland. Maintaining proper nutrition is important in all aspects of good health. A good balance between carbohydrates, protein and fat will provide clients with the best possible nutrition, and trainers that learn about the most popular supplements can help advise clients when certain elements are missing in their clients' diets.

Review Questions

1. The glycemic index is a ranking of _____ based on their simplicity.

2. Dietary guidelines currently recommend 20-30% of your daily calories come from carbohydrates. True or False? _____

3. Fat is necessary for the body in order to:

   a) Help us feel satiated

   b) Transport vitamins A and D

   c) Protect nerve fibers

   d) Form hormones

   e) All of the above

4. Fat is important as a bodily energy source because:

   a) It is converted more efficiently than carbohydrates

   b) It provides more than double the calories per gram than other energy sources

   c) It can be eaten in unlimited quantities without excess storage

   d) It is the body's primary source of energy

   e) All of the above

5. Eating hydrogenated fats can _____ LDL levels.

6. The current method to determine the amount of protein in food is referred to as the PDCAAS. True/False _____

7. When there is an insufficient supply of carbohydrates available for energy, the body will instead use _____ as its primary energy source.

   a) Sugar

   b) Amino acids

   c) Creatine

   d) Fat

   e) All of the above

8. Creatine is an essential nutrient. True or False? _____

9. Caffeine can:

   a) Improve aerobic endurance during short-term, extreme exercise

   b) Increase fat oxidation

   c) Decrease the perception of pain

   d) Allow for more intensity in athletic performance

   e) All of the above

10. When should you advise your clients to hydrate? _____

_____

Answers

1. Carbohydrates.

2. False.

3. e) All of the above.

4. b) It provides more than double the calories per gram than other energy sources.

5. Increase.

6. True.

7. b) Amino acids.

8. False.

9. e) All of the above.

10. Before, during and after exercise.

References

Bloomer RJ. The role of nutritional supplements in the prevention and treatment of resistance exercise-induced skeletal muscle injury. *Sports Medicine.* 2007;37(6):519-32.

Brosnan JT, Brosnan ME. Creatine: endogenous metabolite, dietary and therapeutic supplement. *Annual Review in Nutrition.* 2007;27:241-61.

Graham TE. Caffeine, coffee and ephedrine: impact on exercise performance and metabolism. *Canadian Journal of Applied Physiology.* 2001;26 Suppl:S103-19.

Grunewald KK, Bailey RS. Commercially marketed supplements for bodybuilding athletes. *Sports Medicine.* 1993;15(2):90-103.

Hoffman JR, Falvo MJ. Protein-Which is Best? *Journal of Sports Science Medicine.* 2004;3:118-30.

Hu FB, Willett WC. Optimal Diets for Prevention of Coronary Heart Disease. *JAMA.* 2002;288:2569-78.

Jenkinson DM, Harbert AJ. Supplements and sports. *American Family Physician.* 2008;78(9):1039-46.

Juhn M. Popular sports supplements and ergogenic aids. *Sports Medicine.* 2003;33(12):921-39.

Lattavo A, Kopperud A, Rogers PD. Creatine and other supplements. *Pediatric Clinics of North America.* 2007;54(4):735-60.

Lichtenstein AH, Kennedy E, Barrier P, Danford D, Ernst ND, Grundy SM, Leveille GA, Van Horn L, Williams CL, Booth SL. Dietary fat consumption and health. *Nutrition Reviews.* 1998;56(5 Pt 2):S3-19.

Montain SJ. Hydration recommendations for sport. *Current Sports Medicine Reports.* 2008;7(4):187-92.

Mozaffarian D, Ascherio A, Hu FB, Stampfer MJ, Willett WC, Siscovick DS, Rimm EB. Interplay between different polyunsaturated fatty acids and risk of coronary heart disease in men. *Circulation.* 2005;111:157-64.

Paddon-Jones D, Borsheim E, Wolfe RR. Potential ergogenic effects of arginine and creatine supplementation. *Journal of Nutrition.* 2004;134(10 Suppl):2888S-94S.

Persky AM, Rawson ES. Safety of creatine supplementation. *Subcellular Biochemistry.* 2007;46:275-89.

Phillips GC. Glutamine: the nonessential amino acid for performance enhancement. *Current Sports Medicine Reports.* 2007;6(4):265-68.

Schaafsma G. The protein digestibility-corrected amino acid score. *Journal of Nutrition.* 2000;130(7):1865S-67S.

Tseng YH, Kokkotou E, Schulz TJ, Huang TL, Winnay JN, Taniguchi CM, Tran TT, Suzuki R, Espinoza DO, Yamamoto Y, Ahrens MJ, Dudley AT, Norris AW, Kulkarni RN, Kahn CR. New role of bone morphogenetic protein 7 in brown adipogenesis and energy expenditure. *Nature.* 2008;454:1000-04.

Yamamoto LM, Judelson DA, Farrell MJ, Lee EC, Armstrong LE, Casa DJ, Kraemer WJ, Volek JS, Maresh CM. Effects of hydration state and resistance exercise on markers of muscle damage. *Journal of Strength and Conditioning Research*. 2008;22(5):1387-93.

Chapter 10: Legal/Business

Topics Covered

Legal Issues

Slip and Fall
Equipment Usage
Supplements
Sexual Harassment
Personal Trainer Qualifications
Emergency Response
Confidentiality

Risk Management

Proper Education
Appropriate Training for Each Client
Limiting Liability Through Avoidance, Retention, Reduction and Transfer
Proper Conduct
Proper Training Area
Documentation

Selling Your Services

Marketing Your Business
Determining the Cost of Your Service

Retaining Clients

READ—Rapport, Empathy, Assessment and Development
Customer Service
Key Points for Success
Referrals
Other Incentives
Non-Compete Clauses

Expanding Your Business

Organizing Your Business
The Business Plan
The Budget
Establishing Policies
Clients
Advertisement
Profits

Legal Issues

As rewarding as it can be to work as a personal trainer and positively impact a client's health and fitness, there are some legal issues to be considered. Personal trainers must understand their role when it comes to putting clients at risk for injury. Trainers have to do everything in their power to ensure their clients' safety through proper technique and proper spotting, by not overexerting them and by ensuring that the workout environment is safe. There are some legal terminologies trainer should know and below is a list and a brief detail of their definition.

- Contract Law—Regulates laws that govern individuals who enter into a contract
- Duty of Care—The responsibility one has to protect another from harm, especially in a service-oriented client relationship
- Informed Consent—Ensuring clients understand they are voluntarily entering into the activities set forth by their trainers

- Negligence—Failure to comply with known standards
- Waiver—A document signed by clients that they are knowingly participating in activities that may cause them an injury and that they are waiving legal action should injury occur
- Risk Management—Processes in place to ensure the least amount of harm will come to clients. Essentially being proactive by following safety procedures, properly informing clients of risk and having all proper documentation completed prior to any activities
- Tort Law—Regulates civil wrong-doing

Clients have a right to a safe environment whether their trainer is working for a fitness facility or independently. Ensuring the client's safety is the trainer's duty. Hazards must be taken care of or proper warning must be given. Do not allow a client to workout with faulty equipment. Personal trainers should have a plan as to what workout areas clients are going to be using, so it is wise to make a routine of checking that equipment prior to clients' sessions. Make sure the area being used for a workout is clean of any liquids or hazards.

In a fitness facility environment there are many potential hazards which can harm a client. Make sure there are no water bottles lying around that could be a potential tripping hazard. Any fluid not cleaned up can also cause slippage of hands or a slip and fall. Towels left behind can also lead to accidental injury. Both the trainer and the client must be cautious of bodily fluids—left behind towels can be a source of bacteria or infectious disease. If possible, sanitize equipment before a client uses it. There are so many potential risks that a client can encounter under a trainer's supervision that they cannot all be eliminated; however, personal trainers that are aware of their duties to ensure clients' safety will quickly recognize an unsafe situation. Last and most importantly, trainer should use common sense.

Every year clients make legal claims against personal trainers. This section will briefly discuss some of these and how risk management comes into play when trying to avoid these situations and, most importantly, avoid injury to clients. Below is the list of the most common claims against personal trainers, as compiled by insurance companies:

- Slip and Fall
- Equipment Usage
- Supplements
- Sexual Harassment
- Proper Qualifications
- Emergency Response
- Client Confidentiality

Slip and Fall

Slipping and falling that led to injury was the number one complaint of clients against their personal trainer. As stated previously, ensuring a safe environment is key to clients. This can be accomplished by being diligent about routines. When first starting out, it is easy to develop habits, so trainer must try to make sure the habits developed are good ones. Make it a habit to check a client's workout environment prior to a session in order to decrease the chance that the client may have a slip and fall incident. Obviously a fitness facility is very dynamic, but if a trainer has checked a client's areas prior to use, any out of place items should be very apparent as the workout progresses from station to station.

Personal trainers need to become very observant as part of their risk management technique. Review a client's attire and if, for example, the shoes being worn do not fit properly or are inappropriate for working out, the trainer should bring it to the

client's attention. Clothing that is restrictive or too loose can also cause a slip and fall, so once again, trainers need to make the client aware. If a trainer deems a situation or environment unsafe, the trainer should not continue because in the end, the trainer will be held liable by the employer at the least and also possibly by the client. Clients should be advised of requirements from day one of training: proper shoes and attire are a must. Clients need to be informed that if compliance is not met, their session cannot proceed for their own safety.

Another good habit for trainers to adopt is documenting a slip and fall immediately after the incident and writing down the circumstances. As time passes and the story is retold, information may be mistakenly added or taken out. If trainers write details down immediately, there is a better chance at resolving the issue quickly. Most facilities have their own incident

report documents and trainer notes will help to put as much detail into the report as possible. Another recommendation is that trainers log their precheck of equipment with the date, time and condition of the specific piece of equipment checked. This may seem time consuming and tedious, but it is better to have too much information than not enough.

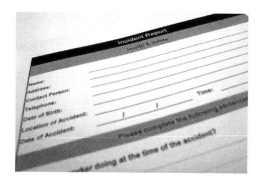

Equipment Usage

Improper use of equipment is the second most reported injury claim against personal trainers. As such, personal trainers need to ensure clients know how to use equipment before they begin a designated activity. Many times clients will say they know how to use a particular machine even though they have never used it. Fitness equipment seems intuitive but, in reality, some of it is quite complicated to set up, and proper technique is a must. Instead of asking clients if they know how to use the equipment, trainers should take the initiative to just show them.

This will keep clients from stating incorrectly that they know how and give trainers the opportunity to demonstrate both proper setup and use of the equipment.

Trainers need to periodically check and document the equipment maintenance record. They may want to inform clients of this documentation if they feel it may be important. There are many pieces of equipment that trainer and clients will use and all situations cannot be covered, but the two main safety rules for equipment usage are proper set up and usage. It is also essential that all working equipment, whether it be resistance bands or high tech machines, be in good condition. All equipment should be inspected for safety.

Supplements

Supplement usage can be a sensitive subject for some people and will most likely depend on

the trainer's own personal beliefs, as there is no law governing what a personal trainer can recommend or sell to a client in terms of supplementation. As a general rule, it is not recommended that trainers sell or advise clients on any supplement. With

that being stated, some personal trainers sell supplements or the company or fitness facility they work for sells them. This aspect of personal training may be part of a job description. This is where education regarding what is being sold becomes of the utmost importance.

There have been liability cases where personal trainers and the facilities they work for have been held accountable for selling supplements containing ephedra to a client. In one case, the client had hypertension and, since ephedra raises blood pressure by increasing heart rate, the client died. As stated throughout this literature, it is absolutely essential that trainers take a detailed initial assessment that includes any chronic illnesses a client has and what medications are being taken. Trainers need to be involved and take own notes versus simply giving clients questionnaires to fill out. Also, trainers should not recommend supplements that they would not take themselves or that they do not know what the active ingredients are and what they do.

There are also illegal substances that are available to clients, such as human growth hormone or anabolic steroids. Trainers may get approached with inquiries about how to obtain such items. We cannot stress enough for trainers not to get involved in this area of supplementation, as it is illegal and highly dangerous. Personal trainers should advocate a healthy road to fitness and stress the importance of hard work. Becoming fit is not an overnight process and a pill will not get a client there. The fact

that a client has sought out a personal trainer means that client is ready to make the necessary changes in daily life. These are the aspects that trainers should stress and they should do everything in their power to deter someone from trying to obtain results through the use of illegal substances. Again documentation is key. Personal trainers should report any attempt at seeking these items to a supervisor; even if nothing comes of it, the trainer will be absolved of any wrongdoing.

Sexual Harassment

Another sensitive subject is sexual harassment. Personal trainers are in intimate situations with clients. Some clients will understand this and others may misconstrue or be uncomfortable with the amount of touching that may occur. This was the third highest claim

made to insurance companies against personal trainers. Sexual harassment comes in all forms—male to female, male to male or female to female.

Some people are just not comfortable being touched by an unfamiliar person. A good initial assessment can address this; so trainers should

not be afraid to ask this question. They should inform clients that, at times, touching may be necessary and ask them how comfortable they are with this. Another aspect of sexual harassment can develop when a trainer and client develop a personal relationship. As stated before, a personal trainer is sometimes in an intimate situation with a client and if a relationship develops, it is unacceptable, inappropriate and unprofessional. Also, there may be certain backlashes once the relationship ends. It is best to end the professional relationship if a personal relationship develops with a client. Most fitness facilities will not tolerate this behavior.

Sexual harassment is a claim that often arises because one person's idea of what is acceptable is not the same as another person's. It is hard to prove and usually rests on the credibility of the persons involved. The best way to avoid any incidence that can be perceived as sexual harassment is to not touch the client. Trainers can demonstrate to clients how particular maneuvers should be conducted by positioning a "barrier" between the client and the trainer; i.e., a trainer could "touch" the client with an object, such as a ball. Trainer should  also avoid private settings where the situation has only the two parties as witnesses. When doing body fat measurements, where touching is required and expected, trainers should have another personal trainer present and document who that person is in case there is any question later. Because sexual harassment is in the eyes of the person being "harassed," the best thing to do is to leave no question, which can be done by avoiding touching. If spotting or touching is required, trainers can use a prop (e.g., a ball), to avoid direct contact.

Personal Trainer Qualifications

Personal trainer qualifications deal more with a fitness facility than individual personal trainers. Those reading this literature are on their way to becoming certified personal trainers. Some clients will claim that

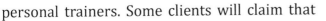

a particular fitness facility staffs improperly certified personal trainers or that the personal trainers do not hold the credentials advertised. Importantly, trainers should not overstate qualifications and should keep certifications handy, as it is the right of any client who may ask to see credentials. People pay for a service from trainers or providers on their behalf and they expect to get what they pay for. If a trainer is not certified and the facility is claiming that the trainer is, it is up to the trainer to set the record straight because this is misrepresentation on behalf of both the facility and the trainer, and it is grounds for legal action should a client wish to take it that far.

Another area regarding personal trainer qualifications is claiming to work with a specific demographic such as elderly people. If a facility advertises this service and the personal trainer assigned to these clients does not have the appropriate certifications to serve this population, the liability is put on the personal trainer. If a trainer wants to work with a special needs group, such as the elderly or those afflicted with arthritis, the trainer needs to get the proper training needed. The bottom line is for trainers not to overstate qualifications or allow their employers to overstate their credentials and to obtain any additional training required to serve special populations.

Emergency Response

A personal trainer will be faced with numerous situations that will require emergency responses. This may be directly, with their own client, or indirectly, in their vicinity. A certified personal trainer is required to be CPR compliant and some certifications require first aid training and automated external defibrillator training as well. If a trainer's certification does not require the latter two as part of the requirements, it is recommended that the trainer obtain this training anyway. Any facility the trainer works for should have a standard operating procedure if an emergency response situation arises and the trainer should be familiar with this procedure. CPR, first aid and AED certifications must be renewed and trainer should keep track of when their certifications expire so they can keep them up to date.

These are also certifications that a client has a right to ask about and see upon request. A trainer does not want to be in the position of having to explain to a client and/or employer why certifications are not up to date. Documentation is also important in terms of the trainer's and facility's liability in an emergency. Proper reporting of the fact is crucial while leaving out any biased opinions of the incident. Most facilities have their own internal form for incident reports, so trainers need to familiarize themselves with them. Independent trainers can generate their own forms to keep on hand in case something happens. During the course of a personal training career, it is likely that the trainer is going to be faced with an emergency response situation, and that trainer may be required to render life saving aid to an individual.

Confidentiality

Confidentiality is one of the most important aspects of personal training. A client is sharing very personal information with a trainer at any given time. It is up to the trainer to maintain professionalism and not discuss or gossip about any information that is given in a professional setting. A client may be hesitant to disclose details about a condition, which can hinder progress or cause injury. It is not necessary, but a trainer may want to become HIPAA compliant. HIPAA (Health Insurance Portability & Accountability Act) is a 2003 law passed by Congress which states that health care professionals are not allowed to release personal health information of clients to third parties.  While a trainer is not classified as a health care professional, it is wise to let a client know that the trainer understands and abides by HIPAA. A client might then be more at ease in disclosing any ailments or medications that may affect training, which will help the trainer tailor a more effective workout. A good initial assessment should include a confidentiality agreement.

Risk Management

Risk management simply means the avoidance of liability in the event that something goes wrong. There are certain steps a personal trainer can follow to reduce the chances of liability

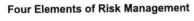

Four Elements of Risk Management

A continuous interlocked process—not an event

when some mishap occurs. Despite taking as many precautions as possible and following all the rules, accidents will happen. Trainers are in a business of serving people. The fact that people will get hurt and people will be unsatisfied is unavoidable. What steps can personal trainers take or what risk management can be put into place that can protect them, their job and their certification when something bad happens? Although this is not an enjoyable topic, it is important that a personal trainer understands how to minimize liability.

Risk can be managed through:

- Proper Education
- Appropriate Training for Each Client
- Limiting Liability Through Avoidance, Retention, Reduction and Transfer
- Proper Conduct
- Proper Training Area
- Documentation

Proper Education

Becoming a personal trainer only requires completing the certification process. If individuals are serious about personal training, they will strive to obtain a higher degree in some sort of exercise physiology area. The more education a trainer has, the less likely that trainer will make avoidable mistakes. Common sense indicates that diet and exercise will gain fitness, so what is a personal trainer bringing to the table? The more education a personal trainer has, the less likely any highly educated client is to question actions. A good understanding of anatomy and physiology is extremely important. What are common injuries? Most people know tearing the anterior cruciate ligament (ACL) is not good, but a good trainer knows where it is located, what movements could result in its injury and what tests are done to confirm any injury. Most clients will not have a clue about anatomy and physiology, but they expect that their personal trainer will. A wise move for a trainer is to invest in a good anatomy book and study basic anatomical structure and typical sports injuries.

Appropriate Training for Each Client

Every client a personal trainer will have will be different, so the trainer should tailor the

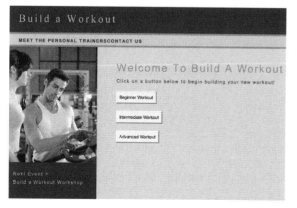

workout to the client. Knowing clients and their needs will greatly reduce their chances of injury and therefore will limit the trainer's liability. If a client has back problems, the trainer should avoid any exercises that could further exacerbate the problem. Remember, not every problem is going to be physical. Some people have physiological or chronic illnesses, such as high blood pressure or heart conditions. Again, it is a personal trainer's job to know this, and the trainer cannot make a client with heart problems run miles at a time. The personal trainer should make sure any client who is under the care of a physician for any condition has a signed release form from that doctor stating it is okay to participate in a physical fitness routine. The bottom line is, take the time to personalize clients' workouts to meet their needs. Trainers should not allow clients to do exercises that will exacerbate any injury. Clients expect personal trainers to remember things, so it may be a good idea to review a new client's information prior to a session until the trainer becomes familiar with the history. This practice will help the trainer to avoid making "dumb" mistakes that may lead to injury.

Limiting Liability through Avoidance, Retention, Reduction and Transfer

Limiting liability is not meant to teach tricks to avoid any wrong doing. It is meant to increase client safety while reducing trainers' risks and protecting their job and certifications. Certifications are easy to initially obtain but are usually difficult to reinstate, so personal trainers want to protect their certifications as much as possible. Liability can be limited by following four steps:

- Avoidance
- Retention
- Reduction
- Transfer

Avoidance

Avoidance simply means to avoid any dangerous action that will lead to a raised risk for injury. Undoubtedly, clients want to be challenged and personal trainers want to provide this, but not at any cost. For example, maybe a client prefers outdoor activities versus a gym setting. While this is fine, a trainer should not take a client cycling or running on busy streets. Instead, the choice should be a park or designated path where there is less likelihood injury.

Retention

Retention of clients is great way to avoid liability because there is a sense of loyalty felt by clients they have developed a good professional relationship with their trainers. Clients are less likely to pursue any action if trainers have retained them for an extended period of time.

Reduction

Within any profession, guidelines are constantly changing and some are mandated while others are not. Trainers are likely to be aware of some mandates, but they should take the responsibility to keep up with all of them. Familiarizing oneself with annual changes will greatly reduce liability, especially when changes affect more of the legal aspect of personal training versus the practical aspect.

Transfer

The most recommended way to transfer legal liability is to obtain liability insurance. This type of insurance requires a fee, which provides trainers with services, just as with health or car insurance. Some of these services include legal representation and any fines set forth by court proceedings. While annual costs will never exceed the annual liability, it is well worth the cost should an event happen that requires paying a large amount of money if found liable.

Just as with any insurance, what goes in is not usually what comes back in return, but it is peace of mind and the assurance of coverage for any mishap that may occur.

Proper Conduct

Behaving in a professional manner, especially in a customer service field like personal training, is a must. Having a crude sense of humor or making inappropriate jokes can lead to unwanted outcomes even though no harm is meant. The best practice of risk management is simply not to do it. Remember, sexual harassment is on a continuum, so what a trainer may deem appropriate may not be in the eyes of others and may leave the trainer having to offer an explanation in an awkward situation. A trainer can also be on the receiving end, which the trainer will want to report and document and potentially end services with that individual. Most importantly, acting professionally can greatly reduce the risk of any reprimand.

Proper Training Area

As discussed earlier, a safe training area is the personal trainer's responsibility and checking areas prior to training will decrease incidences of injury. Also, if the trainer and client are training in a non-traditional area, such as those not located in a fitness facility, the trainer must

make sure the environment is appropriate. Places like parks are an appropriate setting. Trainers do not want to take clients to a place where they will feel uncomfortable. Trainers should use good judgment and common sense, and they should also be cautious of settings that are too intimate or private. A fitness facility is actually the best, most appropriate place to train. Should a client request another place, the trainer should use good judgment when agreeing, which will reduce liability for any wrongdoing. Some employers will not allow off-site training, so the trainer needs to know the policy on this issue.

Documentation

No matter what the occurrence, proper documentation can greatly assist the trainer if a client takes legal action. In the case of an injury, if the trainer properly annotated

that the equipment or the area was checked and can show documentation of that check, as well as proving a history of this practice, the trainer is at much less risk. Most personal trainers will not take the time to check an area, let alone document their check, but trainers should make it a habit from day one. They should keep a small notebook with the date, time and client number. It is wise to never use names when writing informal documentation. When trainers have to fill out incident reports, they use as many details as possible, and they simply state facts, not opinions. Documentation is a good practice for risk management because it allows a record of events when they actually occurred. If an individual is asked to recall something, even the next day, key events are often forgotten. Personal trainers should always document anything they think may be of importance.

Selling Your Services

One of the most important goals in creating a business is obtaining and keeping clients. Getting potential clients in a business can be achieved many ways. Develop a name for the business through various marketing strategies to help expand it successfully.

Marketing Your Business

In this technology-driven age, computers are a convenient and popular information search tool. When trainers work for established businesses, they can work on individualizing themselves from other workers. This can be accomplished

by forming an introductory packet for clients filled with needed information. Creating an identity can help a trainer get noticed at work or can help if the decision is made to open a private business in the future. Trainers considering opening their own business can learn practical skills from their current employer: interviewing, hiring, sales, organization and time management are some important skills for business owners.

Websites

A website is an excellent advertising tool. Constructing a website can be done in three steps. First, decide the purpose of the website and include information, graphics, videos and relevant links. Second, begin to develop the page by figuring out an appropriate domain name that will attract potential clients and choose a reliable Internet Service Provider to register the name. Make the website interactive

and include the intended information. The more visual and interesting (including quizzes, polls, ways to calculate BMI, etc.), the more successful it will become. Remember to update the site with current facts and articles so clients will benefit from the latest changes in health and fitness. There is lots of competition from other websites, so visiting them can help in obtaining information. Links relating to health and fitness websites can also be attached. Finally, the website should be launched in order to ensure continued success. Getting clients to visit the website and spreading its existence through word-of-mouth can help the business expand.

Business Cards and Brochures

Besides developing a website, there are other ways of marketing the business. Personal trainers should develop a consistent logo, color and design to appear on all of their business materials and have business cards available and accessible to clients. The cards should emphasize qualifications and necessary contact information without appearing too crowded. Create brochures and place them by business cards to attract clients. The brochures should include information on benefits not offered by other health centers, the purpose of the business and the

services of personal trainers. It can sometimes replace and be less costly than the client introductory packet.

A useful brochure should contain the following information:

1. Front page: logo, business name, credentials of the personal trainer(s), contact information, mission statement (if business has one)

2. Back Page: contact information, promotions or special deals, positive client feedback

3. Inside: qualifications and experience of personal trainers, more information about the company and owner, brief explanation and general benefits of fitness training, services and programs offered

4. Proper targeting to intended clientele

5. Easy to read, clear layout, limiting word crowding

6. Accurate facts and updates when needed

Steps for Successful Marketing

Selling services requires knowledge of marketing and how to use it successfully. It mainly consists of research to keep the business up-to-date and is not costly or difficult to accomplish. Selling services can be accomplished with the following steps:

1. Identify needs: Find a need that the current marketplace has not fulfilled.

2. Conduct Research: Collect facts related to that need.

3. Satisfy: Make a service that fulfills the need.

4. Promote: Showcase the service to clients so they are aware of the ability of the business to satisfy the need.

5. Distribute: Use advertisements and other information to let clients know about the services.

6. Acquire new business: Make sales and try to keep clients' commitments.

When marketing a business, becoming involved in community activities can be very advantageous. Involvement is inexpensive and useful for individuals who own their own business. Participating in community or public speaking events related to fitness training is a great way to appeal to the media and sell the business. If there is a local newspaper or TV station at the event, highlighting the benefits of a business can be useful and less expensive than placing an ad.

Additional Ideas for Marketing Your Business

Other ways to sell your services include:

1. Create a periodical newsletter and distribute it through mail, email, fax and websites.

2. Highlight a client's positive results (with client's permission) through different sources.

3. Offer gift certificates or discounts.

4. Mail postcards or items with the company's contact information.

5. Develop a line of products like t-shirts, caps, gym bags, etc., with the company's name

6. Promote ads through local TV and radio stations and newspaper.

7. Offer clients and other professionals benefits for referring the company's services.

Determining the Cost of Your Service

Pricing is based on a variety of factors. Think about the salaries of employees and taxes that have to be paid to the government. Also take into account the telephone, uniforms, equipment, supplies and liability insurance. Consider the pricing after completing the following 10-step assessment. It is based on setting up a reliable annual income by answering some questions and doing some math.

1. Determine an annual income, which is the 12-month salary you require.

2. Figure out how much income will be earned weekly (divide wanted annual income by 50 instead of 52 to take into account vacations, sick days, etc.).

3. Next, figure out how many clients and sessions are needed weekly  to achieve the weekly income (divide wanted weekly income by amount earned per session and divide the number of paid sessions by the number of clients).

4. Determine the closing percentage by dividing the number of people interested in a sale by the number who actually signed up.

5. Set a realistic timeframe within which the number of new desired clients needed to fulfill the weekly amount will actually sign up.

6. Divide the number of new desired clients by the closing percentage and determine how long it will take to contact those clients each week.

7. Divide the number from #6 by 5 weekdays to determine how many clients to contact per day.

8. Consider the number from #7 and decide how many clients can be contacted every hour depending on the trainer's daily schedule.

9. Keep a file of new contact information for all clients so they can be contacted for personal sales by showing them a few exercises.

10. Follow-up with clients by sending a thank you card and contact them about a week after that to talk about things to do during the next appointment.

There are several elements to running a successful business. Commit to clients by staying professional and dependable. Take the initiative to create a program suitable for clients. Use clients' feedback as a guide to improve the business in the future. A trainer should always be ready to change the program to better suit a client's needs. Having the ability to keep a professional disposition when providing services, collecting money or listening to complaints can help the business run smoothly.

Use clients' feedback as a guide to improve the business in the future.

Retaining Clients

One of the most important goals in a business should be to produce a profit. However, health and fitness professionals should also focus on getting and retaining clients. When this is accomplished, there is a long-term partnership between both which can be fruitful and profitable.

READ—Rapport, Empathy, Assessment and Development

Because there are a variety of places for people to exercise, excelling in customer service is essential to rise above the competition. This can be accomplished by improving rapport, empathy, assessment and development (READ). When forming a rapport with clients, confidence, enthusiasm and professionalism are very important. When trainers are confident, they are friendly and can explain the importance of fitness training, which will help clients trust them. Clients can see when a person is enthusiastic and willing to help them. They are more likely to stay at a health club with individuals they know are beneficial to them. Clients assess professionalism by what they hear and see from trainers. It is necessary to dress keenly and always be free to communicate with clients. Trainers should not be preoccupied with computers, leaning against furniture or keep clients waiting. They should also have a friendly tone of voice and make eye contact when addressing clients.

For empathy, trainers should strive to understand the thought process behind actions. Motivation helps people make decisions. It is best to understand a client's intentions in personal training by asking a few questions. Trainers should ask which goals clients are trying to accomplish and discuss the importance of reaching them. They should find out how long their clients have been trying to achieve the goals and any past obstacles that prevented them from reaching them. Knowing the motivation behind wanting to workout can help in forming an exercise routine.

During the initial assessment, the trainer should ask the client questions to find out more about the client's requirements, which can help the client feel more engaged in the training program. Questions should be nondirective ones, which require an answer more expanded than yes or no. Understanding the most important needs of the client can help trainers figure out

4 kinds of motivation

Positive
Motivation towards a goal

"Write this report and you get a bonus." *

"I really want to write this report!" +

Extrinsic
Someone wants you to do it

Intrinsic
You want to do it

"Write this report or you're fired!" *

"I really don't want to write this report!" *

Negative
Motivation away from something

* These three don't work—and yet companies keep using them.

+ Only this one creates positive, sustainable motivation.

the best ways to accomplish their clients' goals. Directive questions, in turn, result in a yes or no answer, which can be useful in reassuring a client's responses to other questions. For example, a trainer can paraphrase what the client has just said and ask the client to verify.

A trainer should develop individualized programs by taking into account the client's needs and goals. This should help trainers realize the best course action. The time of day, medical conditions and other factors should be taken into account.

Customer Service

The following is a list of useful guidelines for customer service:

1. Always make time to greet club members (even if off shift).
2. Exhibit a welcoming and professional attitude.
3. Treat each question with careful consideration.
4. Express ideas with clear verbal communication and body language.
5. Be enthusiastic to hear complaints and deal with them accordingly.

Many trainers need to realize the benefits and advantages they have to offer a client. Clients want trainers who can explain how personal training can help their lives. They want someone to give them proper guidance during an exercise to make sure it is safe and effective. A trainer needs to find a way to fit conveniently into a client's schedule. Upgrading the intensity in exercise levels can give experienced clients a refreshing new challenge. Trainers should also be prepared to work with special needs populations, such as people with long-term illnesses or injuries. In order to satisfy a client population, try the following:

1. Have a client introductory packet ready that contains credentials and qualifications.
2. Be certified in CPR & other first aid training.
3. Become a member in professional organizations to show clients an interest in and dedication to the profession.
4. Develop a fitness program based on the client's medical history, needs and goals.
5. Have knowledge of nutrition, which can be advantageous to clients.

6. Seek help from other professionals when needed.

7. Keep up to date on business policies concerning bills, liability insurance, etc.

8. Make safety a priority and practice warming up, cooling down and using equipment properly.

9. Pay attention to client's concerns.

10. Keep each session interesting in order to keep clients coming back.

Key Points for Success

Finding and keeping a clientele is a process. First, trainers should be aware of their qualifications. They should assess whether or not they are educated to deal with different

HEALTHCARE NETWORKING   FOR HEALTH CARE PROFESSIONALS

age or special needs populations. In assessing a client initially, if a trainer is uncomfortable about any information, it is better to let that client train with someone else. Being ill-equipped to deal with a certain client can lead to losing that client and others if the reputation of the business is harmed. Networking with health care professionals and those associated with personal training can help in recruiting clients. A trainer can get in contact with doctors, physical therapists, nutritionists and dieticians and leave business cards or brochures with

them if possible. In making these contacts, a trainer needs to make sure to exhibit maturity and a professional appearance.

Avoid actions that could potentially lose clients, such as failing to follow-up with them. They may lose confidence trainers that are unable to answer questions or lead them in the right direction to find answers. Clients look forward to follow-ups and comments on their progress. Trainers need to make sure to have time to complete current appointments before recruiting new clients. It may be advantageous to hire additional employees when taking on more clients. Take time and consideration when expanding a business.

There are a variety of ways to invest more time with a client including:

1. Take interest in the client outside the training area: Trainers can talk to a client's health care professional if requested or necessary or watch the client engage in physical activity.

2. Become well-rounded: Read a variety of newspapers, magazines or articles not necessarily related to health and fitness. Clients come from different career levels and being well-rounded may help trainers relate to them more easily.

3. Train off-site: Switch workout places from inside to outside to add more variety to routines.

4. Get to know the client: Knowing more about a client's hobbies and interests may fortify the relationship between the trainer and client.

5. Use effective ways to get and keep clients. Mailing clients does carry some cost and can recruit only a few clients out of the hundreds of letters sent. If this is a preferred method, letters need to be sent to a targeted client population. A useful way to attract clients is to have current clients refer them. Referrals are free but can only be successful if trainers provide incentives and helpful reminders to make referrals. Remind clients that referrals are the main way of expanding business and ask them for recommendations to their friends and family. Using this method with close clients can make referrals a reliable way to attracting new clients.

Referrals

Although some trainers maybe uncomfortable with approaching clients to make referrals, there are a few things they should keep in mind. Most clients will understand the importance of expanding a business and acquiring new clients. Long-term clients are usually pleased by their current trainer and will have no problem speaking about the benefits of personal training.

After a referral is made, trainers should do the following to turn potential clients into new clients:

1. Mail a client introductory packet to the potential new client.

2. Call to arrange an introductory meeting; do not wait for the new client to call you.

3. Pay attention to the client's history and disposition to discuss how personal training can be advantageous to them.

4. Listen to the client attentively by using eye contact and mentally recording what is being said.

5. Assess the client's goals to better understand how to successfully achieve them.

6. Close the deal by summarizing what the client has just discussed regarding goals and needs and suggest convenient ways to fit training into the client's schedule.

7. Prepare an outline of the exercises planned and useful information if the client commits to training.

8. Review policies and fees to find what is best suited for the client.

9. Have the confidence to ask a potential client to sign up for training.

10. After completing the introductory meeting, follow-up to close the sale if the client has not already signed up.

Other Incentives

There are several things that can be done to attract new clients. Provide clients with trial offer coupons or the option to purchase gift certificates. People who receive these offers personally are likely to give training a try and may continue once they realize the benefits. If a client was referred, remember to follow-up with the potential new member and thank the client who did the referral. Participate in public speaking events related to training to promote services. Those listening may commit to the services or pass on information about the business. Send thank you notes to clients or other professionals when appropriate.

Non-Compete Clauses

Sometimes health clubs or businesses require a contractual non-compete clause to be signed by trainers before working. This is done in the hopes of preventing trainers from leaving and taking clients with them. However, this contract is very challenging to enforce in court. Should this happen, clients will usually follow a trainer they have been working with rather than start

over with another trainer. If a trainer has a business and employs fellow trainers, it is best to strengthen the relationship between the parties to avoid future conflicts rather than relying on the non-compete clause.

Expanding Your Business

Being a personal trainer is what an individual makes of it. Some people are content with working for an organization such as a fitness center, while others opt to work as a contractor, perhaps working for a company who contracts out the training services. Many personal trainers want to make a business out of their training by seeking their own clients and negotiating their own prices. This next section focuses on those who wish to start their own business or be hired as a contractor.

First the basics. Some terminology to become familiar with are the terms sole proprietor, individual contractor, partnership, corporation and S-corporation. Prospective owners must decide which category best fits their needs.

Organizing Your Business

Sole Proprietor

The trainer is the sole owner/operator of the business. Usually it only requires a license from the particular state/  local government in which the business will be located. This is the least expensive and most simple business model. There a few negatives to this type of proprietorship. One is the large amount of money that must be available up front in order to start up the business. Another is that the personal liability always falls back on the sole proprietor. All legalities or IRS dealings are considered one and the same for the sole proprietor, meaning there is no separation of personal versus business situations, as there is only one owner.

Independent Contractor

This is an individual who provides his services on a hired-out basis for another company or individual. Being an independent contractor allows personal trainers to work at multiple locations and the freedom to make their own schedule. The services provided are not directly paid to the personal trainer by the client. The personal trainer receives payment from the person/company that contracted them out. The downside is that the personal trainer has little flexibility in negotiating salary, as it is usually predetermined and set by the hiring individual or company.

Partnership

A partnership is an agreement between more than one individual entering into a business. There may be formal documentation of the partnership, which is usually handled by an attorney. The partners may also enter into an informal agreement. This is not recommended because if problems arise, proving verbal agreements can be difficult. If the parties are not planning to enter into a formal agreement, they should at least get the agreeing terms in writing and signed by all parties. Federal or state governments do not tightly regulate partnerships. A pitfall to a partnership is that liability is placed on all partners regardless of fault. An advantage is that startup expenses can be shared and all parties will bring their own expertise to the business.

Corporation

Power Fitness Corporation

A corporation is a true business entity and must abide by federal, state and local regulations set forth for corporations. Unlike sole proprietorships or partnerships where liability rests in the owners' hands, a corporation is a legal entity of its own. Managers and owners are not necessarily legally responsible in liability situations. Corporations are governed by charters and bylaws. Investors usually encumber the startup expenses of a corporation. Transfer of ownership is much easier than with other types of business models.

S-Corporation

An S-corporation combines the advantages of all three types of business models and is

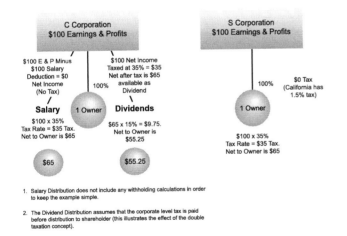

1. Salary Distribution does not include any withholding calculations in order to keep the example simple.

2. The Dividend Distribution assumes that the corporate level tax is paid before distribution to shareholder (this illustrates the effect of the double taxation concept).

usually the best alternative for a small business. It protects the owners from personal asset loss and limits the risk of the individuals involved. In a corporation, usually the owner or owners are taxed on their business as well as their salaries, seemingly being double taxed. However, with an S-Corporation this does not happen. It gives the owners the freedom to distribute dividends as they choose. Basically, the big difference is how the business is classified with the IRS and thus how taxes are handled.

Business Type Comparison Chart

Type of Business	Definition	Advantages	Disadvantages
Sole Proprietorship	Business owned by one person & the operating license is obtained from the state/local city in which the business resides	Work for yourself	Start-up expenses and personal accountability due to any debt
Independent Contractor	A personal trainer who is paid by health clubs in exchange for personal training services	Set schedules, variety of locations, paid per session	Health club may determine amount paid for services
Partnership	Business owned by 2+ people informally or by contract	Compilation of financial resources & talent	Can be accountable for partner's failures
Corporation	Formal business ruled by a contract & bylaws; separate from owners & managers	Investors have limited liability	Costs, regulation
S Corporation	Corporation treated as proprietorship or partnership	Limited risk, no double taxation	

The Business Plan

The Business Plan

Once a decision is made to have a business, the owner's first priority is to make a business plan. This should include plans for the budget, established policies for employees and clients, advertisements and profits. Writing out or making a list of all pertinent processes and costs will help with organization as well as preparation for potential hurdles.

The Budget

Owners can make categories for how monies will be allocated. For example:

Monies required for everyday business operation:

a) Salaries

b) Insurances

c) Equipment

d) Taxes

e) Electricity, phone, water, office supplies, etc.

f) Travel

Monies required for annual training:

a) Certifications

b) Specialized training (i.e., for people with disabilities)

c) Mandated training (This may come up without notice such as when laws that govern areas may overlap. For example, health care information privacy is regulated by the HIPAA act. As of now, personal trainers do not have to be HIPAA compliant, but this may change. If so, owners would have to ensure all trainers employed took a proper HIPAA course.)

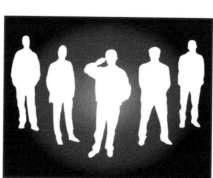

Monies earned:

a) Determine a per session amount—see profits section.

Establishing Policies

Employees

a) How will salaries be determined? Will the arrangement be a baseline with the potential for performance-based raises or will the pay be based on experience, or a combination of both? As an employer, the owner should establish how salaries will be determined and have it in writing.

b) Will health insurance be offered to employees? As of right now, small businesses are not required to offer health insurance to their employees by law; however, owners should be prepared for this to change in case there is a requirement to do so in the future.

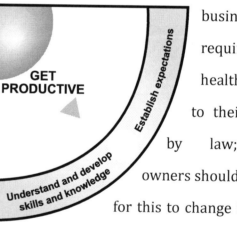

GET PRODUCTIVE

Establish expectations

Understand and develop skills and knowledge

c) How many full-time, part-time or independent contractors will be hired and be on the payroll? This is important when trying to budget expenses.

d) How will vacation, personal time, sick time be handled?

It is better to have established guidelines versus just "winging it." Employees need structure and conflict among them will be better avoided if there are established guidelines.

Clients

a) What sort of clients will services be offered to? This is not meant to exclude any demographic, but to avoid liability. Owners must make sure they are qualified to provide services to people who may require special training. For example, people who have physical disabilities may require a trainer to have more specialized training. If the company is not prepared to offer proper training to individuals who may need specialized training, resources should be able for the company's trainers to refer these clients to known trainers that do offer specialized training. In these cases, however, it is important that these clients understand the company is not refusing to train them but instead considers it wise to encourage them to use a trained specialist.

b) How will clients be charged? Will it be by the session or by the hour? Prices should be competitive.

c) What forms of payment will be accepted? There are three major forms of payment—cash, check or debit/credit card. If debit/credit card payments are accepted, the company may also wish to offer automatic deduction. Many clients view this as convenient and it will assure that payments will be delivered on time, every month.

d) If a client is late to a session, are they allowed to make up the time?

e) If a client is going on vacation, should their sessions carry over?

Having clear guidelines governing employee and client policies is the best way to run a successful business. These lists are not exhaustive or all-inclusive but allow examples of ideas on what to ask. When guidelines are preset there is less likely to be confusion in the future. Policies should always be written in a contract style document that will be signed by the employee or client signifying agreement to the guidelines set forth. It is a good idea to go to several similar businesses and get ideas in terms of how they run their business policywise

because they are likely to be up-to-date with all of the current regulations. Owners must also make sure that guidelines are compliant with current federal, state and local regulations. It is a good idea to outline the business in a mission statement style that highlights key points as to the philosophy upon which it will be operated. Include the vision and important characteristics, such as honesty and integrity. Every person is different and holds various values to varying degrees, but if the owner lays out the design and show clients and employees, they will better understand the type of business person that the owner is trying to be.

Advertisement

A good advertisement will be the key to a successful business.

a) How much do can be spent? In the beginning (at least the first year), the owner should budget more for advertising. If potential clients do not know about the company, how can they seek its services?

b) What type of advertising will be used? After determining how much to spend, this is the second most important area for focus. There are so many avenues to explore for advertising: the Internet, radio, television, flyers and billboards are the most popular.

c) The Internet is where most people find their information in today's world. An owner should strongly consider hiring someone to generate and maintain a website. The ideal website will include the mission statement, any specialized skills the trainers may have, an appointment scheduler, pricing and contact information.

d) The radio is also a good place to advertise, but homework needs to be done to figure out what local stations are the most popular and which are affiliated with the clientele being sought. It is possible to get sponsorships if employees are wearing the station logo in exchange for advertisement. Be creative and explore all avenues.

e) Television is also a great place to advertise but can be very expensive. Again, local channels are the ideal place to advertise, but timing can be an issue in terms of cost. Choose wisely if selecting television.

f) Old fashioned flyers still work and are relatively cheap. Partnering up with other businesses around is a great way to distribute flyers. The company can offer to set up a place for other firm's flyers or business cards and they reciprocate.

Reach out to other local businesses like health stores, especially ones that are locally owned and operated. Owners can also set up incentive programs where a free lunch is given for every five customers they refer.

Make sure money is not being wasted on a demographic that is not likely to become the company's clientele.

g) Billboards may sound old-fashioned, but they still work. People driving by still look at billboards.

h) Who will be targeted? Knowing whom to target can be tricky. Everyone would like to be in shape and have the luxury of having a personal trainer for guidance but realistically not everyone can afford one. Make sure money is not being wasted on a demographic that is not likely to become the company's clientele. Wherever the business location is, the owner needs to examine the area carefully and decide who might be likely to want and afford the services.

i) Where will the target market be? Owners do not want to market in a place that is not likely to gain new clients. Every city is different and it is important to pick the place wisely. Smaller cities are not likely to give much clientele. Success

will be based the your skills to market and sell the company's service. After all, there will be competition in the personal training business, so the owner must figure out what makes the business better/different than the others. That is what the marketing and advertising needs to portray.

Profits

a) How much money does the owner want the company to make? In the first year, and maybe even the first few years, the goal is to not be in the red (negative); furthermore, breaking even is good and being in the black (positive) is excellent. It is important that a good budget is in place to know what expenses are and what amount needs to be made. Pricing must be set such that the firm is competitive but also makes enough money to pay the bills. In order to determine pricing, the owner needs to do some case studies. What are the most successful personal training businesses in the area charging? What are the mediocre ones charging?

b) Next, comparisons need to be made between what the firm's prices are for services and what competitors prices are for those services, and then make prices equal to those of competitors that most closely match the firm's offerings. It is likely that a potential client has been other places and if prices seem higher than competitors, the firm needs to be able to explain why. This is why casing competition is important and why an owner should highlight what makes the company and its training better/different in advertisements. Pricing varies from state to state, city to city and company to company. Only the owner can set the pricing based on the area and business. However, charging inflated prices to make ends meet is not going to work and people will see right through that. Startup money is vital; an owner needs to make sure sufficient funds are available to sustain the business for the first year. In order to save money, minimal hiring should be done until it is determined that the business has the clientele to sustain more employees. The last thing an owner wants to do is have to let someone go because too many people were hired. An owner can be the best personal trainer, but bad business practices are a sure way to guarantee

failure. If a trainer does not feel business savvy, education on running a small business via books or extra classes is a good option. Taking on this endeavor is very challenging and knowing and admitting what one does not know can only help. There are multitudes of ways to help gain the knowledge that may be lacking, so an individual should not be afraid to use them.

Summary

Because of the intensive work and complex interactions with clients associated with personal training, a personal trainer is responsible for many legal issues. It is important to understand all legal issues and responsibilities so they can be accurately addressed. They can include issues of negligence or not fulfilling duty, of failure to provide emergency support and of not gaining the appropriate informed consent. In addition, they can include tort law or legal rights between individuals in relation to civil injuries. Ensuring appropriate exercise regimes for clients is a simple way to avoid any legal problems.

Additionally, many personal trainers operate out of their own facilities and within their own knowledge of personal training. In these situations, it is important to understand any potential legal action that can be brought against the personal trainer. This is important to not only protect the client but also the personal trainer. Risk management through proper education, training, extensive documentation and practicing limited liability can all be used to completely avoid or greatly reduce the chances of liability in case of wrongdoing.

Personal trainers should also be well-versed in business aspects of their profession. It is important to have a sound business model in order to grow clientele and maximize profits. The use of technology to create websites and business cards, identifying current marketplace needs and offering discounts are all important marketing strategies used to grow a business. READ (rapport, empathy, assessment and development) can help a personal trainer connect with clients and excel in customer service. There are many different levels to organized business, with sole proprietorship being the simplest and commonest practice of securing a business. However, getting into business with others in a partnership or a bigger corporation are other possibilities.

Review Questions

1. What is the most common complaint made by clients against their personal trainer? _

   _____

   _____

2. As a personal trainer, you are required by law to follow the HIPAA regulations. True or False? _____

3. Explain how a trainer would deal with a client who has a specific condition that the trainer has not been certified to handle. _

   _____

   _____

4. Liability can be reduced by the following:

   a) Avoidance

   b) Retention

   c) Reduction

   d) Transfer

   e) All of the above

5. List four components of a good website.

   a) _____

   b) _____

   c) _____

   d) _____

6. When considering customer service, the acronym, READ, stands for:

   a) Rapport, Encouragement, Assessment and Development

   b) Reduction, Empathy, Assessment and Development

   c) Rapport, Empathy, Assessment, Development

7. In order to become a personal trainer, an individual needs to obtain a bachelor's degree in Personal Training from an accredited institution. True or False? _____

8. Name the difference between a corporation and an S-corporation. _____

   _____

   _____

9. What are the components of a Business Plan?

   a) _____

   b) _____

   c) _____

   d) _____

10. You should check the _____

    _____ website to ensure that the online certification program chosen is accredited.

Answers

1. Slipping and falling that led to injury is the number one complaint of clients against their personal trainer.

2. False, but that may change in the future.

3. Personal trainers need to ensure that they receive the proper additional training and certification for special needs groups. However, if the trainer cannot achieve the necessary certification in a timely manner, the trainer should refer the special needs client to another trainer certified in the appropriate area.

4. e) All of the above.

5. Any of the following: a purpose; graphics and relevant links to other health and fitness sites; an appropriate domain name to generate and drive the business; interactive content (e.g., quizzes, polls, ways to calculate BMI); up-to-date information.

6. c) Rapport, Empathy, Assessment, Development.

7. False.

8. A corporation is a true business entity and must abide by federal, state and local regulations set forth for corporations. An S-corporation is usually the best alternative for a small business. It protects the owners from personal asset loss and limits the risk of the individuals involved. In a corporation, usually the owner or owners are taxed on their business as well as their salaries, seemingly being double taxed; however, with an S-Corporation this does not happen. It gives the owners the freedom to distribute dividends as they choose. Basically, the big difference is how the business is classified with the IRS and thus how taxes are handled.

9. Budget, established policies for employees and clients, advertisements and profits.

10. National Organization for Competency Assurance at www.noca.org.

References

Eickhoff-Shemek JM, White CJ. The legal aspects: Internet personal training and/or coaching: what are the legal issues? *ACSM'S Health & Fitness Journal.* 2005;9(3):29-31.

Goldman E, Couzelia P. The business side of wellness coaching. *ACSM'S Health & Fitness Journal.* 2007;11(5):38-39.

Malek MH, Nalbone DP, Berger DE, Coburn JW. Importance of health science education for personal fitness trainers. *Journal of Strength Conditioning Research.* 2002;16(1):19-24.

Manley RS, O'Brien KM, Samuels S. Fitness instructors' recognition of eating disorders and attendant ethical/liability issues. *Eating Disorders.* 2008;16(2):103-16.

Melton DI, Katula JA, Mustian KM. The current state of personal training: an industry perspective of personal trainers in a small Southeast community. *Journal of Strength Conditioning Research.* 2008;22(3):883-89.

Robinson EM, Graham LB, Bauer MA. The National Strength and Conditioning Association is the preferred certification for personal training employment in southeastern Massachusetts. *Journal of Strength Conditioning Research.* 2006;20(2):450-51.